the poem is you

the poem is you

60 Contemporary American Poems and How to Read Them

STEPHEN BURT

THE BELKNAP PRESS OF HARVARD UNIVERSITY PRESS

Cambridge, Massachusetts, and London, England   2016

DESIGN BY ANNAMARIE MCMAHON WHY

Library of Congress Cataloging-in-Publication Data

Names: Burt, Stephen, author.

Title: The poem is you : sixty contemporary American poems and how to read them / Stephen Burt.

Description: Cambridge, Massachusetts : The Belknap Press of Harvard University Press, 2016. | Includes index.

Identifiers: LCCN 2016012435 | ISBN 9780674737877 (cloth)

Subjects: LCSH: American poetry—20th century—History and criticism. | American poetry—21st century—History and criticism.

Classification: LCC PS325 .B87 2016 | DDC 811/.5409—dc23 LC record available at https://lccn.loc.gov/2016012435

Contents

the poem is you

Introduction

This book offers sixty poems by American poets, all written or published since 1980, along with an essay about each one. It's meant for readers not already familiar with the exciting, crowded, confusing space of recent American poetry, as well as for readers who know that space—or parts of it—well. It introduces the poems, their ways of working, their techniques, their prose sense (or resistance to prose sense), and, sometimes, their authors' careers, their place in American writing, or whatever other topics—from the history of desserts to the principles of physics—might help us enjoy the poem. Each essay can stand on its own, and readers may traverse them in any order (or, of course, read straight through).

Many books and journals, many critics, present or examine recent poetry. But most of them are specialized or factional; many assume more knowledge than most of us possess. They can also seem almost mutually exclusive: a stage at the Dodge Poetry Festival, a graduate seminar at UC Berkeley, a group of young writers in Charlottesville, an issue of *Lana Turner*, an issue of *Yale Review*, any given coffee-klatsch or Tumblr or classroom—each has its own sense of what to read, of what's important, and few have the space or time to introduce work far from its core tastes and concerns. The venues that do try to look far afield, to see American poetry steadily and see it whole (the series of *Best American Poetry* annuals, for example), are by their nature unable to provide critical contexts for most of their poems. And the best introductions to poetry in general spend much of their time, quite rightly, on poets such as Shakespeare and Emily Dickinson, or Sappho or Bishop or Ted Hughes or Langston Hughes or Li Po or Neruda, rather than focusing only on recent decades.

That's where this book comes in. And yet any approach to recent American poetry as a whole—even this one—raises the problems it tries to solve, much like any attempt to see the United States of America. What should you see if you travel across the country? Where should you live, if you're planning to move? Should you hike in New Hampshire? Meet comic book artists in

Portland, Oregon? Investigate grassland restoration, or the Ojibwe language, in Minnesota? Surf, or help organize unions, in greater L.A.? The answer depends on who you are, where you're coming from, what you like now, what you want to learn to do.

Contemporary American poetry is, in this sense, an image of America: it's vast, and fascinating, and sometimes baffling, because it contains so many subcultures, locales, talents, tastes, and goals. You can also get lost in it. If you're visiting Switzerland, you won't miss the Alps; if you are reading the literature of England around 1600, you will probably brush up your Shakespeare. No single author, style, or feature dominates contemporary American poetry in that way (not even John Ashbery, with whom our book begins). It offers, instead, an enormous and varied geography, whose high points and must-sees can seem very far apart.

That's one reason this book exists. Each essay—like each poem—can stand on its own; together they tell not one story but many overlapping, connected stories about the states of the art. Each essay explains what I find beautiful, important, fascinating, or moving about a poem; each essay also gives contexts for that poem, placing it within the career of an author, a part of American history or culture, the trajectory of a movement or a school. For poems that may baffle readers new to their styles, I spend some time decoding, explaining what happens to people and things named there, or why no consistent explanation can fit. For poems that seem lucid—poems that may not need decoding—I try to show why they work as well as they do.

Here you'll find mothers, fathers, lovers, friends, painters, marine biologists, soldiers, horses, foresters, goths, teachers, teens, post-Marxist saxophonists, more horses, beauty contestants, prophetic undead pianists, and several kinds of kinky sex; you'll encounter slices of life in modern cities, defenses of bourgeois suburbia, and more than one elaborate jeremiad against how we treat our earth, water, and air. You'll find minuscule poems like precisely ground lenses, made of a few dozen words or a couple of lines; you'll also find expansive, even chatty conversations about eyeglasses, marriages, tide pools, antiques, and barbeques, along with corrosive attacks on everyday life under capitalism. You'll find a revelation of supernatural power among children in a Utah national park, and a child's discovery of mortality in a Worcester, Massachusetts, elementary school. You'll find a defense of cake decoration, bedazzled with curlicued syntax and off-rhyme, and an even more elaborate ode to a commercially doomed prefab house. One poet records, with equanimity, an earthquake in daylight hours in greater L.A.; another remembers a choppy ride through New England snow in a dream. You'll encounter a laconic, almost folkloric retelling of the Christian Annunciation, and a cosmopolitan Persian-Urdu-derived lyric of exile, atheism, and *Moby-Dick*. You will hear poems that draw on, or even imitate, doo-wop music, Romantic and classical composition, Osage chants and tribal music, bebop, indie rock, and rap. You'll get jokes, self-portraits, epitaphs, palinodes, erotic invitations, sacred allegories, nightmares, avant-garde conundrums, pranks, and childhood memories. You'll find intricately irregular rhyme, blank verse, free verse of many varieties, prose poems of many cadences, and a poem in terza rima that also sings the blues.

Some essays delve into matters that would seem to lie far outside the study of poetry, except that the poems bring them in: if you read this book from start to finish, you will learn about the history of Angel Island in San Francisco Bay, about the fauna and flora of the Florida Gulf Coast, about early computer fonts and the beginnings of email, and about acrimony over the Vietnam Veterans Memorial in Washington, D.C. Other essays explain matters specific to poetry: What is a sestina? Why are there so many now? What have blogs and Twitter and instant messaging done to, or for, or against the supposedly more durable ways of using language that poems involve? Some essays introduce techniques unique to a decade, a social group, or a generation, such as Carla Harryman's New Sentence. Other essays explain how contemporary poets—Agha Shahid Ali, for example—gather and re-stitch the literary past. Some essays show how poets benefit when they write for wide audiences, including children; others appreciate poets who are, in Douglas Kearney's coinage, "dintelligible," "where what appears as noise in noise to some (thus, insensible but perhaps sensual) is in fact complex contrapuntal signals." In our time, the boundaries of "poetry" blur and shift depending on who is writing: some of the works we call poems (for example, kari edwards's) might not be poems to you, though most of the poems in this book would meet almost anyone's definition, even if they are not to everyone's taste. Some finesse and some resist the changes in culture and media that have made page-based, written-down poetry seem less central to American culture than it was when Henry Wadsworth Longfellow or Langston Hughes published verse.

And yet all sixty poems—whatever else they do—take on at least one of two tasks still best fitted to poetry, rather than to radio, TV, novels, film, comics, *New Yorker* essays, installation art, or video games. First, these poems let us imagine someone else's interior life, almost as if it were or could have

been ours: they project a voice and embody a compelling or attractive individual consciousness, which we can then hear, or speak, or sing, or try on, or
try out, as if it were our own. (If a poem brings you wisdom about your own
life, as many poems from all historical periods can, it also tells you that somebody else got there first.) It's a very traditional goal, one sometimes given the
slightly confusing name of "lyric" (whether or not there are songs involved).
It entails what look like contradictions—how can you see yourself in someone
else, adopt as your own someone else's distinctive words? Yet it is a goal that
many poets, and many readers, have kept in mind; it emerges anew in every
generation. In a poem called "i do not know what a painting does," Juan Felipe Herrera suggests that a poem, like a painting,

> poses for you when you are at your beginnings then
> it follows you passes you dissolves ahead of you where
> it is waiting for you when you get there you will not
> know it until you see that it is seeing you seeing you

Poetry gives you a picture of the poet—but it also "follows you," gets ahead
of you, stays conscious of you, and ends up showing you some part of
yourself.

The other goal is less traditional, but no less important: poetry, because it
uses words in highly patterned ways, because it pays attention to all the parts
of a word (not just those that convey information), because it does not have
to tell a story or tell you how to fix a car, can make language strange; it can
reveal, or upend, the assumptions and habits that go without saying when we
use language in less unusual ways. Some residents of Austin, Texas, used to
sport T-shirts that read KEEP AUSTIN WEIRD. This kind of poem might carry
a similar slogan—it means to keep the world, and the language, weird, either
to keep us alert to the social, political, and economic problems that make the
world worse than it could be or else just to sharpen our sense of what we hear
and see, "to signal imaginative strangeness" (as the literary theorist Jonathan
Culler put it), "resistance to ordinary lines of thought." That alienating goal
may oppose, in principle, the idea of lyric, the poem as a song of the soul, but
in practice the two go together all the time.

The essays in this book often show how they go together within single poems.
The first essay shows how Ashbery at once invites and evades your sense that
his poem speaks to you; the next-to-last essay asks how Brandon Som addresses the inward travail that connects grandfathers to fathers and to sons,

and also how he inverts and renews the sound patterns that came (along with the grandfathers) from China to the United States. Another essay uncovers Lucia Perillo's critiques of American sex and sexuality, comparing how we feel about sex to how we are told we ought to feel, while showing how she makes the American language comically strange. The essay on Rae Armantrout demonstrates how she breaks open clichés while asking you to imagine adopting her not quite resigned, not quite embittered tone. Each poem presents a way of arranging language, and a question about the culture from which it emerged; each poem is a way for a person to live in the world.

There is no main route, no single highway, through all the United States; in the same way, there is no main route, no single argument about American poetry, that connects all these poets and poems. Many cities, though, lie on Interstate 95, and some of the rest can be reached by I-5, I-94, I-10. In the same way, some concerns, some goals, allow us to talk about these poems together, to say how one leads into the next, and what paths many American poets, acting in concert or in conflict, have mapped out.

Those goals emerge from recent literary history. By the late 1960s, many, perhaps most, American poets wrote free verse that could be paraphrased, and that portrayed events in the poets' own lives; these events could be enlightening, moments of beauty, or encounters with nonhuman nature, but they could also be traumatic, moments of shame or stress, in the tradition of so-called confessional poetry, as practiced by Sylvia Plath or Robert Lowell. As more and more writers felt stirred, or obliged, to speak out for racial justice or against the Vietnam War, their poems took part in that speech: eminent midcareer poets not otherwise similar, from Adrienne Rich to Robert Bly to Amiri Baraka, registered either a pressure toward clarity for the sake of political efficacy or a revulsion from familiar, clearly organized, European-derived (hence guilty, or white, or capitalist, or patriarchal) forms. Much poetry of the 1970s tried to be as unmediated, as visceral, as uncomplicated, or as far from expository prose as emotion-laden language can be: influential anthologies had titles such as *Naked Poetry* (1969), *The New Naked Poetry* (1976), and *No More Masks!* (1973).

Like all trends, this one laid the grounds for its own antitheses. Some poets, such as Richard Wilbur, doubled down on their commitments to European-derived, obviously traditional forms, to poetry as a learnèd art, or a craft. Other poets looked to the so-called New York School, the sometimes improvisational, unpredictable, or chaotic set of writers whose first generation included Ashbery, its second Bernadette Mayer: this second generation organized the Poetry Project at St. Mark's Church-in-the-Bowery, which continues to sponsor poems and performances today. Other poets in New York, Washington, D.C., and the San Francisco Bay Area (Harryman and Armantrout among them) became what we now call the language, or L=A=N=G=U=A=G=E, writers (named after a New York-based magazine), trying to get as far as possible outside imitations of voice and prose sense.

Most of the writers in all these groups were white. In years that saw the rise of what we now call (but should never dismiss as) identity politics, poets of color faced questions of their own. Was ethnic authenticity a helpful, or necessary, goal (as the Black Arts Movement, for example, insisted)? If so, must writers who seek it abjure "white" forms? If not, how and where and why do skin color and background, demography and group solidarity, matter? All poets can ask these questions as they become serious about their art, but African American, Asian American, Latin@, and Native writers were more often expected to answer them in public, early on in their own careers. Some styles defined in part by nonwhite identities emerged before 1980 but flowered afterward. Some took their bearings from public performances, from noncommercial theater, and from the protest movements of the 1970s—the American Indian Movement, the Chicano *movimiento*—while others emerged from autobiographical print-based verse. This book includes poets of color who make race and ethnic identities central to their own poetry, and poets who do not; it does not—it cannot—include every identity, every demographic, from which memorable verse has emerged.

Nor can it note all significant institutions. Poets of the 1980s had to handle what had gone before: to negotiate their relationship to modernism, to whatever used to be an avant-garde, to confessional poems, to an international lyric tradition, and to the English and European past. Many of them learned to do so through graduate programs in poetry writing, founded on the example of the Iowa Writers' Workshop; these institutions joined others—from little magazines and popular journals to writers' retreats and even restaurants and bars—that had shaped American poetry since its inception. Poets outside elite universities found it easier than ever, thanks to changes in printing technology, to found presses, create communities, hand down lore; at the same time, economic and medical hardships—including HIV / AIDS—altered, or cut short, many poets' careers.

Accounts of the 1980s *from* the 1980s and 1990s often sorted the decade, calmly or polemically, into schools: New Formalists, neo-confessionals, a free verse "mainstream," performance and proto-slam poets, a post-avant-garde.

Stories about the poetry of the 1990s can be stories about integration, about synthesis, though what is being synthesized varies from scene to scene. Sometimes the integration reflected poets' views of society and politics, and sometimes it seemed internal to poetry: writers of the 1990s—especially those in and around New York City, and those who attended Iowa—read the various productions of an anti-prose-sense avant-garde and the recent accomplishments of a lyrical or voice-based tradition, and tried to find some way between them. "Purists Will Object" (to quote Ashbery once more); other readers, myself among them, enjoyed the ferment of those years, the messiness or the new ambition of poems by C. D. Wright, Lucie Brock-Broido, Mark Levine, and others that almost—but did not quite—make clear prose sense. Capacious anthologies such as *Legitimate Dangers* (2006) and *American Hybrid* (2009), sometimes attacked from a purist left, honored this moment of heterogeneity, eclecticism, and rapprochement.

Stories about American poetry in the twenty-first century can emphasize its responses to public events. The attacks of September 11, 2001, the American military involvements in Afghanistan and Iraq, and the campaigns and elections of 2008 all generated phalanxes of poems, and there are anthologies devoted to each. Hurricane Katrina and its aftermath inspired at least eight whole books (the most celebrated, Patricia Smith's *Blood Dazzler*, is best read whole). It may be that generations to come will read the poetry of our own time principally for its response to global climate change; the Katrina books enter into that response, as does the recent spate of long poems about watersheds, ecosystems, and metropolitan areas, among them Peter O'Leary's book-length *Phosphorescence of Thought* and several long segments in Juliana Spahr's monumental *Well Then There Now*. I do not represent those volumes here, but I do include attempts by Allan Peterson and Jorie Graham, by dg nanouk okpik and James Merrill, to learn from climate science, and to face a rapidly warming world.

Other stories about the most recent poetry highlight controversial schools and explicit programs. Conceptualists such as the wonderfully confounding poet-critic Tan Lin and the outspoken performers Vanessa Place and Kenneth Goldsmith emulated visual artists in their practice of repeating, reframing, or reshaping preexisting, apparently nonliterary texts. (Some of that practice has included racially charged—or offensive—appropriation.) Flarfists, or Flarf poets, flaunt "corrosive, cute or cloying awfulness" (as Drew Gardner put it), looking back to Dadaism and trying to challenge the very idea of taste. The Black Took Collective and its allies, on the page and in performances,

proposed a non-narrative, non-autobiographical "'experiment' or 'innovation' as a means of defining a different kind of blackness," as Dawn Lundy
Martin has explained. "Gurlesque" poets (a label devised by Arielle Greenberg and Lara Glenum in their anthology of the same name) found in apparent "bad" taste, in scandalous extremes, means of resistance to patriarchal
demands. Spurred by classroom needs, by international examples, or simply
by intellectual challenge, poets far from any avant-garde also invented or revived strict forms, from the alphabetical acrostic to Ali's "real ghazal" to the
Golden Shovel, a verse form devised—in homage to Gwendolyn Brooks—
by Terrance Hayes.

If you compare American poetry today to American poetry ten, twenty,
thirty years ago, treating both as if they could be considered whole, perhaps
the most obvious difference is this: African American poets and poems now
seem central, to black and to non-black observers. It's perilous to judge anything by lists of prizes, but it means something that the National Book
Award, the National Book Critics Circle award, the Pulitzer, the Kingsley
and Kate Tufts awards, and the Los Angeles Times Book Prize all went to
more than one African American poet between 2010 and 2015. White poets
in the same years became more likely to write about white privilege and
whiteness: Bruce Smith, Tess Taylor, Ed Pavlic, and Martha Collins have
done so with particular force.

And yet American poetry can no longer be plausibly seen, by observers of
any background, in black and white. The last fifty years—but, even more so,
the last ten—have seen more and more descendants of non-European immigrants publish first, and second and third, books. Many of those poets
wanted styles that fit their multiple or hybrid ethnic identities; some of them,
from John Yau to Khaled Mattawa, worked at once to extend and to discard
ideas about tribes, inheritance, and "voice" that came to them from the confessional, autobiographical poets of earlier years. Asian American poetry, like
African American poetry and like Chican@ and Latin@ poetry, benefited in
the 2010s from institutions and networks built in the 1990s, and it began to
flourish in several places at once. The current renaissance of Native American
poetry, by contrast, has an identifiable source in Santa Fe: the writing program at the Institute of American Indian Arts, where the poet Arthur Sze
taught (for example) Sherwin Bitsui, Layli Long Soldier, and dg nanouk okpik.
Though ethnically specific literary institutions such as Houston's Arte
Público Press long predate the 1990s, the last twenty years saw many more of

them, from the Cave Canem network of African American writers' retreats to the Asian American Writers Workshop.

Nor were all new institutions ethnically marked. Writers devoted to premodern rhymed or metered techniques created magazines, presses, and conferences, such as the West Chester University Poetry Conference, for those goals. Writers who kept up the eclectic, choppy aesthetic of the 1990s, such as Noah Eli Gordon, found new ways to collaborate and discuss their work online, in expansive journals such as *The Volta* that could not have come about before the Web. Very young writers used digital media to conjure poetic communities of their own. And if we count only named institutions, we miss other sources of poetry, styles, and networks created through less formal means. In the late 1990s poets who wanted to capture the informal energies of enthusiastic conversation invented a mode (presented here by Albert Goldbarth) that some proponents called "ultra-talk." Mark Nowak, Craig Santos Perez, Spahr, Claudia Rankine, and others incorporated journalistic research and documentary prose into long poems meant to afflict the comfortable and comfort the afflicted. Epigrams and epigrammatic or witty poetry—hard to find in the America of the 1980s—experienced a revival led by Kay Ryan. Graham Foust, Pam Rehm, and Joseph Massey, among others, revisited the cool observational sides of modernism and the midcentury movement called Objectivism in unadorned, precise miniatures. Some of these schools and movements and institutions and writers are represented in this book. Some are mentioned here because they are not.

If you try to cross the United States using only the interstate highways, you'll get from city to city as fast as possible—but you'll miss most of the reasons to visit each one. In the same way, if you try to discover contemporary American poetry by trying to see what many poems have in common, by figuring out how to think about movements and schools, you will risk passing over, or passing up, most of the reasons you might want to read each poem. I invite you to think about the future of confessionalism, of autobiography, of narrative, and of their difficult opposites, as you make your own way through these sixty poems; I invite you to think as well about instinct, about sex and sexuality and the implicit gender of a poet's voice. I invite you to think about race and representation, about how cadences, words, tones, and arguments situate poets and poems in the multicolored and multicultural history of America and the world. I invite you to think about the past, and the future, of premodern devices and forms—about full rhyme, iambic meters, stanzas and couplets, and their unruly counterparts in the many and fragmented kinds of modern free verse. I invite you to think about music, and about representations of music—jazz, blues, rock, Romantic, and classical—as they provide analogies for contemporary poets and poems. I invite you to think about parents and children; about students and teachers; about sleepers and dreamers and poets who remain uneasily awake. I hope you'll accept at least some of the invitations: I do not expect you to take me up on them all.

I present poems in chronological order by first publication from 1981 through 2015; where poems have two "first publications," one in a magazine, the other in a book, I have felt free to use either year. Where I use magazine publication for order, the table of contents lists both magazine and book dates. I begin in 1981 not least so that you can begin with Ashbery's "Paradoxes and Oxymorons," a poem that does double duty as an invitation to read challenging, slippery poetry and as a claim about the connection between poet and reader, between "you" and "me," that all poems at least attempt to make.

But there are other reasons I start where I do. By that point almost all the poets who shaped American verse before the 1960s had died: Lowell in 1977, Louis Zukofsky in 1978, Elizabeth Bishop in 1979, Robert Hayden and James Wright in 1980. Others had nearly stopped writing (George Oppen) or had already written their best, and their best-known, short poems (James Schuyler, Brooks). The year represents a pivot in political and economic history: the start of the Reagan era, the end of the countercultural dream. And, of course, the book has to start somewhere.

When I set out to write this book I had already identified some of the poems, and some of the poets, I would include; I knew, in broad outline, what I wanted to say about them. I also knew that I would have to look beyond my prior experience in order to make a book that could do justice, not to all, but to enough. "What for so long you and I have observed together, day in and day out," writes the present-day poet William Fuller, "has been constantly modified by what we don't see, leaving one whole side of experience blank." A book like this one should at least try not to leave any whole side of American poetry blank. In making this book I have tried to expand my taste.

And then I have tried to exercise that taste. Picking out the best poems for commentary isn't like trying to say who won a footrace, whose cat has the longest tail, or who got the top SAT score. It isn't even much like judging a bake-off or a balance beam competition, in which aesthetic judgments (grace, poise, risk, deliciousness) generate linear, quantified results. It's a lot more like assembling a dinner party, putting together a radio show, or drafting a basketball team: From a large set of good candidates, which few absolutely must be there? Once they're in, which ones from the remaining pool bring skills, or virtues, or features, that wouldn't otherwise be found? Who would play well together? How many people, or poems, will the league or the table, or (in this case) the word count and the permissions process, allow?

No matter how you describe yourself, you can get more wisdom, more grace, and more of the world if you look beyond your own experience, as well as looking for it, in what you read. Experience isn't identity—much less demography—but they are linked: extreme shyness is an experience, for example, but so is serving in a war; so is driving while black. For some times and places, where literary production—or literacy itself—belonged to the few, that search can feel like a slog. For contemporary America, on the other hand, it's easy for a diligent seeker with a good library and a book budget to find some poems by writers from almost any significant demographic category, about almost any kind of lived experience, or about almost any kind of influence, from D.C.'s go-go music to Lucretius's Latin (for which see, respectively, Thomas Sayers Ellis and A. E. Stallings, who could have been, but are not, in this book). The problem—to which there is no satisfying solution—is when to stop looking, and what, or whom, to leave out. Sixty poems cannot reflect the whole of America: its ethnicities, its personalities, its locales. But the critic who puts those poems together can try.

That critic must also remember that she is assembling not a set of people but a set of poems. The organization VIDA: Women in Literary Arts, established by two poets in 2009, has persuaded many people in the literary arts to go through tables of contents and count the women, count the members of historically underrepresented groups, and then ask whether we can live with the numbers we get. I have counted; I am persuaded. But no poet is here just to represent a group; all the poems are here because I admire them. Ethnic diversity matters, but so does diversity in terms of styles, schools, kinds of poems, topics, and attitudes. Several poems here whose authors are writers of color—like most of the poems here whose authors are white—have no obvious or explicit connection to ethnicity or race.

I have also sought diversity in terms of how prominent the poets and the poems and even their publishers have become. A set of what classical musicians call warhorses, poems already widely republished and studied, would not serve the purpose, but neither would a set of sixty poems no one had ever anthologized before. (In this way, too, a book like this one resembles a radio show: a mix of familiar and unfamiliar works best.) More Americans published more poems, and more kinds of poems, in the 2000s than in the 1990s, and more in the 1990s than in the 1980s; I have tried not to favor unduly the years during which I myself (born in 1971) read new poems. A sequel to this book, assembled thirty years hence, would certainly include more writers of color. It might well include poems predominantly or entirely in Spanish, or in Hmong, or in American Sign Language, which I have not done. Nor do I include poems that cannot be presented effectively using the printed page alone. I have tried for variety both among recognizable forms (the sestina, the anaphoric list, the New Sentence) and among harder-to-classify kinds, with one exception: this book is a sequel of sorts to *The Art of the Sonnet*, by myself and David Mikics. For more of my favorite contemporary American sonnets, you should look there.

Why only American poetry? One country is big enough, and American poetry remains a convenient, indeed inescapable unit, however contested and blurry its bounds. A sequel to the present volume might collect poets writing in English—in many kinds of English—from outside America, bringing Patience Agbabi and Jen Hadfield and Robert Minhinnick and Daljit Nagra and Denise Riley, for example, to what are principally American eyes. Partly because I would put them in such a sequel, I have excluded poets—some of my favorite poets—who live or have lived in the United States but do not seem to consider themselves American, and who are uncontroversially claimed by other national traditions: Anne Carson, Seamus Heaney, Paul Muldoon, A. K. Ramanujan, and Derek Walcott, for example, have been consistently and correctly identified as Canadian, Irish, Indian, and West Indian. They are also in no danger of being ignored. (Nor is Thom Gunn, who might well have been poet number sixty-one.)

Compared to the book I expected to write when I began making this one, six years ago, and compared to the set of contemporary poets I've written about, and enjoyed, thus far, the book you are now reading probably has more poems that tell or at least imply stories, more poems that portray consistent scenes, and fewer contributions from the precincts of contemporary "experiment," from what many of us call the post-avant-garde. One reason is pedagogical: some of those poets require that you have read others—they are, so to speak, more specialized, or more advanced. Many works of the post-avant-garde, from Tan Lin to Susan Howe to John Beer, take the book, not the single poem or page, as their most important unit. The obviously challenging parts of American poetry today—those represented here, and those (such as Lin's and Beer's oeuvres) which are not—may have fewer readers, but they have terrific explainers: if you want more about the contemporary poets whose work places them farthest from prose sense, please see the critics (Altieri, Nealon, Perloff, Reed and Shockley, in particular) recommended in my section on further reading.

I have excluded poets all of whose best works are more than a few pages long, unless those works' short components can stand on their own. Thus, for example, Harryette Mullen's *Muse & Drudge* is represented here, but Theresa Hak Kyung Cha's *Dictée* is not. Nor are Lyn Hejinian's *My Life*, Ronald Johnson's *ARK*, or Cathy Park Hong's exciting narrative *Dance Dance Revolution*. The considerable talents of Nowak and Spahr, like those of Darcie Dennigan, Larry Levis, Ronaldo Wilson, and Rachel Zucker, could be represented effectively by ten-page segments in a ten-poet anthology but cannot flourish within the format of this book. Potential conflicts of interest have led me to hard calls, and much second-guessing, in both directions: while I have included poets known to me personally, I decided not to consider several—especially those of my own generation—either because I know them so well or because they published and supported my own work so frequently for so long.

Influential scholars now argue that we should study not poets' styles so much as, in Stephen Voyce's terms, their "practice": "not a particular author or work" but the ways in which "experimental forms of writing are inexorably linked to experiments in forms of collective life and action"—who paid to publish that page, what happened to it, what social difference it could make. This introduction might help you do just that. Some poets might not separate life and art. But the essays in this book often must; if we could not sever poems from their poets, at least provisionally, it would be very hard for those of us not already acquainted with their social circles to discover new poets to read. This book includes poets who sometimes say or imply that they do not believe in individuals, who want poems that do not rely on notions of individual consciousness, feeling, or voice. Such poets, in our time, have done some of the strangest, most individual work, and it has been appreciated, shared, and imitated by individual writers, most of whom used their individual names.

As I put this book together I wrote, sometimes, exactly what I expected to write. At other times I was surprised: I liked a poem less, and discarded it; I liked a poet more; I discovered that one or another poem meant almost the opposite of what I, teaching, had taken it to mean. The best surprises came when I asked myself to investigate a category, a kind of poem or a set of poets, I had previously overlooked, and then discovered a poem I turned out to love.

I was slightly surprised, by the end of the selection process, at the ratio of so-called lyric to anti-lyrical poems, at how many of the recent poems I chose to include had consistent scenes, and speakers and senses of voice: readers attached to the present-day post-avant-garde may find in this book, not a case against it, but a claim that it's not the only game in town.

The biggest surprise, though, had little to do with any individual poet or poem. In writing these essays I realized just how long ago, how far away, 1981 seems. What we now call the "poetry world"—what its participants sometimes called (and occasionally still call) "po-biz"—was smaller, whiter, and more dependent on New York trade presses such as Farrar, Straus and Giroux or Alfred A. Knopf, which play a role, but a smaller one, in the poetry scenes of the current century. Some poets performed their work in theaters and nightclubs and outdoor public gatherings, but the term "poetry slam" had not been coined, and many of the "little magazines" that would be online today relied on mimeographs. St. Mark's was thriving, but there was no Dark Room Collective, no Cave Canem, no Kundiman, no Asian American Writers' Workshop, no Electronic Poetry Center at the University of Buffalo, no genius.com, no poems.com, no Internet. There was no *Best American Poetry* annual, no competing *Best American Experimental Writing* annual, and of course most of the writers we now see as the old guard were midcareer poets or just starting out. I have tried to look back at the early 1980s with a clarified sense of what was possible then, as well as to look around at what we have, at what practicing poets find valuable, now.

When I started to write this book I was excited: there were, and are, so many contemporary poets and poems I like, and for so many and various reasons! Some seemed, and seem, inexhaustible, practically demanding the attention I wanted to give them; others seemed, and still seem, unduly neglected, overdue for the frames that this book can provide. When I was midway through, I was happy but tired: there was so much to learn, so much to discover, so many poets and poems and ways of reading poetry that I had not encountered, or had not been encouraged to practice, before. (Unsurprisingly, these poets and ways of reading were less often white, and less often from the Northeast, and less often examined by critics I knew.) Now, at the end, I'm still excited, but also sad, and certainly apprehensive: there's so much that I could have put in but had to leave out, so many poems that could have been number sixty-one or sixty-two or sixty-five, and—perhaps more consequentially—other poets whom my peers admire but whose work has left me lukewarm, if not cold. I'm sad, too, about the poets I've left out because they cannot fit our format, the poets whose best poems are twenty pages long, or are whole books, or are audio files, or were written too early to count; I can describe—sometimes I have described—their work elsewhere.

"No kind of book is easier to attack than an anthology," remarked the Canadian critic Northrop Frye. Yet no kind of book is more useful for readers new to a field, or for experienced readers who want to expand their own taste. Some readers will find my selections too obvious, or too "mainstream"; others will think them idiosyncratic to a fault. Others still will find this book marked too obviously, too deeply, by my own experience and temperament: I'm a white Anglo fortysomething writer and teacher with two genders, two kids, an expensive education, and an adult life sponsored by college English departments in the Northeast and the Midwest, not to mention classical piano training, college radio experience, and a habit of buying comic books; an athletic Filipino critic raised in Denver surely would not choose all the poems I chose. My title—"The Poem Is You"—means not that all the poems here reflect you exactly (not even the poems you might write yourself can do that) nor that all the poems will speak to you; instead (as the first essay in this book explains) it means that the poems invite you to try out, or try on, or simply encounter, the identities, the kinds of language, and the ways to see the world, that each poem opens up.

Still other readers might well object to this book on the grounds that a real critic ought to pick not sixty or thirty poets from her own time, but three or four. Randall Jarrell quipped that previous eras suffered from "what T. S. Eliot called 'fools' approval': most of the poets were bad, most of the critics were bad, and they loved each other." Yet Eliot himself averred that when we are reading the poetry of our own day, there's no point in trying to decide who is truly great: it's hard enough to say what is, in his term, "genuine." Eliot said so by way of introducing Marianne Moore, a poet who seems to many of us better—or greater—than she did to most critics during her writing career; the same qualities that made her seem minor, eccentric, twee, overscrupulous, limited, Baroque, or (not coincidentally) feminine have magnified her influence today, as a few poets in this book (Angie Estes and Robyn Schiff, for example) imply.

"Some books are undeservedly forgotten," quipped W. H. Auden; "no books are undeservedly remembered." I have no regrets about the poems I have put in, but many about the poets and poems I left out. I am delighted that a book originally planned to include fifty poems, as if for the fifty states, now encompasses sixty, not least because America is more than its fifty states

(I, for example, grew up in and around D.C.). I am grateful for the pressure that creating this book has put on my own tastes, on my own sense of what I like and what I choose to read, and why. And I take heart from the knowledge that no collection, no canon (whatever that means), no single set of favorite poems, is final: like any such work, this one will be replaced by future collections, future commentators, who will—if I am lucky, if I have read carefully—admire, and enjoy, and learn something from, some of these sixty poems.

JOHN ASHBERY

Paradoxes and Oxymorons

This poem is concerned with language on a very plain level.
Look at it talking to you. You look out a window
Or pretend to fidget. You have it but you don't have it.
You miss it, it misses you. You miss each other.

The poem is sad because it wants to be yours, and cannot.
What's a plain level? It is that and other things,
Bringing a system of them into play. Play?
Well, actually, yes, but I consider play to be

A deeper outside thing, a dreamed role-pattern,
As in the division of grace these long August days
Without proof. Open-ended. And before you know
It gets lost in the steam and chatter of typewriters.

It has been played once more. I think you exist only
To tease me into doing it, on your level, and then you aren't there
Or have adopted a different attitude. And the poem
Has set me softly down beside you. The poem is you.

Poems are complex, and sometimes opaque; poems aspire to transparency. Poems are speech from the soul, embodied emotions; poems are modes of resistance, ways to get around our relentless, high-pressure insistence that everything have a clear meaning and use. Poems are intellectual challenges; each one should look new. Poems are what poets *must* write: each one should sound authentic, like real speech. Yet poems, in a literate culture, are not speech at all—modern poems should puncture the illusion of speech, making us notice that these are words put on paper, where our imaginations must lend them voice or sound.

Intelligent, well-informed readers have made all these claims about contemporary American poetry (and about poems from other places or times). All fit some of the poems in this book. Ashbery's intimately evasive not-quite-sonnet belongs at the start of this book and gives us our title, not just because it's such a delightful (if baffling) invitation but also because it addresses each of these claims; it may even satisfy them all.

Since those claims seem to contradict one another, a poem that supports them all is a paradox (a seeming self-contradiction), if not an oxymoron (a real self-contradiction). Earlier poets used paradoxes too: the lovers in Renaissance sonnets burn with icy fire; Christ is God and man. Ashbery's title points back to those serious paradoxes, as well as to the comic ambience of "oxymoron," a word that implies a mistake. And this poem, when it starts, does not sound paradoxical, or witty, or even deep: it's determined to make poetic use of truisms and clichés, from "very plain level" to "set me down softly" and "wants to be yours."

Ashbery's stanza calls our attention—casually, offhandedly—to our own role in making these familiar words seem to speak: if you "look" at the poem, you'll see no talker there. "Paradoxes and Oxymorons" thus begins by teasing its reader, and then describes itself, and you, as having been teased. "Miss" can mean "miss the meaning," "misunderstand," and also "long for; regret the absence of." The poem remains over *there*, and you wish it were *here*: more comprehensible, closer to you. In one sense all poems work that way: they do not make their authors, their authors' absent loved ones, or our loved ones physically present, even when we wish they could. One theory has it that poems come about *because* of that wish, because we are isolated in our own lives ("each in his prison," as T. S. Eliot had it). Poems are the speech that we never hear in real life, releasing us from the prisons of our skins. Ashbery's poem supports that serious theory.

Then it asks if we would like to play a game. Eliot also called poetry a "superior amusement"; traditions older than English highlight not the emotional charge in poetic words but their power as riddles and puzzles, their form of "play." (For more on "play," see the poems in this book by John Hollander and Lucia Perillo.) Like any game, this one has rules, though the rules can change; as with many games, from baseball to kickball to chess, those who love it can give it additional meanings, make it "a deeper outside thing."

No wonder, then, that our best-loved poems—whether or not they also seem paradoxical—can seem to give us "grace": like a perfect summer day, poetic language can make a pedestrian moment sublime. To see poetry in this way—a way that the poets we now call Romantic could see it—is to align the best poems with unspoiled nature, with the outdoors, with spontaneous speech, as against prepared texts, white-collar work, and modern technology, "the steam and chatter of typewriters," including the typewriter on which Ashbery probably wrote, or retyped, this poem. Twelve lines on, "Paradoxes and Oxymorons" has incorporated a kind of supercompressed history of ideas about poetry, from oral cultures' riddles to industrial modernism: "It has been played once more." But to what purpose? What next?

In other words, to whom will a poem such as this one speak? To novices, to initiates, to everybody who wants to learn its codes, to members of one or another subculture or school? "Paradoxes and Oxymorons" evokes the situation of all poems, or all people—trapped in our separate selves, hoping that someone will "tease me into doing it" (whatever "it" might be). But it also speaks to the feeling that serious poets once had readers but no longer do. That feeling has seemed contemporary for every generation since about the 1830s, when novels became more commercially successful than poetry in Britain and the United States. "Is verse a dying technique?" asked the critic Edmund Wilson in 1928.

How to address that feeling, or its basis in fact? Poets might find aesthetic as well as social success by speaking to subcultures, to particular demographics. Ashbery is a gay man who grew up before Stonewall; in Ashbery's indirections, John Shoptaw and other critics have seen versions and echoes of midcentury gay code. Poets might instead address imagined readers, not real ones; maybe they need only address one (and that one is *you*). Most poems that give the illusion of intimacy—Shakespeare's sonnets make fine examples— address someone for whom the reader stands in: a lover, former lover, parent, child, God. Or else the poet speaks to herself. But in many of Ashbery's poems (as the critic Bonnie Costello points out), "you" is really, literally, any person who has been reading this poem. His poems show how "writing and reading," as Costello remarks, "require the very silence and solitude they are designed to dispel." "As we respond to the 'you' in Ashbery's poems, uncertain whether we are addressees or bystanders," the effect can be cute, exhilarating, or even (as Costello concludes) "a repeated experience of embarrassment." We blush as we read; we feel addressed, then overlooked, as the poem comes "down" to "your level," then rises away.

Compared to other poems by other poets, "Paradoxes and Oxymorons" might seem elusive, winking, or even bizarre; compared to many other poems by John Ashbery, it is the soul of clarity. During the 1950s and 1960s (much of which he spent as an art critic in Paris) Ashbery seemed strange, or marginal, or part of a limited school (the New York School, which also included Barbara Guest and Frank O'Hara). During the 1970s he came to seem central—at least among white Anglo poets—for critics and schools who agreed on little else. Harold Bloom and others read him as a Romantic prophet, or a failed prophet, in the tradition of Wallace Stevens and Hart Crane; language writers and their allies could admire his slipperiness. Still other poets and critics saw him as the latest development in a more or less traditional personal lyric, finding new ways to present the pathos of memory, the tenuousness of friendship, and the disappointments of erotic love. "There is a meditative Ashbery, a formalist Ashbery, a comic Ashbery, a late-Romantic Ashbery, a Language poet Ashbery, and so on": so Susan Schultz began *The Tribe of John*, her 1995 book about his influence. There is even a minor subgenre of poems about him.

And he can seem aware, if not of his fame, then of his place in a crowded field. More than many poets, and even in these relatively pellucid, traditionally arranged near-pentameters, Ashbery depends on our awareness that other poets have come before him, that he writes for self-consciously literary communities, even when he sounds like he is talking to himself. "Paradoxes and Oxymorons" seems to know that it is far from the first poem in history; it is not even the first poem in its collection, occurring third in Ashbery's *Shadow Train*, a book of poems in four quatrains (sixteen lines) that sometimes resemble sonnets but do not tell a story or make up a sequence. (Many hold other jokes: one is entitled "Untilted.")

Like several other poems in *this* book, Ashbery's almost jocular late-summer non-sonnet is an ars poetica, a poem that designs to tell us what poetry—this kind of poetry, his kind of poetry—does. It presents both a warning and an invitation, like a sign at the entrance to an amusement park ride: you must be at least this sophisticated to ride here; you must be at least this able to tolerate double and triple puns, irresolutions, cases in which a meaning is really a tease. "Ashbery's work famously resists attempts to extract a program, method, or message," writes the critic and memoirist Michael Clune. "His poems can seem like ingenious machines for making nearly any statement look faintly ridiculous, especially any statement about the principles of the poetic machine's construction."

That versatile, volatile ridiculousness is itself a statement about what poems say and mean and do. In some ways it is not "plain" at all. And yet it is "concerned with language on a very plain level": it, or the person it represents, feels lonely, and wants to join you. It wants to know what happens to you when you sit down to read, not a long novel, not a restaurant check or an op-ed, but (whatever you consider to be) a poem. And what happens is that, however self-consciously, belatedly, or tongue-in-cheek, you imagine that some other soul, some "I," shares something with you that could not be shared without poems.

Yet the same poem that solicits interpretation (asks us to decide what it means) and solicits companionship (asks you to join it) also resists those things, pushing the reader slightly away; we are told as clearly as Ashbery ever tells us anything that what the poem means for one reader cannot be quite what it means or does for another. This poem may fit your feelings perfectly, or describe feelings you did not know you had (in which case it "is you"); at the same time it does something else for someone else.

For all that it is an Ashbery poem, a foxy, teasing, slippery New York School poem, "Paradoxes and Oxymorons" thus resembles (and tells us that it resembles) and introduces (and tells us that it introduces) many other kinds of poems, even poetry in general. In particular, it resembles the rest of the poems in this book: even as I attempt to guide you through them, the poems can and should stay weird, slip away from assigned meanings, speak to other readers in other ways. Critics can—I can—guide you into their workings, help them make more sense, show you some of their intricacies, invitations, special abilities; but the rest is up to you.

TATO LAVIERA

tito madera smith

(for Dr. Juan Flores)

he claims he can translate palés matos'
black poetry faster than i can talk,
and that if i get too smart,
he will double translate pig latin
english right out of webster's
dictionary, do you know him?

he claims he can walk into east harlem
apartment where langston hughes gives
spanglish classes for newly-arrived
immigrants seeking a bolitero-numbers
career and part-time vendors of cuchi-
fritters sunday afternoon in central
park, do you know him?

he claims to have a stronghold of the
only santería secret baptist sect in
west harlem, do you know him?

he claims he can talk spanish styled in
sunday dress eating crabmeat-jueyes
brought over on the morning eastern
plane deep fried by la negra costoso
joyfully singing puerto rican folklore:
"maría luisa no seas brava,
llévame contigo pa la cama," or
"oiga capitán delgado, hey captain delgado,

mande a revisar la grama, please inspect
the grass, que dicen que un aeroplano,
they say that an airplane throws marijuana
seeds."

do you know him? yes you do,
i know you know him, that's right,
madera smith, tito madera smith:
he blacks and prieto talks at the same time,
splitting his mother's santurce talk,
twisting his father's south carolina soul,
adding new york scented blackest harlem
brown-eyes diddy bops, tú sabes mami,
that I can ski like a bomba soul salsa
mambo turns to aretha franklin stevie
wonder nicknamed patato guaguancó steps,
do you know him?

he puerto rican talks to las mamitas
outside the pentecostal church, and
he gets away with it, fast-paced i
understand-you-my-man, with clave
sticks coming out of his pockets hooked
to his stereophonic 15-speaker indispensable
disco sounds blasting away at cold reality
struggling to say estás buena baby
as he walks out of tune and out of
step with alleluia cascabells,
puma sneakers,
pants rolled up,
shirt cut in middle chest,
santería chains,
madamo pantallas,

into the spanish social club,
to challenge elders in dominoes,
like the king of el diario's
budweiser tournament
drinking cerveza-beer
like a champ.
do you know him?
well, i sure don't,
and if i did, i'd
refer him to 1960
social scientists
for assimilation
acculturation
digging
autopsy
into
their
heart
attacks,
oh,
oh,
there
he
comes,
you can call him tito,
or you can call him madera,
or you can call him smitty,
or you can call him mr. t.,
or you can call him nuyorican,
or you can call him black,
or you can call him latino,
or you can call him mr. smith,
his sharp eyes of awareness

greeting us in aristocratic harmony:
"you can call me many things, but
you gotta call me something."

There is no Tito Madera Smith, but there should be, and there are certainly real people like him. Pluripotent snappy dresser, domino champion, slang-slinger, street style icon, virtual guardian angel and patron saint, the man in the poem (Laviera has said he is fictional) unites in his own person the virtues, the tastes, and the semisecret knowledge of African American, island Puerto Rican, and Puerto Rican New York immigrant culture, which did and do overlap and fuse, especially but not only in New York City.

That fusion—and, sometimes, New York Puerto Rican identity generally—has gone by the term "Nuyorican." Originally a pejorative island designation for Puerto Ricans who sounded or acted black, "Nuyorican" during the 1970s became a neutral or laudatory description both of an ethnic group and of a poetic style, as in "Nuyorican poetry" and the Nuyorican Poets Café, both of which Laviera helped to create. Tito Madera Smith, both the man and the poem, serves as a positive example of the inherently mixed, and proud, Nuyorican.

Laviera's verse takes part in other traditions too, both verbal and musical, Puerto Rican and international. "tito madera smith" is a praise poem, an encomium: such poems go back at least to Pindar, the ancient Greek poet whose odes celebrated athletic champions. Like Pindar, Laviera uses the occasion of a hero's life to celebrate a culture and to defend it against detractors—not only white Anglos but (as the poet and critic Urayoán Noel has explained) also the Puerto Rican nationalists of the 1970s, who wanted to separate island culture and language from an English-dominant mainland.

Laviera's pride says otherwise. Among the Nuyorican writers of the 1970s and 1980s, Laviera wrote perhaps the most often quoted single poem, the manifesto of sorts called "AmeRícan." All Laviera's books hold poems wholly in Spanish, as well as poems in standard English and poems like this one that mix standard English, standard international Spanish, island-only spoken Spanish, and black American dialect. "I have five hats, all Puerto Rican," Laviera told one interviewer: "the Latino hat, the urban hat, the black hat, the Boricua hat, and the hemispheric hat." Like other founders of Nuyorican poetry in the 1970s (Pedro Pietri, Miguel Piñero), Laviera also wrote stage plays.

Nuyorican identity in poetry—and not only for Laviera—strives to sound like a stage performance, to feel not only alive but "live," as if the poet were presenting his body before an audience. It evokes both spoken stage dialogue and live musical performance, especially the call-and-response of the Puerto Rican musical genres *bomba* and *plena*: "oíga capitán delgado" ("listen, [police] Captain Delgado"; "hey, Captain Delgado") quotes the refrain from a frequently performed *plena*.

That poetry also thinks about the physical location of Puerto Rican bodies in urban space, about where they must go, where they are prohibited from going, what happens to what kind of body where. It may describe a barrio or the routes between barrios, it may strike back against physical segregation, and it often works to make the body of the poet present—in fact or in imagination—to the people who hear the poem. Quoting the late New York University professor, activist, and scholar of Puerto Rican culture Juan Flores, to whom Laviera dedicates this poem, Urayoán Noel explains that Laviera "embodies a community by performing its unincorporated language." His performance style, Noel continues, "hews to the humorously rhythmic and high-energy delivery of oral poets" such as the street-based (and, at one point, homeless) Jorge Brandon, "often savoring syllables and stretching out word endings . . . Laviera performs an Afro-Latino vernacular as a creative signifying of urban space." (Both Laviera and Pietri wrote encomia to Brandon, nicknamed "El Coco Que Habla," "the coconut that speaks." Laviera's "jorge brandon" doubles as an ars poetica: "poetry is the incessant beauty called / a person by an action that takes form.") Like the real street poet Brandon, and like the heroic Tito within the poem, the implied author who speaks Laviera's poem has to be imagined as reciting it, using techniques fit for recitation, techniques that readers who knew the neighborhoods would not have to stop to decode.

But that does not mean you must be Puerto Rican, much less Nuyorican, to read him. Laviera begins by praising bilingualism and a kind of biculturalism that unites the street to the book, oral to written poetry, original composition to simultaneous translation, and simultaneous translation (literally, the rendering of one language into another in real time) to the cultural translation or code-switching that almost all immigrants learn to perform. "He blacks" (acts black, does black things, speaks black vernacular in English) and "prieto talks" ("prieto" being U.S. Latino slang for a black or dark-skinned person) "at the same time"; he also boasts, and he seems to do most of the things he boasts about.

Half the poem comprises Laviera's, or Smith's, tour of places, languages, practices, and tastes where that biculturalism would serve him well. Luis Palés Matos (1898–1959) brought African and Cuban themes and symbols into the poetry of Puerto Rico; simultaneous translation from Palés Matos's "black" Spanish into English, or black English, would be intellectually impressive, but perhaps on its own "too smart," too academic, to show the full range of Smith's supposed gifts, whereas the pig Latin shows a sense of the ridiculous, as well as a man who can think on his feet.

He can also go places with those feet: from the Puerto Rican Lower East Side to east Harlem, for example, where connections between Puerto Rican identity and black American literature go back for generations. Langston Hughes translated works by Nicolas Guillén, the poet of Afro-Cuban identity, and often treated blackness and black literature as hemispheric or global phenomena, though he may not have taught "Spanglish" to anyone. A *bolitero* is a numbers runner, someone who works in illegal lotteries; *cuchifritos* are fried pork, street food; Santurce is the Puerto Rican town of Laviera's birth. Chatting up "mamitas" and then taking part in the old people's game of dominoes, this Smith unites generations as well as neighborhoods, though he remains insistently male. "Do you know him," like most of the best poetic refrains, changes meaning as it recurs, but it also means one thing for Nuyorican people, and another for the rest. If you do know these urban spaces, these folkways, you can take pride in the knowledge; if you are not Puerto Rican at all and you do not know any Puerto Ricans with a connection to black culture, then Laviera will at least show how you have missed out.

"tito madera smith," for all its anatomy of city life, thus has less in common with the "social scientists" whom the poet mocks (who wanted to understand, improve, or control the neighborhoods they would study dispassionately) than with the modernism of, say, T. S. Eliot's "The Waste Land," where poetry shows us, directly or by allusion, what we should know because the poet cares for it. For example, we should know the music: love songs ("maria luisa"), drug songs, the black American music of Stevie Wonder and Aretha Franklin, and claves (pronounced "KLA-ves"), sticklike percussion instruments important to Latin styles, including the *guaguancó* music of the percussionist Carlos "Patato" Valdez. (*Clave* in Spanish means, literally, "key": "tito madera smith" first appeared in Laviera's book *EnClave*, whose title makes one more bilingual pun.) *El Diario* names several newspapers, but Laviera must mean the Spanish-language daily based in New York. Smith's hypothetical

day concludes with a drinking contest, the least dignified among his achievements, as simultaneous translation is the most.

So far "tito madera smith" follows the conventions of praise poetry and of
enthusiastic oral performance—it might be taken as representative Nuyorican
poetry (though no more so than, say, Stanley Kunitz's work is representative
post-confessional poetry). Its standout rhetorical elements—quasi-refrain at
the end of each verse paragraph, iterations and repetitions, long sentences made
out of accretive short phrases—help the verse feel "live," and they portray
Smith as a perfect example of hybrid black and Puerto Rican identity, someone
who demands, and gets, respect for all that he is.

But I have been writing as if Smith were real, and as if Laviera knew him.
Laviera admits—and the lines change radically, growing much shorter, as he
admits—that "i sure don't." But he would like to: indeed, a few lines later,
Smith seems to arrive—"oh, / oh, / there / he / comes." He must be acknowledged, never ignored, and he must be spoken to, not just spoken about:
people like Smith will exist if only we imagine them hard enough, and if we
show the right kind of respect for the people he resembles now.

Such people should hold themselves in high regard—but they should also
make jokes. If you do not call Smith by his given names or his family names,
"you can call him mr. t," *T* for Tito, or for Tato Laviera (the actor Mr. T, in
1981, was a prominent pro wrestler, not yet the co-star of *Rocky III* or *The
A-Team*). "Mr. Smith" could be an American everyman: and what if the de-
fault American hero, the everyman—say, the Mr. Smith in some future remake of the film *Mr. Smith Goes to Washington*—were black, Latino, Nuyorican? (What would Laviera have thought of *Hamilton*?)

Thus the poem ends not with the coming of Laviera's composite hero but
with his second coming. By his triumphant return, Smith (and hence Laviera)
has incorporated all four of the stages in what Flores called "the Puerto Rican's coming-to-consciousness," a process that Flores said he came to understand (it "dawned on me") as he was reading Laviera's poems. First, the Puerto
Rican reacts to the northern city; then he remembers the island. Third, he
reenters a working-class multiethnic city where "the life of poor people is a
legitimate and abundant source of cultural energy." Fourth, he reacts to
"Anglo-American society," with its white tastes and its standard English, from
a position of greater confidence. The last examples of code-switching and dialect mixing—after the poem has shifted back out of its monosyllables into
the earlier eight-to-ten-syllable line—takes place not between Spanish and English but between levels of English, from the "aristocratic" polysyllables back

to the street talk of "gotta." If someone exactly like Smith could exist, with every one of Smith's skills and his justified pride, then we could experience in fact, from day to day, the kind of "aristocratic harmony," the pride in new, mixed, Nuyorican styles, that Laviera's exclamations both imagine and strive to make real.

RICHARD WILBUR

The Ride

The horse beneath me seemed
To know what course to steer
Through the horror of snow I dreamed,
And so I had no fear,

Nor was I chilled to death
By the wind's white shudders, thanks
To the veils of his patient breath
And the mist of sweat from his flanks.

It seemed that all night through,
Within my hand no rein
And nothing in my view
But the pillar of his mane,

I rode with magic ease
At a quick, unstumbling trot
Through shattering vacancies
On into what was not,

Till the weave of the storm grew thin,
With a threading of cedar-smoke,
And the ice-blind pane of an inn
Shimmered, and I awoke.

How shall I now get back
To the inn-yard where he stands,
Burdened with every lack,
And waken the stable-hands

To give him, before I think
That there was no horse at all,
Some hay, some water to drink,
A blanket, and a stall?

Does poetry change? Should it change much from generation to generation? Richard Wilbur's long career seems to stand for the idea that it need not: from the 1940s through to the present day, the Second World War veteran and second poet laureate of the United States has offered carefully wrought examples of a metrical craftsmanship that could have been honored and recognized in any era from Shakespeare's to our own. His poetry is "conservative" in that sense: it insists on historical continuities.

It is also "conservative" in the sense that it often hopes or tries to save (conserve) things in danger of disappearing, being crowded out, overwhelmed, or overrun (in this sense Greenpeace is conservative too). In this poem such things include a dream-horse, a path almost erased by snow, a familiar ethic of mutual assistance and respect for labor, and an idea of imagination itself. Wilbur's stanzaic gallop through the veils and storms of nothingness becomes both an existential claim about what poetry and imagination can and cannot do and a nod to the real world of real people and service animals, in which Wilbur's careful, kind, skeptical, and politically liberal imagination begins.

Before we can see what the poem does with political liberalism, we have to see how it figures imagination. Imaginative discoveries, like poems, like dreams, can seem hard to recapture once lost. W. S. Merwin, a contemporary of Wilbur's, imagined the poems he had not been able to write: "How many times have I heard the locks close / And the lark take the keys / And hang them in heaven," reads Merwin's poem "The Poem." Percy Bysshe Shelley compared the imagination to a fading coal. Such earlier poets' efforts to keep visionary discoveries alive give Wilbur the precursors for his own dream-trip: he is nothing if not aware of what came before him, even if the snowed-out vistas and the smooth surfaces of his stanzas make it harder to see.

But what does it mean to keep a vision alive? Wilbur's balanced phrases ("the ice-blind pane of an inn") and his exact rhymes suggest a poet who relies less on inspiration than on conscious skill. Yet his choice of stanza and meter—trimeter quatrains rhymed *abab*, so-called ballad stanzas, with free substitutions of triple feet for double (to the VEILS of his PAT-ient

BREATH)—strongly recall the supernatural ballads of the Romantic poets, such as John Keats's "La Belle Dame Sans Merci," where the poet or his hapless stand-in is overcome by a force from another realm. Wilbur does not present the poet as a prophet with a divine message, but neither does he present himself as a craftsman working to order. Instead the poet and the reader join each other on a ride across the territory that constitutes the poem—and they have help. They need it, too. Wilbur's generous steed renders survivable, and exciting, what in other hands would be (literally still is) a night-mare.

That steed also adapts and renders tolerable the secret nightmare inside an all-too-famous poem by Robert Frost: who doesn't know "Stopping by Woods on a Snowy Evening"? Wilbur, who has lived in western Massachusetts and taught at Amherst College (which he attended) for most of his life, often presents himself as the heir of Frost, especially in the New England seasonal poetry of Wilbur's later volumes. These "spare lines," the critic Bruce Michelson agrees, "recall the famous Frost scene and perhaps the Frost voice." Wilbur presents himself, as Frost once presented himself, on a horse, in the dark, in the New England woods; the horse (as in "Stopping by Woods") appears to know the right way better than he does.

Like many of Frost's best poems, "Stopping by Woods" wraps in a popular cloak of homely wisdom something close to existential despair: there is really nobody out there, nothing to see, and no such thing as society to receive the poet after the long night. Wilbur's horse is an answer to Frost's, and the horse (like many of Wilbur's animals) has a politics, something like the tragic liberalism of Reinhold Niebuhr, which sees in mortality and in recent history reasons we can, and should, use the institutions of society for mutual assistance. As James Longenbach explained in a pathbreaking essay, Wilbur has been for decades "that rare thing: a seriously misunderstood poet," both in terms of his politics and in terms of the metaphysics his forms imply, which are consistently liberal and gently secularist. Horses, even magic ones in Wilbur's world, require "stable-hands," and riders owe something—housing and food, for example—to the animals that carry them, and to the strangers who care for those animals, no matter what "magic" the journey seems to contain.

For those who know the rest of Wilbur's work, it is tempting (though it might be overreading) to see, in the reliable, powerful horse that keeps his rider safe and warm, the horse that risks vanishing from memory now, a kind of preemptive elegy for the welfare state, which America rode through the Great Depression and whose growth over decades—and whose subsequent sabotage by political conservatives—Wilbur lived through. In 1987–1988 he was the second writer to bear the title of poet laureate (earlier poets held similar duties as consultants in poetry to the Library of Congress); the only poem Wilbur published during his year in the job, "A Fable," was an Aesopian caution against President Ronald Reagan's program of nuclear missile defense.

It might go too far to see, in "The Ride," a full defense of the New Deal, or the Great Society, in the Reagan era. At the least, though, we can see in "The Ride" a rebuke to poets who consider themselves self-made men, who credit themselves and only themselves for their acts of imagination, who hold themselves up (as Frost sometimes did) as autonomous, inimitable examples ("the exception / That I like to think I am in everything," Frost called himself). The Frost of "Stopping by Woods" made his own decisions, wryly overruling his inquisitive horse. But the Wilbur of "The Ride" has to trust his equine companion, not only to get him through snow to his destination but also to know where he is going and to keep him from hypothermia ("chilled to death"). Wilbur's own wry and careful vision begins in helplessness, requires credit to someone or something outside the poet, and concludes with measured and timely acts of obligations inside a larger, precarious social life. That vision includes not just death but taxes, imaginary hay as support for the arts, not a "burden" without justification but a matter of mutual gratitude.

Whether or not "The Ride" becomes directly political, it is a poem of pathos about the fleeting and yet articulable nature of inspiration, and about how one writer's moments of transport depend on the labor performed, sometimes invisibly, by other people (and animals) at other times. The dreamed ride comes from a dreamed horse; the real poem comes about because the real poet has the time and resources to write, and who supplied those? Stable hands, and horses; not demons, nor gods. Wilbur's consciously balanced, artificial form, working against the onward rush of his sentence, also "resists any mystical sense" (to quote Longenbach) "of the poet's ability to transcend the boundaries of language or thought." "The Ride" admits, at the same time, that we wish poetry *could* do such a thing, that we go to poetry to see that wish shared. Wilbur's imagined stable, so full of nostalgia, also recalls the stable in Thomas Hardy's Christmas poem "The Oxen," another great poem in rhyming quatrains, by a disillusioned political liberal, about reluctant post-Christian disbelief.

Many of us would like to have a religious or quasi-religious belief in something that could steer us through all the difficulties of waking life. But "magic ease," like thrilling horror, like anything supernatural, belongs to the night. Come day, we must make choices, credit our sources, feed the hungry,

compensate service workers, get down and walk. The old-fashioned confidence
that Wilbur's rhythms suggest does not control his tone, which begins in some
fear and ends in the familiar sadness of an unmet obligation: animals and
people (real and imaginary) continue in their needs, and the poet does not
know how to help them out.

"The Ride" came first in Wilbur's 1987 *New and Collected Poems*, making
it both a way to greet the times and an introduction to the inspiration—and
the craft, the care—that guides Wilbur's entire oeuvre. The kind of care that
a good rider and stable hands can show a faithful horse becomes Wilbur's
figure for the poet's work, even as the life-threatening ride through harrowing
winter weather becomes (to quote Frost again) the figure a poem makes. The
blanket at the end is the blanket under which we sleep, or would like to sleep,
or would like to continue our sleep in the morning, even though we must wake
to perform our practical tasks, our real-world obligations to real-world colleagues, students, parents, partners, or children. But we may also—so Wilbur
suggests, in his measured way—have obligations to our dreams: we should
take time to feed, thank, preserve, and shelter them, before they fade away.

LUCILLE CLIFTON

my dream about the second coming

mary is an old woman without shoes.
she doesn't believe it.
not when her belly starts to bubble
and leave the print of a finger where
no man touches.
not when the snow in her hair melts away.
not when the stranger she used to wait for
appears dressed in lights at her
kitchen table.
she is an old woman and
doesn't believe it.

when Something drops onto her toes one night
she calls it a fox
but she feeds it.

Clifton characteristically combines compression and demotic language (there is no word here that grade-schoolers would not understand) with many-layered allusion, starting with her title. Clifton could easily have called the poem "Motherhood" (which would ally it with other poems about working-class mothers, such as Gwendolyn Brooks's "the bean eaters") or "Annunciation" (since it *is*, after all, an annunciation, an angel bringing news about her conception to Mary; for another 1980s Annunciation, see Jorie Graham's "San Sepolcro"). Instead, Clifton renders approachable, comic, and domestic that normally masculine triumph, the Second Coming. Her Jesus will not return in light as an adult, separating the sheep from the goats with a sword. Nor will he be (as in Yeats's "The Second Coming") replaced by a beast of pagan war. If the world will change radically, the impetus will come from a mother, a Mary, a shoeless one too, here conjoined to the biblical Sarah, a woman who thought herself too old to have children (Genesis 18:11–14).

To say "mary is an old woman without shoes" is to sever the Christian topos of charity, the Gospel's focus on the poor and unserved, from the traditionally Christian interest in virginity, purity, youth: it is to embrace the former and ignore the latter. The skin on her pregnant belly, with its stretch marks, recalls "the print of a finger" (women can touch it too). The burden of the unborn Christ makes Mary seem not prematurely grown-up but notably younger ("the snow in her hair melts away"), and the angel or "stranger" who comes with good news reminds her of someone (perhaps an unreliable partner or father) who has now come home.

But Clifton's Mary is not, after all, young; like Sarah, "she is an old woman and/doesn't believe it." The free verse here resembles, without quite becoming, dactylic lines alternating three and two feet (NOT when the SNOW in her HAIR melts a-WAY). Clifton also flaunts a refrain ("doesn't believe it") that turns into a near rhyme. These shortest lines make a statement of their own: Mary does not have to accept the religion that makes her holy, that tells her she will bear the Son of God, in order to perform the charitable act that religion ought to promote, exists to promote.

Mary does not have to call her new baby Jesus: she can call it whatever she likes. She can even call it a thing ("Something," not a person, though the capital S means it's holy). She can call it by the name of an animal strongly associated with trickery and theft. What's important is that she feeds it. Love— here as in 1 Corinthians 13:13—is more important than faith; and love, as in 1 Corinthians, might also be translated as charity. The kingdom of God will come when we can all behave as mothers, as Marys, nurturing everybody and taking in strays, even strays that appear to be predators, like the real fox that scared Clifton when it kept on appearing in her southern Maryland yard. Mary is "old," but her readers may not be: like many other poets attracted to the parable form, Clifton has created a verbal space open to adults and to readers of grade-school age, who may well share Mary's own reaction to the "good news" the angel or stranger brings. It even becomes a space of worship: as Rachel Harding has explained, Clifton's comfort with spiritual visions, her willingness to rewrite stories from Christian religion, speaks to the specifically black version of women's empowerment named (by Clifton's contemporary Alice Walker) "womanism" and to the history of "black religion, in both its churched and extra-church forms," as "a protected space."

Clifton's friend Adrienne Rich, in *Of Woman Born* (1976), argued that we must see mothers as individuals, responsible to themselves, not only or always to their children. White feminists (Rich among them) often focused on reproductive rights, including abortion, and on ways to make women's embodiment (including pregnancy) less salient in professional and political life. But Clifton and her Mary have other objectives. A mother of six writing after the death of her husband, in her own late forties or fifties, Clifton tended to valorize fertility, the bearing and nurturing of children, along with intuitive, more or less feminine access to language and truth. One of Clifton's most discussed later poems (from 1991's *Quilting*) is "poem in praise of menstruation," which envisions no "river / more beautiful than this / bright as the blood / red edge of the moon"; she also wrote "poem to my uterus," anticipating and dreading a hysterectomy ("where can I go / barefoot / without you / where can you go / without me"), an ingenious and deliberate echo of the Emperor Hadrian's famous Latin poem to his soul. In the poem just before "my dream about the second coming" in *Next* (1987), "my dream about falling," Clifton calls herself "a fruitful woman," then compares herself to "an apple" who "thought / that the tree / was forever / fruitful . . . the fact is the falling. / the dream is the tree."

Clifton herself became a fruitful tree, a resource, for poets who came after her. Her celebrated first books, *good times* (1969) and *good news about the earth* (1972), drew on the aesthetic of the Black Arts Movement (sometimes abbreviated BAM), the late 1960s and 1970s program that asked black poets, playwrights, and novelists to write for black audiences, using black—and eschewing European—language and forms, making work fit for oral delivery, in the populist service of revolutionary struggle. BAM position pieces (the most famous remains Amiri Baraka's "Black Art") and BAM-affiliated poets (Baraka, Sonia Sanchez, Nikki Giovanni) were celebrated as examples of black empowerment, but also excoriated for their advocacy of violence, their sometimes brazen sexism and homophobia. Debates between BAM and non-BAM standards would vex, and inspire, black poets whose careers began in those years. Some black writers, such as Yusef Komunyakaa, proved able to sidestep the harshness of such debates by creating their own aesthetics from jazz. Others, such as the future U.S. poet laureate Rita Dove, responded directly: in Dove's early poem "Upon Meeting Don L. Lee in a Dream," the BAM-era poet and publisher "starts to cry; his eyeballs / Burst into flame," his aesthetic apparently superseded by her cosmopolitan technique.

Later black poets—as the critic Walton Muyumba has explained at length—
would find ways neither to reject BAM entirely nor to confine themselves
to its vision. To do so they would have to find models who were populist
without being exclusionary, demotic without becoming flat and predictable,
and compatible with many radical visions of social justice without depending on visions of imminent revolution. Clifton turned out to be such a
model—for some poets, the single most important model. Her poems project
an unassuming charisma, and their reliance on cadences of black speech
seems to give all readers (including quite young ones) some chance to join in.
Elizabeth Alexander went so far as to say, on Clifton's death in 2010, "I do
not think there is an American poet as beloved as Clifton, or one whose
influence radiated so widely." Clifton took from BAM a demotic simplicity
and a commitment to oral forms. She found in its free verse, and in much
older folk song and story, new directions for the American miniature, the
poem of compressed anecdote or single remark, also practiced by Emily Dickinson, Langston Hughes, Lorine Niedecker, Samuel Menashe, even Kay
Ryan. Like Hughes, Clifton wrote for all ages, often depicting families and
children; she also contributed to the musical *Free to Be . . . You and Me*
(1972–1974). Like Hughes and Niedecker, she assembled sequences: she can
be hard to anthologize, since her poems gain power when they need not
stand alone.

"my dream about the second coming," for example, first published in
Virginia Quarterly Review in 1982, comes in a series of seven "my dream"
poems, all either sonnet-sized or in very short lines, within *Next* (1987). The
first is called "my dream of being white"; the last is "morning mirror," in which
Clifton looks for her own mother in her grown face: "my mother her sad eyes
worn as bark / faces me in the mirror." As the poet goes on she realizes that
she cannot, will not, should not become her mother after all: "my mother refuses to be reflected." (Clifton's own mother, Thelma Moore Sayles, died in
1959, long before the poet began to publish.) What is eternal, what is continuous, what should we cherish, what can we learn, from mothers, from mirrors,
from ourselves as mothers, from the embodied experience that older women
possess?

For one thing, we can learn to stop equating feminine power with innocence, or with virginity, or with girls; we can appreciate what women, especially poor (shoeless) black women, have been through, not as a reason for pity
but as a source of a power that they can pass on. Seeking that friendly power,
Clifton's later poetry also explored the vulnerabilities in her own body: her

treatment for breast cancer, for example, and the kidney she received from her adult daughter. Her remarkable life story, as told in interviews and auto-biographical verse, has sometimes overshadowed the achievements in her other sorts of poems. But the life and the poems, the spiritual vision and the in-terest in womanly bodies, are, as her own poems say, interdependent. This Mary, like Clifton herself, like Clifton's Eve, and like the biblical Sarah, asks us to take a special interest in the female body not as a site for potential autonomy, liberated from everyone and everything else, but as a locus of nur-ture and interdependence, a source of life that is not hers alone.

CARLA HARRYMAN

Possession

Inside, the ear spins beautiful webs.

"With one clear picture of an individual collective abstraction is exposed. There is no smoke rising from over there.

"Let me tell you," he swallowed her and spit her out, "it is a bargain."

"Sing to me," she slipped.

"I don't intend," he said, "to imitate poetry but to be imitated by it."

"I live in a fabrication near something I have never said before. I can't see my doctor and when he . . . I do see him he pelts me syntactically. My assignation burns toward abstraction. Because imperatives never blow over, get on your feet! Stumbling through this padded interstice, my body has limits. Yours doesn't compare notes.

"But let me tell you a story. I am civilized:

"The high illusion constrains the pent-up trees. We float beneath them tortoises bathing in the night. It is primitive. We creak in the fog. The outboard motor racket mutes the wall like a powwow. A small echo fishes with a person's features. Me talking fuses to you. Puberty here, fantasy there." He paused, basing his headtrip on the profile of a sated barbarian. Then proceeded to deliver his child with unconscious mirth.

Surprised by his use of words, the moral presence swelled to veracity plunging the social salad into the contemporary fork. She looked deep into the merchandiser's past. "Yes," she said, "but you enjoy suffering."

Because there was nothing else, he waded across the pool, fading into a mental fog, which, to this day, fuels its maws with the purest minds.

A robot adjusted her seat in the ornate theater. If this was merely an eidetic image why did she want to be nursed? Nothing stuck out.

It was hot, beautiful. True and the same at the same time. The scooped-out center of the continent described the middle of life without describing a figure. Standing around in serialized plateaus was enough to make you cry. But fleeting mammals sucked up revolt.

Oversensitivity was wrong. She wrenched her mind from its wasteland of souvenirs. "Where is that bastard?" She couldn't get enough.

He was behind the door, hiding from the spirit of the new world.

If our selection from John Ashbery seems challenging, you might find this prose poem, or poetic project, simply incomprehensible; if "Paradoxes and Oxymorons" seems pellucid, this text might baffle even you. If you want to skip ahead to other kinds of poems and come back to this one, go ahead; most of the poems in this book, and most American poems of the 1980s and afterward, aren't nearly this far from prose sense. But some of the best poems are.

Is it really a prose poem? Is it a piece of experimental fiction (akin to the short stories of Donald Barthelme)? An advanced psychology experiment, designed to test our perception, to strain our ability to perceive coherence in fiction, perhaps to the breaking point? A series of dreamlike jokes? A scenario for an avant-garde play? Harryman's prose could be any of these, or none; like much of her work (almost all of it in prose, or else printed as stage drama), it will not let us settle in one category of literature.

It does, however, belong—however uneasily—to the categories she and her peers in the San Francisco Bay Area developed during the late 1970s and 1980s. Most of those peers—with whom she collaborated, both at live events and in publishing projects—were poets, among them Rae Armantrout, Lyn Hejinian (whose Tuumba Press first published this work), and Harryman's husband, Barrett Watten. Like other language writing, Harryman's work strives for what Hejinian called "the rejection of closure": it seeks "a necessarily open-ended and continuous response to what's perceived as 'the world'" (in Hejinian's words), trying to show what it might be like to encounter people, or things, or places, or words, while shaking up or trying to escape our assumptions about what they should mean. (You might say it seeks a revolution in language, or a "spirit of the new world.")

Harryman's work does not only occupy the gap, or cross and recross the line, between poetry and prose, or between prose poem and experimental fiction; with its questions about poetry, imitation, and image, its self-consciousness about its own intellectual moves, "Possession" also crosses the multiple lines between poetry and criticism, between creation and analysis, between what happens to us when we are reading (whatever we already see as) poetry and what happens when we are reading about it. The prose works almost sentence by sentence to describe what happens when we read a more traditional, or more clearly poetic, poem: we envision characters and scenes, even though they are made up ("a fabrication"). We enter "illusion," imagining that we can hear people speak ("we talking fuses to you"). We enter an "ornate theater" that we recognize as located in our heads ("merely an eidetic image") and yet, from that theater, we derive some comfort, we may even feel at home (we "want to be nursed"). Parts of that prose lead us into their fictive world, inviting us to imagine characters, as in conventional fiction ("he waded across the pool") or symbols for emotions, as in lyric poems ("the scooped-out center of the continent"). Yet Harryman's prose also works against the very effects (of absorption into scene and plot) that it describes; its disconnected but not unrelated units represent what another of Harryman's peers, Ron Silliman, dubbed the New Sentence: each stands *almost* alone.

Prose and / or poetry of this kind (a kind that another language writer, Charles Bernstein, calls "anti-absorptive") can make you feel like Charlie Brown kicking a football: no sooner do you approach the pigskin (no sooner do we feel that we know what is happening) than Lucy (the author) once again yanks it away. The secret to enjoying such writing—to deriving pleasure and not only instruction from it—is to put yourself also in Lucy's position, to enjoy the prankish strangeness the experience brings, and to observe what kind of expectations have been mocked, undermined, or removed. Lucy is, among other things, exacting a girl's revenge on the repetitious, injurious, masculine game of American football—although she's also mean to Charlie Brown.

"Just about everything we do requires framing of some kind, most of it done so continuously and unconsciously that we don't notice it," wrote the Berkeley cognitive scientist and linguist George Lakoff, who contributed to the language writers' flagship critical organ, *Poetics Journal*. "If we notice framing at all, it is when there is a problem. Are we still in a friendly conversation or has it become an argument? . . . Does the shooting amount to a civil war or a foreign invasion?" A genre label ("prose poetry"; "wilderness story"), is what Lakoff referred to as a frame: it sets our expectations about the kind of thing that we are encountering, before we can know what the individual thing is. Shifts in reference and situation within and between Harryman's sentences create the kinds of problems that call attention to frames: she sets up situations, gives us cues about what to expect—a lyric poem focused on its own sound ("the ear spins webs"), a critical dialogue, an "assignation"—and then renders those cues inapplicable. What Lakoff wrote about other Bay Area artists applies to Harryman's prose as well: "The partialness of the framing is part of the art form, and an indispensable part, since this kind of art requires the audience to try constantly to categorize and frame, while never being totally successful. Things unframed gradually become framed, and through the piece there is at each moment some partial framing. . . . It is this *partial local coherence* that holds the piece together, and . . . holds our attention."

That partial coherence, for Harryman, involves both sentence and story. "I prefer to distribute narrative rather than deny it," she has written. For her— as for Lakoff—certain kinds of concepts, among them narrative and character, might be hard-wired features of human brains, even though other features once thought hard-wired (patriarchy, for example) are alterable consequences of social life. "Narrative exists," Harryman continued in her essay "Toy Boats," "and arguments either for or against it are false"; even the most innovative "structure of writing . . . must borrow from the things of this world in their partiality." Harryman's own imaginative writing shows the effects—sometimes comic ones—of such skillful borrowing.

Like "Paradoxes and Oxymorons," "Possession" is a kind of ars poetica, making a case for the kind of experience that it gives: that experience can be as much fun, if you are in the right mood, as any more realistic or more consistent attempt to "tell you a story," to make a durable image, or to conjure up another, better "new world." And like those other attempts at an ars poetica, "Possession" does not exclude emotion: its blind alleys and cul-de-sacs of defeated references and impossible situations (barbarian, tortoise, childbirth, salad fork) construct a frustrating but also curious, almost Alice-in-Wonderland sort of world, in which we may find ourselves burrowing deeper and deeper, investigating first the sonic patterns ("beautiful webs") and then something else.

The parts of "Possession" may not work together to tell one story, but they do work together to raise questions. Is a poem a "picture of an individual collective," the oxymoron by which poetry supposedly brings out both what we have in common and what makes us uniquely ourselves? Should we regard poetry (as Aristotle regarded it) as a kind of imitation? As a way of becoming "civilized," as a set of "beautiful webs," patterns, or traps? As a "moral presence," or (as in Plato's *Ion*) as a fraudulent copy of a copy? Has poetry—have earlier kinds of poetry—trapped us in "a fabrication," let us believe lies? For example, are we really best understood as "individuals"? Do we follow "imperatives" (for example, "pay your bills," "keep your promises," "avoid what is publicly shameful") of which we are not entirely aware but which constitute being "civilized"? Do we live in a "high illusion" of bourgeois safety? Does fiction, culpably, reinforce that illusion?

Are there important distinctions, for example, between a wilderness scene out of Hemingway or Richard Ford (with an "outboard motor racket") and a novel of high manners (with salad forks)? Or do both sorts of realist fiction offer the same sort of limiting characters, making the same sort of limited choices (should I go back to my wife? Should I find a new job?) that poetry ought to open out, or reject? Are there important distinctions between the kind of poetry that seeks, above all, to be memorably concrete ("eidetic image") and the kinds that seek wisdom, or comfort ("to be nursed")? Is there a way that we can find, through arrangements of language, alternatives to the confessional poet's notion that the truth about us is the truth about our deepest wounds (so that a "doctor" who "pelts me syntactically" is the equivalent of a poet, teaching us to "enjoy suffering")? Can we use language to open our minds, rather than just to play on familiar emotions, "to make you cry"? Harryman and her allies imply that we can: they may not tell us what we should do or how the world will look once our minds have been opened, but at least—so their techniques suggest—we can start to find out.

JOHN HOLLANDER

Songs & Sonnets

When we were all fourteen, the sharper our visions were
—Say, of the body of the neighbor's girl at her bath
Framed in the half-opened window across the courtyard,
Say, of her memory of young Heathcliff on the black
And white screen that afternoon—the more distant from touch.
Staying in a sense fourteen, even as we were all
Getting older, kept something alive—the girl's image
Blurred as she lay beside us in the bed of springtime,
The actor's face coarsened into color and substance,
Yet the Sublime kept climbing its ladder as the flood
Waters rose from the cellars; something beyond contact
Kept touch constantly aspiring to it, even when
The mind wandered, even to being fourteen again.

The structures and agitations of the older ways
Of handling matters of love, then housed and empowered
Other spirits—it was as if an old tomb could be
Recast and made into a series of monuments
Of reconsideration, with the base as of old,
A new frieze, somewhere in which the antiquarians
Might discern an image of the old tomb as it was,
And a new roof open to the stars. But these places
Are empty now: neither lovers, nor thinkers in the
Light of the afternoon, lurk about them any more.
But they stood for so much more than they were built to bear,
And for so long, memorials to the masonry
Of the ideal, as if love hung ever aloft.

The age of sixteen, in its infinite wisdom, puts
Lightly aside mere fourteen's joys and terrors. And thus
With our larger histories: the temples all rebuilt,
Modern love went at it all the better, hung two more strings
On the old, echoing instrument, strung two more lines
Across the alley-way to hang the dirty laundry
Out, for the truthful wind to comment on in detail
(Underpants flapping like the triumphant flags of love
Smocks blown into the clefted folds they had been worn to
Conceal). Now, when love and thought take their evening walks
They linger to talk along the widened peristyle
And slightly lowered elevation of a folly
Like this one in the public gardens we know so well.

Though honored over his long life for his poetry, Hollander was at least as famous as a literary scholar, critic, and polymath; when he died in 2013, his Yale colleague J. D. McClatchy compared the loss to the burning of the ancient library at Alexandria. This three-stanza poem deploys Hollander's intricately allusive mind and his mastery of classical, biblical, Renaissance, and Victorian poetry in the service of naive pursuits: teen lust, embarrassment, sexual satisfaction, as well as the memories of those things in art. Do we learn anything as we grow up? Does love get better or less frustrating—or just less vivid and salient? To find out, Hollander draws on what he knows.

He also asks, wryly, how and why old poems survive. When is a song (or a poem, or a sonnet) a monument, and when does it become a neglected tomb, or just an airing of dirty laundry? Hollander's argument for the "visions" of age fourteen is also a defense of older love poems: both the young people and the long-ago sonnets deserve respect from the older, less excitable readers that we modern adults have become.

What makes teenage lust more intense, and often more memorable, than the lust of adults? Hollander's answer has nothing to do with hormones and much to do with the not-yet-ness, the futurity, the aspiration, of youth, praised in the first stanza and then set beside adult retrospect in the third. To stay in touch with the ideal versions, the "sharper visions," of our own desires, for Hollander, we must "stay . . . in a sense fourteen." We can do that through memory or through film: we can watch Heathcliff, for example, as portrayed by Laurence Olivier in the black-and-white 1939 film of *Wuthering Heights.*

Hollander does not say (as Shakespeare does in Sonnet 129) that sex, consummation, real contact with the object of lust, makes us hate love, or hate our objects of desire ("enjoyed no sooner but despiséd straight," as Shakespeare has it). Instead, Hollander's extended sentences, their conclusions so elaborately postponed, argue that we, or some parts of us, would like to postpone that sexual consummation, to put off discovering truths about real life. We, or some part of us, prefer distance to contact, imagination to reality, sight to touch, a figure on a "screen" to the figure up close: we might thus prefer poetry to reality, old poems to new ones, or being fourteen (and inexperienced) to being sixteen.

Like John Ashbery's *Shadow Train*, Hollander's volume *Powers of Thirteen* (from which "Songs & Sonnets" comes) collects many poems in one new, un-rhymed form, in this case a grid of playful syllabics: 169 stanzas, each with thirteen lines of thirteen syllables apiece. The title "Songs & Sonnets" reminds us that the poems resemble sonnets (fourteen-line poems). But *Songs and Sonnets* is the usual title given to John Donne's lyric poems about erotic love (which are "sonnets" in the sense of "little songs," though almost none have fourteen lines). Those poems survive as "memorials" to the (formal, antique, rule-bound) ideas about love and poetry that they contain, or entomb.

We could simply enjoy those old poems. Or we could neglect them, as most people do: their temples are empty now, their styles passé, their words of courtship "hung aloft" in the sense that they are unreachable (like a constellation) or in the sense that their instruments go unused (like the harps hung on willows in Psalm 137). If we do not play them and do not look up to the stars, it may be because we have our eyes on the alley—or our minds in the gutter. Hollander responded with asperity to what he called "the rise of excessively literal . . . versified autobiography," to the so-called confessional poets of the 1960s and 1970s who used real names, dwelled on their traumas, and otherwise aired their "dirty laundry," forgetting that "indirection is the soul of poetry." "The older ways / Of handling matters of love," which had more rules (in poetry and in real life), look better to him, at least in retrospect; they "empowered / Other spirits," unavailable now.

Hollander's triptych about young love and old verse risks becoming—but does not become—a complaint about kids today, or about the 1960s and sexual revolution, or about the death of chivalry. Instead, it takes a breath and attempts a long view: Hollander's deliberate, patient, bemused, involuted sentences liken changes in poetic style from era to era to changes in dating habits from decade to decade, and both to the way that people change as we grow up. His central joke here is that we moderns, confessional poets, supposedly liberated contemporary writers, may think we are to the writers of the past as grown-ups are to fourteen-year-olds, but really we are to the writers of the past as sixteen-year-olds are to fourteen-year-olds: we have fewer illusions and less patience, but most of the time we only think that we know better. We should not condescend to the fourteen-year-olds, and we still have a lot to learn.

We might even want to return to their more idealistic, less experienced attitudes, which predisposed them to enjoy older, more apparently innocent, and more formal verse. Rule-governed, indirect, formal erotic writing (like Donne's?) might better excite desire, much as those vexing underpants reveal—excitingly—what they were "worn to / Conceal." At this point, though, Hollander's sentences let us think not just about kinds of adolescence, but about satisfied adults. "Love and thought take their evening walks" together like a married couple; they represent a union that seemed impossible for the teenagers, who could not think clearly about consummated love, and they walk together through the accessible if slightly less exciting ("widened . . . and slightly lowered") versions of the same architecture, the same poems, whose decay Hollander bemoaned. "Folly" puns on a general meaning (foolishness; wasted effort; "expense of spirit") and on a meaning specific to architecture (an ornamental, often roofless structure in which nobody could live). Once we have read enough, once we are out of our teens (and perhaps even before then), the articulation of unrealized or unrealizable desire becomes less like spying, less like airing dirty laundry, and more like taking a walk through such a folly, placed not at home but in "public gardens," open to all.

For Hollander, poems—whether old or new—should not be tombs; they might, however, be follies that we can explore. Like architectural follies, poems can incorporate in-jokes, variations that look like repetition, and paradoxical flourishes ("lowered elevation," for example, or the French-English false cognates in "comment on"). Hollander's burdensome clotheslines, stroked by the wind, parody the once-famous Aeolian harp, a stringed instrument "played" outdoors by moving air: "the archetypical music of English Romanticism," Hollander wrote in 1975, "is the aeolian harp, activated by the wind, eventually coming to stand for the poet himself," and becoming "a figure for poetic form." "Truthful wind" blowing through underwear is also a fart joke.

Avoiding both the potential forcefulness (what Donne called "masculine persuasive force") and potentially stately pace of iambics, Hollander's thirteen-by-thirteen syllabics give an impression of careful pattern nonetheless, leaving room for his characteristically digressive, spiraling sentences, a contrast to the urgent teen lusts he describes. The thirteen-by-thirteen grid, an alternative to the fourteen-line, ten-syllable sonnet, also associates sonnets' fourteen lines with how it feels to be fourteen. Compared to the sonnnet's fourteen-by-ten statements, these thirteen-by-thirteen units both go farther, and fall short.

What about being sixteen? The Victorian poet and novelist George Meredith added "two more strings" to the sonnet in his famous series of sixteen-line sonnets, *Modern Love* (1862), which depicted the grueling end of his marriage. Adding two strings to his clothesline, two more non-sonnets to his first thirteen-line non-sonnet, Hollander has—like Meredith—expanded his "old, echoing instrument"; and "echo," as Hollander wrote in 1981, has been another symbol for poetry itself. "The delay between prior voice and responding echo in acoustic actuality" (or in an alley) can "become a trope of . . . difference between prior and successive poems." In place of Meredithian progress from illusion to disillusion, fantasy to reality, Hollander offers a three-part scheme: dressed-up old formal poems, then too-naked confessional poems, then new poems (like this one) that look back on both; fourteen (inexperience), then sixteen (more experience), and then the longer walks of adult life, the "elevation of a folly" (perhaps love, perhaps romance, perhaps companionship, perhaps poetry-writing) in which convention never gets old.

In her splendid book on poems' titles, the critic Anne Ferry considers what happens when titles get reused: "Because the title is borrowed, it defines the new poem as something retold," "something that belongs to age-old experience." Hollander's quoted title does so with relish, and in a way that this book cannot fully replicate: all the titles for poems within *Powers of Thirteen* are printed below the poems, like the labels on old picture frames, so that you do not know what a poem is called until you have already read it. Such "titles designed to escape the effects of conventional framing," says Ferry, "tend to do to the poem what they purport to free it from," by making us more aware of conventions and frames.

And romantic love itself, for Hollander, is also a convention. Though we feel we've just discovered it, it is always already constructed for us by others, just as our ways of looking (even our ways of looking at hot naked people) reflect the ways in which we have learned to look. That does not make them insincere or unimportant, but it does make Hollander self-conscious. At this late moment in literary history, "we," the poet and the reader, the strolling couple of "love and thought," revisit the formal spaces that let us "linger," with no alleyways, no urgency, and no flood. There we find ways to enjoy older models without trying to make any one of them stand, nakedly, for the whole history of poetry, let alone for the truth about love.

CARL DENNIS

More Music

This one thinks he's lucky when his car
Flips over in the gully and he climbs out
With no bones broken, dusts himself off
And walks away, eager to forget the episode.

And this one when her fever breaks
And she opens her eyes to breeze-blown,
Sky-blue curtains in a sunlit house
With much of her life still before her
And nothing she's done too far behind her
To be called back, or remedied, or atoned.

Now she'll be glad to offer her favorite evening hours
To Uncle Victor and listen as he tells again
How the road washed out in the rain
And he never made it to Green Haven in time
To hear the Silver Stars and the Five Aces.
And she'll be glad to agree that the good bands
Lift the tunes he likes best above them to another life,
And agree that it isn't practice alone
That makes them sound that way
But luck, or something better yet.

And if Victor thinks he's a lucky man for the talk
And for his room in his nephew's house
Up beneath the rafters, and the sweet sound of the rain
Tapping on the tar paper or ringing in the coffee can,
Should we try to deny it? Why make a list

Of all we think he's deserved and missed
As if we knew someone to present it to
Or what to say when told we're dreaming
Of an end unpromised and impossible,
Unmindful of the middle, where we live now?

Like Thornton Wilder's *Our Town*, Dennis's poetry commits itself determinedly and deliberately to "the middle," to an outlook you might call
middle-class, or Middle American, or middlebrow. If you think that's an insult, please go back and read it again. His style in general, and this poem in
particular, examine and defend the middle tones of ordinary speech—
conversational, affable, or regretful, careful not to take over a room. They
defend too the compromises, settlements, and muddlings-through that make
up the better part of so many relatively fortunate adult lives. Against other
kinds of poetry implying that our way of life is an unsustainable disaster, that
authentic art must end in protest, or that we must live out our deepest truths
no matter what, Dennis insists on compromise, on accommodation, giving
two cheers for the way many of us in fact live.

At the same time his poetry reminds us what that way omits, and how hard
it can be. Learning to think themselves "lucky" for not faring worse, Dennis's girl and her penniless uncle (likely, but not incontrovertibly, the gully-
accident survivor) learn to inhabit their lives the way Dennis inhabits his
sentences: they take the unobtrusive, mild middles for what they are, and do
not hold out for a more spectacular end. The man in the car accident who
"walks away," "no bones broken," could have complained, could have sworn
a blue streak. He might think about how he could have avoided the accident,
and whether it was his fault. Instead, a subdued optimism—or is it pessimism,
not expecting any better?—leads him almost blithely forward, into a life that
will end in doublings-back.

As for the girl, who sees only "Sky-blue curtains," she's lucky not to die, of
course, though she's also unlucky to have fallen ill in the first place. (Dennis
has said that these characters are wholly fictional; we cannot know how she
got sick.) Mild praise for her state, her childhood in which any deed can be
"called back," suggests—very lightly—that adulthood is awful, that it consists largely of mistakes, missed chances, and accidents from which we cannot
walk away. This nameless girl—she could be eight or eighteen—could do

many things with "her favorite evening hour," but in what we could call generosity, or gratitude, or selflessness, or pity, or low expectations about her other options, she chooses to spend evenings with the ironically named Uncle Victor, who survived, but never saw the Silver Stars, just as he never got his own place, only a "room in his nephew's house" (which would make the girl his grandniece).

Victor never got to hear his favorite bands play live, but now he has "more music" than he might have expected, more than we might think, since he redefines "the sweet sound of the rain" as music. ("Where are the songs of spring? Ay, where are they?" John Keats asked in "To Autumn"; "Think not of them, thou hast thy music too.") His grandniece might soon have more to do with "her favorite evening hours," but right now she's "glad" (Dennis repeats the adjective) to listen to him. We would be churlish to question her sentiments.

We might remember, though—and she might know—that other people spend their senior years in far more comfortable quarters. Dennis, as his later poems make clear, is no political conservative arguing against public help for the poor, but a political liberal reminding other liberals not to hold poor people's circumstances in contempt. (A more recent poem envisions an "other life" in which Dennis works "to bring the union / To a non-union shop, and then, / Helped by a union scholarship, / I earn a degree in labor law.") It is because he has no alternative to rain in the coffee can and holes in the roof, because he has nobody who can provide him with anything better, that Uncle Victor has learned to like what he has.

Or has he? Dennis knows how Victor felt after "the road washed out," how the girl felt when she woke up; but he makes Victor's current luck into a question: "And if . . ." The otherwise unrhymed poem includes a couplet right where it tells us what we *should* not do, what Dennis won't write. We should not, he will not, "make a list / Of all he's deserved and missed": there is no one (no God) we can "present it to." But we could make such a list, and easily too: it might start with a roof that doesn't leak. Things obviously could have worked out better for him. And—even if we have a sound roof over our head, concert tickets, a home of our own—things could always have worked out better for us. Rather than fight them, Dennis takes those thoughts as given and writes to help us move on, even though (as the poet has said in an interview) his "narrator . . . feels that these characters are leading more narrow and impoverished lives than they should have to lead, that they deserve more."

Don't we all? Or, at least, don't we all feel that we do? "And yet, the ways we miss our lives are life," wrote Randall Jarrell, the American poet and critic who must be the most audible influence on Dennis's lines. Uncle Victor seems to have missed his life—the story he tells again and again shows "how . . . he never made it." He gets defined only by what he has not done. If we feel superior to him, we may also see how we have been shaped by our missed opportunities. "Beside any path actually taken from one point in time to another runs a myriad of ghostly paths of the might-have-been," Dennis has written, "and this perspective means that poetry . . . has to find an important place for regret."

Even the band names reflect missed changes and regrets. They imply doo-wop, or early R&B. But while the Four Aces had several vocal hits, including "Mister Sandman" (1952), there were no nationally successful pop groups called the Silver Stars or the Five Aces; even the tunes that matter most in Uncle Victor's world mean nothing in ours. Even if they existed, the Five Aces' greatest hits could not have changed music history in the way that "Earth Angel," "Maybelline," or "Will You Still Love Me Tomorrow?" did. And Dennis wants us not to care: he wants us to ask not what's important for every-body but what would have been enough for one man, once.

"The primary task of the writer," Dennis has also said, "is to construct a speaker whose company is worth keeping": the poem should behave like a friend (for more on poems as friends, or "hermeneutic friends," see the work by Allen Grossman and Ross Gay, later in this book). Dennis's speaker really means to befriend us, to stand beside us, to give us wise advice that applies to him as well (as when he says "we"). That tone works for him not only because he sometimes gives genuinely wise advice but also because it lets us focus on pace and syntax, on how voice unfolds over time; that pace, and that syntax, might help us grow patient, learn to listen to one another more closely, and above all slow down. That unobtrusive style also implies a refusal to compete with the poets who strive for grand effects. Like the girl in his poem "At Becky's Piano Recital," Dennis is "free of the need to be first / That vexes many all their lives."

The poet's collection *The Near World*, from which "More Music" comes, also contains a memorial poem to the fiction writer and critic John Gardner, who prescribed a stern realism of his own: "If a writer's work is fully successful," Gardner believed, "we are likely to say . . . that the work is 'true.'" Dennis seeks truths too—truths about many real people. Because Dennis's descriptive flourishes are short and not especially innovative (the car "washed out," "the sweet sound of the rain"), the abstract parts of the poem are the parts that stand out. That effect—the reverse of the workshop adage "Show, don't tell"—means that we can assimilate the poem to earlier, familiar experience of similar pathos: we might have Uncle Victors of our own.

Writing about how we miss our lives, how we might like what we get, how we might settle, Dennis has landed on reasons we might not. What began as a guide to small pleasures, even a sermon in favor of complacency, demonstrates—smoothly and almost reluctantly—the omnipresence of regret. We might be "eager to forget" the recent past, but we will not; Uncle Victor did not. We might try very hard to reach the point of view of Emily in *Our Town*—"Do any human beings ever realize life while they live it?"—to appreciate "Mama's sunflowers. And food, and coffee." We should think ourselves lucky; we should try to be satisfied with middling results, with second choices, with the blue sky given to children, even if we ourselves have grown up (whatever that means). But we cannot help imagining "another life," and art cannot help doing so for us. Dennis's calm, patient style, with its composite characters who try hard to be good, might really help us listen harder, stay calmer, show more patience for difficult uncles or for persistent children. Complete satisfaction, however, belongs to the dead.

LIAM RECTOR

Saxophone

Not by money—
   Markanthony Mastro

When younger, money for pleasure.
Older, money that creates money.
Oldest, money for medicine, protection
from the elements that have become
the elements of money.

Pleasure, protection,
Guilt money, gold the color of wheat
grown on "real estate,"
Farm money, Wage Earners, their "careers,"
their cities, Car money for the suburbs,
subways to bring them in for their money,
Bank money, trust, savings, standing in line
for Cash money, Coin money for the machines
to wash the Clothes money, Laundered money,
Drug money, the sons and daughters
of Economists' money, Boat, Plane and Get Away
money, The Arts money, I-Love-You-Honey money
for the dinners whose table and atmosphere
are the discreet sauce of Food money,
my money, your money, our "tax" money,
Pound's money, money for an ounce, a half-gallon,
a fifth, Milk money, money for the containers
containing the distribution of money.

Promotion money, earning "good money,"
having no money, doing it for money.

Money turned to power no longer
money, money through time, the spirit
of money—secular, psychological money.
Who's Got and Where Can We Get
some money?

You and I, our money. Their money.
Our pleasure and fist full of money.
Laughter over money, serious laughter
over money. Too much, too little,
fluid money. The saxophone, color of wheat,
purchased through Hock Shop money, saxophone
splitting the night, our air, blowing money.

Repetition—the coming back around of recognizable words and ideas—is by some accounts the basis of poetry, whose memorable features let it be remembered, repeated, and transmitted in cultures without writing. Poetic forms can be sorted by what they repeat: rhyme repeats a final stressed vowel plus all the sounds after it, alliterative meters repeat initial consonants, complex forms from Wales and Thailand repeat other sets of consonants and vowels, ghazals (like Agha Shahid Ali's in this book) repeat words, villanelles repeat entire lines. Rector's informal, insistently American, and bitterly contemporary tour de force turns up the rate of repetition while eschewing all those traditional forms.

Instead, Rector repeats, almost to the point of fatigue, "money," which can occur at any place in a line: the effect is both to reject older, more intricate, more predictable kinds of repetition and to imply that money is now the root not just of all evil but of all experience in the modern world. Exhausting—or showing that we cannot exhaust—the many meanings of money, Rector at once makes a protest against its ubiquity and turns it from a necessity into a plaything, a term that he can pick up and throw around.

He also imagines it as a kind of trauma. "Money" itself—the word and the idea—burrows and charges through context after context, insistently, unavoidably, almost annoyingly, as if our dependence on money, our persistence in a society where (as the pop song put it) money changes everything, were itself a trauma to be worked through; but there is no way to work it through, to leave it behind, without leaving capitalism behind, which few of us believe that we know how to do. To figure out how to master "money" would be to use it accurately in a sentence—and there is not one complete sentence in Rector's poem.

Once we start thinking in terms of money—and what adult can avoid thinking about it daily?—we start to see all of life in terms of what Marxists call "exchange value" (a thing is worth what other people will pay for it) or what economists call "market price." Soon we are seeing the world transactionally, quantitatively, through lenses that make it impossible for us to treat human beings as human beings, much less to value the communities to which human beings belong. (One such community was the contentious 1980s literary magazine *The Reaper*, in which Rector and the otherwise mysterious Markanthony Mastro both published poems.) As we move through the poem we see how money, exchange value, quantity, and market value infiltrate and replace every concept that comes to hand, in the course of a life and in the culture that Rector surveys.

Young people's pleasures often cost money, from Little League registration fees to the sky-high rents in Greenpoint and Williamsburg; adulthood ("older") requires us to view our time and energy as an investment, maximizing our returns for the sake of retirement, a mortgage, or a family. Because we depend on our savings to shield us in old age, to pay for drugs and to keep a roof over our head, the "elements" in the sense of wind and rain can be kept away only by the "elements" of personal finance. By the time "machines / to wash the Clothes" come up, we can anticipate the pun on money laundering, since a form of money laundering—making a morally illegitimate financial practice look respectable—has engulfed us all. Even if you have "Boat, Plane and Get Away / money," you cannot get away *from* money. And even the rhetoric of intimacy ("I-Love-You-Honey") seems to conceal a quantifiable exchange.

The philosopher and social critic Georg Simmel, toward the end of his 1907 study *The Philosophy of Money*, argued that changes in the use of money affect a society's sense of rhythm and time. A well-ordered capitalist economy frees buyers and sellers from having to live according to the slowly repeating seasons, as preindustrial people lived: "money is the most decisive . . . means for transposing the supra-individual rhythm" of premodern life "into the harmony and stability that allow a freer, more individual and more objective confirmation of our personal energies and interests." But those harmonies, and their individual patterns, may not last: during a time of high inflation, when it is in "everyone's underlying interest to transact his economic operations as quickly as possible," life seems unstable; rhythms collapse, or speed up. Both the absence of premodern rhythms (associated with modern money in general) and the effects of financial insecurity, the scrambles produced by inflation (a much-debated problem in America in the years just before Rector's poem), might be heard in his unsettling, uneven lines.

Rector is hardly the first poet to pursue the pathologies of money, or to attack the way that we see money now. But he does not name even one of the many who have subscribed to Marxist critiques: not even Bertolt Brecht, who figures in Rector's other work. Instead, there is Ezra Pound, who believed in the fringe economic theory of Social Credit, propounded by Major C. H. Douglas. Douglas's theories—which promised to reduce the power of bankers—proved congenial to anti-Semites and fascists, including Pound himself, who wove them into his unfinished long poem *The Cantos*. To put the obsessive modernist "Pound's money" so close to "my money, your money" is to suggest that the financial obsessions that (as most readers see it) sent Pound astray are not far from the attention to credits and debits, prices and paychecks, that characterize an ordinary life. In the same way, once you see life in terms of money, "a half-gallon" (as of milk) is not so different from "a fifth" (presumably of hard liquor): both are potable liquids, and consumer goods.

See life this way, in terms of exchangeable quantities, and we truly have been taken over by "the spirit / of money," a term whose paradox (can money be spiritual?) Rector emphasizes with a line break. The spiritual questions of Western history—for example, "What shall it profit a man, if he shall gain the whole world, and lose his own soul?" (Mark 8:36)—have been replaced by the more practical question "Who's Got and Where Can We Get / some money?" Irregular capitalization, in that question as throughout the poem, points to the difficulty of determining what's important, what's proper (as in "proper noun"), and what's unique when everything is for hire or for sale. (It also suggests the German of Marx and Brecht, in which common nouns are capitalized.)

It would not be wrong to see the irregular, constant repetition in Rector's poem as a cri de coeur, a blast of feedback, a loud protest against the experience of life under capitalism. The sense that we are all "doing it for money" is not (perhaps alas) a defense of sex workers but an attack on everybody else; under capitalism, in a society organized around scarcity, "we are all prostitutes," as the erstwhile punk rocker Vic Godard sang. But if the poem, in that way, resembles punk rock—and it does—in other respects its irregular changes, double meanings, and unpredictable rhythms resemble jazz, the kind of music most likely to have a saxophone for lead instrument, and more particularly the kind of skronky, challenging music called free jazz (Ornette Coleman's, for example), played in small combinations, sometimes dissonant, and not ordinarily fit for dances. (Other poets, many of them African American, have fashioned whole aesthetics out of bebop and free jazz: Yusef Komunyakaa, represented later in this book, credits his line shapes to it, and the twenty-first-century poet Fred Moten imitates it in distinctive prose-block forms.)

If money falsifies what it represents, might words—might language—do the same? Perhaps, in order to work against that falsehood, we need to change language, to make language rise above, or react against, its ordinary business as a medium of exchange. And Rector's language does so: it sounds strange, could not be part of a conversation, stands apart from ordinary speech, just as the saxophone at the end of the poem stands apart from everything—from the pawn shop where it was purchased, from the musician, from the "night"—blowing (as in wasting; as in making instrumental music) until all the money, and the word "money," is gone.

Though invented by a white Belgian, Adolphe Sax, saxophones, as jazz instruments, carry associations with black America; the "serious laughter" at the end of the poem comes to Rector from Langston Hughes (author of *Not Without Laughter*) and from other poets of African American life. The disrupted, repeated rhythms are like free jazz, too, in resisting conventional notation: the lines have obvious rhythmic force, but God help you if you attempt to explain it with scansion. The shape of a tenor or baritone saxophone also resembles the physical, typographical shape the poem makes on a page. Jazz is, moreover, a music of improvisation, built around solos, never the same way twice. Gifted improvisers have to figure out—eventually—where and how their improvisation will end. Rector tries to end in a happy place: by the end of the poem he could be on a date, out at night with enough cash to have some fun, postponing worries—and brow-furrowing critiques of capitalism—for tomorrow. The jazz that is at once an analogy for this poem's music and a counterpart to it, a voice of freedom, thus ends up "splitting the night," opening life back up, committing the conspicuous waste, the jubilant excess, that is also life itself: worth blowing money on, tonight.

CZESŁAW MIŁOSZ

Incantation

Translated by Robert Pinsky and Czesław Miłosz

Human reason is beautiful and invincible.
No bars, no barbed wire, no pulping of books,
No sentence of banishment can prevail against it.
It establishes the universal ideas in language,
And guides our hand so we write Truth and Justice
With capital letters, lie and oppression with small.
It puts what should be above things as they are,
Is an enemy of despair and a friend of hope.
It does not know Jew from Greek or slave from master,
Giving us the estate of the world to manage.
It saves austere and transparent phrases
From the filthy discord of tortured words.
It says that everything is new under the sun,
Opens the congealed fist of the past.
Beautiful and very young are Philo-Sophia
And poetry, her ally in the service of the good.
As late as yesterday Nature celebrated their birth,
The news was brought to the mountains by a unicorn and an echo.
Their friendship will be glorious, their time has no limit.
Their enemies have delivered themselves to destruction.

There is something arbitrary, and something frequently cruel, about national boundaries: decisions about who gets to be American (or Costa Rican or Thai) determine who has to move and who can stay put, who gets police protection and gainful employment, and—far less consequentially—what gets to be in this book. "American poetry," now as in 1980 and 1960 and 1920, makes sense as a durable category for teachers and students and for readers and writers, since most American poets are closely related, in their influences and in the language they use, to other American poets. Ongoing relations between American English and other Englishes, between American readers and poets who hail from Armagh, Johannesburg, Oxford, Barbados, or Dunedin, could and should be the subject of another book (perhaps a sequel to this one). Poets who live in the United States but developed their English-language styles elsewhere—the clearest examples are Irish and West Indian: Seamus Heaney, Paul Muldoon, Derek Walcott—would be well represented there.

Poetry in translation is another matter, affecting American poetry in discrete and sometimes overwhelming waves. A book that covered only the last ten years might address the Russian-language poetry brought into Brooklyn by Ugly Duckling Presse; the shocking or disconcerting or extreme poets, such as Kim Hyesoon, disseminated in English translation (and accompanied by invigorating polemic) through Action Books; the U.S. reception of Palestinian poets, such as Mahmoud Darwish and Taha Muhammad Ali; or the major Latin Americans—especially Raúl Zurita—now being brought into English by Forrest Gander, Daniel Borzutsky, and others (as well as being read in the United States in their Spanish originals).

All these poets get addressed regularly, in 2016, in literary journals and blogs. In part for that reason, I've chosen, as the one poem in translation within this volume, a poem that belongs not to the literary present so much as to the recent past, rendered from Polish by the Polish Nobel laureate and a future U.S. poet laureate, and subject to sustained attention during the 1990s and 2000s. It is a link at once between the United States and Eastern European literature, between the poetry of the 1960s and that of the 1990s and afterward, between two very public poets, and (not least) between ancient hopes and contemporary beliefs about what poetry can do. Miłosz's "Incantation" shows what American readers in those years and afterward wished to find in him, and from Eastern European and Russian poetry in general, and it points up some troubles those wishes contain. But the same great poem also shows what Miłosz could do, what Miłosz thought that poetry could do, to satisfy us in hard times, to give hope without falsehood, to envision a power in poetic language that looks like, but is not, a power of collective action, of authoritative social speech.

Miłosz wrote the Polish version of "Incantation" in Berkeley, California, in 1968, during the year of worldwide student revolts, just after tanks crushed the Prague Spring, and seventeen years after the poet chose exile in France and then in the United States over government service in communist Poland.

Though celebrated by determinedly international critics (such as the British transplant Donald Davie), Miłosz had little prominence in the United States until he won the Nobel Prize in Literature in 1980; a flood of attention, and a new demand for his work in translation, followed. "Incantation," in English, appeared in a 1982 chapbook and then in *The Separate Notebooks* (1984), a volume translated by Pinsky and Robert Hass; the three poets would have known one another through long residence in and near Berkeley, where Pinsky taught English, and Miłosz Polish literature. "Incantation" then reappeared in Pinsky's own new-and-selected poems, *The Figured Wheel*, in 1996, alongside another anthology favorite of Miłosz's, the much earlier "Song on Porcelain" ("Of all things broken and lost / Porcelain troubles me most").

The poem went on to a grander career. Heaney, who won the Nobel Prize in Literature in 1995, quoted about half of "Incantation," including the first and the last few lines, in the *New York Times Book Review* for August 26, 2001. Heaney was writing on the occasion of the United Nations Conference Against Racism, which had met that summer in postapartheid South Africa: Miłosz's lines, Heaney said, "express the fundamental beliefs upon which the fight against racism must be based . . . It is thrilling to hear the ideal possibilities of human life stated so unrepentantly and unambiguously." Two weeks later came September 11, 2001. Pinsky—who had recently ended his three-year term as U.S. poet laureate—would read "Incantation" repeatedly at public events after that, and three years later at the dedication for a 9 / 11 memorial.

What does "Incantation" tell us, and what does it promise? Its end-stopped lines lend gravity, as well as something like a public self-assurance, to its pace and tone as it says something that most of us want to believe. Yet only in a certain willful, subjunctive sense can the poem believe it: its antique machinery of allegory—not reason but talking reason, personified, and eventually Philosophia—says what modernism in the arts, and modern history with its gulags and its famines, suggests that we can no longer believe.

Not necessarily an intuitive pairing (as Plato knew), poetry and reason team up—so Miłosz and Pinsky say—against recent history, where barbed wire prevails: the *longue durée* will show how the laudable allies win out after all. No mere personal consolation, no theological claim about another world, the poem (like Derek Walcott's "The Season of Phantasmal Peace") very calmly projects an apocalypse, another world, in this one. And the poem seems to know it: like much of Miłosz's later work (some of it witness to the poet's idiosyncratically Catholic faith), the poem says what it thinks we need to hear, what poetry as such ought to have told us, because we will never get that sort of claim from honest, responsible prose. It projects a counterworld that we can imagine as we go about in this one, aware that things may not really turn out so well, but fortified by our ability to think that they still can.

Miłosz's antagonists, early in the poem, suggest a Soviet-backed regime: the enemies of reason ban books, pump out propaganda, and put up barbed wire (rather than, say, setting off car bombs). The poem in English speaks to the America of the 1980s—of Reagan, and of liberal poets such as Pinsky who wanted a national pride that was not Reaganesque, nor parochial, nor militaristic. But the same poem works hard to become international: it speaks of the ancient world, and speaks to a future when communism and anticommunism, Soviets and internal exiles, will not be the issues of the day. A reason that "does not know Jew from Greek or slave from master" is a reason allied to the world of the New Testament, to Christ and St. Paul: this reason trusts us, as Christ could trust the Apostles, with its "estate."

If as poetry—not "human reason" but human verbal imagination—"puts what should be above things as they are," then it does what Aristotle and Philip Sidney and Samuel Johnson claimed it has always done, being better, and better for us, than the facts. Poetry and wisdom ought to be friends—"their friendship will be glorious"—but that friendship belongs to the future; are they friends now? Miłosz concludes with a pagan Annunciation, in which—the phrase is almost a giveaway, almost a way to undermine what Miłosz has been hoping he can make himself, and us, try to believe—"a unicorn and an echo" announce the good news. We can believe in the triumph of "human reason" over barbed wire, the eventual downfall of repressive regimes or genocidal dictators or kleptocrats or ignorance, but only if we can also listen to, if we can also believe in, unicorns.

And perhaps we should. "Nature's kingdom is not our home," Miłosz wrote in prose: "we belong to it, and yet we do not belong. In nature's kingdom necessity is the only good: not so for us." Poetry for him—more clearly, more self-consciously, than for any of the wholly American poets in this book—allows us to envision another world, one that can help us because it is not our home: one where justice prevails alongside unicorns. If we could not imagine such a world, we might not be able to bring ourselves to improve this one; we would give up on language, on society, on ourselves. Heaney's essay pointed out that "in the original Polish, there is a certain frantic, even comic pitch to the meter and tone of 'Incantation,'" which "saves [the poem] from illusion and sentimentality." In English, the lines cannot sound frantic or hurried, but they can admit a kind of hush that is almost uncertain, a tone on the cusp between belief and disbelief. Miłosz and Pinsky's "Incantation," in English, consists entirely of the sort of thing we say to ourselves and to one another in the hope that it might still be true.

Miłosz himself, in the America of the 1980s, became a kind of unicorn. The exiled writer, his style, and his career represented, for English-language poets, a kind of mission and clarity and force for poetry that (at the very least) white Anglo poets, writing in American English on American subjects, largely believed that they could not have. He also represented himself, in such poems as "Incantation," as a self-conscious bearer of universals. These parallel sentences on the triumph of reason, this allegorical new birth, could speak to the particular struggles of (for example) Deaf people, or farm workers, or Armenians, but they could not be reduced to any one struggle, nor to any one national literature—they spoke to the "human," considered as a whole. "What entrances [Miłosz's] readers is the plangency and certainty of his tone," Heaney wrote in an earlier essay, along with "the cadence of a wisdom that is, against all expectation, unwearied and resilient." He wrote of universals, in tones of wisdom, and he seemed to write from an experience that was not his alone: those tones (even for readers who knew nothing about Miłosz's eventful biography) let us trust him as we could not trust any more identifiably, or merely, American style.

Yet Miłosz's other poems warn us not to trust poems such as this one. "The true enemy of man is generalization," Miłosz wrote in "Six Lectures in Verse"; "The true enemy of man, so-called History / Amazes and terrifies . . . Don't believe it." What is "Incantation" but a set of generalizations? One answer is that it is a public poet's way to get outside mere facts, mere headline news, and—in this sense—outside what other poets and critics might consider the poet's social responsibility. Miłosz had lived through the Second World War in Warsaw—his poems of the 1940s record the experience—and when he became famous in the anglophone world, his life in the war years was not far from critics' minds. Americans wanted to see him—and to see other survivors of terrifying regimes in Russia, in Eastern Europe, in Latin America—as a bearer of testimony, or an instructor in social responsibility, or a living piece of history.

Miłosz would not let himself be read that way. When the British critic A. Alvarez praised Miłosz in a 1987 essay in the *New York Review of Books* called "Witness," Miłosz snapped back: "Perhaps some Western writers are longing for subjects provided by spasms of historical violent change, but I can assure Mr. Alvarez that we, i.e. natives of hazy Eastern regions, perceive History as a curse and prefer to restore to literature its autonomy, dignity and independence from social pressures." The critic and translator Clare Cavanagh, who quotes the passage (she is also Miłosz's biographer), has shown how Miłosz's "brand of poetic witness" rejected the roles of martyr, recorder, and political leader in order to open up a space for the unpredictably individual imagination, a space where neither he nor anyone else would let history or society tell us what to make or do.

That is the world that "Incantation" appears to predict, and works to bring about, and it is a world whose characteristic poet (to quote Cavanagh again) "builds bridges between pasts—his own, his nation's, and that of the human race as such . . . to change breadeaters into angels, to save the species itself and restore its true homeland, the fallen earth." "Miłosz's reputation in the West as exemplary poet-witness was hard-earned," Cavanagh continues. "But Miłosz is also an escape artist." Indeed, "escape is evidently as a rule very practical, and may even be heroic. . . . Why should a man be scorned if, finding himself in prison, he tries to get out and go home?" That last quotation comes not from Miłosz or Pinsky or Cavanagh but from J. R. R. Tolkien's essay "On Fairy Stories": such stories, too, belong to the realm that Miłosz's reason defends. Escape from the demands of history, from a public monophonic voice, from time itself, is part of "the good." "Incantation" is not and cannot be a model for public, responsible, socially aware poetry, much less for any poetry of witness; its "austere and transparent phrases" instead defend (among other things) philosophical idealism, a vision of apocalypse, the idea of a truly international poetry, and unicorns.

Nothing is slangy in Miłosz and Pinsky's "Incantation"; almost every term is dignified, fit for "universal ideas." And yet the lines never dissolve into translationese: they have a formality almost never associated with successful American poetry, but they do echo the greatest American oratory—the cadence of Pinsky and Miłosz's ending even recalls the Gettysburg Address. Other decisions set the language apart from the speech of contemporary America: "Philo-Sophia" belongs in Constantinople or Athens or Krakow, not in Peoria or Queens. Some sentences take on a biblical cadence, even replicating the psalmist's strong midline break. Miłosz, or his persona in Pinsky's English, says these things, makes these pronouncements, propounds these predictions, not because he believes they are already coming true in his America, not because they are supported by what we can see around us, but because so often, and especially in public events, they are not. We need to hear these claims shored up in poetry because we will not find good enough evidence for them anywhere else, and we need to hear them in this dignified and international English so that they can be more easily contemplated, if not entirely believed.

ROBERT GRENIER

SHOE FROM THE WAVES

```
oh he got a shoe from the waves
```

That's the whole poem—the title plus one line. Or maybe it's not one poem: maybe it is one piece of a larger whole, such as the page from Grenier's 1984 volume *A Day at the Beach*, which—like every other page from *A Day at the Beach*—contains three poems, or three units, each with its own title. Maybe the relevant whole is, instead, part one of that book, called "Morning." Maybe the whole book is one poem; maybe its poetic aspects include its type-writer face, its page layout, its front and back matter (which includes six grainy, or sandlike, black-and-white photographs), and even its physical weight in the hand. Maybe the book itself is just one part of a collaborative multi-media project by Grenier and like-minded writers in California—in Berkeley, where he lived while writing *A Day*; in San Mateo County, whose beaches he visited while writing it; and in Bolinas, California, the unusual seaside vil-lage where Grenier settled in 1989, and where some of his friends, among them Robert Creeley (whose *Selected Poems* he had edited), lived in the 1970s and 1980s. All of these frames and contexts can help us react—with amuse-ment or dismay or fascination—to Grenier's shoe.

What do we mean when we call this a poem? When we say "call," or "a," or "this," or "we"? Grenier (who coedited an avant-garde journal called *This*) raises such questions throughout his body of work. His poetry—like Carla Harryman's poetic prose—asks how we know where the frame for a work of art ends and begins, and it shows how much the reader, spectator, or listener must decide, or assume, before we can say what it means. Grenier's most fa-mous project, *Sentences*, completed in 1978, consists of five hundred index cards, each with a single sentence or sentence fragment, which can be read in any order; the first edition came in a box (as of 2015, a digital version resides at www.whalecloth.org/grenier/sentences_.htm). Grenier's recent work (some of it visible at http://writing.upenn.edu/pennsound/x/On-Natural-Language .php) involves words written, or drawn, in an initially almost unreadable hand-writing, and cannot be duplicated in print.

All these projects (including *A Day at the Beach*) pursue philosophical territory opened up by the so-called Minimalist artists and writers of the late 1960s and 1970s: Donald Judd, with his series of smooth steel boxes; Dan Flavin, whose sculptures were neon tubes; the Robert Creeley of *Pieces*, whose poemlike units were sometimes single words; Aram Saroyan, whose most famous poems include "lighght" and "eyeye." Minimalists make art in units so small, and with so few clearly separable features, that they require us to examine ourselves and to fall back on our own experience rather than looking only "within" one work. Very short or apparently featureless works cast our attention back on the empty air, the "negative space" on the page: "spaces solids those are spaces too," another of Grenier's poems declares. The space of the page around the lines, in *A Day at the Beach*, also stands for the beaches themselves.

No wonder the poems have proven so important to later boundary breakers and avant-gardes: the first *This* (1971), Bob Perelman recalled, was "as much of an originary movement as language writing can be said to have." Grenier's works, as Perelman concludes, at once valorize the "Here and Now," the single moment at which you exist and read, and try to escape the set meaning-making procedures of the literary past. For Grenier (as for Perelman), "the more fully and finally legible a poem is, the less compelling." How can you render finally legible, fully interpreted, one sentence about one shoe?

When we praise works for resisting, or subverting, our expectations and axioms, skeptics may wonder why we need more than one such work: once the assumptions are subverted, why go on? Sometimes that question has no clear answer. With *A Day at the Beach,* however—and with this diptych—there's always more going on. Each sentence says, does, and means things that other paradoxical or minimal works of art, or anti-art, would not; each also discloses one moment at one West Coast beach.

Though Grenier in 1984 had not yet moved to Bolinas, he already belonged to its social circles, and we can take Bolinas as a symbol for part of what his supershort poems tried to do. Bolinas is and was a tiny community famous for its isolation and for the writers—part hippie and part avant-garde—who clustered there in the 1970s, Saroyan, Creeley, Ted Berrigan, Alice Notley, and Joanne Kyger among them. Residents have a tradition of stealing the road signs so that outsiders could not find the town. Bolinas style was anti-analytical, sometimes to the point of seeming anti-intellectual, about being, not doing; exploring, not accomplishing; process rather than finished thing. It could incorporate Taoist or Buddhist advice, as in these additional lines from *A Day at the Beach*: "you have to do the work / that the boat is doing & you have to go / in the direction that the boat is going."

Bolinas also made writing hard to separate from other day-to-day activities, in particular (not to put too fine a point on it) dropping acid and smoking pot. Heightened attention, directionless introspection, and distance from practical goals—all associated, since the nineteenth century, with aesthetic experience in general, and with poetry (as opposed to prose) in particular—can seem like more or less desirable effects of marijuana. You may take that similarity as an objection to certain versions of post-Kantian aesthetics, or as a reason to get high. *A Day at the Beach* at least suggests the latter, in a quatrain entitled "FOR WALTER PATER": "the effect / if not the result of / marijuana is gained by smoking / my own home-grown weed." (The same page, in a pun on sunburn and cannabis, warns us about "eyeballs . . . getting baked.")

But what is that "effect"? What attitude, what form of attention, does Grenier encourage, or produce? His challenging 1985 essay "Attention" tries to explain: "What if life remains to be discovered? What if language could still be used to wrest 'objects' from 'experience' toward reality in the literal strata of the words?" That sort of guide to presence—that sort of trip—saturates Grenier's *Day*. And that day brings us back to his lost and found shoe, a found object that stands for any object, for words as objects ("words must be 'somehow' the same things as things," "Attention" concludes), for Grenier's ability to throw our focus back on the process of mental discovery in addition to the thing (in this case, the shoe, the wave, the beach) described.

But Grenier leaves more for that shoe to do. It is, among other things, *one* shoe, not two: there's not much you can do with one shoe, even if it does fit. Two dry shoes would be what the philosopher Martin Heidegger called "ready-to-hand," significant thanks to what we can do with them: one wet shoe is, instead, "present-at-hand," without practical use, hence able to provoke reflection about why there is something instead of nothing, or about what sort of thing this thing could be.

And poetic language, for Grenier as for many other poets (some of them not remotely avant-garde), should be like one wet shoe, not like two dry ones: present-at-hand, remote from practical use. Grenier's line appears without any clear purpose other than "to be a poem" or "to make us ask 'what is a poem?' "—almost as the shoe appeared from the waves. We might even say, punningly, that the shoe, like the line, "waves" good-bye to any idea that we can distinguish for good between art and non-art. The line may also represent something Grenier overheard: it may be a found poem, analogous to

Marcel Duchamp's readymades, or to William Carlos Williams's "This Is Just to Say."

In any case, it is a poem about what someone found, what made someone say "oh." You can say "oh" with delight ("Look, a shoe! How odd!") or with a shrug of dejection ("Oh, that's just a shoe"), though you cannot do both at once. You can also hear this funny "oh" by the Pacific as a demotic, American answer to the European and classical "O" that opens many older poems, the "figure of apostrophe" that the literary theorist Jonathan Culler has singled out as *the* defining feature of lyric. Percy Bysshe Shelley may call out "O wild West Wind," but the contemporary American poet faces the potential sublimity of the Pacific waves with "oh." The poem above this one in *A Day at the Beach* reads "HI SEAL / hi seal / hello seal," greeting the seals known to live at Bolinas, and also teasing at the way that prior poets, from Shelley to Elizabeth Bishop ("At the Fishhouses"), greet the nonhuman and the unseen.

Williams, and many poets who tried to follow him (the language writers included), sometimes said that they were breaking from Shelley's, or from Bishop's traditions—from Romanticism, from efforts at spiritual expression, from the European lyric past. Yet to see how many echoes of that past—the seaside poet, the "oh" or "O," the peripatetic quest—inhere in this tiny poem is to see how hard, and how paradoxical, that breaking away could be. The difference between "oh . . . a shoe" and "a shoe" (or just "shoe") is the difference between language that implies a speaker with an attitude, language that has to come with a tone and a pitch, and language that could have come from anywhere.

Other parts of *A Day at the Beach* (as the poet has pointed out) portray a dog named Boom: is that dog Grenier's "he"? Is the reader who searches for meaning like a dog who happily fetches, over and over, the otherwise useless fruit of the ceaseless sea? It may be, and the critic, or dog, may be none the worse for it: poetry, a game played with language, may be as pleasurable, as engaging, for certain humans as a game of fetch is for the right dog. Both fetch (with a dog) and poetry (with people) also defy the demands that a larger society places on verbal or physical action: that it have an end product, that it turn a profit, that it pay for itself.

In this sense Grenier's avant-garde poem is almost a proleptic lament for the Bolinas where Grenier would later live. The journalist Kevin Opstedal in 2001 called the town "the last holdout" for its countercultural way of life. "Of all the poets who lived in Bolinas during the sixties and seventies," he added, "only John Thorpe, Bob Grenier and Joanne Kyger" remain (Grenier has since relocated to Vermont). Read in this way, Grenier's line becomes elegiac, even as it produces a teasingly slight tool, like a lock pick, with which to prise open literary traditions.

Some of my paragraphs about this poem may seem to tack up a literary history where ideas matter more than the words that pursue them. Others may seem like attempts to place on a single jocular sentence more weight than it supports. Yet that kind of overreading—sometimes comic, sometimes deadpan, sometimes philosophically ambitious—might be what poetry, in general, rewards. And such poetry—not just Grenier's poems or avant-garde-ish poetry generally, but this book and this line and this shoe in particular—requires us to realize what might get hidden by other discussions of other kinds of poems: there is no generalizable, consistently persuasive, or objective way to distinguish "overreading" from simply "reading." We go to a poem, or to poets or to schools of poetry, not as we show up for a standardized test but as we go to the beach. Once we get there, we see what other people have found. We might expect an experience similar to theirs (the same kind of discoveries, the same kind of poetry), or similar to what we saw last year, but we should also get ready for a surprise.

RITA DOVE

Lightnin' Blues

On the radio a canary bewailed her luck
while the county outside was kicking with rain.
The kids bickered in the back seat;
the wife gasped whenever lightning struck
where it damn well pleased. Friday night,

and he never sang better. The fish
would be flashing like beautiful sequined cigars.
This time he'd fixed the bait himself,
cornmeal and a little sugar water
stirred to a ball on the stove,
pinched off for the scavenger carp.

So why did the car stall? And leap
backwards every time he turned the key?
Was Gabriel a paper man, a horn player
who could follow only the notes on the score?
Or was this sheriff the culprit,
pressing his badge to the window to say
You're lucky—a tree fell on the road ahead
just a few minutes ago.

Turned around, the car started
meek as a lamb. No one spoke
but that old trickster on the radio,
Kingfish addressing the Mystic Knights of the Sea.

The fifty-four one- or two-page poems in Rita Dove's *Thomas and Beulah* (1986) follow Dove's maternal grandparents through their adult lives, telling first Thomas's story (in twenty-eight poems), then Beulah's (in twenty-six), remaining in the third person but sticking closely and consistently to one perspective, either Thomas's or Beulah's, throughout. *Thomas and Beulah* made Dove the first black woman to win the Pulitzer Prize, and it has been well attended since: the volume, writes Pat Righelato, "has been valued as black history, as family memorial, as gender critique, and as formally innovative." Dove's poems trace familiar swaths of American history, among them what we now call the Great Migration: Thomas, like hundreds of thousands of black Americans, has left the rural South for opportunity in the industrial Midwest, and he finds it—along with Beulah—in Akron, Ohio. There he adopts a respectable middle-class life, joining a church choir, and becoming a father to four girls ("Girl girl / girl girl," Dove writes in "Compendium"). Beulah, who begins by "Taking in Wash," endures the trials and the longueurs of motherhood, "irons alterations / in the backroom of Charlotte's Dress Shoppe," and outlives her husband into old age. (Dove's real grandparents were Thomas and Georgianna Hurd: the poet has said that she changed Georgianna's name because it "seemed too male based," and that she took other small liberties with biographical facts.)

"Lightnin' Blues," with its irony and its brief narrative, makes an ideal example for Dove's understated technique. Every detail in the poem points— pathetically or comically—to the freedom to roam and the playfulness that the adult Thomas has lost, and also to the security that this working-class black family man has achieved. The poem can be read as a way to think about adulthood, fatherhood, responsibility. But once we see its trick ending, it can also be read as a commentary on ways of writing, on the vocation of the poet (or at least of poets such as Dove), on the enduring appeal of the pastoral—of poetry as a release from necessity—and on the ways in which practical, social, and literal constraints, including the constraints of racism and race, come back to us however we try to escape.

Thomas is driving himself, Beulah, and their young daughters into the country, where they will spend a weekend, and he will go fishing. Another black poet might emphasize the contrast between this black family, traveling over water in Ohio for fun, and the earlier generations of former slaves who crossed the water to Ohio and freedom. Dove instead emphasizes the security and the relative comfort of a car big enough for the whole family, with a backseat. Beulah keeps a caged canary herself ("usurper / of his wife's affections,"

Thomas calls the bird in another poem), but the canary on the radio has to be a chanteuse or a jazz singer, though there is no jazz standard nor 1930s pop hit entitled "Lightnin' Blues." Instead, it is Thomas who gets the blues, worried (for good reason) about the lightning and thunder: they mock him—they go where they please, whereas he's a family man—and they will ruin his fishing trip, to boot.

"Lightnin' Blues" is not a blues (it does not repeat lines and it does not follow twelve-bar form), but it is a poem in an old—a blue—tradition, a monody about the failure of pastoral: the poet tries to imagine a better, carefree life in the country, then must turn around and give up. As Malin Pereira notes, Dove literally chose blues—variations on the color blue, "designs that featured blue"—for all her book covers from *Thomas and Beulah* up through her service as U.S. poet laureate between 1993 and 1995. Dove told an interviewer that during the writing of *Thomas and Beulah* "I was playing a lot of music, everything from Lightnin' Hopkins to older [blues musicians] like Larry Jackson or some of the recordings that Al Lomax made of musicians . . . all the way up to Billie Holiday, stopping about in the '50s" (some critics identify the "canary" with Holiday).

Thomas would know some of their repertoire. Thomas and his best friend, Lem, in their youth roamed the South as itinerant musicians: Lem played mandolin, and Thomas sang. Then Lem drowned. (Thomas still has Lem's mandolin; it hangs on his wall, rarely played, "a frozen / teardrop.") It's a shame if Thomas truly "never sang better," since he barely has an audience now, as he sings along with the radio: his children quarrel rather than listening, and Beulah cares more about what she sees (the hazardous storm) than about what she has heard. Yet Thomas, for a while, can look ahead, projecting a future to fit the past he recalls, in which "he'd fixed the bait himself."

Himself: ending her line with that word, Dove sets up a contrast between the solitary man's activity—meant for him to catch literal fish—and the "fishing" of a courtship that lies in the past. Rough weather makes the county resemble a dance party ("kicking") that no human being can attend; only trees will enjoy this "Friday night," and then only until the stanza break, till the trees fall down. Thomas's work at the stove resembles, or parodies, the work that Beulah has ordinarily done in the same kitchen, feeding their children; the fish that Thomas imagines he will catch resemble the cigars traditionally handed out by fathers of new babies, so his preparation for the fishing trip recapitulates and parodies what a new father goes through.

Of course, Thomas won't go fishing, or not this weekend. "Why did the car stall? and leap / backwards?" The literal answers—wet weather made cars of that vintage hard to handle—won't do. It seems to him as if some entity had planned for the weather to prevent him from enjoying a holiday. That entity could be the devil, or it could be the angel Gabriel, associated with trumpets and with the Christian Annunciation, hence with parental responsibility. "A paper man" (an insult in jazz circles) is a musician who can't improvise; if Gabriel is a paper man, then he cannot deviate from a pre-set (divine) script. To be a responsible father is to be, like Gabriel, committed to a plan. Any angel—perhaps especially Gabriel—would want Thomas to do good, to stay with his family, rather than escaping even in imagination. An angel, and not a devil, will send Thomas home: the cop who stops them is on the side of the Lord.

Not all cops are so helpful to black men—not now, and not during the 1930s. A "sheriff . . . pressing his badge to the window" could have become "the culprit" in a hate crime. Instead, he delivers a friendly warning: Thomas and Beulah are "lucky" in several ways.

But not in all ways: they've been cheated out of a holiday. No canary, no fish, no cigars, no symbols of secular freedom or pleasure remain; instead, the car has become a tractable lamb, as if they rode back to town by God's command. And so no one sings, not even over the airwaves: "no one spoke / but that old trickster on the radio." Thomas and Beulah can no longer tune in music, only the once extraordinarily popular comedy show *Amos 'n' Andy,* the longest-running program in the history of American radio, whose recurring character Kingfish Stevens extolled his devotion to his fraternal order, the Mystic Knights of the Sea (a parody of the Masons). Notoriously, white voice actors played the black characters, whose grandiloquent or ne'er-do-well habits reinforced racial stereotypes.

Righelato believes that "Lightnin' Blues" "wittily adjudicates between feminine priorities" (such as the safety of Thomas's family) "and masculine pleasures and pursuits," like fishing: "between 'canary' and 'Kingfish.'" But the poem ends up sadder than that, since neither security nor pleasure can be reliably had: a falling tree might have crushed the car if not for the dumb luck (the good luck!) of being stopped by police; the "Kingfish" is a white entertainer pretending to be a foolish black man.

And this Kingfish is the only "fish" in this "sea": he is not a real fish, nor a king. Nor is "Lightnin'"—the name of another comically foolish *Amos 'n' Andy* character—admirable or fast. Glitter and light disappear from the poem, along with the near-rhyming sound effects that light up the ends of Dove's lines ("cigar," "carp," "leap"); instead, a new pattern of rhymes and near rhymes comes in ("show," "radio"; "ahead," "started"; "say," "sea") to guide the ride home. In lines whose pace matches the drive out and the drive back, in a vocabulary that plausibly matches Thomas's own, Dove has written a poem that might depict any midcentury paterfamilias who won't get—not for a weekend, not till the kids leave home—the kind of freedom he once enjoyed.

But Dove has also crafted a poem about dilemmas specific to black life: everywhere Thomas turns, in the country or in the city or on the radio dial, he finds reminders of race. America may be kind or cruel, but it can never be color-blind. What does it mean for a car driven by a black man to "leap / backwards," to become "meek as a lamb"? Is it a metaphor for slow progress, for patience (like that recommended by Booker T. Washington), or is it just a car that won't start? Why can't Thomas and Beulah hear anything on their discouraged trip home except *Amos 'n' Andy*? Literally the answer may be that their radio won't get any other stations, but at the level of allegory the answer is also that in the great network of signals that constitutes American culture, racial markers and racial stereotypes are something we can't help but hear: the same events (a radio show, a sheriff who stops a car, even the preparation of cornmeal) have meanings that change with the racial markers involved.

Before her graduate work at the Iowa Writers' Workshop, Dove was a Fulbright scholar in Tübingen, Germany, and many of her early poems (especially those of her second volume, *Museum*) pursued European or international subjects. Pereira writes that with *Thomas and Beulah* Dove began to "chart a path back home." Yet, as Pereira argues, Dove's careful techniques, with their multiple sources, both Anglo-European and black American, suggest personae who can travel from place to place: "her work signifies on the concept of home and neighborhood, refusing any sort of nostalgic embrace." Thomas has left his home in the South for a sometimes precarious middle-class life in Akron; Thomas and Beulah in "Lightnin' Blues" literally have to go back home, but only because a tree blocks their road.

A. R. AMMONS

Target

In spring the high twig tip
puts out a blur that,
if not undershadowed, represents

itself below with a
correspondent invention on the ground:
the sun lengthens

drawing longer and longer northerly
arcs
until the leaf, if not undershadowed,

declares its full singular shape:
the sun eases back wintering
south

and the high
leaf, acorns cracking,
dives into its shadow running on the ground.

Ammons studied chemistry and biology at Wake Forest University and worked for a biological glass company for twelve years, becoming its vice president, before his career as a poet took off. That earlier career helped make him great: no other poet in American history has shown such comfort with the natural sciences, not only with their data or their terminology but also with their methods and ways to examine the world. In very long poems such as *Sphere* (1971) and *Garbage* (1988), in tiny ones (see *The Really Short Poems of A. R. Ammons* [1990]), and in focused works of more conventional length, Ammons used his unmistakable syntax and his idiosyncratic punctuation (all colons, no full stops, till the very end of a poem) to embody a worldview consonant with observation, verification, and quantification, with the sense of wonder that motivates those activities, and with the absence of evidence for intention in the observable material world. Ammons models his poems (almost all in free verse) on unfamiliar, mathematically intricate shapes, rejecting "straight lines, blocks, boxes, binds / of thought," as "Corsons Inlet," his most famous early poem, says. Things, plants, animals, and landscapes change and rise and fall according to patterns, but those patterns incorporate randomness, and they do not serve a conscious end.

This poem's single sentence traces some of those patterns. Its five stanzas plot the rise and fall of one leaf in air, the growth over time of its shadow on the ground, and the daily change in zenith, in the sun's position at noon, over three seasons' worth of sky. To get everything out of the poem, you might want to envision, as you reread it, a series of black-and-white photographs, with bud, leaf, or twig and shadow; a series of Cartesian-coordinate graphs (height of leaf versus time; size of leaf versus time; length of shadow versus time); and an equation (likely involving derivatives) that would probably connect them. In these plots spring becomes summer; at the end of the summer, the leaf meets its shadow (the shadow of its own death) and reaches, or buries itself on, the ground. Where another poet might get from those time scales a sense of urgency or a sense of fear—the old *carpe diem* theme—Ammons finds comedy, or else equanimity. This is what happens in nature; these are the overlapping, sometimes circular, sometimes progressive, entropic processes that govern terrestrial life.

Ammons's leaf rises, "represents / itself" by extruding its shadow, reaches upward, and then—as the sun recedes—falls. We can read the poem as a purely visual exercise, an attempt at attentive transcription, but we should not read it that way and no other, since we can also let it stand for human life and death. Ammons portrays the twig, bud, leaf, and shadow, rising and falling, growing and coming down, as if its end—when the leaf touches its own shadow, having fallen—has been the leaf's "target" all along. Human life too has its usually unintended destination, its own ironic "target," in the grave. Ammons's three-part sentence shapes and three-part stanzas may therefore represent three seasons, or three parts of a life (as in John Keats's sonnet "Four seasons fill the measure of the year"): childhood (where we try out many parts, in a "blur"), early adulthood (where, if we are lucky, we find our one shape), and maturity, which concludes with sudden decline. The "high twig tip . . . represents / itself" with a lengthening shadow as a leaf grows out of a bud. Its cluster of long *i*'s, a cluster of monosyllables, itself lengthens into a string of abstract, Latinate words, literally describing a shadow, perhaps standing also for the way that a young person works to imagine a bigger, more capable, newer version of herself.

As much as it offers a figure for human life, "Target" also pursues the aspiration—familiar to Ammons from the modernist poetry of William Carlos Williams—to do almost photographic justice to the appearance of found things, things in themselves, things not conventionally beautiful. The poem owes a lot to Williams's own poem about a treetop twig, "Young Sycamore," itself indebted to a famous photograph by Alfred Stieglitz, "Spring Showers." Ammons admired Williams, learned from his line breaks, and traveled to meet him in 1960, near the end of the older poet's life; when Williams died, Ammons wrote a poem entitled "WCW." Williams also insisted that poets learn from the local, from the shape of the land where they lived, and Ammons took that advice, at first in New Jersey and then in Ithaca, New York, where he lived and where he taught at Cornell University from 1964 until his death in 2001. The short growing season, the emphasis on summer sunlight (because winter brings so little sun), the struggles of single deciduous trees, and the attention to whether the sun sits in its "northerly" sky before "wintering south" all reflect Ammons's Ithaca point of view.

Ammons alternates very long lines and very short ones ("arcs," "south"), evoking the bends and the sudden release of a bow, though no bows and no arrows appear in the poem. There is, however, the word in the title, "Target," as if someone—the leaf?—might be aiming at something. So it seems to the patient observer, the poet who has been following the twig, bud, leaf, and shadow all year, as if he were watching a time-lapse film. Until the last lines, it has been a silent film. Then we hear "acorns cracking": the whole deciduous tree can now reproduce, and the leaf, having outlived its purpose, falls. But in Ammons's line it does not "fall" or die, but "dives," as if to complete itself by merging with the image of its alternate life.

If the leaf is a life, what's odd about that life, or about the photographic, filmic, botanical figure that Ammons gives? For one thing, it's exceptionally alert to the counterintuitive natural processes (how the tilted earth generates seasons) from which its tentative metaphors come. For another, it's neatly mimetic—short broken-up lines represent high leaves dangling, "longer and longer" lines tell us they're getting longer, and the longest lines end up (twice) "on the ground." It's enticing in its mix of local chaos (breaking lines on "a" and on adverbs and adjectives) and in its overall sense of order: the poem begins with a traditional invocation, "In spring," and a gymnast would say that it sticks the landing. Other poems from *Sumerian Vistas* (1987) emphasize the ongoingness and the overlapping workings of natural processes, one at a nadir while the other hits a zenith—"The filled out gourd rots, the / ridge rises in a wave / height cracks into peaks, the peaks // wear down," as Ammons says in "Motion's Holding." Here, instead, the poem follows, and ends with, its single leaf.

But Ammons has more to do, and more to say. What does it mean to say that the "full singular shape" of the leaf involves the shape of the shadow ("if not undershadowed") on the ground? We know a leaf should not be *over*shadowed (it may not grow if something above blocks the sun), but why should we care whether it is *under*shadowed? We might just say that Ammons seeks unlikely symmetries, thinking like a photographer, or like the serious painter he also was.

We might also say that it is of the essence of his scientific method that Ammons does not always accept the boundaries of familiar words and things. A branch is a thing, as is a leaf, and a bud, and a dog, but so is the unit leaf-branch-shadow; so is the unit hillside-sun. So is an ecotone; so is a quadrat; so is one slice of a surveyor's arc. The world does not stay divided into the "singular" units that our preexisting words give us, but operates according to its own logic of interdependent systems, which may or may not correspond to the names that we give. We may humanize things in nature, the better to see them ("dives," "eases," etc.), but we will enjoy them more, and understand them better, once we see patterns in them that are not ours.

These patterns, in turn, can stimulate human invention. "Target" is itself a "correspondent invention," a new thing that "represents" what the poet could see. The word "correspondent"—the longest in the poem—gave a title and a thesis to M. H. Abrams, the scholar of Romantic poetry who was Ammons's colleague for decades at Cornell: "air-in-motion," wind that could move leaves, gave the Romantic poets (so Abrams argued) a way to describe inspiration that came right from nature, without the mediation of inherited gods. To William Wordsworth, "a corresponding creative breeze" could bring "the holy life of music and of verse." Yet it would not be right to call Ammons's leaf, or leaf-shadow unit, holy: its patterns, like all the patterns in the mature poetry of A. R. Ammons, are emergent, not intended, and belong to the physical world.

Ammons in several interviews, as his biographer Roger Gilbert recalled, "described an experience he had in the Navy that he felt represented a turning point for him. He was sitting on the bow of a ship looking at an island, thinking about the level of the water and the level of the land and of all of the physical forces that were contributing to this relationship between land and sea, and at that moment he became aware of the universe as a place that operated according to its own laws. Suddenly there was no God in charge of things." Commitment to the real universe with its own laws—and to the sense of wonder they can bring—seems, in the intricate balances of poems like this one, almost a conscious substitute for the no longer credible Pentecostal, Baptist, and Methodist creeds of Ammons's North Carolina childhood.

Ammons seems, in life, to have been shy, and often depressed or anxious. Here, though, Ammons approximates not just a mathematical elegance but an equanimity that belies the leaf's speedy, irreversible end. In some ways a very traditional poem on mortality, "Target" even echoes the medieval literary mode called *de casibus*, about the fall of kings and other people who once were "high." But Ammons's scientific mind made "Target" an untraditional poem too. Nothing in it tells us how to feel or what to do. It contains no verbs of feeling, no subjunctives, no imperatives, no verbs in anything other than the present indicative (unless you count verbal adjectives). We see, simply, a botanical and meteorological process, one unpredictable in its details but every year predictable overall. Its pattern of literal "representations"—the leaf represents its own outline—might resemble ratiocination or literary making, but it can offer no moral or metaphysical or practical advice. The leaf cannot really consider the ground a "target," any more than it consciously tries to grow long and green, but we, as observers, can watch it more closely, learn more about it, and more about ourselves.

YUSEF KOMUNYAKAA

Facing It

My black face fades,
hiding inside the black granite.
I said I wouldn't,
dammit: No tears.
I'm stone. I'm flesh.
My clouded reflection eyes me
like a bird of prey, the profile of night
slanted against morning. I turn
this way—the stone lets me go.
I turn that way—I'm inside
the Vietnam Veterans Memorial
again, depending on the light
to make a difference.
I go down the 58,022 names,
half-expecting to find
my own in letters like smoke.
I touch the name Andrew Johnson;
I see the booby trap's white flash.
Names shimmer on a woman's blouse
but when she walks away
the names stay on the wall.
Brushstrokes flash, a red bird's
wings cutting across my stare.
The sky. A plane in the sky.
A white vet's image floats
closer to me, then his pale eyes
look through mine. I'm a window.
He's lost his right arm

inside the stone. In the black mirror
a woman's trying to erase names:
No, she's brushing a boy's hair.

"Facing It" reflects (in many senses of the word "reflect") Komunyakaa's own experience in Vietnam, where he reported for the military newspaper *Southern Cross* in 1969–1970. It also reflects on his own and other visitors' experience of the Vietnam Veterans' Memorial, the right-angled walls of black granite inscribed with the names of the American war dead, designed by Maya Lin and built, to much appreciation and some controversy, in 1982 in Washington, D.C. Komunyakaa addresses and even attempts to explain the Wall's power as a public symbol, analogous to (but not the same as) a book, a poem, a photograph, a mirror, a wound, a cemetery, a grave.

Placed last in Komunyakaa's 1988 volume *Dien Cai Dau*—all of whose poems concern the Vietnam War—"Facing It" also contemplates its own potential status as the poetic landmark that it has in fact become: by far the best-known, most often cited American poem about the war in Vietnam. At the same time it speaks to far broader questions of poetry and memory. Can poetry speak for the dead, or seem to bring inanimate objects (such as carved tombstones, printed words, or mute statuary) to life? Can it serve as a mirror, showing us to ourselves? Or do poems—by coming to an end, by stopping us in our tracks, by speaking for and to the dead, with a text that is always the same—reduce the living to mute monuments, powerless listeners, versions of death in life?

For the literary theorist Paul de Man, autobiography, memorial poetry, and even the simple names on graves (like the names repeated on the memorial) were versions of "de-facement," leaving readers and listeners "condemned to muteness," since their words, as dead symbols, would replace and erase the absent human being. "I'm stone. I'm flesh," the poet tells himself, too old, too manly, or too deeply moved, or too absorbed in his own thoughts, to cry. Can we cry for each one of the Vietnam war dead? Can anyone cry for them all? Lin's black granite wall—on which the poet sees first himself, then "the names," then one after another visitor's face—seems meant to raise such questions: it reminds us that the American war dead (3.1 million dead Vietnamese people are not represented) were people with their own histories, their own lives, even as their time and place of death unifies them into a discrete, somber part of public history.

The memorial, though praised by art critics, faced objections before and after it opened. "Lin's design proved instantaneously divisive," writes the art historian Elizabeth Wolfson. "Many veterans, politicians, critics, and the general public read its refusal to explicitly glorify the war or frame the listed soldiers' sacrifice in recognizably heroic terms as an ideological statement, proof of Lin's—and the memorial's—purported anti-war position." The novelist and Vietnam veteran Jim Webb, later secretary of the navy and a Democratic senator from Virginia, blasted the design as a "black gash of shame." Critiques from the right objected to the lack of empedestaled heroes; critiques from the left objected to the wall's sense of closure, to its false proposition (as Subarno Chattarji put it) that "ghosts of the war can finally be laid to rest." Chattarji quotes another veteran poet, W. D. Ehrhart, whose own poem contrasts the opening of the memorial with the contemporaneous U.S. invasion of Grenada: "I didn't want a monument," Ehrhart wrote, "not even one as sober as that . . . What I wanted was an understanding / that the world is neither black-and-white / nor ours."

"Facing It" thus approaches and defends what was still, when Komunyakaa wrote, controversial public art. In observing the wall, Komunyakaa allies its reserve to his own, careful not to encroach on other veterans' or visitors' views. He will speak for himself, not for them. "The stone lets me go": the poet turns away so that he no longer sees his own face in the sheer granite wall. He then turns back to keep reading. He will not find his own name there, because he survived.

He does, however, find a name he knows. The most famous man named Andrew Johnson was the seventeenth president of the United States, whose pro-southern, anti-black attitudes would hinder post–Civil War Reconstruction. Johnson became president upon the assassination of Abraham Lincoln, whose own memorial stands a few hundred yards from Lin's black wall. But this Andrew Johnson (so interviews reveal) was a man Komunyakaa knew, whose own death the poet had apparently seen. "Facing It" does not tell us whether Johnson was African American, white, or neither; his death, however, came as a "white flash," opposed both to the black granite and to Komunyakaa's dark skin. Johnson's death was also instantaneous: it was an event in time, like a bird's passage overhead, like the shimmer of light on moving fabric, like the motion of the woman (the only woman in the poem) who "walks away." Poem and wall together contemplate the almost frightening power of memory and mourning, the way that the dead can haunt the living through loneliness, incomprehension, or survivor guilt.

But Komunyakaa will not voice overt complaints: not against the baffling, almost paralytic function of memory; not against the controversial war itself (more than a decade after he himself came home, just nine years after it ended); certainly not against the stark architecture of the memorial. Like the memorial itself, "Facing It" is somber and contains no celebration, but it also contains no overt objection, no policy position: it does not resemble the flotilla of poems written in the late 1960s and early 1970s advocating American withdrawal from Vietnam, most of them by poets who had never been there. Komunyakaa's rhythms participate in that restraint; his three- and four-beat free verse, which in other poems evokes the syncopations of jazz, here holds tightly to the confines of its sentences, more stately than playful, more restrained than free.

Why would Komunyakaa imagine his own reflection as a "bird of prey"? Perhaps because, set below the ground level of the surrounding National Mall and parkland, the Vietnam Veterans Memorial can make visitors feel exposed and vulnerable. Why would "a plane in the sky" attract special attention? Are we to think of military airplanes, hostile surveillance, bombs? How can Komunyakaa see himself, or his own experience, in the experience of the other (black or white) veterans? How can we go from mere names, mere words, to an imagined face? Those questions concern not only this poem, not only memorial poetry, not only war memorials, but poems in general, whose lines allow us to pretend that we get to know the poet or her persona, that we can go from mere words about an absent imagined person to a feeling of presence, the feeling that we see a face.

That pretense can seem uncanny; it makes reading a poem sound a bit like seeing a ghost. And Komunyakaa, when "a white vet's image floats / closer to me," sounds as if he had seen a ghost: "his pale eyes / look through mine." That veteran may be seeking his own name, or seeking the name of a comrade (perhaps Andrew Johnson). Whatever he finds, he disappears from the poem, as part of him (his right arm) disappears into the reflective surface "inside the stone" (an effect of the wall's right angle).

Do poems, as de Man argued, really erase their readers, turning us all into tombs? Does the act of writing erase the life of the writer? Does the memorial (that black gash) paralyze us with its gloom? Or do poem and memorial enable us to see one another more clearly? Even ambiguous, somber poetry that avoids conclusions or prescriptions—perhaps especially that kind of poetry—can (far from erasing us, or making us stony) help us face one another, and face the shared past: so "Facing It" shows. The people—East Asian or

American, still living or dead—in the rest of *Dien Cai Dau* need that kind of help; often they find that war has severed connections between generations. One poem portrays a Chinese "sergeant major's woman": "Once I asked her about family. / 'Not important, G.I., she said." At the wall, in D.C., connections among Americans, at least, might be repaired. As the poet Robin Ekiss writes in her own superb guide to "Facing It," the poet "mistakes the woman's gesture for a futile attempt to remake the past, but then changes his mind, and ultimately sees . . . an act of motherly tenderness."

Komunyakaa's compressed and halting poem becomes at once a defense of poetry, which helps the living see one another's faces, rather than de-facing, taking a face away; a defense of the Vietnam Veterans Memorial; and a justification for its own laconic, nonjudgmental approach. We can see the wall, or the poem, as a reason to pause, to consider life and death, but if we imagine that they erase other possibilities, other ways of naming, or that they ought to take a position (on the justice of the war itself, for example, or on the one right way to commemorate), we have made a mistake, just as Komunyakaa makes a mistake when he misreads the visitor's gesture as erasure. Instead, she tends to the living (perhaps to her son), representing the next generation, who may come back later to revisit the memorial, seeing the faces, rereading the names.

DIANE GLANCY

Hamatawk

Just it was (crow tongued) he was saying a caw.
Then wings fold up the Indian
if antlers deer give up
totems of the head the anyhow of them.
This coat gets smaller each year
like the tepee I come from
when I (back) to the (space) I was born,
the small *hohum* of it,
old ones all reversed
smaller the autumn trees than I remember
(the way) old language breaks.
Hum way to *hum hum* the buzzled wiggle
of the tall grasses smoothed down
by the path of them (to woods) through the field.
I'm going and if not
I come back smaller.
Then he (the crow) sings like this
his mouth he opens. *Caw. Caw.* The grasses
(wave) they take flight the crow wings (grasses
burnt) all fields shrivel
next the new world.

It is just possible to read this almost teasing, almost bitter poem from Glancy's collection *Lone Dog's Winter Count* (1991) as if it told a clear story with a
reliable, consistent narrator: such a narrator would have to "come from" a place
and time where people grow up in tepees, a Native American tribe from
the Great Plains. She or he would have to be old enough to miss that time,
to "remember" the "old ones," whose way of life was on the wane, like a coat

that "gets smaller each year." Feeling the old Native ways recede into memory, and then into oblivion, this speaker feels almost as if his or her birthplace were being erased, becoming not a "place I was born" but a mere "(space)," a vague parenthetical. In a wild, culturally appropriate place, amid "tall grasses smoothed down / by the path" of previous humans, or of migrating animals (buffalo?), this speaker encounters a crow, whose important message cannot be rendered into English. This crow, who says "caw," says what carrion birds often say: that we will die, that time moves only one way, that we are moving from summer into autumn and winter, and into "the new world."

Read this way, the poem would echo familiar claims in famous lyric poetry—time passes, we grow up, we should seize the day. It would also echo familiar claims about American Indians: the claim that their culture and language belong to the past, "old language breaks," "all fields shrivel," tepees are museum pieces, assimilation cannot be helped, and time moves on.

But the poem—given closer attention—will not let itself be read in that way. Glancy never denies that time passes, that people grow up, that tall grass can shrivel in autumn. Nor does she deny—far from it—the history of American Indians and other people on the Great Plains. Glancy spent her first decades in Oklahoma and Missouri, the daughter of a German American mother and a Cherokee father who managed slaughterhouses in Kansas City; she has written a novel about the Trail of Tears, and all her many books address Native concerns. But in doing so they often work against cliché; they acknowledge and then dispel familiar stories, that of the doomed, nostalgic, folkloric Indian among them. Full of non-words, confusing punctuation, syntactic blind alleys, and non sequiturs, Glancy's poem does not try to give us a narrative—the fact that we can find one anyway (as we might realize upon rereading) testifies to the all too easy availability of the dominant narratives that the poem works to displace. And what emerges from the poem instead, once we reject the nostalgic, elegiac, single-voiced reading, is an attention to nonhuman animals, to ways of being that do not depend on language; an attention to the complexities of Native and tribal heritage, some of it linked to oral, unwritten tradition (itself a more complicated matter for Cherokee people than for many Native groups); and a strong link to traditions of lyric poetry that extend far outside Glancy's Great Plains.

What is a "hamatawk"? Not a hawk, and not a tomahawk, that sometimes offensive symbol of "Indian" life; the word sounds like both and like neither, and like "talk," a way of talking that garbles and pushes back against "Indian" stereotypes, as the rest of the poem will do. The crow comes to warn us, alert us, befriend us, or call to other crows, ignoring us; we hear only "caw." "The crow is an old Trickster, an observer, a mimic," Glancy has written. "He shows us ourselves." Yet we cannot finally understand him. In the same way, we cannot understand other people and their concerns if we treat them as "totems," magical problem solvers, or tokens. Glancy makes fun of Anglo readers' tendency to treat "Indian" as a single category, as if all totems and teepees belonged to one tribe: she also, perhaps, pushes back against oversimplification within Native writing itself.

"This coat gets smaller every year," the burden of representation more constraining. The language gets small and stays small, too, the English words all very common, and often repeated, even at line breaks ("grasses . . . grasses"), so the words that stand out most are not in fact words: the title, and then "the small *hohum*," apparently not a word in Cherokee but the English word meaning "blah." The lesson that you can't go home again, that one's aging relatives are almost always "smaller . . . than I remember," does not belong to particular ethnic groups; nor does the lesson that your hometown, when you go back to it, having left it, can be blah. Disillusioned, terse, almost bored, the poet seems to want to leave the space she occupies, to get away, through the "tall grasses" whose "buzzled wiggle" lets her coin an attractively onomatopoetic phrase.

When she gets away from the ho-hum home, as if getting away from expectations, her grammar goes haywire—"I'm going & if not / I come back smaller" (i.e., perhaps "I will come back"); "his mouth he opens," a fancy and unidiomatic word order. Does she have a vision? Does she encounter a real crow, or dream one? Does she see a grass fire, or a future of ecological disaster, something a crow might warn us about? America was the New World to its European explorers and settlers; does Glancy direct heavy irony at that use? Or is this New World something else?

Is it heaven? Glancy's other poems and prose have been outspoken both about her environmental convictions and about her Protestant Christian beliefs. Or is the lowercase new world simply a place we can't go, a home for something we can't know? Perhaps the crow knows. A poem that toys with, and rejects, clichés about the plains and about American Indians becomes a poem about the incomprehensibility of nonhuman nature: we try to interpret the crow in our words, but we fail. We cannot "tawk" with him; we hear only "caw," and we have to envision the rest.

Or is he a messenger after all? Does Glancy find not alienated creatures but animal kin, even "totem animals" in the widest, psychological sense—first deer, then crow? If she does, she's not telling; she can "(wave)" good-bye to the implied reader who gets shut out, concisely and sharply, from the end of the poem. "Hum way to hum hum" sounds like a ceremonial chant, but it could also be an instruction—hum this way, not in another—or a warning: if you are not from around here, the scene with the field and its grasses may seem ho-hum, though it exhilarates me. Don't linger here; it's not for you.

The whole poem, in fact, with its clipped complaints, its short lines, and its restricted vocabulary, has the affect of withholding: Glancy does not want to tell us everything she knows. Instead she conveys a sense of self-protection. "Hamatawk" (whose title sounds like but is not a kind of "talk") explores the desire to keep some things secrets (because secrets give power, because revealing them would make her vulnerable), not just as a feature of a character but as an aesthetic effect. The poem, like many of her poems, says in effect: "Here's why I won't tell you everything." Glancy's fractured consciousness sometimes brings her close to the truths—unspeakable in anything like English—that her crow may experience, even as they remind us that we are not crows.

Glancy's prose, like her poetry, sometimes supports ways of reading and listening in which the authentically poetic, the oral, and the truly Native, stand up for the land, and for nonhuman nature, against invidious, technological, textual, white intrusions: "Something like poetry is come upon," she writes in *In-between Places* (2005), "when the real self connects to an otherness" that modern "America pushed out of the way: the sacredness, the horse, the animals, the land, the understanding of that place where they began." But Glancy takes care to complicate those ways of reading too. The horse, of course, came to North America with Europeans, and the history of Cherokee people (as Glancy goes on to write) defies any "Native American belief that our stories cannot be separated from the land," since—generations before Glancy's father pursued an urban career—Cherokee people were severed from their land, "forced to march west on the 1838 Trail of Tears." Cherokee language, moreover, thanks to Sequoyah, has since the late 1810s had its own written syllabary: it has never been confined to English terms.

A Cherokee poesis thus rewards "an attitude of place located in the mind. The geography of thought," as Glancy writes, rather than any simplified attempt to go "(back) to the (space) I was born" (which certainly was not a tepee). A map of such thought, or a form of writing adequate to it, would not correspond easily to single places on a U. S. map, nor to easily transmitted oral forms: no more than Glancy's "Hamatawk:" corresponds to a single site or a single animal, and no more than her phrases correspond easily to sentences that you, or she, might write as prose, or say.

"What are written words but the voice tamed?" Glancy asks in her experimental novel *Designs of the Night Sky* (2002). Does wild expression become tamed when written down? "Hamatawk" asks that we imagine bird calls, sounds that cannot be adequately written down, because they are not human speech; but we might have the same reaction to speech in a language we did not recognize, or one that had no adequate written form. "The written word, like the spoken word, can disappear," Glancy's protagonist, a librarian, muses. "But instead of ashes, the remains of written words are barbed wire against the sky."

They may be less confining if kept alive. Resistance to prose sense, to the fixity of writing, in Glancy's series of experiments—including this self-consciously experimental poem—is like Native resistance to white rule: appropriate, attractive, a basis for art and for ethically urgent thought, but only when mediated, not absolute: and the mediator, the limit-setter, the peace-maker, for the devout Glancy, are names for Christ, with whom souls may "take flight."

As much as it is a Great Plains poem, a Cherokee poem, a poem about mediation, about taking flight, and about the mystery of salvation, "Hamatawk" is also about a nonhuman animal, an overheard crow And in this dimension Glancy's early poem anticipates the body of writing—sometimes called critical animal studies, and represented well in 2015 by the radical vegan poet Gabriel Gudding—that asks us in what sense, if any, we have any claim over other animals' being. "It is a sure bet that the Umwelt," the perception and experience, "of the turkey is similar to that of the pig and that of the human," Gudding insists in *Literature for Nonhumans* (2015); his poetry, like his morality, tries to "recognize the imperatives of bodily and mental sovereignty for those whose nerves obligate them to turn away from pain." Glancy grew up in a Kansas City of slaughterhouses, cattle, and hogs. Though she eats meat—she has endorsed Michael Pollan's call for "animal welfare," rather than animal rights—she has written feelingly, in biblical cadence, against factory farms: "when will EVERY CREATURE, even the PIG, praise its Maker—when the last hog barn has been wiped from the earth?" How close can our mediated consciousness come to the consciousness of other animals, if we can call them conscious? Why should we not live like crows? Should we do what crows do? How—within our human language—can we even know?

Poetry can ask us to do the impossible—to imagine other species-beings; to establish authentic relations to the land, or to a tribe, or to all humanity— while reminding us that we cannot; poetry can ask us to get outside our own language while showing us that we cannot (unless we learn another language, which comes with its own limits); but poetry can also let us leave our place of origins, our "humdrum" problems, behind. A defense of the taciturn, of the unsayable, "Hamatawk" also mimics flight, linguistic escape, not least an escape from the human-built environment. Glancy's "new world" is a world in which "old language breaks," in which we can distance ourselves from stereotypes by attending to oddity, by swerving away from prose sense. It is a world in which she (but perhaps not we) can fold herself up and imagine becoming a crow. But it is also a world in which very old kinds and functions for lyric poetry have a place. As much as Glancy's wiry, scrambled poem belongs to a line of midwestern experiments, and to a body of Native American verse, it is also a poem in which human problems get solved when the speaker encounters, and understands, birds. These wise, wild birds can occur in medieval lyric, and in William Butler Yeats ("Cuchulain Comforted") and in Seamus Heaney ("Sweeney Astray," based on the medieval Irish language poem in which a bard becomes a bird). "The buzzled wiggle/of the tall grasses" could only occur in these tallgrass plains, but the avian vision—or something very like it—has happened elsewhere as well: that excited, mysterious, international, interspecies vision is part of what saves the figure in the poem, even if it will not save me too.

LUCIE BROCK-BROIDO

Domestic Mysticism

In thrice 10,000 seasons, I will come back to this world
In a white cotton dress. Kingdom of After My Own Heart.
Kingdom of Fragile. Kingdom of Dwarves. When I come home,
Teacups will quiver in their Dresden saucers, pentatonic chimes
Will move in wind. A covey of alley cats will swarm on the side
Porch & perch there, portents with quickened heartbeats
You will feel against your ankles as you pass through.

After the first millennium, we were supposed to die out.
You had your face pressed up against the coarse dyed velvet
Of the curtain, always looking out for your own transmigration:
What colors you would wear, what cut of jewel,
What kind of pageantry, if your legs would be tied
Down, if there would be wandering tribes of minstrels
Following with woodwinds in your wake.

This work of mine, the kind of work which takes no arms to do,
Is least noble of all. It's peopled by Wizards, the Forlorn,
The Awkward, the Blinkers, the Spoon-Fingered, Agnostic Lispers,
Stutterers of Prayer, the Flatulent, the Closet Weepers,
The Charlatans. I am one of those. In January, the month the owls
Nest in, I am a witness & a small thing altogether. The Kingdom
Of Ingratitude. Kingdom of Lies. Kingdom of How Dare I.

I go on dropping words like little pink fish eggs, unawares, slightly
Illiterate, often on the mark. Waiting for the clear whoosh
Of fluid to descend & cover them. A train like a silver
Russian love pill for the sick at heart passes by

My bedroom window in the night at the speed of mirage.
In the next millennium, I will be middle aged. I do not do well
In the marrow of things. Kingdom of Trick. Kingdom of Drug.

In a lung-shaped suburb of Virginia, my sister will be childless
Inside the ice storm, forcing the narcissus. We will send
Each other valentines. The radio blowing out
Vaughan Williams on the highway's purple moor.
At nine o'clock, we will put away our sewing to speak
Of lofty things while, in the pantry, little plants will nudge
Their frail tips toward the light we made last century.

When I come home, the dwarves will be long
In their shadows & promiscuous. The alley cats will sneak
Inside, curl about the legs of furniture, close the skins
Inside their eyelids, sleep. Orchids will be intercrossed & sturdy.
The sun will go down as I sit, thin armed, small breasted
In my cotton dress, poked with eyelet stitches, a little lace,
In the queer light left when a room snuffs out.

I draw a bath, enter the water as a god enters water:
Fertile, knowing, kind, surrounded by glass objects
Which could break easily if mishandled or ill-touched.
Everyone knows an unworshipped woman will betray you.
There is always that promise, I like that. Kingdom of Kinesis.
Kingdom of Benevolent. I will betray as a god betrays,
With tenderheartedness. I've got this mystic streak in me.

At once messianic and ingenuous, "Domestic Mysticism"—the first poem in
A Hunger, Brock-Broido's first book—is both an ars poetica and a self-portrait:
it introduces, rapidly and passionately (the passion informs the long, fast-
moving lines), the ample prop closet that will serve her increasingly elaborate
later books, from *The Master Letters* (1995) to *Stay, Illusion* (2014). The poem

announces what will become her unmistakable persona: immortal and innocent, magically wise and deliberately childlike, "slightly / Illiterate," likely to
step outside the bounds of prestigious taste, but also drawn to a sophisticated—
or else a mock-sophisticated—range of reference and speech.

In *Stay, Illusion* (its title taken from *Hamlet*) Brock-Broido commemorated
her mother, her father, victims of the death penalty in America, and the drying-
out, the disenchantment, and the lowered expectations that age and change
bring to so many people and things. Her ornamented, involuted sentences
(sometimes run-on sentences), and her range of reference (Northern Renaissance and Baroque art, Emily Dickinson, the Brontës) played her own liking
for lacy, stormy wildness against subjects so serious and unyielding that they
might seem fit for plainer speech.

Here, though, she can have fun, and the cascade of props and cos-
tumes—for all their seriousness about poetic vocation—may let the right
reader have fun: that's why "Domestic Mysticism," though not her subtlest
poem, probably makes the best entry point for her oeuvre—it reads as if
assembled with that function in mind. This poet, returning after 7,500 years
(30,000 seasons), becomes a dramatically feminine revision of Yeats's "rough
beast" from "The Second Coming," who brings a new era to a post-Christian
world. She comes from another "kingdom," like Christ (who will also "come
back to this world"), or rather she comes to us from many kingdoms, some of
them magical, fraudulent, or satanic ("Kingdom of Lies"). She is also a ghost,
an innocent, a girl returning to earth in the manner of spirits summoned by
mediums, teacups, and Ouija boards. Given her glamour and mystery, "Wandering tribes of minstrels" might follow her, paying homage to her work, "the
kind of work which takes no arms to do" and is "least noble of all." That work
makes her a "witness," but also a liar, someone who takes liberties: it must be
the work of writing and reciting poetry in a post-confessional age, "dropping
words" that sound both wrong and right, both fictive and accurate, "often on
the mark."

Not poetry in general, then, but this kind of poetry—extravagant, unpredictable, unsettling, excessive, yet intimate—is Brock-Broido's "work," and it
allies her to a succession of misfits: "the Flatulent, the Closet Weepers, / The
Charlatans. I am one of those." Others mock them, but she will defend them:
she belongs among them. That mission defines poetry as uncouth, as excessive,
and—as the critic and poet James Longenbach wrote about that earlier self-
dramatizing poet, Ezra Pound—"the poem's excess, like any poem's excess, is
driven by the wish not to die; but because the wish is experienced in such a

primal form, the poem dramatizes its romance with excess excessively." With its overtones of gothic fantasy, its invitation to a supernatural scene, Brock-Broido's poem echoes young-adult fantasy novels, whose readers can escape into (and then see their own troubles represented in) magical otherworlds. Such novels had a lower cultural profile—and less prestige—in the 1980s than they do today, but they were widely available (think of Marion Zimmer Bradley, or Diana Wynne Jones), and they drew—as Brock-Broido does—on Renaissance Europe and neopagan practice.

Cluttered and vaunting, urgent in its axiomatic devotion to self-expression—and involved in a feminist argument about it (express yourself, women, or men will do it for you)—Brock-Broido even anticipates the unsettled extremes of what the recent critics Alicia Eler and Kate Durbin name, approvingly, "the teen girl Tumblr aesthetic," with its clusters of pop and high culture allusions, its "altered self-portraits, and writing that is personal and vulnerable." In such self-portraits the poet is risking embarrassment, presenting her soul, by sharing her tastes, rather than telling the story of her life. Its gathered tableaux promise more power to their constructors than any straightforward narrative could entail—though, like confessional and narrative poetry, it courts accusations of self-indulgence. The famously judgmental critic and poet William Logan, reviewing *A Hunger*, accused Brock-Broido of "haute couture vulgarity." Brock-Broido then made that phrase into a title for one poem in her next book.

It is no mistake to identify Brock-Broido's early way of writing, at once heightened and drawn to escape, with adolescence: it will, after all—so the poet says—take a millennium for her to become "middle aged." Poetry is a way for the poet to keep away from the central preoccupations of adult life, "the marrow of things"; it is, in fact, a kind of magic spell, capable both of resurrection and of spiritual protection, and what it protects is the space of special meaning, the small whole world, that we may construct and share with childhood friends, or siblings. Other poems in *A Hunger*—"Birdie Africa," "Lucie and Her Sisters"—also envision communes, secluded households, shared fantasies, and private languages, sometimes macabre ones. Her poem "Elective Mutes" takes place between real twin sisters, June and Jennifer Gibbons (born 1963), who "refused to communicate with any adult," "living and speaking in an invented world of poems, novels and diaries based on the lives and rituals of their dolls," until "they began to think of murdering one another." (The real June Gibbons, after her sister died, went on to a quiet, not at all murderous village adulthood.)

Devotion to girlish, secluded creations can go badly wrong—it can become a fatal addiction—but it can also become the richest part of a varied life-world, and "Domestic Mysticism," its story not over, leaves open both possibilities. Brock-Broido's verbal imagination will create not only an escape but a refuge, like the Brontë sisters' Gondor, a made-up world on a Yorkshire moor, or like the pantry in which herbs may grow. The stanzas themselves, with their crowds of concrete nouns, resemble those plant-friendly, propitious closets as well.

The poet as teen girl collector, imaginative maintainer of private worlds: "Domestic Mysticism" offers and even recommends that archetype, but it also presents the same poet as prematurely old, dressed in Victorian fashion, surrounded by cats, "In the queer light left when a room snuffs out." Not quite Miss Havisham, but close; even closer, perhaps, to the kind of self-confident gothic persona adopted by pop stars from Joanna Newsom to Stevie Nicks. Brock-Broido appropriates—one might say with a vengeance—the slur that poetry, or her kind of poetry, is good only for teenage girls and old ladies: such people are just as important as the kinds of people (able-bodied adult men) who do not appear. Dwarves are important too, and they can have sex—they are "promiscuous," which also means that they don't hide. Brock-Broido does not say whether she intends Wagnerian metalworkers or very short human beings (now usually called little people); either way, this domestic pagan space belongs to them too.

It is also, if we wish, for us. "I want a poetry which is fetishistic, a-Moral, obsessive, erotic, a poetry of Commission, a poem of pre-meditation, beneath (not above) the law," Brock-Broido wrote a few years after *A Hunger*, in a manifesto called (quoting Emily Dickinson) "Myself a Kangaroo Among the Beauties." The very arbitrariness, the freedom to act out selfish emotions and embodied desires, that this returning ghost with her "mystic streak" claims for herself appears to be a domain marked as adolescent, or as secluded, or as its own "kingdom." In fact, though, Brock-Broido's poetry attempts to open that domain for us all—as long as we do not mind knowing that it will "betray" us. No matter how open it seems, how much or how little it lets us in, the best verbal art comes about—in Brock-Broido's view—to satisfy the creator's inner needs: no matter how weird it looks, nor how long (perhaps 30,000 seasons) it can take.

KILLARNEY CLARY

Above the Inland Empire today the sky is off the desert, deceptively active in a ridiculous heat. The whole country is hot, colored red-orange on the news. We are stuck here on earth with no breath of air. Coolers rumble all over town; I actually consider making lemonade. If there is a remedy, I will stay.

I was born into my skin and its future, the planet and its promise or demise. Each day a similar sun, the almost predictable moods of the moon, seasonal weather holding its shape for planned vacations.

After the earthquake this morning, the day broke sizzling with monstrous clouds to the east—what Mama once called "earthquake weather." I stood in the doorway until the windows quieted, and went back to bed, sleeping easily, rocking, anchored through dreams to the shifting plate. I trust the blatant forces, and worry only about that which grows and moves unseen, the odd cell, thriving.

Eileen, there is no way to practice traveling alone; you just go. And you might finally hear for yourself the stories you told us from your sleep. Maybe. Doesn't seem to matter how hard you try, you don't leave when you intended, and it's the idea of a cure, the reassurance of your own power, that defeats you. The world fails and you are failure—not finding the impossible recovery that was set for you.

All disasters are natural. The heart shudders; the flood fills. No one knows what to die of.

Lines break; sentences connect. That sentence itself seems too general to be true over a wide range of verse and prose, but it's the impression you might get from many a prose poem, where the pacing of verse, the stops and starts, is absent, and rhythm emerges from syntax. Rather than stitching together disparate units, prose poems such as Killarney Clary's present experiences, memories, impressions, and ideas already put together, as if they had always belonged together, and almost request that we take them apart. (Like all Clary's prose poems, it lacks a title; as in the tables of contents for Clary's books, we refer to it by its first phrase.) In one way such poems resemble the kind of poems where a poet looks around, describes a landscape, and then reflects on her interior life (this book contains many of them), but in another way such prose poems might seem closer to the stream-of-consciousness parts of a modernist novel (say, a novel by Virginia Woolf), in which we simply ride through a character's thoughts, intuiting the associations that link them.

"Above the Inland Empire," in that respect, represents Clary's consistent genius, still too little known. It also stands out for the way that its sets of sentences interact with its topics (earthquakes, dry summers, Eileen's mortality) and with the prose poem form: the unpredictable endings of its sentences and paragraphs—whose music can go on and on almost indefinitely before stopping (as lines cannot), and which can shift abruptly from very short to very long phrases and sentences—come to reflect the unsettling nature of illness, and our unsettled tenure on earth.

Clary has spent her whole life—bar a stint at the Iowa Writers' Workshop— in California, most of it in and around Los Angeles, though she now lives in Arctos, near Santa Cruz. "Inland Empire" refers to the Southern California cities and towns—among them Claremont, Riverside, and Ontario—south of the San Bernardino Mountains, west of the desert, and east of L.A. The area is long-settled, economically varied, often suburban, and (like much of California) dry: it is also, for Clary, a place of heritage, where "Mama" introduced her to the atmosphere, the nonverbal cues, that presage earthquakes.

The earthquake—a quintessentially Californian danger, almost a cliché— provides one occasion for this poem, and it does not scare this Southland native: "I trust the blatant forces," she writes. Clary "went back to bed, sleeping easily." Earthquakes are well defined, like the ends of paragraphs and sentences: we know what they do and what to do when they strike (stand in a doorway, for example), and we can know when they come to an end.

What frightens Clary a little, and saddens her more, are the progressive, insidious, perhaps illimitable, often invisible causes of death and destruction: for example, the cancer—"the odd cell, thriving"—that seems to be killing her friend (or relative) Eileen. As in most of Clary's best prose poems, the characters get some definition, but not as much as they would get in realist fiction: like a private, signed letter, the poem is addressed *to* Eileen, who does not need to be told how old she is, nor what her relation to Clary might be. If the poem acknowledges other readers besides Eileen, it provides not a full picture of Eileen's life but a scene, an attitude and a set of ideas that Clary brings to the end of that life, which has not come yet but may come soon.

Clary's first paragraph evokes the stillness of windless heat: the sky, "deceptively active," changes colors, but the ground feels just the same, its unpleasant menace accentuated by the color-coded drought maps on televised news. Lemonade as a "remedy" for heat is an American cliché, and poets avoid clichés, but Clary will risk it: the summer day, though exceptionally intense, represents any day, every day, in an "almost predictable" middle-class life, one that follows the calendar's seasons through childhood and adolescence into adulthood, making room for "planned vacations." "Weather holding its shape" is weather that will not change, as the seasons will not change in greater L.A., as a healthy child's sense of her own body before puberty may not change, as the middle-class parents' promise of security may not change. All these kinds of security, making space for "planned vacations," stand for one another, as adulthood, the earthquake, and (more seriously) Eileen's illness disrupt them all.

Aging is constant and gradual; earthquakes, however are sudden, and just as Californian as drought. Knowing her locale, knowing the building codes, knowing a bit of seismology, Clary finds them predictable, almost reassuring—they remind us where we are. No wonder, then, that she can go "back to bed, sleeping easily, rocking, anchored through dreams to the shifting plate," as in a cradle. The sentence itself rocks: scan it as you would scan verse, looking for strong (loud) and weak (soft) syllables, and you will find a preponderance of dactyls ("STOOD in the," "QUI-et-ed"), whose triple rhythms faintly suggest the 3/4 cadence of a lullaby.

But the poem is not all lullaby, not all ironic reassurance, not all earthquake or childhood or California. What disconcerts Clary—and breaks up the dactylic rhythm—is her friend's cancer, introduced in consonant-heavy mouthfuls, with phrases that have no triple feet: the poet will "worry only about that which grows and moves unseen, the odd cell thriving." It might feel bad to wake up stuck in the heat, or odd to wake up to a seismic event, but at least that experience is shared. To die, however, is to leave the space and the place that we share with others: "there is no way to practice traveling alone." Cancer, like other progressive diseases, defeats our ideas about agency, not least because it defeats our expectation—as bourgeois as Claremont, as bourgeois as a planned vacation—that we can control our destiny, manage our path through life's seasons, down to life's ending. Eileen may feel like a failure, "not finding the impossible recovery that was set for you."

She may, but Clary wishes she would not: her prose poem is not just a letter to the ailing Eileen, not just a piece about Southern California's climate and weather, but also a general meditation on the life course, with its unpredictable ending. "All disasters are natural" in that they show the limits of the unnatural artifice by which we think to keep ourselves safe. The very American tradition of telling us that we can simply put mind over body, that we can decide "what to die of," that we can will ourselves to health—a tradition also associated with Southern California, despite its roots in Mary Baker Eddy's New England—is, to put it simply, something Clary's prose tries mightily to reject.

And it has to try hard: there is no more persistent form of wishful thinking that the belief that our beliefs come true, and there are few kinds of guilt harder to shake than guilt about one's own incapacity. *If only I were a better person, tried harder, had more focus, had more faith,* the sufferer says to herself, *I'd get well.* Patients can even get worse because contemporary culture makes them feel guilty about their lack of "positive thinking": the British newspaper columnist Oliver Burkeman (*The Antidote*) and the American journalist Barbara Ehrenreich (*Bright-Sided*) have both written cogent books about that effect. Clary's "Maybe" advises Eileen not to feel guilty for not knowing how she ought to feel, and not to feel bad about feeling afraid.

That advice comes in surprisingly choppy—and almost shockingly short—sentences, by far the shortest in the poem. Clary's prose serves up spondees: "the HEART SHUDders; the FLOOD FILLS." "The stream of consciousness, like the stream of time, does not provide any principle of termination," as the literary theorist Barbara Herrnstein Smith remarked. But the end of life does. Human lives are unlike verse lines—they are more like prose sentences—in that there is a way to describe their irregular shape, but no way to say in advance even approximately where they are going to end. The shape of the prose poem, with its unpredictable sentences, now half a page long, now supershort, thus fits a poem about the unpredictability of the human life span.

What would it mean to "know what to die of"? It would mean a sense both of moral rightness and of predictability in human life and the natural world. We live without such a sense, as people in the Inland Empire live without the predictability of Oxford's or Boston's seasons. If only we could face chronic illness, the deaths of our parents, or the deaths of our friends with the same equanimity that native Californians bring to a seismic event.

Prose poetry, says the polyglot scholar Steven Monte, in its French origins and in America now, invites us "to construct a history around an abstraction," to figure out how we have learned to decide what a "poem" is. Some prose poets, such as Harryman, double down on the resistance to story and "sense" that define their sort of poetry anyway. Others, with roots in the European Surrealists, seek the uncanny illogic of dreams, the refreshment of comic relief, or (like the much imitated, never equaled Russell Edson) both. Clary, on the other hand, stays close to the objectives we sometimes call "lyric." "There is a pattern, not a story," Clary writes in a later prose poem, "a game of perception" in which we look for fleeting objects, "shown for only a moment" before "the tray is taken into another room": that poem (from *Shadow of a Cloud but No Cloud,* published in 2014) describes at once a party game, a psychological research experiment, and Clary's own artful goals.

JOHN YAU

Modern Love

The clouds continued swelling like poisoned fish
While the boy listened carefully to the story
That was being invented by the girl
Who, like him, had been abandoned in the city.
They were, she whispered, itchy to avoid the forest
And reach the little red motel by the stream.

However, when she came to the edge of the stream,
She began trembling like a fish.
She was going to have to enter the forest,
After all, and hear the birds laughing at her recital of a
    story.
"I've become as soft and defenseless as a drug infested city.
I might as well eat rags and dust," muttered the girl.

Suddenly, the boy was scared of the girl,
And wondered how to cover the stream
Of invectives she was leaving all over their city
Owned apartment: "Perhaps, if I steal a fish,
Pick some flowers, and beg you to finish the story,
You will remember how to lead us past the forest."

Remembering that no one had ever circumnavigated the forest
Before, she tried to pretend she was just another pretty but deranged
    girl.
"Don't be afraid: if you happen to fall off the edge of my story,
Remember that paper is made from trees that have crashed into a
    stream.

It is only frightening if you are a fish."
She put on her best stupid smile and she looked out at the city

Which had spread further than any other city.
Still, no one had been able to map the forest.
"Before you go out and cadge a fish,
I should teach you how to swim," said the girl.
"There is something lurking at the bottom of the stream,
And it may attempt to break into my story."

This happens every time she tells a story,
He thought, as evening's shadows absorbed the city.
I can no longer be sure of the meaning of "stream."
Of what is immeasurable about the forest.
If I am lucky, I will be able to convince the next girl
That life's pleasures consist of warm rows of oily fish.

"Actually, the story is about two fish
Who leave their stream to live in the forest.
It is a parable about our life in the city," began the girl.

The sestina is a thirty-nine-line form in which the same six line-ending words repeat seven times, in a preset order, so that the last line-ending word of one stanza becomes the first in the next, the first becomes the second, the fifth the third, until the last stanza, the envoi, where all six words reappear in just three lines. The form originated in Provençal (southern French) medieval love poetry, and it has strong associations with frustration—it's almost impossible to write a coherent sestina that isn't about going around in circles, or getting trapped, or feeling stuck. The first sestina in English, Philip Sidney's "Ye Goatherd Gods" (1590), is a double sestina (twelve six-line stanzas) about two shepherds' unrequited love.

The form also lends itself to comic absurdity: John Ashbery's cartoonish, bizarre sestinas, especially "Farm Implements and Rutabagas in a Landscape" (about Popeye and Olive Oyl) would become models for dozens of sestinas by younger poets in the 1990s and 2000s, culminating in *The Incredible Sestina Anthology* (2013), compiled by Daniel Nester, who edited the sestinas-only poetry section for *McSweeney's* magazine. But Yau got there first, or (counting Ashbery) second; though there are earlier models—Elizabeth Bishop's heartbreaking "Sestina," about childhood mourning, and W. H. Auden's "Have a Good Time," about symbolic sexual quests—Yau's torqued, interrupted, embittered fairy tale might be the first after Ashbery to advance the form.

Yau turns the frustrated repetitions that the form itself provides into anger against clichés, against expectations around sex, love, and romance. His sestina pushes back against—even as it also tries to tell—a story in which a mistreated boy and an inventive girl fall in love, conspire, and escape to the country, where they do what comes naturally. It's the story of *Romeo and Juliet,* and it doesn't end much better for Yau's nameless couple than for Shakespeare's doomed teens. The latter die by misadventure and suicide; the former are, so to speak, destroyed by their language, kept from any happy ending by sexist and heterosexist assumptions that (for Yau, here) turn any love story into a fish story, and any escape from a culturally dominant narrative into an impossible dream. Yau's harsh attitude, his brusque, almost hasty pace, and his sometime disgust or self-disgust distance us further from the desperate, unfortunate girl and boy, even while their stories, and their sexual culture, could be our own.

So could their "Modern Love": George Meredith used the same title for his scandalous 1862 sonnet sequence about infidelity in a disintegrating marriage (also a reference point for John Hollander; Yau must have also heard David Bowie's 1983 pop hit "Modern Love," though Bowie's optimism would not fit well here). Yau's modern lovers have not yet encountered the adulthood, nor the disillusion, with which Meredith's sequence began: they are more like the many Shakespearean lovers who flee the city or court for another green world. These lovers, though, seek not an Edenic clearing but a far-from-pristine "motel"; they'll have to cross a stream (symbolically, lose their virginity) to get there.

Is the stream polluted? Is the very atmosphere polluted? Is sex itself polluted? Are the fish poisoned? Women's genitalia are associated with water and with fish (decades-old drag queen argot calls female authenticity "fishiness" and cisgender women "fish"). The girl may feel like a fish, something meant to be caught; she may feel more like a target, or an object, than like another actor in the boy's own story about his triumphant escape. If they have sex, will people laugh at her? Will she feel defenseless, or compromised, or dirty, like ungentrified 1980s New York? Are the boy and girl like Adam and Eve, liable to become conscious of mortality and guilt, "rags and dust," if they ever complete their "little red" sexual tryst?

Her fears scare him—perhaps adult femininity scares him; perhaps he's scared that she'll leave him alone. Nevertheless, he makes the offer that countless men have made to countless women, some of them sex workers, some of them brides: if the woman meets the man's emotional needs ("finish the story"), he will provide her with physical sustenance and material comfort (fish and flowers). And she accepts the offer, for a while: the story she tells, the story they inhabit, the story on which the sestina insists, "is only frightening if you are a fish." Hearing the girl's doubts, the boy becomes dismissive as well as impatient (we might say that he has blue balls): Yau sandwiches his "lyrical" phraseology, "as evening's shadows absorbed the city," between sarcastic, exasperated lines. Sick of the way the girl turns away from him, sick of the way her stories do not end, unsure of himself, the boy wants to find a new girl, one who will be satisfied with something simpler, or perhaps with more sex— "warm rows of oily fish."

This account makes a plot clearer than it can possibly be while you are reading the poem; that false clarity shows how much Yau wants to muddy the waters, to prevent you from losing yourself in the story or in the familiar symbols from which such stories come. What lies beyond them? We don't know: Yau's fairy-tale characters cannot know. Like the characters in Auden's sestina "Have a Good Time" (whose end words include "country" and "wood," analogous to Yau's "city" and "forest"), they're stuck in the story of their quest-romance, which is to say that they are stuck in a life story designed for certain straight people, a sexist and heterosexist story that promises happy endings few couples reach. (We could set Yau's resistance to love, or to love stories, beside Diane Glancy's resistance to claims about animals, and to Native stereotypes.) Yau's "Something lurking at the bottom of the stream" could be the body itself, or the Freudian unconscious, or the unruly oddities of bodily desire, which can be kinky, or predictable, or hard to get to know. (If you think I am looking too hard for sex in this sestina, consider all the sex in Yau's short stories, collected in *Hawaiian Cowboys* and the punningly titled *Forbidden Entries*.)

Yau's sestina thus becomes a more and more pessimistic, more and more ridiculous, more and more embittered "parable about our life" inside a culture obsessed with erotic fulfillments and happy endings, one that tries to pair off each boy and each girl. The grating elements within Yau's style—its inexactness, its sometime clunkiness, as in the frequent passive constructions ("was being," "was scared")—serve the critique: if meter and form cast a spell, then those elements, and especially Yau's final, ametrical, distractingly lengthy line, break a spell, directing us away from the world that the boy wants to know. The poem thus evolves (like Carla Harryman's writing) into a critique of story itself: we find ourselves trapped in, we flail as we try to escape, not only one story about sex but also the whole idea that our lives should be like stories, that we should be able to describe ourselves as protagonists whose choices cause events, and whose events reveal our character, or (worse yet) our origins.

Critics who write about Yau at length have, so far, concentrated on his ethnicity (his parents were Chinese and Chinese American) and on his most obviously Asian American work, such as the sarcastic antinarrative verse sequence called "Genghis Chan, Private Eye." Yau's style can seem to attack invidious stereotypes about Asian Americans (especially Asian American men) by flaunting not just agency but the emotions and reactions—anger, rudeness, spontaneity, violent strength—that stereotypes about them exclude. A 1994 essay or manifesto has Yau refusing all stereotypes, all categorical origin myths, in caustic terms: "I am the Other," Yau writes, paraphrasing Arthur Rimbaud, "the chink, the lazy son, the surrealist, the upright East Coast Banana . . . You have your labels, their falsifying categories, but I have words. I—the I that writes—will not be spoken for." ("Banana"—yellow outside, pale inside—is a very offensive label for East Asian Americans who seem or act white; Asian American cultural politics, in those years, had their center on the West Coast.) Yau's best critic, Timothy Yu, writes ingeniously that Yau's work, neither antireferential nor autobiographical, presents an "unstable but storytelling 'I,' one that is constantly in revision"; when it toys with "explicitly ethnic signifiers," then refuses to tell us how to read them (as in the "Genghis Chan" sequence), Yau's poetry therefore presents "the nagging sense that we do not know what it means to be 'Chinese.'"

Nor do we know what it means to love, or be in love. We are not ("Modern Love" says) like the protagonists of folk tales, of the Eden story, of romantic comedies; we are more complicated, more double-minded, more unpredictable, perhaps less in control of what we do, than the characters in the stories we tell, and we ought to know it. Yet we can't escape from it, any more than fish can "leave their stream to live in the forest," or sestinas can escape their repetitions: we live in "story," alas, just as fish live in lakes and oceans and streams.

Writing about Frank O'Hara—like Yau himself, a New York City–based poet and art critic—Yau says that the earlier poet knew "art doesn't solve a problem forever . . . each answer it provides produces more unexpected questions." The repeated words in this sestina, each one a kind of answer to the questions of the form, reject familiar stories—romances, love stories—in favor of those not yet told. Yau also praises O'Hara's "ability to be simultaneously vulnerable outrageous and self-mocking. He is self-possessed and provocative, distanced and theatrical." We could apply the same adjectives to Yau's style, though we might have to add—taking "Modern Love" as an example—that the poems sound harsh, brusque, always dissatisfied, unwilling if not unable to settle down.

ROBERT CREELEY

Oh

Oh stay awhile,
sad sagging flesh
and bones gone brittle.

Stay in place,
agèd face, teeth,
don't go.

Inside and out
the flaccid change
of bodily parts,

mechanics of action,
mind's collapsing
habits, all

echo here
in mottled skin, blurred eye,
reiterated mumble.

Lift to the vacant air
some sigh, some sign
I'm still inside.

Published in *Windows* (1990), when Creeley was only sixty-four, "Oh" sounds
like the work of a figure in poor health indeed (in fact, the poet lived till 2005).
It extends to the depiction of what W. B. Yeats called "bodily decrepitude,"
and to a very traditional mode of poetic complaint, the new means, new

rhythms, and new ways of using small words that a younger Creeley developed for other goals.

Creeley began writing and publishing during the 1950s, in close correspondence with Charles Olson, the charismatic poet, teacher, and theorist (their correspondence fills ten published volumes); "It is really Charles Olson I must thank," Creeley remembered later, "for whatever freedom I have as a poet." Creeley, Olson, Ed Dorn, Denise Levertov, and others were sometimes called the Black Mountain School, after the experimental college in North Carolina where Olson served as rector from 1951 until 1956. Olson's 1950 essay "Projective Verse" (which quotes Creeley) asked poets to proceed from "the HEAD, by way of the EAR, to the SYLLABLE," and from "the HEART, by way of the BREATH, to the LINE." Projective verse should reflect the physical outflow of air, the patterns of breathing, the somatic life of the poet; the process by which the poem entered the air was the shape of the project the poet undertook, the pattern the poet's body gave the world.

Breath and its physicality—or ideas about it—would direct his subsequent work. Creeley's early poems, gathered in *For Love* (1962), often portrayed balked or baffled erotic desire. At the same time, some of those poems—and, even more so, Creeley's poems of the late 1960s—pointed away from persons and situations, toward sounds and words explored for their own sake: one poem from *Pieces* (1969) read (it's the whole poem) "One, and/one, two/three." Creeley's mischievous or deep hypothesis, explored most fully in *Pieces*, that poems are pieces before and after they are wholes, that "the 'piece' . . . is not a fragment of the whole, but a whole with provisional status" (to quote the poet and Creeley scholar Ben Friedlander), remained a key to his work. One poem from the 1970s imitates blues: "You don't/love me/like you/say you do, you // don't do me/like you/said/you would." Another, much later poem is called "Box": "What do you think/he's got it for // unless/he means to use it" ("it" might be a coffin).

But the Creeley of head-scratchingly radical practice, the Creeley who most resembled his sometime editor Robert Grenier, did not outlast the 1970s. Creeley left California in 1976 to visit New Zealand, where he met his third wife, Penelope. After the new couple settled back in America, in Buffalo, New York, and then Providence, Rhode Island, Creeley produced a series of quieter books in whose short poems and sequences overt experiment took a backseat to emotion and voice, to pathos, domestic warmth, and diffuse regret. The scholar and critic Mark Scroggins, normally sympathetic to Black Mountain and its heirs, complained that "far too many of [Creeley's late] poems, for my taste, linger on the discomforts and indignities of encroaching age."

"Oh" is one such poem. To begin a poem with that syllable, spelled that way, is to establish an intimate connection between poet and reader (no vaunting "O" here), and also between the poet and his own breath: the poem may express surprise, or dismay, or delight, or (as here) subdued desperation, but it will also acknowledge its pneumatic dimension, as Grenier's own "oh" did too. Creeley wrote earlier and later poems entitled "Oh" or "Oh No" or "Oh Love"; the earlier "Oh" begins "Oh like a bird / falls down // out of air."

Pursuing absolutely ordinary, millennia-old anxieties about old age, Creeley has managed to arrange around those anxieties elegant courses of sound: alliterations in *s* and *b*, internal rhymes such as "place" and "face," consonants in long *a* and then in long *o*. It is not quite what Olson would have called "projective," nor does it exactly duplicate the effects of Creeley's ultimate sonic model, William Carlos Williams, who more or less invented enjambment-driven, demotic American free verse; instead it uses short breath, the sound of the body, to build up short and irregular lines in which the spirit or soul of the poet becomes again what the ancient Greeks called it: *pneuma*, the spirit or breath that the body contains.

Can that spirit be used up? The Roman emperor Hadrian wrote a very famous poem about his soul, beginning (in Latin) "Animula, vagula, blandula," asking his soul where it would go when his body died and the soul could no longer play jokes on (or with, or in) it. Creeley's nearly playful but finally mournful poem asks after his *pneuma* or *animula* in the same way, nor does it stop by acknowledging the way that the physical body runs down as we age. Does the mind run down too? Does perception fade? Do the emphatic cadences of argument in prose or verse turn into a "reiterated mumble"? Does the soul change as the breath changes, as the body that generates the breath grows less robust and ultimately feeble?

These lines come close to strong accentual meter—two units in every line, whether the unit has one syllable ("don't" and "go") or four ("mechanics of," "reiterated"). These lines in turn add up to six stanzas, five with strong closure at the end. The exception, the one enjambed stanza, asks whether we have lost "all." "Oh" shows how a way of writing designed to highlight the vigor of breath, the dependence of soul and intellect upon body, poetic spirit on pharynx and teeth, can be used to ask what happens to poetic spirit when teeth go bad and breath fails. But Creeley is not exactly, or not only, complaining; after his first two requests, he manages a long declarative sentence (the main verb is "echo") as if he were stating facts, or rather arranging those facts into his short, irregular, breath-driven lines ("all // echo here"). He has already asked "flesh / and bones," "face," and "teeth" not to get any worse. They may not obey him. Yet they have already shown that there is something—however short, or short of breath—Creeley's faculties can still do.

As in most of Creeley's best poems from the 1950s through the early 2000s, the poet's emotions can be simply stated: as Scroggins put it, he "never hid his own emotions." Most of his words are simple indeed. What's strange and new, and far from simple, comes in those words' small-scale arrangements, which remind us that poetry comes from the breath of a person, that words may convey the spirit, and yet are also physical air. Such poetry—unlike, say, medical manuals—might remind us that language comes from the body, that verbal signs represent aural events, that words are not just marks representing ideas. Unlike most poems about old age and impending disability—from our period or from any other—Creeley's six-stanza exclamation emphasizes its status as something produced, something literally exhaled, from the very body whose troubles it laments. We have to understand its words on a page (whether we read it silently or aloud), its "reiterated mumble," as Creeley's instructions to himself (which he can, in fact, follow) to convert his worries into actions taken by lungs and pharynx, or else by his writing hand.

That physical engagement—that use of what Olson liked to capitalize as "BREATH"—gives Creeley just what he seeks in the final stanza, which turns again to something like a secular version of petitionary prayer: "Lift to the vacant air / some sigh, some sign / I'm still inside," Creeley asks, and his poem has done exactly that. The poem is itself the "sign" that Creeley is "still inside" his aging, "sad, sagging" body: his "I," himself, inheres in these rich sounds. They are the "sign," sent into (and by means of) "air," that there is some life, some spirit, in this author yet.

CHARLES WRIGHT

December Journal

God is not offered to the senses,

                         St. Augustine tells us,

The artificer is not his work, but is his art:

Nothing is good if it can be better.

But all these oak trees look fine to me,

                           this Virginia cedar

Is true to its own order

And ghosts a unity beyond its single number.

This morning's hard frost, whose force is nowhere absent, is nowhere
    present.

The undulants cleanse themselves in the riverbed,

The mud striders persevere,

                  the exceptions provide.

I keep coming back to the visible.

                I keep coming back

To what it leads me into,

The hymn in the hymnal,

The object, sequence and consequence.

By being exactly what it is,

It is that other, inviolate self we yearn for,

Itself and more than itself,

                the word inside the word.

It is the tree and what the tree stands in for, the blank,

The far side of the last equation.

———————

Black and brown of December,

             umber and burnt orange

Under the spoked trees, front yard
Pollocked from edge feeder to edge run,
Central Virginia beyond the ridgeline spun with a back light
Into indefinition,
                charcoal and tan, damp green . . .

Entangled in the lust of the eye,
               we carry this world with us wherever
                        we go,
Even into the next one:
Abstraction, the highest form, is the highest good:
Everything's beautiful that stays in its due order,
Every existing thing can be praised
                when compared with nothingness.

       ————————

The seasons roll from my tongue—
Autumn, winter, the *integer vitae* of all that's in vain,
Roll unredeemed.
             Rain falls. The utmost
Humps out to the end of nothing's branch, crooks there like an
    inchworm,
And fingers the emptiness.
December drips through my nerves,
               a drumming of secondary things
That spells my name right,
         heartbeat
Of slow, steady consonants.
Trash cans weigh up with water beside the curb,
Leaves flatten themselves against the ground
                  and take cover.

How are we capable of so much love
             for things that must fall away?

How can we utter our mild retractions and still keep
Our wasting affection for this world?
                                        Augustine says
This is what we desire,
The soul itself instinctively desires it.
                                    He's right, of course,
No matter how due and exacting the penance is.
The rain stops, the seasons wheel
Like stars in their bright courses:
                                        the cogitation of the wise
Will bind you and take you where you will not want to go.
Mimic the juniper, have mercy.

                            ——————

The tongue cannot live up to the heart:
Raise the eyes of your affection to its affection
And let its equivalents
                            ripen in your body.
Love what you don't understand yet, and bring it to you.

From somewhere we never see comes everything that we do see.
What is important devolves
                                from the immanence of infinitude
In whatever our hands touch—
The other world is here, just under our fingertips.

You can recognize a Charles Wright poem—or at least a mature Wright poem—at a glance: his characteristic work relies on the integrity of long, balanced, end-stopped lines, making the line and the sentence as important (if not more so) than the putative unity of the poem. These lines give acoustic form to a consistent elegance, and an understated confidence, that Wright's metaphysical, or antimetaphysical, diffidence belies. His poetry can thus tell us to give up on clear doctrines, to trust in the senses and live in a moment's experience, carrying us with rare élan into the moments it tells us to cherish, and then allows us to let go.

Raised in the rural South, on the border between Virginia and Tennessee, Wright "began writing poems in the Army in Italy" (as he once put it), in 1959: there he fell hard for the northern Italian landscape, Italian art, and modern Italian poetry, and for that American Italophile and Sinophile, Ezra Pound. "It wasn't until I stumbled onto *The Selected Poems of Ezra Pound* that I discovered a form that seemed suited to my mental and emotional inclinations—the lyric poem . . . that didn't depend on a narrative structure but on an imagistic one, an associational one." Wright's mature poems conjoin literature and landscape, linking what he can see—in the Blue Ridge, by the Pacific, in Venice—loosely to propositions derived from his reading; the poems tend to quote, and then to reject, large claims about the nature and purpose of being, seeking instead a way to live without doctrine or program amid the transient yet transporting pleasures of this world.

Here that search begins, as in a true sermon, with a widely revered text. Wright has rearranged propositions from St. Augustine's *Of True Religion*, which Wright's notes confirm that he read in J. H. S. Burleigh's translation: "It is sin which deceives souls, when they seek something that is true but abandon or neglect truth. They love the work of the artificer more than the artificer or his art, and are punished by the error of expecting to find the artificer and his art in his works, and when they cannot do so they think that the works are both the art and the artificer. God is not offered to the corporeal senses, and transcends even the mind." The Augustinian God resides not amid the created world ("his work") but outside it, omnipotent, omnibenevolent—if He is good, He must be as good as He can be; he must be better than anything in this world. Against such propositions (each on its own line) Wright sets his own apparent satisfaction with the imperfect world and the plant life in it: folksy monosyllables ("all these oak trees look fine") dissolve into more complicated language fast. "Ghosts" is a verb: the cedar "ghosts a unity" because it stands for all cedars, if not for all Virginia trees. For Augustine's omnipresent, invisible deity, Wright substitutes "hard frost," nowhere seen, everywhere felt; here and for several more lines, the poet keeps "coming back to the visible," trusting what he can see, or feel on his skin.

If the poem ended there, we could call it anti-intellectual. Instead, Wright inquires within himself: how can it possibly be (he asks) that the hungers formerly satisfied by religion, a hunger for explanation, for first and last things, for some sense of overarching order, might be satisfied in Wright himself by the contemplation of newt trails, ice slivers, or whatever animals he designates as "mud striders"? (Mud *sliders* are freshwater turtles, native to Virginia and often kept as pets; perhaps the turtles stride.) Wright's answer is itself theological: "this Virginia cedar," "true to its own order," like the maybe-turtles in their stride, are perfect examples of whatever they are, and to contemplate them is to feel that the world makes sense, that it adds up as an equation adds up, to have the feeling that faith provides.

Yet to trust in "the senses" is to leave an important equation "blank." What happens on the other side? What, if anything, happens after we die? Poems about December, about the New Year, or about winter often pursue such questions. The most famous such poems in English—consider Keats's "In drear-nighted December," Christina Rossetti's Christmas carol ("In the bleak midwinter"), Wallace Stevens's "The Snow Man"—depict a December in which nothing grows. Wright, however, lives in "central Virginia," where the first hard frost may postdate New Year's Day: his winter is like a New England fall, "charcoal and tan, deep green," a figure for our inability to leave the beauties of this world behind.

And why should we? Can we consider everything beautiful? Wright tries: this way of seeing, this way of writing, owes something to Pound but more to Walt Whitman as it tries to see the beauty in everything and to tell us why. "Every existing thing can be praised." Even lice? Even your least favorite candidate? Why? Because it beats "nothingness." Better to have something than no things at all. Wright's balanced long line projects a kind of assurance—who could feel otherwise?—that itself provides evidence for the beliefs Wright seems to want us to have.

Wright tells us not that we already love, say, trash cans full of rain but that we are "capable of so much love" for them; how much more love might we muster for human beings? And now we are back with St. Augustine, who wrote in one of his final sermons that the early Christian martyrs "thought of how much they should love the things eternal; if they were capable of so much love for things that pass away." The Church father continued: "You do not want to die. And you want to pass from this life to another in such a way that you will not rise again, as a dead man, but fully alive and transformed. This is what you desire. This is the deepest human feeling: mysteriously, the soul itself wishes and instinctively desires it." That passage occurs not in *Of True Religion* but in Augustine's *Sermons*; it is quoted in several biographies, including a well-known 1969 life of the saint by Peter Brown.

Augustine's point (here and in the passage from *Of True Religion*) is that our love for this world ought to help us look beyond it and help us attend to the next one, just as the martyrs did. Wright's points, instead, are that we are the sort of beings who can entertain Augustinian ideas without accepting them; that we love the world so much (and therefore want so fiercely not to die) that we have sought metaphysical beliefs, equations, as part of our effort to preserve it; and that he can be content without them now. Wright redeploys Christian theology in the service of something like epicureanism, asking us to see this world as enough, and something like Taoism (invoked with explicit approval in his other poems), asking us to appreciate a nonteleological nature, a Way. (A yard "pollocked" from edge to edge is painted unevenly in orange, as if in Jackson Pollock's expressionist style: another nonteleological Way.)

For a dweller in images, a lover of dewy particulars and sound effects, Wright can turn out to be a surprisingly systematic, or at least essayistic, thinker: almost a maker of sermons, a giver of sound advice. He knows his Bible too: in fact, one way to think of Wright's style is as a heaven-to-earth, Christian-to-post-Christian translation machine, in which the most confident cadences of a certain kind of sermon get transfigured so that they celebrate—with appropriate humility—the transient things and people of this life. In Judges 5:20 "the stars in their courses fought against Sisera," helping the Israelites defeat the pagan general. Here the rain and the seasons and the stars bring an equally inexorable fate, but a fate in which no one wins: we are subject not to a God who exalts one people and trashes the rest but to the seasons, to entropy, to mortality ("the word inside the word" respectfully inverts a Christian image as well, since it comes close to quoting T. S. Eliot's "word within a word, unable to speak the word").

For a reader who "wants more than the emotionally freighted image," Helen Vendler has written, "the poems by Wright that linger most may be those that repeat religious promise in undoctrinal form." The promise that this poem repeats, or transfigures, is not so much a promise of salvation, of rescue from death, but a promise—derived from those earlier salvific promises, in Augustine and in the Gospels—that contemplation of death can teach us how to live. Wright's sonic debt to Pound's *Pisan Cantos* notwithstanding, few American poets have done more with the Hebraicized English of the King James Bible, of its Psalms with their two-part lines. "Raise the eyes of your affection to its affection"—let yourself look at the things you love. That's what you get when you run through Wright's heaven-to-earth translation machine—a passage such as Isaiah 51:6: "Lift up our eyes to the heavens, and look upon the earth beneath: for the heavens shall vanish away like smoke, and the earth shall wax old like a garment . . . but my salvation shall be forever."

No, it won't—at least not in this poem: Christian eschatology has rarely had more positive, more respectful dissent, if indeed it even is dissent, since "Love what you don't understand yet, and bring it to you" could be advice about how to tell faith from proof. Peter Stitt writes that "December Journal" and some of Wright's other "journal" poems "use the same strategy of false statement followed by a correction" in order to show that "abstraction is not truth." But neither, taken on its own, is concreteness: no concrete examples make sense to us without some prior sense, some implicit rule, about how to take them.

As Robert Denham (who wrote two books on Wright's poetry) has put it, "For Wright the visible world is never the material world only," and the inextricability of the tangible from the intangible, of sight from thought, is part of "what Wright opposes [in] Augustine's separation of body from soul." Wright developed his characteristic way of writing in the late 1970s and early 1980s, toward the end of a period when (as the scholar Charles Altieri explained) many American poets worked hard to reject "transcendence," the search for great truths in another world or in a realm of abstract thought, in favor of "immanence," finding their truths in this one. Other poets rejected argument, rhetoric, and syntax; Wright never did. He may be hard to paraphrase, but he is easy to quote: his best poems, like this one, positively ask to be quoted. They also give useful, and even joyful, advice.

ALLEN GROSSMAN

The Piano Player Explains Himself

When the corpse revived at the funeral,
The outraged mourners killed it; and the soul
Of the revenant passed into the body
Of the poet because it had more to say.
He sat down at the piano no one could play
Called Messiah, or The Regulator of the World,
Which had stood for fifty years, to my knowledge,
Beneath a painting of a red-haired woman
In a loose gown with one bared breast, and played
A posthumous work of the composer S——
About the impotence of God (I believe)
Who has no power not to create everything.
It was the Autumn of the year and wet,
When the music started. The musician was
Skillful but the Messiah was out of tune
And bent the time and the tone. For a long hour
The poet played The Regulator of the World
As the spirit prompted, and entered upon
The pathways of His power—while the mourners
Stood with slow blood on their hands
Astonished by the weird processional
And the undertaker figured his bill.
——We have in mind an unplayed instrument
Which stands apart in a memorial air
Where the room darkens toward its inmost wall
And a lady hangs in her autumnal hair
At evening of the November rains; and winds
Sublime out of the North, and North by West,

Are sowing from the death-sack of the seed
The burden of her cloudy hip. Behold,
I send the demon I know to relieve your need,
An imperfect player at the perfect instrument
Who takes in hand The Regulator of the World
To keep the splendor from destroying us.
Lady! The last virtuoso of the composer S——
Darkens your parlor with the music of the Law.
When I was green and blossomed in the Spring
I was mute wood. Now I am dead I sing.

With its debts to antiquity, to Jewish and Christian tradition, and to European painters, poets, philosophers and composers, "The Piano Player" may seem forbiddingly learned, as well as semantically tricky. At the same time the poem acknowledges that poetry cannot work only by ideas—it has to have its music too. Grossman enjoyed a long, admired career not just as a poet but as a teacher and as a theorist of poetry, explaining in philosophical prose (such as his magisterial "Summa Lyrica"), as well as in richly allusive, resonant verse, what high purposes poetry could serve.

This poem follows those explanations; it also tells jokes. The corpse (as a student of Grossman's, Jamey Hecht, put it) represents "the tradition of poetic knowledge to which Grossman has devoted his life's attention, a tradition which is always dying and returning to life and being killed, as in the story of Orpheus," the poet-musician of Greek myth, whose music animated wood and stone, and whose talents almost let him bring his beloved Eurydice back from the dead. Grossman's dense, majestic allegory builds itself up around that story as Grossman understood it, a story about the purpose of poetry in general. In it, the poet makes spirits or souls present for other people, rescuing them from oblivion, conjuring them out of nothing, bringing them back from the dead; but his poetry also acknowledges that he will die.

Such Orphic goals require immense authority, which Grossman's style at its best—its booming Miltonic pentameters, its high diction, its mysterious symbols, not without humor—attains. "Orpheus is . . . the archetype of the *regulator*," Grossman explained, enunciating "language in service of the order of the world." A poem at once creates (depicts, makes present, conjures up) a person through the sound of an imagined voice. A true poem thus resembles the head of Orpheus, which sang after the Maenads tore him apart: "the Orphic machine is the poem: a severed head with face turned away that sings." The messianic piano is that machine.

Chosen by the poet as a fit introduction to his work, placed first in his 1991 new-and-selected poems, "The Piano Player" seems aggressively modern in some ways, especially in its wealth of apparent allusions. The "bared breast" belongs not to Pre-Raphaelite practice but to earlier depictions of classical goddesses; it might have appeared on an eighteenth-century canvas, or in ancient Rome. Yet the poem evokes the Victorian era of the Pre-Raphaelites and their beseeching women with long red hair (such as D. G. Rossetti's "Blessed Damozel"), an era when middle-class families had pianos in their parlors.

And that is why it uses a piano. Invented during the eighteenth century, pianos in general (as the pianist, teacher, and critic Jeremy Siepmann writes) have become "a symbol of the Romantic age, with its glorification of man over nature and science over God"; the piano and its history link the "master craftsman" who superintended its origins to "the commercial and technolog-ical triumph of the Industrial Revolution," which put pianos in hundreds of thousands of homes. Starting with Ludwig van Beethoven in the 1810s and crystallizing later around Franz Liszt, the figure of the piano virtuoso would incarnate quintessential goals of Romantic art: sublimity, emotion, individu-alism, emancipation from doctrine, high seriousness, attention both to the natural (what comes before technique) and to the apparently supernatural (the sublime, the amazing).

Grossman's poet-singer as pianist incarnates, or resurrects, those Romantic goals. For the philosopher François Noudelmann, "piano playing privileges an old-fashioned or even intimist Romanticism." "One has to master the in-strument," Noudelmann writes, "possess the keys . . . but to take pleasure in playing, one has to submit to the piano's mechanics and to learning a piece of music." As with the piano keyboard, so with poetic language: we may not know when the piano player controls the Messiah, the Regulator, the spirit of language itself; when the so-called Messiah controls the man; or when it is best to regard them simply as one. Grossman's brief note on the poem mused that poetry itself was, "in the world in which we live," "like the piano in a middle class living room which no one can play and no one can remove." In his lines "the poet," the observing "I," and the piano itself, given wholly sepa-rate pronouns and points of view before the paragraph break, merge into "we," and then into "I," at first a god figure, a sender of demons, and then a figure for the piano itself.

Such a piano played by such a poet (Grossman called it "the poetic instrument") would serve the contradictory functions of the Orpheus myth; it would regulate (give a law to) the bodies in nature, including the body of the player himself, and it would at the same time "stand apart" from ordinary life. It would let us communicate with the dead, and it would acknowledge their death. It would bring down to earth, "regulate," and harmonize an otherwise intolerable afflatus, and it would serve as a symbol both for poetic technique and for the part of poetry that lies above and below any conscious technique: Jennifer Lewin connects it both to the Aeolian harp of Romantic poetry, "unplayed" by human hands because played by the wind, and to the harp of Psalm 137, which the disconsolate, conquered Jews hang from a tree.

The nameless poet who can play this "Messiah" recapitulates not just the task of Orpheus, but also the feats of Odysseus, bending his bow, and of King Arthur, pulling sword from stone. As for the composite "composer S——," both Robert Schumann and Franz Schubert died young, with prominent works published posthumously, and both were Romantic composers known for piano and chamber works as well as for lieder (art songs). Musician-poet, composer and piano together perform the work of the Messiah, the work that Christians attribute to Jesus Christ: they re-order the world and revive the dead. Though this poem (unlike many of Grossman's poems) has no unmistakably Jewish content, Grossman writes as a Jewish American poet: for Jews, the Messiah has yet to arrive.

If poetry does the work of religion, it also poses a threat to religious orthodoxy. The corpse at the start of the poem, whose resurrection overturned natural laws, was killed again by the mourners, who, like the Pharisees in the Gospels, prefer the laws they already know. The mourners also emulate the Greek maenads, who rip Orpheus apart because he does not love *them*. But the spirit of poetry cannot be killed. It proceeds from poet to poet, performer to performer, inspiration to inspiration, until it makes the poet sit down "at the piano no one could play" and play what is, of course, a "posthumous work." True poetry thus turns a funeral, a "memorial," into a "weird procession," a near resurrection; it alters the very air.

We do not hear the music that the magic piano can play; we can only hear or read about it. Yet Grossman turns back to the piano, retelling the scene from a new perspective marked by present tense, as if we *could* hear. In this retelling, which starts at "We have in mind," the messianic piano waits not at the funeral of a particular person but in a darkness that stands for death, for autumn, and for evening, who roams like a gleaner, like Demeter, like Ruth. The poet at the piano must respond (as "To Autumn" responds) not to the funeral of an individual but to the presence of death in the world: now, however, the intimidating piano has become "the perfect instrument," whose poesis will "keep the splendor from destroying us." Words and music, rightly arranged, will yield what the critic Geoffrey Hartman called an "anti-apocalyptic view of regeneration": poetry will combat the solipsism of unchecked sublimity and enable us to live within the limits of social and natural life.

Form in general, and meter in particular, can signal the acceptance of such limits. Grossman's metrical choices look back to Shakespeare's plays: blank verse punctuated by occasional rhymes ("say"-"play"), with a clinching couplet at the end, and a last line that adds emphasis by consisting entirely of one-syllable words. Literally, that last couplet means that the piano's wood made no sound while it was a tree. In the allegory of poetic making, it means that the poet-piano must die out of his real life, with all its literal distracting circumstance, in order to make or become the voice of the poem, the answerer, who keeps us willing to live in this world.

If it stands with Grossman's other work in the heft of its theories, "The Piano Player" stands out for the quality of its jokes. They begin with the title, as if this ambitious set piece were no more than a sheepish excuse, and they continue through the hesitation forms ("to my knowledge," "I believe") that retard the propulsive blank verse. Then the jokes go away: once the first person refers not to the poet-observer but to a creator-figure who can summon a demon, Grossman has switched from the mock- to the real sublime. Grossman's piano player moves from a third person to a first person plural to a first person singular, speaking at first for nobody, then for us, and then for his instrument. By ending as it does, the poem reminds us that the making of poetry, for Grossman, means both a bringing to life and a version of death. The artist dies into his art: the poet-singer becomes the instrument, and together they say, at first, "now I am dead," and only then "I sing."

ADRIENNE RICH

An Atlas of the Difficult World XIII (Dedications)

I know you are reading this poem
late, before leaving your office
of the one intense yellow lamp-spot and the darkening window
in the lassitude of a building faded to quiet
long after rush-hour. I know you are reading this poem
standing up in a bookstore far from the ocean
on a grey day of early spring, faint flakes driven
across the plains' enormous spaces around you.
I know you are reading this poem
in a room where too much has happened for you to bear
where the bedclothes lie in stagnant coils on the bed
and the open valise speaks of flight
but you cannot leave yet. I know you are reading this poem
as the underground train loses momentum and before running up
    the stairs
toward a new kind of love
your life has never allowed.
I know you are reading this poem by the light
of the television screen where soundless images jerk and slide
while you wait for the newscast from the *intifada*.
I know you are reading this poem in a waiting-room
of eyes met and unmeeting, of identity with strangers.
I know you are reading this poem by fluorescent light
in the boredom and fatigue of the young who are counted out,
count themselves out, at too early an age. I know
you are reading this poem through your failing sight, the thick
lens enlarging these letters beyond all meaning yet you read on
because even the alphabet is precious.

I know you are reading this poem as you pace beside the stove
warming milk, a crying child on your shoulder, a book in your hand
because life is short and you too are thirsty.
I know you are reading this poem which is not in your language
guessing at some words while others keep you reading
and I want to know which words they are.
I know you are reading this poem listening for something, torn
    between bitterness and hope
turning back once again to the task you cannot refuse.
I know you are reading this poem because there is nothing else left
    to read
there where you have landed, stripped as you are.

To read the poems Rich wrote in the 1980s and later is to read a poet writing
in almost constant, sometimes painful consciousness of herself as a public
figure. Admired in the 1950s for her conventional, shapely poetry, and selected
(by W. H. Auden) for the Yale Younger Poets Award before she graduated from
Radcliffe, the poet transformed herself during the 1960s into a far more challenging author, adopting a harsh, self-critical form of free verse, and giving
her energy to one cause after another: opposition to the war in Vietnam, open
admissions at the City University of New York, and—most important for her
own reception—feminism. *Diving into the Wreck* (1973), still her best-known
book, codified Rich's commitment to women's solidarity and to a poetry that
could defy patriarchy.

That volume won the National Book Award, which Rich accepted "on behalf of all women." Rich's "Twenty-One Love Poems," reprinted in *The Dream
of a Common Language* (1978), was the first widely noticed and unmistakably
lesbian set of love poems in American English. By the early 1980s Rich was
surely America's best-known feminist poet, a movement leader, public speaker,
and editor. She had also moved house, from New York to Vermont, where she and
her partner, Michelle Cliff, coedited the lesbian journal *Sinister Wisdom*, and
then, in 1983, to California, where she resumed teaching, at Stanford, San Jose
State University, and the University of California–Santa Cruz.

California's landscape, its sublime coast, its thrillingly isolated mountains,
and the counterpoint of its exploitative agriculture, animate many of her later

poems, "An Atlas of the Difficult World" (the title poem in her 1991 book) among them. "Within two miles of the Pacific rounding / this long bay, sheening the light for miles / inland, floating its fog through redwood rifts and over / strawberry . . . fields," she wrote in section I, "this is where I live now. If you had known me / once, you'd still know me." Yet, she continued, "This is no place you ever knew me." There and throughout her late works she tried to explain to herself and to her readers how she could have been so many things—mother, wife, partner, lesbian activist, Maryland native, Radcliffe graduate, New Yorker, Californian, teacher, speaker, skeptic, leader—and still remain true to herself.

She tried to be true to other people as well. "Someone writing a poem," Rich has said in prose, "believes in a reader, in readers, of that poem." And readers she had. By the time of her death in 2012, her books—according to her publisher, W. W. Norton—had sold almost 800,000 copies in all. Her repeated "I know" in this last segment of "An Atlas" carries a metaphysical confidence like Walt Whitman's (as her lists of people echo Whitman's "A Song for Occupations"), but it also carries the empirically verified confidence of somebody who spent years with blizzards of fan mail.

Rich has arranged her list of imagined readers in approximate order of decreasing privilege, from an overburdened white-collar worker to an almost entirely abandoned figure who may not have long to live. First, the white-collar worker, for whom "this poem" comes as a supplement, a source of energy, "one intense yellow lamp-spot" in an otherwise enervating life. (Her firm trusts her to leave the office last, and to turn out the light.) Then we meet someone geographically far from Rich, "far from the ocean," in the snowy plains. "Standing up" means this reader will not buy the book: perhaps she cannot afford it; perhaps she works in the store, and her boss will not permit her to sit down. Rich also leaves open the possibility of the resisting reader, who opens and skims but will then reject her work: this is the reader envisioned in Rich's slightly earlier poem "Negotiations," to whom "I'll say, But damn, you wrote it so I / couldn't write it off You'll say / I read you always, even when I hated you."

However it might be written, distributed, and read, Rich also wrote, "poetry dwells in a web of other social practices historically weighted with enormous imbalances of social power." Within the web of historical, economic, sexual, material causes and dependencies, the poem forms relatively egalitarian networks of its own. And it connects relatively fortunate, though hurried or stressed-out or lonely, readers to people in acute distress. The person "in a room" with disordered bedclothes may be a woman fleeing domestic violence, or a captive, or a hotel worker whose bad memories—so vaguely presented—encompass a sexual assault. The next reader has come lately to a big city—the subway seems new to her—and seems to be meeting, or seeking, same-sex love. Kinds of persons, not individuals, are the point. The sentences may even ask us to catch ourselves applying stereotypes: the television viewer could be Palestinian but need not be; the reader with "failing sight" could be elderly, or youthful and diabetic. Then there is the reader who incarnates an earlier version of Rich herself, the stressed-out mother with too little help, whose "thirst" for more than domestic responsibility, more than domestic rewards, gave Rich the principal subject of her breakthrough third book, *Snapshots of a Daughter-in-Law* (1963). She gets a stanza break to introduce her, and three whole lines on her own.

John Ashbery's "Paradoxes and Oxymorons" insisted on the privacy and the oddity of the poem's encounter with "you," with a reader (one reader per encounter), before it insisted on anything else. "Dedications" does not deny that idiosyncrasy but asks us to see instead how many kinds of "you," how many kinds of encounter, are possible, as well as how thoroughly Rich, with her public, ethical—or, if you prefer, political—mission, wants to reach them. Dana Gioia's much debated 1991 essay "Can Poetry Matter?" began from the premise that very few people read, or would read, most contemporary poetry. But Rich knew that many people read *her*. They also read, during the 1970s, poetry of the feminist and Black Power movements, by authors whom Rich would continue to champion, such as Judy Grahn and June Jordan. In those years those poets spoke of women, for women. But "you," in this poem, need not always have the same gender, much less the same race or affliction or social station or age.

"In this last line," Rich told the television reporter Bill Moyers, "I thought first of all of someone dying of AIDS. . . . But finally I was thinking of our society, stripped of so much of what was hoped for and promised and given nothing in exchange but material commodities, or the hope of obtaining material commodities. And for me, that is being truly stripped." This figure also recalls migrants, emigrants and immigrants, who have fled Ireland, Germany, Somalia, El Salvador, and so many other countries, with the hope of a new life in America, and who had to start near the bottom once they arrived.

For the poet and scholar Piotr Gwiazda, *An Atlas* "acknowledges the impossibility of speaking to two kinds of readers at once, the specialized poetry community and the general audience that is always on the verge" of coming into being. Yet Rich already had that general audience, in part because she knew how to write to and for the many kinds of needs, the many kinds of demands, maintained by the people who made up that audience—and their sisters, and their cousins, and their troubled neighbors, and their home health care aides. Rich insists, speaking to all these sorts of "you," that she has not forgotten them; that she does not write just for herself; that she knows they have various interior lives and various levels of excitement, fear, confusion, exhaustion, desperation; that she knows they differ; that she knows they are there. As often happens in Walt Whitman, the lengthy lines conclude with something a bit like formal meter, in this case a strongly bifurcated, decasyllabic line, whose sound marks the gap between poetry and other language.

Rich's lines do not only acknowledge her readers; they remind her why she writes poetry, and not only hortatory or polemical prose. In this formulation, poetry is the Other both to the bad instrumental language of commerce, to the materialism of commodities, and to the good but limited instrumental language of radical politics, which brings people together for a previously defined, clear common cause. (Czesław Miłosz and the determinedly democratic Robert Pinsky might both agree, though Miłosz's third-person universals stand very far from Rich's first-person acknowledgment that we do not all come from the same place.)

Poetry speaks to us differently depending on what we need, on where we began, on how we are affected by headline news; yet it remains, as Jahan Ramazani has written, a kind of language in "vexed dialogue with the news," responding to headlines, to matters of public urgency, while gesturing away from their specifics, toward the "recursive and ritualistic norms" of prayer. Poetry is what we want when more specific, more instrumental, more practically useful kinds of language have been "stripped" away. And this haunting negative definition of poetry, of what poetry is good for, seems more satisfying—to Rich and to many others—than any positive claim about the use or the worth of (particular) kinds of poetry, about how it can "matter" in particular societies or in particular ways. Poetry brings us together, tugs on the web that connects us, and speaks to us as individuals, caught in—and yet also weaving—that web; it tells us that we have been "listening for something," even if we cannot agree, with Rich or with one another, on what it is.

LOUISE GLÜCK

Lamium

This is how you live when you have a cold heart.
As I do: in shadows, trailing over cool rock,
under the great maple trees.

The sun hardly touches me.
Sometimes I see it in early spring, rising very far away.
Then leaves grow over it, completely hiding it. I feel it
glinting through the leaves, erratic,
like someone hitting the side of a glass with a metal spoon.

Living things don't all require
light in the same degree. Some of us
make our own light: a silver leaf
like a path no one can use, a shallow
lake of silver in the darkness under the great maples.

But you know this already.
You and the others who think
you live for truth and, by extension, love
all that is cold.

Glück's style evolved by subtraction. In her late teens and twenties, partly due
to anorexia, Glück undertook an unusually demanding psychoanalysis.
"Analysis was what I did with my time and my mind," she has recalled.
"Analysis taught me to think." In her first book, *Firstborn* (1969), she could be
recognized as a confessional poet, presenting traumatic memories in forceful
lines that could recall Robert Lowell, or Sylvia Plath, or her teacher Stanley
Kunitz. Confessional poetry—one branch of "Freudian lyric," as Helen

Vendler calls the midcentury genre—understood human development and expression through the lens of psychoanalysis: the poem expressed painful truths at the core of the id or psyche or soul or personality. And in a way, Glück was still a psychoanalytic poet when she wrote *The Wild Iris*, the book from which "Lamium" comes: her poems still drill down, or cut down, or carve away inessential details in order to present an imagined listener with the disagreeable, counterintuitive, taboo, or dangerous truth of a self.

In other ways Glück's durable poetry—starting with *The House on Marshland* (1975) and continuing to the present day—does not feel psychoanalytic, or "confessional," at all: it pares down its selves, its speakers, to a few essential attributes, such as plots from Greek myths, or single bits of conversation, preserved for their comedy but stripped of detail. "You don't love the world," she accuses herself in *Meadowlands* (1996): "If you loved the world you'd have / images in your poems." Her spare language seeks truths that do not change, generalizations—about herself, about alternative versions of herself, or about all of us—that other people might be afraid to see. The images that she does admit serve that end.

Which brings us to *The Wild Iris*. In some ways very traditional—a book about flowers and gardens, the seasons and God—the book was in others *sui generis*. About half its poems are spoken *by* the flowering plants that the book's human gardener observes. These articulate flora let Glück use her spare, condensing sensibility to present personalities very unlike one another, though each speak either *to* or *for* some part of herself. "Violets," for example, cannot see themselves as individuals. "We do not grieve / as you grieve, dear / suffering master," the violets say; for them, "the soul's nature . . . is never to die." Actual violets spread through tendrils and runners, so they grow in bunches and patches, never one at a time. Yet the violets also know what the psychoanalyst knows: "in our world / something is always hidden."

In this company "Lamium"—the plant of that name speaks the poem— stands out as an ars poetica, a justification for the poet's style, which this shade-tolerant ground cover represents. The plant, like the style, looks unforthcoming, never very far off the ground, averse to the hypotheses and the elaborations—grammatical, metaphorical, philosophical—that other poets would erect in air. This ground cover speaks artfully, carefully, strangely, surprisingly—the poem, read aloud, requires that we read it slowly—but it also takes care to stay plain.

No wonder it sounds so sad. Glück's memorably conclusive sentences can have the quality both of hard-won psychoanalytic discoveries and of what academic psychologists call "depressive realism," in which people with certain depressive disorders make more accurate—because less illusioned, less self-serving—predictions. Glück's diction does not vary much from poem to poem—it is rarely adventurous, often "flat"—but her choice of line and sentence shapes varies. Here several lines are, or could be, single sentences, and each of them describes both the plant, and the poem. And those descriptions look like a case for depressive realism: the cold-hearted plant sees what warm-hearted humans would not. Indeed, the plant prefers to live with its own characteristic substance, its leaves, blocking most of its sun.

Human beings who spoke this way might come off as sullen, or sad; they might, instead, be defending shyness or introversion, a style of life or a choice of profession out of the public eye, like the piano tuners, fact-checkers, and translators chronicled in David Zweig's study *The Invisibles*, who "don't seek attention the way most of us do." Glück's leaves work collectively, and they are introverts: they see what people and flora who demand exposure, or who try to look on the sunny side, will not. The single prominent simile—"like someone hitting the side of a glass with a metal spoon"—stands out, and it says that a simile *ought* to stand out. Such glimpses of other worlds, such ways of reaching beyond bare summarized experience, ought to be cherished, because they are rare, and—like a spoon struck on glass—they command our attention even if they do not suggest melodies.

"Lamium" stands not only for Glück's attitude, but also for her method of composition. The genus *Lamium* includes a few dozen species of flowering ground cover, though Glück does not notice the flowers; all prefer shade, and some spread aggressively, crowding out adjacent plants. Its common name, "deadnettle," comes from the way that its leaves can resemble the leaves of the stinging nettle, though lamium does not sting. The overlapping leaves, which often show silvery patterns, do block one another, so most of the plant does not get much light; the plant is not only shade-tolerant but cold-tolerant, surviving frosts. Toothed, arrowhead-shaped, the leaves point in every direction (hence leading nowhere, "like a path no one can use").

This process of uneven growth, in which leaf hides leaf (and leaves often represent pages, as in *Leaves of Grass*) suggests the unpredictable process of growth and erasure involved in revising a poem. The paths of poetry too might lead us nowhere, might not solve our problems or make us happier or more fulfilled, even as that same poetry, Glück's sort of poetry, lights up a sort of darkness in the soul. And lyric poetry of this sort in particular—small-scale, darkness-loving, spare and without elaborate allusion, and yet late in a tradition that goes back quite far—might look, to the poet, like a small flowering plant below or beside the great tradition, the "great maples," of older American and European poems: a "lake of silver," not a sea of gold.

"Lamium" places the poet's voice not in a tree but in a plant that can never get off the ground; it also, however, represents Glück's liking for conclusions, for things seen whole. Early in *The Wild Iris* Glück's son, Noah, defines her alleged depression as an inability *not* to see the big picture:

> Noah says this is
> an error of depressives, identifying
> with a tree, whereas the happy heart
> wanders the garden like a falling leaf, a figure for
> the part, not the whole.

We may say that we do not want a sugary poetry, or a poetry of fantasy, or a poetry of partiality; we may say we prefer the kind of poetry that Glück writes, "a poetry that does not soothe or placate or encourage," as the critic Joanne Feit Diehl put it. We may believe that, as readers, we "live for truth." But Glück's aggressive ground cover has come to tell us that we get ourselves wrong. "Humankind," wrote T. S. Eliot, "cannot bear very much reality," and Eliot is, for Glück, the great example of "hunger for meaning and disposition to awe," a poet whose "compulsion of speech is to find and say the truth." Glück's stark lines work by a similar compulsion—they ask to be judged not on their fancies, not on what they do for us or with us, but on how far they have gone toward some ground of human motivation, some unanswerable—and previously unstated, because unpleasant or harrowing—truth.

What might such hard truths be? Glück's earlier poetry is full of them: "I hate sex"; we "can make / no forms but twisted forms"; childhood "came to mean being always alone." Maybe we want to believe that we have found the darkest, coldest, lowest, or most deeply hidden truth, so that we can celebrate the discovery and move on. But that belief would itself perpetuate comforting illusions. Lamium, "trailing over cool rock," keeps on going, spreading out, rather than drilling down or climbing out: it has depths, and hidden darkness, but (as "Violets") no one root or core. There is always more cold, more darkness, hence more to investigate, if we can bear to contemplate what we find.

JAMES MERRILL

Self-Portrait in Tyvek™ Windbreaker

The windbreaker is white with a world map.
DuPont contributed the seeming-frail,
Unrippable stuff first used for Priority Mail.
Weightless as shores reflected in deep water,
The countries are violet, orange, yellow, green;
Names of the principal towns and rivers, black.
A zipper's hiss, and the Atlantic Ocean closes
Over my blood-red T-shirt from the Gap.

I found it in one of those vaguely imbecile
Emporia catering to the collective unconscious
Of our time and place. This one featured crystals,
Cassettes of whalesong and rain-forest whistles,
Barometers, herbal cosmetics, pillows like puffins,
Recycled notebooks, mechanized lucite coffins
For sapphire waves that crest, break, and recede,
As they presumably do in nature still.

Sweat-panted and Reeboked, I wear it to the gym.
My terry-cloth headband is green as laurel.
A yellow plastic Walkman at my hip
Sends shiny yellow tendrils to either ear.
All us street people got our types on tape,
Turn ourselves on with a sly fingertip.
Today I felt like Songs of Yesteryear
Sung by Roberto Murolo. Heard of him?

Well, back before animal species began to become
Extinct, a dictator named Mussolini banned

The street singers of Naples. One smart kid
Learned their repertoire by heart, and hid.
Emerging after the war with his guitar,
He alone bearing the old songs of the land
Into the nuclear age sang with a charm,
A perfect naturalness that thawed the numb

Survivors and reinspired the Underground.
From love to grief to gaiety his art
Modulates effortlessly, like a young man's heart,
Tonic to dominant—the frets so few
And change so strummed into the life of things
That Nature's lamps burn brighter when he sings
Nanetta's fickleness, or chocolate,
Snow on a flower, the moon, the seasons' round.

I picked his tape in lieu of something grosser
Or loftier, say the Dead or Arvo Pärt,
On the hazy premise that what fills the mind
Shows on the face. My face, as a small part
Of nature, hopes this musical sunscreen
Will keep the wilderness within it green,
Yet looks uneasy, drawn. I detect behind
My neighbor's grin the oncoming bulldozer

And cannot stop it. Ecosaints—their karma
To be Earth's latest, maybe terminal, fruits—
Are slow to ripen. Even this dumb jacket
Probably still believes in Human Rights,
Thinks in terms of "nations," urban centers,
Cares less (can Tyvek breathe?) for oxygen
Than for the innocents evicted when
Ford bites the dust and Big Mac buys the farm.

Hah. As if greed and savagery weren't the tongues
We've spoken since the beginning. My point is, those
Prior people, fresh from scarifying
Their young and feasting in triumph on their foes,
Honored the gods of Air and Land and Sea.
We, though . . . Cut to dead forests, filthy beaches,
The can of hairspray, oil-benighted creatures,
A star-scarred x-ray of the North Wind's lungs.

Still, not to paint a picture wholly black,
Some social highlights: Dead white males in malls.
Prayer breakfasts. Pay-phone sex. "Ring up as meat."
Oprah. The GNP. The contour sheet.
The painless death of History. The stick
Figures on Capitol Hill. Their rhetoric,
Gladly—no, rapturously (on Prozac) suffered!
Gay studies. Right to Lifers. The laugh track.

And clothes. Americans, blithe as the last straw,
Shrug off accountability by dressing
Younger than their kids—jeans, ski-pants, sneakers,
A baseball cap, a happy-face T-shirt . . .
Like first-graders we "love" our mother Earth,
Know she's been sick, and mean to care for her
When we grow up. Seeing my windbreaker,
People hail me with nostalgic awe.

"Great jacket!" strangers on streetcorners impart.
The Albanian doorman pats it: "Where you buy?"
Over his ear-splitting drill a hunky guy
Yells, "Hey, you'll always know where you are, right?"
"Ever the fashionable cosmopolite,"
Beams Ray. And "Voilà mon pays"—the carrot-haired

Girl in the bakery, touching with her finger
The little orange France above my heart.

Everyman, c'est moi, the whole world's pal!
The pity is how soon such feelings sour.
As I leave the gym a smiling-as-if-I-should-know-her
Teenager—oh but I *mean* she's wearing "our"
Windbreaker, and assumes . . . Yet I return her wave
Like an accomplice. For while all humans aren't
Countable as equals, we must behave
As if they were, or the spirit dies (Pascal).

"We"? A few hundred decades of relative
Lucidity glinted-through by minnow schools
Between us and the red genetic muck—
Everyman's underpainting. We look up, shy
Creatures, from our trembling pool of sky.
Caught wet-lipped in light's brushwork, fleet but sure,
Flash on shudder, folk of the first fuck,
Likeness breathes likeness, fights for breath—I *live*—

Where the crush thickens. And by season's end,
The swells of fashion cresting to collapse
In breaker upon breaker on the beach,
Who wants to be caught dead in this cliché
Of mere "involvement"? Time to put under wraps
Its corporate synthetic global pitch;
Not throwing out motley once reveled in,
Just learning to live down the wrinkled friend.

Face it, reproduction of any kind leaves us colder
Though airtight-warmer (greenhouse effect) each year.
Remember the figleaf's lesson. Styles betray

Some guilty knowledge. What to dress ours in—
A seer's blind gaze, an infant's tender skin?
All that's been seen through. The eloquence to come
Will be precisely what we cannot say
Until it parts the lips. But as one grows older

—I should confess before that last coat dries—
The wry recall of thunder does for rage.
Erotic torrents flash on screens instead
Of drenching us. Exclusively in dream,
These nights, does a grandsire rear his saurian
    head,
And childhood's inexhaustible brain-forest teem
With jewel-bright lives. No way now to restage
Their sacred pageant under our new skies'

Irradiated lucite. What then to wear
When—hush, it's no dream! It's my windbreaker
In black, with starry longitudes, Archer, Goat,
Clothing an earphoned archangel of Space,
Who hasn't read Pascal, and doesn't wave . . .
What far-out twitterings he learns by rote,
What looks they'd wake upon a human face,
Don't ask, Roberto. Sing our final air:

Love, grief, etc. ★★★★ for good reason.
Now only ★★★★★★ STOP signs.
Meanwhile ★★★★★ if you or I've ex-
ceeded our [?] ★★★ ~~more than time~~ was needed
To fit a text airless and ★★ as Tyvek
With breathing spaces and between the lines
Days brilliantly recurring, as once *we* did,
To keep the blue wave dancing in its prison.

The longest poem in this book (by number of lines) comes next to last in *A Scattering of Salts*, the last book by James Merrill, who died in early 1995 while the book was in press. (The poem appeared, three years earlier, in the *New Yorker*.) By turns lighthearted and deathly serious, the poem speaks self-consciously from near the end of his life, and (so Merrill speculates) from near the end of the history of the kinds of high culture that Merrill's work could represent. A poem about democracy and equality, laying out mixed feelings about both, it also considers aging and death: Merrill sees how the ebullient, uncomprehending young become the bemused, uncomprehending old. It is a poem—appalled, amused, proud, double-minded—about the snobbery of which Merrill and his friends could be accused. And it is, at last, an ecological poem, one that addresses the planetwide emergencies, the continuing insults to "nature," that emerged in Merrill's lifetime: first "the nuclear age," and then global climate change, with its threat of rising waves. Can poetry alleviate those emergencies, or even face them in good cheer?

Merrill also responds to the poet Elizabeth Bishop, whom he knew and admired (a poem from the same book, "Overdue Pilgrimage to Nova Scotia," pays her explicit tribute). Bishop's first characteristic poem, "The Map" (1935), describes a colorful map of the world: "Land lies in water; it is shadowed green . . . The names of cities cross the neighboring mountains." Her map makes a delicate, harmlessly artful counterpart to the real, and bloody, events on the land it represents. It also lacks room for human bodies: it is a flat, static, two-dimensional thing.

Merrill's map isn't like that. It's bold, even garish, and stronger than it looks ("unrippable," though "seeming frail"), able to fit around a moving body (for example, the poet's, as he walks or runs to the gym). "The windbreaker (which Merrill owned and wore: he didn't invent it) suggested to him a symbol of daily life in the post–Cold War global economy, which unites the people of the world as consumers," writes Merrill's biographer Langdon Hammer. Is it a union we ought to want to join? Is it in good taste? Like Bishop (see her "Filling Station"), Merrill at the start of the poem can sound like a snob as well as an aesthete: something not only repels but even offends him in the "vaguely imbecile" shop where he nonetheless bought his jacket. The shop's bad taste suggests that we—the civilization that buys and sells this stuff—cannot tell gems from paste, or (worse yet) nature from art. We save cassette tapes instead of saving real whales, and make "lucite coffins" while we destroy the real sea.

Our wish to make copies, to manufacture duplicates, had been for Merrill, in his earlier work, a reason to celebrate, allied to camp rather than kitsch.

"The essence of camp is its love of the unnatural: of artifice and exaggeration," wrote Susan Sontag in a 1964 essay that popularized the term. Moreover, "camp . . . is one way of seeing the world as an aesthetic phenomenon." (It has also had a special appeal for gay men.) But camp knows what it is; it knows that there is something else, something more earnest, less self-conscious, more fallible, perhaps more consequential, elsewhere in the world. The shoppers who buy up kitsch objects such as "rain-forest whistles," on the other hand, may think (like diners at a Rainforest Cafe) that they are saving the planet.

If shopping at eco-emporia is a poor way to fight back against oblivion, what would be a good way? Perhaps Roberto Murolo's. Reckless human beings have endangered things worth preserving for a long time, though not "back before animal species began to become / Extinct" (the phrase is a joke: trilobites bit the dust long before *Homo sapiens* emerged). Merrill's jocular, almost condescending tone implies that he is speaking to a young and badly educated listener, perhaps a teen, like the one he will meet later on: we are presumed unfamiliar not only with Roberto Murolo but with Benito Mussolini as well. But Murolo deserves more attention than Mussolini, since he did something good: "He alone" allowed Neapolitan song to survive.

Murolo's songs are neither camp, nor kitsch, nor expensive, prestigious high culture like opera; instead, they have "a perfect naturalness"—they fit into "the life of things." (Merrill is citing William Wordsworth's "Lines Composed a Few Miles above Tintern Abbey": "With an eye made quiet by the power / Of harmony, and the deep power of joy, / We see into the life of things.") Such songs, which inspired the anti-fascist resistance, might inspire the poet to resist kitsch and bad taste . . . or to resist his impulse to condemn them. Clad in his "world map," earbuds in, Merrill is trying to figure out how a belated art such as his own, an art less natural-seeming than Murolo's, can help him live in a world both tacky and doomed.

As he does in parts of his epic science fiction poem *The Changing Light at Sandover* (1976–1982), Merrill implies here that individual human beings are not the right units of value—rather, we ought to try to preserve the "Air and Land and Sea," the biological systems that let human beings in general flourish on what is not, or not only, *our* world. "Human Rights" and "innocents evicted" are not as important, to Merrill, as "dead forests, filthy beaches," the filth in "the North Wind's lungs." His windbreaker, showing the Earth at human scale, divided into manmade countries, gets the planet wrong.

At this point a poet who began gaily, even lightheartedly, descends into an intensity of disgust. Why would "gay studies," as an academic discipline, offend this sixtysomething out gay man? Perhaps it seems drearily earnest, indifferent to aesthetic merit, or else it seems reductive and presentist, an unworthy rival to "literary studies" or musicology. As Hammer notes, the early 1990s saw shrill arguments over college and high school curricula: defenders of the so-called canon (Dante, Shakespeare, Milton and so on) viewed their opponents as both irresponsible and immature. Bright colors (like those on the windbreaker), consumerism, and affable democracy put Merrill off (even though he wears the windbreaker) because they are characteristics of immaturity: they might be American too. "America's youthful imagination, its liberation of youthful energies, colors, forms, products and narratives," writes the philosopher and social critic Robert Pogue Harrison, "appeal directly to what is most neotenic and childlike in our nature." Harrison's book *Juvenescence* complains that these days everyone wants to be young. Merrill seems to agree: adults who are "dressing / Younger than their kids" are trying to live outside the history for which they ought to hold themselves (as Murolo did) responsible. That childish lack of interest in history is also a lack of interest in consequences, an inability to connect the dots: no wonder we cannot get together and figure out how to stop the "greenhouse effect" (the standard name for global climate change in 1992) from sending "blue waves" over our coasts.

Merrill's form itself speaks to history: each block of eight pentameters begins and ends with the same rhyme (call it *a*) and contains, usually, two rhymes in between (the second stanza, for example, rhymes *axbbccxa*). "Forms," Merrill said in an interview, "tide one over"; "they *do* change, but they change as slowly as the forms in Darwin." W. B. Yeats's later poetry made frequent use of *ottava rima*, the Italian-derived stanza rhyming *abababcc*, and Merrill's stanza casts him as a belated Yeatsian; Yeats, too, complained that history had let him down (see, especially, Yeats's "Coole Park and Ballylee, 1931," which concludes with a "darkening flood"). Beginning as they conclude, with varying contents, the stanzas also mimic other containers, such as rectangular tape cassettes and the "mechanical lucite coffins" that Merrill at first disdains. All these rectangles, by the end of the poem, come to stand for a civilization. Can it be saved?

The impulse to save everything, to gather in farflung materials, struggles throughout Merrill's mature poetry against the impulse to make a poem that is seamlessly, faultlessly beautiful: as Merrill passes "strangers on streetcorners," we hear that struggle take place, and it sounds as if Merrill wanted to let the democratic (and international) impulse win: "the carrot-haired / Girl in the bakery" touches his heart. Poet and bakery girl share a "wave," a pun that oscillates through the whole poem, as Merrill oscillates between the desire to include himself in contemporary culture and the impulse to run from it.

That oscillation describes his feelings about civilization and his internal debate about the role of taste, a debate whose ethics he describes by quoting Pascal, and whose intellectual basis can also be found in a book published after Merrill's death by the pop music critic Carl Wilson. Wilson wrote a whole book on the singer Céline Dion in order to figure out why so many people like Dion when he himself loathed her. (The book was called, after her album, *Let's Talk about Love*; a second edition added the subtitle *Why Other People Have Such Bad Taste*.) "Our guts tell us certain kinds of music are for certain kinds of people," Wilson wrote. Should we trust our guts? Are Wilson's dislike of Dion, Merrill's dislike of the Rainforest Cafe, and Merrill's liking for the now obscure Murolo nothing but badges of superiority or markers of class position?

Merrill's tastes, whatever else they do for him, set him apart from the intimidating, unintellectual, and largely heterosexual ("folk of the first fuck") crowd. They also speak to his extraordinary wealth. Merrill's father cofounded the brokerage Merrill Lynch; the poet never had to work for a living and could travel almost wherever he liked. Merrill's other late poems reflect on his upper-class upbringing, sometimes in poor-little-rich-kid mode, and on the sometimes invisible line between snobbery and educated taste. Even so, he fears being caught up in the "swells of fashion," "Where the crush thickens," punning again on seas and waves. (Wilson wrote, sarcastically, "It's always other people following crowds, whereas my own taste reflects my specialness.") Merrill thus includes himself in his condemnation of fashion, of always-evolving "styles," all of which (kitschy, authentic, sophisticated) can conceal unchanging truths.

One of those truths is that we are going to die. Harrison's culture of perpetual youth is also a culture that denies that truth. Honest art instead frames it (as the Lucite boxes frame waves), but it isn't enough: art gives us inadequate compensation for the loss incurred by age. If we get old enough, we no longer experience "erotic torrents" firsthand; that is one reason Merrill does not imagine he has much in common with the teenager in "his" clothes, or with a culture of juvenescence. The poet feels as far from his own childhood as humanity from dinosaurs; and, since he had no children, he could not restart their process of descent.

Merrill learned in 1986 that he had HIV, for which in the early 1990s there were no effective treatments; "Self-Portrait" has also been read as his plan for his funeral, a self-elegy complete with choice of coffin. As Helen Vendler explains, by the penultimate stanzas Merrill has decided that the original windbreaker, "white with a world map," cannot be his shroud: the "black celestial twin of his jacket," however, strikes him as "a garment for death not only appropriate but beautiful." The heaven of the constellations ("Archer, Goat") invokes artistic standards that will not compromise with democracy. Up there an "earphoned archangel" works alone and "doesn't wave": he is not ours and has no obligations to us. Instead, he represents art as a perfect, and perfectly other, world. In death, we—embodied by our art—might go there.

Or we could listen to one another on earth, with all the imperfections and compromises that such listening entails. Wilson came to believe that truly listening to other people's music, and to their reasons for liking it, was an important, unselfish ethical act: "grappling with people and things not like me," leaving space for them in our heads, is an act of democracy, and "through democracy, which demands we meet strangers as equals, we perhaps become less strangers to ourselves." We may even be moved to "collaborate with strangers."

Merrill's last stanza is such a collaboration: it puns on the constellations, since it's filled with stars, but it relies on us to fill in the spaces with words that preserve the meter. We might even cross out, or fill in, the suggestion in Merrill's struck-through phrase that our undertaking needs "more than time." Merrill's earlier poem "Losing the Marbles" had used a similar typographical device to consider lost memories: here the device admits that "you or I" with our "Love, grief" do not want to spend our listening lives alone. We do not want our texts "airless," nor do we want our works of art so solid or remote that they do not move; we would like them, instead, to leave room for "waves."

"People who enjoy kitsch in a naive way may lack good taste," writes the critic Josh Glenn, "but at least they haven't lost the capacity to feel." Nor has Merrill, though he feels wryly, in a regretful, camp-inflected way. We will need "more than time," more than poetry, more than "STOP signs," to do something (if we can do something) about the "greenhouse effect," the "guilty knowledge" of mass extinction and climate change, and some of us may come to hold all or most of humanity in contempt. But such contempt would be a mistake: we cannot dismiss people simply because they like "gay studies," or Céline Dion, or the Rainforest Cafe. It would be better to try to treat them better: to give other people, strangers, "breathing spaces," to make room in our imaginations for their past or future contributions, even if they are not likely to wear our clothes.

LINDA GREGERSON

Salt

Because she had been told, time and
        again,
           not to swing on the neighbors' high hammock,

and because she had time and again gone
        back, lured
           by the older boys and their dangerous

propulsions, because a child in shock (we
        didn't know
           this yet) can seem sullen or intran-

sigent, and because my father hated his life,
        my sister
           with her collarbone broken was spanked

and sent to bed for the night, to shiver
        through the August
           heat and cry her way through sleep.

And where, while she cried, was the life he
        loved?
           Gone before she was born, of course,

gone with the river-ice stored in sawdust,
        gone with the horses,
           gone with the dogs, gone with Arvid Anacker

up in the barn. 1918. My father was six.
　　　　His father thought Why
　　leave a boy to the women. Ole (like "holy"

without the h, a good Norwegian
　　　　name)
　　Ole had papers to sign, you see,

having served as county JP for years—
　　　　you
　　would have chosen him too, he was salt

of the earth—and Arvid's people needed to cut
　　　　the body down.
　　So Ole took the boy along, my father

that is, and what he hadn't allowed for was
　　　　how badly
　　Arvid had botched it,

even this last job, the man had no luck.
　　　　His neck
　　not having broken, you see, he'd thrashed

for a while, and the northeast wall of the barn—
　　　　the near wall—
　　was everywhere harrows and scythes.

It wasn't—I hope you can understand—
　　　　the
　　blood or the blackening face,

as fearful as those were to a boy, that, forty
                    years later,
            had drowned our days in whiskey and dis-

gust, it was just that the world had no
                    savor left
            once life with the old man was

gone. It's common as dirt, the story
                    of expulsion:
            once in the father's fair

lost field, even the cycles of darkness cohered.
                    Arvid swinging
            in the granular light, Ole as solid

as heartwood, and tall . . . how
                    could a girl
            on her salt-soaked pillow

compete? The banished one in the story
                    measures
            all that might heal him by all

that's been lost. My sister in the hammock
                    by Arvid
            in the barn. I remember

that hammock, a gray and dirty canvas
                    thing,
            I never could make much of it.

But Karen would swing toward the fragrant
                    branches, fleshed
          with laughter, giddy with the earth's

sweet pull. Some children are like that,
                    I have one
          myself, no wonder we never leave them alone,

we who have no talent for pleasure
                    nor use
          for the body but after the fact.

Gregerson's compact and frightening poem gives a model to poets who want
to use verse to tell stories: three generations, six characters (counting her child),
the parallel symbols of swinging hammock and dangling corpse, and the
central concern of much realist prose fiction—how did this person get to be this
way?—thread through questions and answers, explanations (the poem begins
"Because") and anticipations ("you see," "you see," "it wasn't") that keep the
narrative clear while turning inside out the order of events. It's also a way to
think about bodily trauma, and about why children seem to enjoy having
bodies, playing and running and swinging and so on, as adults often do not.
In addressing how trauma gets passed on, how adults ignore or misunderstand
children, Gregerson can pursue the responsibilities that she takes on as an
adult, as a parent, as a mother determined to face scary facts, and to prevent
whatever happened to Karen, and Ole, and indeed to Arvid, from happening
to her never-specified "child."

    Scholars of narrative distinguish between *fabula* (what happens to the char-
acters) and *sujet* (how and in what order a narrative shows these events). Here
the *fabula*, the order of events as they happened, runs like this: Arvid hangs
himself, and "botch[es] it"; Ole takes Gregerson's father to cut down the body
and sign the papers; Gregerson's future father (at the time, a child) sees Arvid's body; Gregerson's father (now adult) drinks to excess; Karen, a child,
swings in the hammock and likes it; father warns Karen, who swings again
anyway; Karen breaks her collarbone; father "spank[s] / her and [sends] her to
bed." Long after that, the poet becomes a mother.

The *sujet*, however, runs like this: father warns Karen; Karen breaks collar-bone; father sends Karen to bed, where Karen cries; Ole goes to the barn; Arvid hangs; father drinks; Karen swings. The contrast suggests not a timeline so much as a circle: the last event predicts the first. And events whose causes are circular cannot be stopped: they are the consequence of eternal laws, like the law that Gregerson seems to enunciate in her tearful final lines: adults never leave children alone; adults must protect children (and often fail); adults resent children, who have not been hurt as we have, and who love their bodies as we do not love ours; adults care about bodies only if bodies are dead.

It is a terrifying view of human maturation, and a plausible—if partial—one even for those of us who have not undergone traumas like Karen's, or like Karen's father's. Adults who are not clinically depressed do experience pleasure, but few adults know the untroubled pleasure, the "glad animal movements" (as William Wordsworth put it) of a child on a swing. And this reflection—this reason to cry, this bit of salt—is what cues the whole poem. Is it true—does the poet seem to think that it's true—that "we" adults, we who read this poem, "have no talent for pleasure" compared to children, that we have "no . . . use / for the body" until it becomes a corpse? It is true, at least, that Gregerson feels this way; so we might feel, had we been raised by an adult who wants to punish the world and the children in it for whatever he himself lost.

This poem about "cycles of darkness" thus becomes a poem about failures of parenthood. Gregerson's father became "the banished one" when he lost not only trust in the literal integrity of the human body (having seen a dead body in pieces) but trust that his father, Ole, would do right by him. Ole wanted to inure his boy against the hazards of this world. Ole's son, Karen's father, seems to want to punish his daughter for having what the father no longer has: fun, and fun with her body, and fun taking risks, and the ability to literally rise into the air on a hammock whose dangerous arc repeats the swinging of the dangling, dying Arvid.

Karen in her hammock and Arvid "up in the barn" in turn repeat the back-and-forth swinging of Robert Frost's famous poem "Birches." "Earth's the right place for love," that poem says; "I don't know where it's likely to go better" (he did not say what he thought of its chances here). As if to counter the dregs of Frost's supposed optimism, Gregerson has written a poem of disillusion, of generational succession, of a Fall and subsequent, repeatedly inherited, original sin.

But she has also written a tender, resigned poem of motherhood, or parenthood. How can we sympathize sufficiently with children? How can we make sure that we never behave as Ole or as Karen's father behaved? No matter how much we learn about children's behavior, there is always something they cannot tell us, something "we didn't know . . . yet." Adulthood itself is a kind of asceticism, like being "holy," but with something gone; childhood is, by definition, sooner or later lost, "gone with the horses, / gone with the dogs," something that enters the past and becomes an object of nostalgia, like the commercial ice trade, something that cannot keep, like river ice. Even if we try to preserve it, it goes.

That dilemma has prompted beautiful laments (among them William Wordsworth's "Ode on Intimations of Immortality from Recollections of Early Childhood") by poets who look back at their own early years. It also creates a problem for parents. If you try too hard to sympathize with your child, you will not be able to prepare her for the world, you will not let her fail, you will prevent her from learning what it means to take risks. But if you do not try hard enough, you may end up putting a child to bed who will "cry her way through sleep," because you did not listen. How to square this circle? How not to envy, nor overmother, nor underparent, nor spoil your child?

Gregerson was hardly the first poet to write about parenthood (check out the terrific, still underrated nineteenth-century poet Sarah Morgan Bryan Piatt), but she wrote in a moment when poems by mothers, about motherhood, became suddenly much more common: Bernadette Mayer's book-length poem *Midwinter Day* (1982) probably marks the beginning. Longer, sometimes more chaotic poems about mothers and children came slightly later, from Laura Kasischke, Rachel Zucker, and others (you can find more of these poems in the big 2007 anthology *Not for Mothers Only*).

Many of these poets write about motherhood as a matter of shared or linked bodies. For Gregerson, though, motherhood is responsibility, a drive to keep her child from what befell Karen (and Ole and Arvid), hence a temptation never to leave her child alone. (In real life, the poet has two children, both girls.) Where other poets write from their own childhoods, Gregerson sounds decidedly adult: she complained in 2001 that during the 1980s, when she herself was learning to write, America asked women poets to "write as ingenues . . . willing to simulate youth even as you age, willing to cultivate a freshness impervious to experience." "Salt" in its point of view, as in its syntactic and narrative complexities, pushes back hard against that restrictive program.

It also uses Gregerson's characteristic form, what the poet and critic Dan Chiasson calls "a three-line helix-like stanza with a corseted middle line." It has clear precursors in poets of the 1980s (such as Stephen Dunn and the young Jorie Graham), but it has become hers, and it has proven especially useful for the control of pace, slowing down, speeding up, and focusing on single— sometimes incongruously small—words. The fact that the middle line could be nothing but "the" heightens the force when the emphasis falls, for example, on the horrible half-rhyme "luck" and "neck."

Chiasson also writes that Gregerson's real subject is "coincidence," "the adjacency of fortune and misfortune," and certainly there is misfortune here. Like many of Gregerson's poems, it reflects on bad luck from a position of better luck: the poet herself has not been hurt in this way. But "Salt" is also a poem about inevitability, about the way that trauma and family history, once set on a certain path, repeat themselves like marbles in a marble run, or rivulets flowing downhill. Gregerson's father passes on a terrible stoicism to Gregerson's sister just as Ole passed on a false stoicism to him: because they try to teach their children to live in a sad and dangerous world without complaining or taking risks, each patriarch makes his children's world sadder than it has to be. The three-line stanzas resemble three generations, with insupportable pressure on the enjambed single word, or the one man, in the middle—the father, or the "the."

Gregerson's poem conforms so closely to realist models of story and character—it is like the kind of film we expect to win Oscars—that it might be a surprise to see how thoroughly it also instantiates weighty, supposedly abstruse theories. French poststructuralists of the 1960s and 1970s, such as Jacques Derrida, Luce Irigaray, and Hélène Cixous, while they hardly agreed on everything, did agree that Western culture had been formed and deformed by the mistaken belief that words and statements and texts had single fixable meanings, meanings handed down like laws (sometimes they *were* laws) from the speech of authoritative father-like figures (such as the Jewish or Christian God). Ole, a justice of the peace, must carry out local law; showing his son the law in operation, he also passed on the "law of the father," as it were, showing him how to be a man. It is an ugly business, involving denial and silence in the face of obvious, disconcerting, grotesque pain; the father performs the same business, acts out the same law, when Karen breaks her collarbone, punishing her for disobedience without noticing what her body might say.

The law of the father is a law about who gets to say what happens to bodies, which is to say it is also a law about sex. Gregerson's terms, and her word choice early on ("lured / by the older boys"), might lead readers to expect a poem about sexual abuse. But there is none depicted, or even mentioned, here. Such cases may seem far from Gregerson's story, but they go back to the roots of psychoanalysis, to Freud's Dora (another case in which adults, Freud included, could not leave a child alone), and they show collectively what Gregerson's poem also shows: how hard it is for adults under patriarchy—a system designed to regulate both sons and daughter—to create and maintain a space where a child can simply and safely be.

What is sweet and leisurely and gives pleasure, in this poem, always belongs to the past, to an unrecoverable innocence. The taste of experience is its opposite: salt. Ole is "salt/of the earth," reliable, trustworthy, unpretentious, representative of his rural community. Karen cried salt tears. Salt preserves meat and produce—without ice, and before refrigeration, it could be the only way to preserve those foods. Salt also figures in some of the tales on which Shakespeare drew for *King Lear*: rather than saying nothing, the truthful daughter, the model for Cordelia, tells the foolish king, "I love you more than salt." The epigraph to *The Woman Who Died in Her Sleep* (1996), the book in which "Salt" appears, includes that phrase.

Yet salt, which preserves food, also prevents agriculture: when the ancient Romans conquered Carthage, legend has it, the victorious army sowed the ground with salt so that nothing would grow. "Salt" is a poem about growing up in farm country, among the ethnic Norwegians of the upper Midwest, but it is also what critics call antipastoral, a poem where farm life and its symbols suggest not innocent pleasure but pain and hard work. The "harrows and scythes," which ought to sow and reap grain, instead mutilated a human body; the hammock, a space of leisure, an object meant for rest, not only is unattractive, "gray and dirty," to the poet ("I never could make much of it") but comes near to breaking Karen's neck.

A scholar of Renaissance poetry and an expert on the poet Edmund Spenser, Gregerson has argued that Spenser's "withheld and belated backstory," with its "digression and deferral," reflects the two genres (classical epic and Renaissance romance) to which Spenser's long poem *The Faerie Queene* belongs. Gregerson's far shorter narrative poem belongs to two genres as well: it is at once a warning about what we can prevent, about how trauma can be (but need not be) passed on, about how patriarchy (which we might resist, or replace) can harm kids. But the same poem amounts to a sophisticated complaint about what nobody can prevent: we grow old, we die, and children learn about death and pain as they grow. What children experience as "the earth's/sweet pull" is in fact the body's tropism toward its own undoing: we repeat experience "time and again" until it ends in disillusion and death. Such ideas are, at the least, half true: they are what mothers, and other parents, do not want to let our children see. Instead, if we are poets of Gregerson's gifts and Gregerson's temperament, we might share them with other adults, in clear, and yet understandably halting, lines.

Emptiness

Emptiness cannot be
compressed. Nor can it
fight abuse. Nor is there
an endless West hosting
elk, antelope, and the
tough cayuse. This is
true also of the mind:
it can get used.

All the aspects of this poem—its wryness, its knowing, almost superior attitude, its proverb-like caution addressed to all of us, its short lines, casual diction, and densely irregular rhyming (including full rhyme at the end)—mark it out as the kind of poem that Kay Ryan has written since the early 1990s, a kind that she largely invented (despite debts to Marianne Moore) and that has now been imitated in any number of first books. It gives us a sense, as do all memorable poems, of what kind of person the poet might be. But the Ryan persona is not the persona of most first-person poems, in which the poet takes action, suffers, or tells us about something (growing old, falling in love, traveling to Barbados) that might have happened to her. Ryan's poems always generalize, almost never use "I" or "me," and almost always take place in the simple present tense reserved, in contemporary English, for general truths: one and two make three, the sky is blue, and "Snails / make mucus" (as Ryan's poem "Diamonds" puts it). We pick up not her life but her ideas and her tastes, her judgments and moods, learning to see the world as she has seen it, applying to our own experience her quips and claims.

Ryan belongs, in other words, to the venerable tradition of the epigram, the moral or witty saying that covers many lives at once. Epigrammatists are in the generality business, whether carving on drinking vessels, as in antiquity, or publishing in the *New Yorker*, as Ryan has often done. (For decades a teacher at a community college in Marin County, California, Ryan became well known quite rapidly in the late 1990s; from 2008 to 2010 she served as U.S. poet laureate.) Epigrams try to bite, or at least to nip, to puncture illusion, but also to convey prudence or wisdom; they are related to proverbs, to jokes and to warnings, and (though they would prefer otherwise) to clichés. (One of the most famous verse epigrams in English is Sir John Harrington's couplet: "Treason doth never prosper; what's the reason? / For if it prosper, none dare call it treason.") Epigrammatists' personalities—often cynical or jaded, almost always witty or experienced—stand in contrast to the often surprised or naive, and avowedly personal, figures in some lyric poems, which start from one person's experience, in one place, once: epigrams instead lead with the general case.

Ryan's eight lines about "the mind" could thus fit minds in general: open minds, so-called "empty" minds, can be abused, or filled up, or used up. The same lines might have a special bite for residents of the American West, taken as "empty" or available by white settlers throughout the nineteenth century, often to the detriment of the people and animals who already lived there. The space of the plains and the mountain West has been "used," or misused, and yet remains visually, physically "open," though unable to defend itself: the big skies are big skies, the long distances lengthy still. Yet Ryan warns that the West and things like the West (for example, your own mental capacity) are not "endless"; her warning applies not only to wild ungulates but to "the / tough cayuse" (not the Native American Cayuse nation but the feral pony). The poet and critic Alan Williamson has suggested that the literature of the American West, from Nebraska to California, "repeats . . . the trajectory of American literature itself," a century late: Ryan's late twentieth century poem, like many late nineteenth century novels and poems from Twain to Piatt, considers the end of a promised transcendence, the limits to supposedly open space.

As much as it draws on real warnings about the real West, the poem also asks us how we might protect the "emptiness" in our own minds. You can't compress "emptiness," but you can fill it with garbage, or with flowers, or with flour: being a void, it cannot fight back. We should take care of it, protect its purposelessness, save some of our language and some of our energy for activities (the writing of poetry, perhaps) that seem to have no "use": if you try to "use" all of your mind, you will use it up, block it up, fill it up, kill it off. (The consonant shift from the *s* in "abuse" and "cayuse" to the *z* not in "use" but in "used" suggests the unwelcome change.)

Ryan has said that she discovered her vocation for poetry on a mountain in Colorado, on a bicycle trip that took her across the Rockies. The West has been, in that sense, her welcome "host," but it cannot do everything for its guest: she had to ride the bike and write the poems herself, and keep herself in shape in order to do so. This analogy between the life of the poet and the force in the poems seems illuminating, even inescapable. At the same time it seems incompatible with, even hostile to, the insistent, cleverly managed, and sneakily authoritative lack of a personal story within her poems. That absence too may be a Western choice. One tradition of Western writing, from Robinson Jeffers to Edward Abbey, emphasizes the vast spaces' distance from civilization, from human values and human scale, and Ryan puts that rocky, majestic tradition in play, though she never shares its haughty or misanthropic tones. Not only the open spaces of the mountain West but its indifference to a single life, to autobiography, resonates with Ryan's poetic goals: she seeks not intimacy but trustworthiness, and she is never autobiographical, never exposed. We might even say that she keeps her poetry open and her mind free.

Ryan's last word has the implication "used up," but also the subordinate sense in which we can say that a person was "being used," that a bad friend or a bad boyfriend is "just using" someone: a mind, in this sense, is a terrible thing to use. Nor should we treat the language that way: we should give it space in which to play. We cannot hear Ryan without becoming aware of her lines' rhythmic ebb and flow, nor without hearing her dense full rhymes, which avoid regular patterns: they make their own rules, respecting neither the ends of lines nor the boundaries of English words. The "ness" in "emptiness" rhymes with the "ess" in "compressed" and in "West"; "tough" rhymes with "of," the "o" in "hosting" is the same "o" as the final vowel in "antelope," while "abuse" rhymes with "cayuse" and with the "you" sound in "used."

These cadences give some finality, some sting, to that briefest, last line; they also—as is normal in a Ryan poem—make the poet sound whimsical, even when she is giving us serious warnings. Ryan's poems try to be fun, even to be funny, as do Albert Goldbarth's and Lucia Perillo's, but her humor is dryer than theirs (it might even be compared to Rae Armantrout's). She invites us in all seriousness to adopt as our own (perhaps warily or ruefully) the general truths or rules that she underwrites. One of those rules advises that we not adhere strictly to mental rules. That sense of freedom from "use," that wildness of spirit, that sense of a space in which we could go anywhere and do not have to serve one goal or live out one life, might define Ryan's kind of generalizing, witty art; it might also fit other poets' and other thinkers definitions of art in general, which—so said the philosopher Immanuel Kant—offered "purposiveness without purpose," the feeling but not the fact of a thing made for use.

The literary critic and Tolstoy scholar Gary Saul Morson, who wrote a book attempting to classify epigrams, proverbs, and other very short literary genres, names one genre "wisdom literature," as in the biblical books of Proverbs and Wisdom, in which "natural and human nature derive from an underlying, fundamentally moral order." Against these "wise sayings" Morson sets "sardonic maxims" such as those of La Rochefoucauld, whose advice is finally cynical (Harrington's couplet would belong here). Opposed to both, in Morson's scheme, are "thoughts," *pensées*, such as those of Blaise Pascal, which prompt us to further, perhaps endless, reflection. All these categories jostle and fuse within Ryan's fruitful, compact poem, which gives us wise advice (don't let your mind fill up; keep some of it productively empty) that provokes unpredictable thought (that's what will happen if you *do* keep your mind open) and reminds us (as a cynic would) how often we Americans, we Westerners, we human beings, defeat ourselves. Her apparently impersonal analogy cannot save all the elk or cayuse in Montana (elk are not endangered anyway), but it might save your ambitions, your career plans, or your weekend: it might even help you live your own life.

ALBERT GOLDBARTH

"A Wooden Eye. An 1884 Silver Dollar.
A Homemade Explosive. A Set of False Teeth.
And a 14-Karat Gold Ashtray"

says my wife, and then she looks up from her book
called something like *Cockamamie Facts* and tests me:
"What's their common denominator?"—right. As if
we still believe some megamatrix substrate (God,
or atoms, or Imagination) holds the infinite unalike dots
of *its* body in a parity, and daily life reflects this. As if
all of our omniform, far-post-lungfish, nuttier-than-Boschian
evolution, crowned by any ten minutes of channel-surfing
the news and (little difference) entertainment possibilities here
at the bung-end of the millennium, hadn't knocked that idea
out of our heads and onto what my father would have charmingly
    called
its bazoonkus. Common denominator—sure. And yet

it's Sunday night—my wife is reading in bed, with the grim
conviction that the work-week upcoming is going to be one
spirit-dead, hellacious spate of days—and so her mood,
her mind, increasingly assume the über-darkness of the night
itself, the way "industrial melanization" means those moths
in the factory districts gradually blackened to match
their new, soot/city background: and I see, now, how
the sleepless nun, and the lycanthrope in a skulking prowl,
and the warehouse watchman telling the face of his friend
the clock his griefs, his griefs . . . are all subsumed and
equalized into the night, as into a magpie's hoard: so
maybe some Ultracommodiousness, some Great Coeval, does

exist (it might be the Night, it might be almost any of our
pancultural abstractions) and welcomes us into its organizational
gestalt. If so . . . if so, it's more than *my* day's scan
of newspaper cullings and letters can ever rise above itself
to see. I learn someone's investigated the annual global methane emission
in cattle gas; that every seven years a god will fill the toad
attached to the tip of a ritual ribboned pole, and glow like a lamp
in its warty belly—then it rains; that only yesterday a girl,
eleven, was found with the name of a rival gang, the *Lady Satans,*
carefully cut in her thigh and rubbed with drainpipe acid. Somewhere
there may be a world where such as these are equally legitimized, but
not here in the thick and swirling mists of Planet Albert. So

imagine my confusion today at a letter from friend Alane,
who's sweet enough to read and like my poems, and praises
my "inclusiveness," and writes "I'm watching a man with nothing
below the waist on television. He's saying he can do anything.
He walks on his hands, he has a lovely wife. Now, *you'd*
know what to do with him. Me, I just shake my head &
take my hat off." I can't guess at how reliably the toad god
zaps the crops with rain—I do know that this faith
in *me* is wholly undeserved. And as for lovely wives . . . the answer
is: *"Those are the weirdest items tuxedo rental-shops reported
finding in pockets of suits returned to them this year,
a fashion magazine says,"* and with that

thematizing of what had looked like data chaos, she
turns out the light, and fluffles the pillows, and
starts her billowy downslip into sleep. And leaves me
wakeful—leaves me wildly trying to think of pockets adequate
to everything: The ashtree staff of the hermit
on his mountaintop for seventeen years. The latest Nintendo
epic, *Callow Drooling Wombat Warriors.* The doctors

cracking open Nicky's sternum like a matzoh—he was five.
The perfect wedge of brie John found one dawn on his car hood.
Gunshots. Twill weft. Owl-hoo. Storm, and calm.
The poem as fit receptacle. Sure. Right.
I'll know what to do with them.

Where other poets try to remove inessentials, to compress and condense, to make poems (as Ezra Pound quipped) into "gists and piths," Goldbarth does the reverse: his gregarious poems (he has published over a thousand) try to fit everything in, juxtaposing the serious concerns that have been the traditional domain of lyric—love, death, anomie, God, depression, joy—with trivia, ephemera, facts from any field of human knowledge, and other items that seem too awkward, too inconsequential, or too absurd to find a place in a more conventionally, or more densely, organized poem. No living poet—if we can judge by the poem—would do better on *Jeopardy!* Goldbarth entitled his 2007 selected poems *The Kitchen Sink*, as in "everything but the kitchen sink"; other titles from *The Kitchen Sink* include "Some Common Terms in Latin That Are Larger than Our Lives," "Astronomy / A Pulitzer Prize Winner's Statement That Bears upon Early American History / Cakeology," "***!!!The Battle of the Century!!!***," and "Things I've Put in This Poem."

"'A Wooden Eye'" is (like many of Goldbarth's poems) both a love poem and an ars poetica: as it pays homage to his wife, Schuyler, it shows us what his style tries to do, why we might object, why he—and we—might cherish it anyway, and what only Goldbarth's chatty, approximate, fast-paced poems can do. The poet and critic Mark Halliday has dubbed this sort of writing "ultra-talk poetry": an "ultra-talk" poet, in Halliday's words, sounds "like a practiced raconteur extemporizing," making easy-to-follow connections among "seven or eleven things . . . swirling in my head," so that he might "go . . . over well with a not-especially-literary crowd." Halliday was praising David Kirby; readers soon applied the term to Goldbarth, Barbara Hamby, Campbell McGrath, and Halliday himself. Among these writers, Goldbarth began publishing first; he also has the least predictable syntax, the clearest engagement with literary history, and the widest, most eclectic range of reference. Indeed, that range is one subject for his poems, as it represents one part of real life—one part of many people's inner lives—that sharper, slimmer, more songlike poems cannot address. It is the part, at once extroverted and geeky, that almost frantically collects information, trivia, ideas; tchotchkes, secondhand-store finds; and people, acquaintances, friends with stories to tell.

"'A Wooden Eye'" does not just demonstrate ultra-talk style; it shows what emotional work that style performs. To read Goldbarth is to watch his mind connect one fact to the next, and the next, as if talking and association were life itself. To stay on one topic, on the other hand, or (worse yet) to shut up, could mean death. More than half of Goldbarth's only novel, *Pieces of Payne* (2003), consists of digressive explanatory notes, introduced with an epigraph from John Muir: "When one tugs at a single thing in Nature, he finds it hitched to the rest of the Universe." The short "main" text of *Pieces of Payne* concerns a friend's cancer.

Restless, associative collection, both a subject and a project for Goldbarth's poems, becomes a pleasure in itself. But it also has a protective function: Goldbarth's accumulation of surfaces, of facts that fascinate for a bit, then slough off, suggests that depth, contemplation, remaining on one big topic for too long could be dangerous to our mental health, since the deepest topics of life—how should we live? what do we owe our loved ones? what should we do about death?—represent questions that do not have good answers. No "megamatrix substrate (God, / or atoms, or Imagination) holds" the solutions we seek. We can live with those questions only by asking more questions, by distracting ourselves and entertaining our friends.

Goldbarth's ultra-talk poems thus recall the proverbial shark, which must keep moving to keep breathing: they also suggest the work of a stand-up comedian, who has to keep entertaining at any cost. Goldbarth's wife, Schuyler, who figures in many of his poems, teases him with the expectation—more than reasonable, for another poet—that he can get organized, that his poetry can provide what Robert Frost called "a momentary stay against confusion." But Goldbarth says that he cannot: he is too riveted, too distracted, by the "omniform, far-post-lungfish, nuttier-than-Boschian" diversity of the facts at hand, which have no apparent reason to stay together, and no profound pattern they let us behold.

How can a poem built along such lines stay together? What do antique and modern, cosmetic and practical, dangerous and harmless, metal and wood, "Twill weft, and owl-hoo," "storm, and calm," have in common? How would you know? Can such knowledge turn out to be adaptive? Peppered moths, who depend on camouflage to hide them from avian predators, grew darker as the air in the north of England grew more polluted, a famous example of evolution by natural selection; can a poem help us get "darker" in order to better adapt ourselves to our dark world? Can a poem help you adapt to the "spirit-dead, hellacious . . . *über*-darkness" of a terrible job, or of a depressive episode?

Writing in 1995, Goldbarth seems to anticipate the distracted, twitchy, mul-titasking reader, or nonreader, of the Internet age, with ten browser windows open at once (even though as of 2015 Goldbarth himself uses a manual type-writer and refuses email). Albert, like Schuyler, wants his eclectic, collector-oriented, inclusive, fast-moving mind and language to help us—and to help Schuyler—adapt to the weird, demanding world, "here / at the bung-end of the millennium." But Albert does not think his poems can do it. The kind of adaptation he hopes to enable, a kind of camouflage like the peppered moth's, is "more than *my* day's scan / of newspaper cullings" and so on can ever perform. There's just too much weirdness out there—too much embarrassment, too many warts and farts, too much violence, and too much pain, such as the gang-inspired torture of an eleven-year-old.

Poetry cannot do justice to such events. Nor can it offer a smooth escape: Goldbarth's poems are no heterocosm, no "Planet Albert" distinct from Earth, but rather an inadequate attempt to keep up (as other poets with other goals do not even try to keep up) with the flood of news about what's real. This ars poetica also addresses insomnia, and it ends after its grammar nearly breaks down: a cannonade of nouns and noun phrases, followed by speech particles—"Sure. Right"—resolves on a final, atypical, self-contained short sentence: "I'll know what to do with them." He pretends to believe that he doesn't know what to do, what poem to write, though he has just written it.

Goldbarth has been accomplishing, or perpetrating, what rhetoricians call paralipsis, saying he is not going to do, or cannot do, what in fact he has done. The poet has not justified evil, nor has he explained why gang members burn kids with acid, but he has composed a poem that finds a place for these bi-zarre discoveries, a poem that knows "what to do with them"; we have just read it. Moreover he has, with his fast, talky, apologetic style, provided a model, an attitude, a way to live with the crazed profusion of anecdotes and facts on Planet Albert, and on your planet too.

Goldbarth lets us admit what he thinks we already know: the world is disor-ganized, and only a baggy, unteleological, comic literary form can reflect it. Goldbarth's ultra-talk style, with its debts to stage comedy (in American English and in Yiddish) shows that he shares our fluster, our confusion, and that he can make it more bearable by telling jokes, by emphasizing—rather than trying to avoid—the clutter of facts (some horrible or disgusting, some simply amusing) that fly at him. If some of the facts provoke horror, others provoke awe, or awe and horror at once (perhaps the doctors' quick action saved Nicky); others still promote innocent fun, or even suggest that the world has become less dangerous, more amusing—not Homeric warriors, but video wombat warriors (who drool). Goldbarth's poems cannot wish horrors away, but their juxtapositions insist that the horrors are never the whole story—the jokes, and the spiritual questers' staves, and the random Brie, and the fact that we will know what Schuyler does if Goldbarth writes, not "fluffs" but "fluffles," are facts about the world too.

It is a world that fits—so to speak—Goldbarth's talky, improvisational style, into which nothing finds an exact "fit" but anything can find an approximate one. Other than "tuxedo-rental shops' weirdest finds," no rubric includes these and only these objects, from eye to ashtray. In mathematical terms, no function can generate exactly this set; in philosophical terms, no intensive definition could produce them. But there are other rubrics, other functions, other labels, that could include them along with thousands of other things: "data chaos" is one, and "everything" is another. The title could also describe an update on the Renaissance visual art works called memento mori, since each object could stand for fleetingness (ash in an ashtray), for the hypocrisy of worldly pursuits (gold and silver), for violence (explosive), or for bodily decay. That rubric perhaps explains why Goldbarth's imagination moves to bad news, to news about death, so fast—though it does not stay there for the whole of the poem ("Twill weft" gets in too).

Tuxedos should also "fit"; their pockets are "receptacles." John Milton wrote that he wanted *Paradise Lost* to fit this world to the next, "to justify the ways of God to man," and that he hoped it would speak to the very best (best-educated or most upright) readers, "fit audience find though few." Goldbarth's long-lined, irregular, American poem shrugs away, almost sadly, Milton's ambitions: it asks us to join him in his shrug. At the same time it thanks a real person, the "lovely wife" to whom " 'A Wooden Eye' " also counts as a note of thanks. Not even Goldbarth can make the world as experienced look like a credible unity; not even Goldbarth can truly fit into a well-organized poem—or even into a slapdash, moderately organized, overstuffed poem—everything from theodicy to terror, from the Lady Satans to the kitchen sink; not even if Schuyler asks. But it is Goldbarth's cheerful vocation to try.

HARRYETTE MULLEN

honey jars of hair
skin and nail conjuration
a racy make-up artist collects herself
in time for a major retrospection

her lady's severe beauty
and downright manner
enhance the harsh landscape
positioned with urban product

mule for hire or worse
beast of burden down when I lay
clean and repair the universe
lawdy lawdy hallelujah when I lay

tragic yellow mattress
belatedly beladied blues
shines staggerly avid diva
ruses of the lunatic muse

At once playful and baffling, childlike in their sound play and alert to adult sexuality and to history, Mullen's lines aim to integrate disparate ways to think about speech and writing; to ask what sounds natural, and to whom, and why; to show what goes without saying in American spoken English and what has to be contested or written down. Mullen's book—and these lines in general— at once evoke the history of black womanhood as a symbol and as a lived experience; take back, and push back against, stereotypes about black women; and give that pushback a confident place in the still distressingly white American avant-garde.

This poem, or unit, comes from Mullen's book-length sequence *Muse & Drudge* (1995), which (Mullen has written) "employs a ubiquitously traditional form, the quatrain or tetrastich, common to ballads and other folk poetry, and well represented within the history of English verse." Four such quatrains appear on every page of *Muse & Drudge*, and many of them (not only those above) present African American women in terms that can be confrontational or salacious: another page includes the quatrain "breaks wet thigh high stepper / bodacious butt shakes / rebellious riddem / older than black pepper." Sometimes ungrammatical, rich with puns, hints, and half-hidden associations, both semantic ("beast" leads to "of burden") and sonic ("belatedly beladied"), the links that lead Mullen from word to word do not lead back to the start, nor to some clear whole. Mullen has also likened her quatrains to "women's work," "piecework, like quilting," with its squares of disparate origin, as against the presumably masculine ideal of a unified, sculptural poem.

Mullen came to this way of working by bringing together separate parts of her own career. She published three books of poetry (as well as a great deal of scholarly prose) before *Muse & Drudge*: one book of more or less clear, speech-like poems of African-American experience, *Tree Tall Woman* (1981), and then two collections of prose poetry, *Trimmings* (1991) and *S*PeRM**K*T* (1992), explicitly indebted to Gertrude Stein. The prose poems had feminist, and antiracist, politics—the first imitated descriptions of clothes, the second the aisles and products in supermarkets—but they did not feel like speech. *S*PeRM**K*T*, for example, began, "Lines assemble gutter and margin. Outside in, they straighten a place. Organize a stand. Shelve space." Such choppy prose phrases evoke supermarket shelves; they also tell us that Mullen does not want to marginalize herself, to make a mere product for sale, to stand in line.

These two books—as Mullen has also said—situated her among writers who paid more attention to written language than to spoken, writers of the so-called avant-garde. "Any theory of African American literature that privileges a speech-based poetics or the trope of orality to the exclusion of more writerly text," she has argued, "results in the impoverishment of the tradition." Nonetheless—and (so she implied) alas—those books changed Mullen's audience: where she once read to African Americans at community events, she now saw overwhelmingly white readers on college campus after college campus.

Muse & Drudge responds to that change. Its succession of quatrains, quotations, and near quotations, its bluesy, allusive, fabricated "speaker," at once individual and collective, attract readers familiar with the avant-garde, readers who want to see poetry that relishes its status as artifice, but it also answers readers who seek ethically and politically forceful versions of black women's experience. "The making of the voice in the poem," Mullen told the critic and poet Calvin Bedient, "is the recycling of tradition," incorporating "a generic 'I,' a traditional 'I,' the 'I' of the blues."

Set beside other avant-garde texts, *Muse & Drudge* resounds with African American folk and popular terms and expressions, and it has a clear, consistent subject: the cultural history of black womanhood. Set beside other explorations of African American female experience, though (Lucille Clifton's, for example), *Muse & Drudge* looks forbiddingly nonlinear, even bizarre, not to mention thrillingly or maddeningly allusive. "I wrote this book to bring the various readers of my work together," Mullen has concluded, and the quatrains' resonance tries to do so, even if they also seem to pull apart any impression of any unified voice.

And what one voice could speak for all black women? None could, though some (especially in the 1970s, when Mullen was a college student) have tried: black women, like any demographic (and more than most), are brought together not only by lived experience but also by the persistence of stereotypes, not least the two that Mullen's book title names—the source of inspiration, the sexualized font of (men's) art, the Muse, and the low-status worker, often performing domestic or unpaid labor, the Drudge. Both sorts of stereotype are, of course, "made up": both satirical and euphoric, even giddy, Mullen's quatrains on this particular page try to own, or to take back, the implements and stereotypes of (so to speak) that "make-up."

As in much of *Muse & Drudge*, almost every phrase permits a double meaning. "Honey jars" could be women's sex organs ("honeypots"), so often alluded to in blues, though they could also be jars of shampoo or pomade; "conjuration" could be the magic worked by a good hairdresser, a fine nail parlor, though it could also be the "conjure" of black folk medicine, or of Haitian vodun. All these are systems of knowledge and practice designed to shape black women's bodies, and "made up" both by women and by men. No wonder some women, and some men, become "make-up artists," seizing the terms by which they are to appear.

How different is makeup (cosmetics) from making things up (creativity), or from the special kinds of creation involved in poetry or the so-called fine arts? (Shakespeare asks the same question in Sonnet 83.) Is an art show (an artist's retrospective) the same as a display of some "lady's beauty," and does it matter whether the lady is dark? "Severe beauty" (killing beauty, beauty of the kind that Geoffrey Chaucer admired when he wrote "Your eyen two wol sley me sodainly") "enhances" the work of male poets all the time. That work too is a "product" and might make women into exchangeable "product," passed from male writer to writer through a male gaze.

But "product" also means a paste or oil for hair care; "urban product" implies black hair. Is a black woman who works hard to look like a beautiful lady well "positioned with urban product"? Or—by participating in the beauty myth, by working hard on her makeup—has she just made herself into another servant of patriarchal expectations, a "mule for hire or worse / beast of burden," the sort of woman a man will try to "lay"? If the stereotype and the experience of black femininity are both burdens, how can she give them up, "lay" her burdens down, as the song has it, without ceasing to be black? ("Lay" can also mean a narrative ballad, as in Walter Scott's *The Lay of the Last Minstrel*.) Feminine beauty, whatever its race, is at once something made, an accomplishment, and something that often represents submission to somebody else's unchosen norm. Can women get out from under that paradox without having to "repair" the whole "universe"?

Such questions could go on indefinitely. They give us not a single imagined speaker able to answer them, but a strong notion of an imagined author, an author who put these bits of words together. The same lines can give us a sense of an imagined audience, a set of ideas, a mood (knowing, frustrated, socially alert, playful), and a set of aesthetic goals. One of those goals is to find beauty in confusion, in a state where not much gets resolved: Mullen's quatrains, like the players' play in *Hamlet*, could be a "ruse" designed to unmask hypocrisy, or the work of a "lunatic muse." They might also be an homage to the spiritual known as "Glory, Glory" (also called "When I Lay My Burden Down"), though they also point to nonblack compositions (the Rolling Stones' "Beast of Burden," inescapable on the radio in the 1970s) and to concepts from other religious traditions ("repair the universe," for example, translates the Jewish moral precept *tikkun olam*).

"Since no single reader is likely to 'get' all of her far-ranging allusions," writes the poet and critic Elisabeth Frost, "Mullen effectively short-circuits ideas of mastery." To read Mullen's quatrains with any degree of attention is to notice that different audiences will hear them in uncommonly different ways. As for these particular quatrains, Frost continues, "this appropriation diva might redefine the literary trope of the 'tragic mulatto' (deflated to 'mattress') or the 'yellow gal,'" while an "avid diva" delights in the play of language as such— in palindromes, for example, like "avid diva," and in rampant homophones. Such compositional methods also link Mullen to the Continental school of poetic production called OULIPO, also invoked by Brandon Som.

But Mullen's lines also pay homage to African American music. "Shine" and "Stagger Lee" are black heroes of blues and folk song: Stagger Lee escapes from everything, including the sinking *Titanic*, as this poem's black phrases escape from our attempts to give it syntactic unity. Mullen and her fragmentary alter egos represent, of course, an experimental poet, one who pursues philosophical disjunctions. Yet they also include what the critic Kimberly Nichele Brown calls the "black revolutionary diva," a black woman who addresses a black audience in empowering terms, a woman who refuses to stick to the true story of her life (the kind of true story white readers expect), who can "talk about black subjectivity in terms of duality and multiplicity" as a cause for celebration, whose unpredictable imagination makes her seem larger than life. Mullen's lines at first may seem both halting and baffling, but they stretch out, resonate, and even empower, once we can understand what—and whom—they include.

STANLEY KUNITZ

Halley's Comet

Miss Murphy in first grade
wrote its name in chalk
across the board and told us
it was roaring down the stormtracks
of the Milky Way at frightful speed
and if it wandered off its course
and smashed into the earth
there'd be no school tomorrow.
A red-bearded preacher from the hills
with a wild look in his eyes
stood in the public square
at the playground's edge
proclaiming he was sent by God
to save every one of us,
even the little children.
"Repent, ye sinners!" he shouted,
waving his hand-lettered sign.
At supper I felt sad to think
that it was probably
the last meal I'd share
with my mother and my sisters;
but I felt excited too
and scarcely touched my plate.
So mother scolded me
and sent me early to my room.
The whole family's asleep
except for me. They never heard me steal
into the stairwell hall and climb

the ladder to the fresh night air.
Look for me, Father, on the roof
of the red brick building
at the foot of Green Street—
that's where we live, you know, on the top floor.
I'm the boy in the white flannel gown
sprawled on this coarse gravel bed
searching the starry sky,
waiting for the world to end.

Halley's Comet will probably never hit Earth; it will, however, return in 2061, having passed close to us in 1986—when Kunitz probably started writing the poem—and in 1910, when Kunitz was a five-year-old boy in Worcester, Massachusetts. The famous comet thus serves the elderly poet as a symbol for childhood memories, those that never fade and those that, after a long while, return. As those memories gather in his mind's eye, the comet that prompted them also becomes a symbol for other things we can seek in the heavens, and for that other heaven where the dead may live on.

Like most of Kunitz's best late poems, "Halley's Comet" bears at once the clarity of a child's eye and the experienced confidence we may associate with old age. It does not require analysis. And yet it rewards analysis nonetheless. Kunitz's poem tries to replicate, to speak for (but not exactly "in the voice of"), the consciousness of the child whose day and whose night it depicts, as if the poet were trying to use only words and ideas his first-grade self would know. (Its diction, its pace, and its subject, as well as its unrhymed trimeter, owe much to another poem about a child "in Worcester, Massachusetts," Elizabeth Bishop's "In the Waiting Room.") The poem conforms so closely to the rules of a storyteller's narration that readers may not even notice syntactic shifts. Yet the shift from past-tense lines addressed to the reader into present-tense exclamation addressed to the father ("Look for me") does a great deal of emotional work, the more so because the poet never shifts back. We are left "waiting" along with his five-year-old self, staring up at the sky, looking for something to see before the world ends.

That something could be the comet, easily visible to the naked eye in 1910, less so in 1986. It could also be the poet's father, whom he never met. Solomon Kunitz, a dressmaker who had gone bankrupt, took his own life before Kunitz was born. "The first grand concept I had was of death," the poet recalled; "I could not sleep at night thinking about dying." The poet's mother removed all trace of his father from his boyhood house, destroying the one image of him that the boy found, and slapping his cheek (as Kunitz recalled in "The Portrait") to punish him for the discovery. The adult poet knew about Solomon "practically nothing aside from his name." The first grader thus seeks his father's image nowhere on earth, but instead in "the starry sky," where nothing but a sublime emptiness can be found.

Relatively simple in its acoustic patterns, the stichic poem—like Kunitz's earlier stanzaic lyric "Three Floors"—makes intricate use of imagined space and time. Kunitz moves from one room, across town, into another, and then up into the open; from the astronomical time of the comet's return, the eschatological time of the roaming prophet, to the hour-by-hour schedule of a child's day, with an early bedtime and a way to sneak out after dark. The white-on-black chalkboard at the start of the poem prefigures the "starry sky" of the close; the questionable "tomorrow," in Miss Murphy's mind, points to the future time of the final sentence, where "I'm the boy" refers to the adult who writes the poem. The child's innocent apocalypse reverses not only life and death but also floor and ceiling, up and down: his bed, his "gravel bed" (as if he lay out in a construction site), is the top of the building, and his absent (or buried) father looks down from above.

Why "tracks"? In 1910 a train is the fastest, most forceful thing teachers can name. Why "wandered"? Neither the teacher nor the student understands how thoroughly comets are governed by physical law (they go only where gravity and inertia take them). "You know" means both that everyone should know where the boy lives (as children assume adults know) and that the father, particularly, ought to know: the boy has—or seeks—such unusual certainty here that the poem breaks into iambic pentameter. Why "even," in "even the little children"? The mad preacher wants even the children to repent. He shouts at them, as if they too should feel guilty. But this boy pointedly does not blame himself for his father's disappearance, nor for anything else in this world; rather, he believes that he will be saved, as—in one sense, having lived to write this poem—he was.

"When I was a child, I spake as a child, I understood as a child, I thought as a child: but when I became a man, I put away childish things. For now we see through a glass, darkly; but then face to face": standing in the dark, exclaiming, "Look for me," Kunitz echoes that famous passage from St. Paul (1 Corinthians 13:11–12). The biblical language suggests at once that we will understand why people die, once we have the right faith; that we will meet our loved ones after death; and that our lives on this earth are like childhood, best lived in preparation for what comes next. It is a statement of Christian faith that Kunitz would expect readers to recall.

But Kunitz himself was the son of Jewish immigrants; indeed, after earning his M.A. from Harvard, he was told not to pursue academic English with the absurd excuse that only Christians could teach a Christian tradition. (During the 1970s and 1980s he became a celebrated teacher of poets at Columbia University—where he encountered Louise Glück and Lucie Brock-Broido—and at the Provincetown Fine Arts Work Center, which he helped to found.) The father who never shows his face recalls the Father-God who does not answer when Jesus asks, from the cross, "Why hast thou forsaken me?" (Mark 15:34). Yet he, or He, is also the aniconic God of Rabbinical Jewish tradition, whose Messiah has yet to come, and who cannot be seen.

Though schooled in Worcester, Kunitz spent childhood summers on a farm in Quinnapoxet, Massachusetts. There, "out in open territory," he recalled, "I was a transformed character. . . . It was such a different environment from home, which I felt was too enclosed a world, a house of sorrows," where "the shadow of my father's suicide loomed over my family." Many of Kunitz's late poems take place in New England woodlands, at the beach, on farms, or in the poet's Provincetown garden. Not by coincidence, many of those poems emphasize the cyclical, hardy endurance of earthly life.

"Halley's Comet," however, is a city poem, without natural renewals; what appears gone from its spaces will not come back in recognizable form, or not until too late. Kunitz's poems with rural or garden settings often reach instinctive certainties, intuitive knowledge that brings us good advice: "Live in the layers, not on the litter": "I am not done with my changes." Among such pronouncements, "Halley's Comet" stands out for its quiet emphasis on scientific (astronomical) information, for its urban setting, and for its dramatic irony: we are left with the child, thrilled as well as scared to stay up indefinitely, and we know what he cannot, which is that the world will not end and his father will not show. The child is not maudlin, not lost in mourning; instead, he seems almost eager for what will come next. As much as the poet remembers missing his late father, he also remembers excitement. The other world above the Worcester buildings, with its "fresh night air," seems preferable to this one: the boy wants to be rescued by his father almost as kids in later science fiction and fantasy want to be rescued by aliens or faeries, transported to a less humdrum, less saddening place.

With its wrenching turn from indicative to vocative ("Look for me, Father"), "Halley's Comet" turns emotionally on what we know that the child does not know: the dead do not come back, time moves only in one way, what goes down into the earth does not come back up. The child is old enough to know these things. But he is *not* old enough to articulate, or to admit, why that knowledge makes adults so sad: he imagines the afterlife as a lark, as a better residence (with no school). A less hopeful poet would tell—or induce his readers to tell—the child why he was wrong. But Kunitz's final sentence, which stays with the child in the present tense, does no such thing. Just as Halley's Comet is still the same comet after each cyclic return, Kunitz is still the same Kunitz, transported easily back into a past where he cannot believe that his father is gone. That belief becomes, in the adult, not a religious faith but a capacity for figuration, for pretending, for seeing beyond today's sorrow—and for making poems.

MICHAEL PALMER

Letters to Zanzotto: Letter 3

Our errors at zero: milk for mist, grin
for limbs, mouths for names—or else hours

of barks, stammers and vanishings, nods
along a path of dissolving ice. The sign

we make for "same as"
before whatever steps and walls,

shutters flapping in the lighted body
called null or called vocative. I'd wanted to ask

about dews, habits of poplar, carousel,
dreamless wealth, nets, embers

and folds, the sailing ship "Desire"
with its racks and bars

just now setting out. This
question to spell itself. And the waves of us

following what follows,
retelling ourselves

what we say we've said
in this tongue which will pass

Like Carla Harryman and Harryette Mullen, Palmer resists the tools that we use to interpret prose: he asks what those tools enable and what they prevent. Like Harryman and Rae Armantrout, Palmer lived and worked in the Bay Area in the 1970s, when the group now known as language writers coalesced, and critics have often treated him as one of them. But he is not: Palmer owes more to the transcendentally ambitious postwar poets of the European continent, among them Paul Celan, Edmond Jabès, and the Italian poet Andrea Zanzotto (1921–2011), to whom he dedicated this set of eight poems.

Palmer seeks what defies familiar language: experiences of discovery or transcendence that we cannot even imagine having until we get more prosaic kinds of sentences out of the way. Yet Palmer (like Celan, like Jabès) is almost always asking whether such experiences can be authentic or whether they are our "errors" alone. Palmer has cast many of his poems as "letters," both letters of the alphabet ("Dear X," "Dear L," they begin) and letters in the mail. A much earlier poet, Gerard Manley Hopkins, complained that his poems felt like "letters sent to him who lives, alas!, away," to a God who would not respond. Palmer's letters can also feel like messages to a celestial emptiness. His poems seem at once to reach for the moon and the sky—or the sun; an earlier book is called *Sun*—and to imply that we never get there, that our messages, or "letters," or "signs," never get where we wish they could go.

Here they are letters from shipboard. "Letter 3" imagines human life as a trip on a ship, "the sailing ship 'Desire,'" which we ride, or sail, or follow, in our passage from infancy to old age (a very traditional metaphor you can also find in the work of Lucia Perillo). When we are born, we know nothing, and therefore make no mistakes, "our errors at zero," as a compass pointing north is also "at zero." As babies and children attempt to interpret the world, we learn the difference between "milk" (such as breast milk) and "mist," between what we do with the muscles of our face (grin) and what we can do with our limbs; we also learn the phonic differences (linguists call them minimal pairs) that separate similar sounds, such as "milk" and "miss."

That process of learning—a process of "stammers and vanishings"—leads us down the barely navigable stream of childhood toward fluency in a language: we learn to speak, as we grow up, by learning what words, what sounds, what things, what experiences, are similar (thus covered by the same or similar words) and which ones are the same. This sense of language as a set of signs, related to one another rather than, or more than, to things in the world, comes to Palmer from Continental philosophers (Ferdinand de

Saussure, Jacques Derrida), but you don't have to read those philosophers in order to follow Palmer's poems.

With some phrases philosophy will not help. What are those "shutters flapping in the lighted body"? If the shutters are body parts that help us speak—the tongue, for example, or the uvula—then Palmer must be referring to the vowels: to *O*, or "oh," or zero, and to *U* or "you," the exclamations and pronouns that in English indicate the vocative (aka the "second person"). Shutters also separate indoors from outdoors and light from darkness; the shutters of a lighted body might reveal, or conceal, a soul, an inner light. No sooner have we learned to speak—learned to make signs, learned what is the "same as" what—than we encounter what cannot be put into words.

There are means of expression that do not use words. Palmer has worked as artistic advisor and collaborator with the Margaret Jenkins Dance Company on at least thirty-six works over four decades. The gestural repertoire and the embodied energies of modern dance can give us analogies for Palmer's goals. Yet this poem does use words, and the words mean things: consider the range of wet things denoted by "dew," of hot and formerly hot things denoted by "embers" (including the embers from Shakespeare's Sonnet 73), of straight or hard or confining or painful or sandy things denoted by "bars" (including the boundary between life and death in Alfred, Lord Tennyson's once very well known short poem "Crossing the Bar").

All these things point back to the human life course. Opening out into its unanswered questions, its array of common nouns, Palmer's sentence—the only grammatically complete sentence in the poem—pays homage to the many possibilities, the openness, in any life that has yet to come to an end, though especially to the life of somebody still young, somebody "just now setting out." We are all in the same kind of boat, "the sailing ship 'Desire,'" traversing "the waves of us." And we never reach our preferred destination: we are always "setting out." Life does not answer our fundamental questions, but replaces them with more questions: each question must both articulate ("spell" as in spell out) and put to rest ("spell" as in relieve) some earlier version of itself. The stories we tell or retell are the same kinds of stories, no matter how much their details ("nets, embers // and folds") differ: they show how we grow up, pursue our goals, succeed or fail, and then die. Not only will we, as individuals, pass away, but the very language in which we describe our lives, in which we ask each other such hard questions, will itself "pass," as did Assyrian, Latin, and ancient Greek.

Read this way, Palmer's letter-poem concludes in an almost stoic, not quite serene resignation. We are the frangible, fragile waves of our speech, unable to get outside ourselves, fated to sail along in the language we use. That is one version of Jacques Derrida's famous saying "Il n'y a pas dehors-texte," often translated as "there is nothing outside the text," though a better version would be "there is no outside-text," no context-free, absolute, and reliable way to interpret: "what we say" has to emerge from "what we've said." We can never get outside our body, or outside language, or outside the boat.

We can, however, share our stories about it, and gesture—as dancers might—toward questions we cannot explicitly ask. Palmer characteristically avoids proper nouns, as he avoids descriptive adjectives and common nouns that would set the poem in one particular place or time. This generality—this sense that the poem evokes many people, many occasions, rather than only one—might be a property of lyric poetry (as opposed to, say, novels) in general, but many modern poets work against it, specifying real places or material things; Palmer, instead, accentuates the general property, the sense of abstraction, that his brand of writing shares with much older lyric verse.

Palmer's poetry has not usually been read alongside much older verse: his own interviews and essays (collected in the volume *Active Boundaries*), as well as his strongest supporters (such as the poet and critic Norman Finkelstein), emphasize his ties to West Coast modernists such as Robert Duncan and Robin Blaser, as well as to Jabès, Zanzotto, and Celan. Palmer has called himself "a poet committed to an exploratory prosody, an assertion of resistance to 'meaning' and 'expression' as givens, and a radical questioning of our means of representation." Yet he said so in an essay about Percy Bysshe Shelley (1792–1822), who—like Palmer—set the ancient resources of song, sound, and selfhood, against themselves, attempting (as Palmer put it) to speak "out of difference," never affirming one thing at once.

If Palmer—and Shelley—end up also evoking familiar facts (that we age and die; that words can elude us), we may well conclude that those facts are not "conservative" mystifications but permanent aspects of life; we may even conclude that one of the permanent uses of poetry, with its distance from merely familiar language, is to help us tell permanent facts of life from political mystifications, to keep those two things apart. This use or reuse of "the lyric," of poems that can resemble song, separates Palmer from all the language writers, and also (as Palmer's essay goes on to say) from poets who wear their politics and their ethics on their rolled-up sleeves. His own work recommends instead a kind of slowing down, a taking care, a skepticism that channels and does not preclude the reverence suggested by his tone.

This poet does not seem to care if we know his sources: as the scholar Nerys Williams put it, he "is clearly not interested in poetry as pedagogy, and suggests that the reader's focus should be on the indeterminacy enacted by the text, as opposed to an excavation of intertexts in the poetry." And yet the intertexts can help. Williams herself goes on to show what Palmer gets from Zanzotto, who may well have read Palmer's eight-poem sequence when it appeared. Within Zanzotto's long career, Palmer has been most drawn to his poetry of the late 1960s, as in the 1968 collection *Beauty* (*La Beltá*), a radical, sometimes nonsensical, and yet deliciously elaborate efforts toward (in the words of Zanzotto's most frequent American translator, Patrick Barron) "estrangement from known semantic fields and reading habits." Compare, to Palmer's halting lines, a passage from *Gli Sguardi i Fatti e Senhal* (1969), in Elizabeth Wilkins's English version:

> —"No, I am not me yet
> no, I was not born me
> no, I knotty nest of no's   diamond of never
> no, I was the glided beside.

Zanzotto used nonsense, foreign words, collage, interruptions, and baby-talk (in Venetian Italian, *petèl*), along with explication and description, not to sow chaos or simply subvert expectations but to create a space where readers might ask: if we can get ourselves to stop looking for prose sense, to stop assuming that our existing perceptual habits allow us to get the world right, what else might we be able to find?

It is a question asked by religious mystics and skeptical philosophers, from the ancient world's sophists to modern social constructionists. Palmer pursues it without putting forward an answer; instead, his sets of signs, his unfinished journeys, imagine a space where we might look for answers ourselves. They also—thanks to Palmer's extraordinarily recognizable (and by now much imitated) style, with its euphonies, its repetitions, its floating nouns—convey an elegant calm, a confidence in the poem's direction, even when we cannot know where it wants us to go.

ROBERT HASS

Our Lady of the Snows

In white,
the unpainted statue of the young girl
on the side altar
made the quality of mercy seem scrupulous and calm.

When my mother was in a hospital drying out,
or drinking at a pace that would put her there soon,
I would slip in the side door,
light an aromatic candle,
and bargain for us both.
Or else I'd stare into the day-moon of that face
and, if I concentrated, fly.

Come down! come down!
she'd call, because I was so high.

Though mostly when I think of myself
at that age, I am standing at my older brother's closet
studying the shirts,
convinced that I could be absolutely transformed
by something I could borrow.
And the days churned by,
navigable sorrow.

Literally breathtaking (the short lines at the end require short breaths) as well
as immediately, intensely affecting, "Our Lady of the Snows" is also atypical
for Hass: the former U.S. poet laureate normally writes longer, looser, poems,
focused (in general) on the present moment, his family life, his travels, or the

news, and his works are normally ratiocinative, accretive, and essay-like, rather than pithy and dense. Hass's religious allusions are usually Buddhist or East Asian: *Sun Under Wood* (1996), which contains "Our Lady of the Snows," also includes a twelve-page poem that begins with a mantra ("Creekstones practice the mild yoga of becoming smooth") and ends at a Korean Buddhist shrine. Yet Hass was brought up otherwise. "I don't remember exactly when, in what stages, I shed Catholicism," he has recalled. "I had grown up inside, or halfway inside, a religious communion. My mother was, not devoutly, but deeply, culturally, a Roman Catholic." The poet's father "seemed, for whatever private reasons, to like the idea of sending his children to school to priests and nuns, and managed also to convey a sense of mild wonder at the church and its doctrines."

That mild wonder comes here to good account. Hass has written a religious poem of sorts, one that shows what a religious attitude—alert to another world, seeking help from elsewhere, out of this life—can do for ultimately nonreligious people. He has also written an unlikely rejoinder to some parts of American poetic history, in particular to the confessional poetry written by Robert Lowell and his followers in the late 1950s and 1960s, and to the earlier, more elaborate Lowell of "The Quaker Graveyard in Nantucket," one of the first modern poems Hass loved. And he has managed to fit around his apparently unlikely subjects—alcoholism, trauma, prayer, first and last things—the attitude that typifies his poems: a hard-won calm, a diffidence as close to melancholy as to happiness, a resolve to take things as they are.

"Our Lady of the Snows" is one among many traditional names for the Virgin Mary, derived from a miracle in ancient Rome, where the Basilica of St. Mary Major stands on the site of a legendary summer snow. Several Catholic churches with that name operate today in California, though there appears to be none in San Rafael, where Hass grew up; his title may designate a church now renamed, or the altar and chapel within a larger church, or the white statue of the Virgin herself. Describing its surface and setting, Hass makes Mary's "unpainted statue" an almost excessive, or deadpan, figure for innocence, inexperience (like his own), and—in the fourth line— Shakespearean forgiveness. "The quality of mercy is not strained," says Portia in *The Merchant of Venice*, in a speech once standard for high school recitations; "It droppeth as the gentle rain from heaven / Upon the place beneath." (Not by coincidence, Portia is speaking to Shylock, the Jew, who will later, under compulsion, "become a Christian.") *The Merchant of Venice* is, technically, one of Shakespeare's comedies, but it is not often funny, and it requires the "scrupulous," clever young Portia to set its plot aright, as the intercessory figure of the Virgin (so many Catholics believe) sets real wrongs right.

What follows could scarcely sound more personal, if "personal" means "autobiographical" or "about a shameful past." And that is what the personal meant for the so-called confessional poets—the Robert Lowell of *Life Studies*, W. D. Snodgrass, Anne Sexton, John Berryman—prominent in the early 1960s, when Hass (born in 1941) was in graduate school (his first book would not appear until 1973). In that sense "Our Lady of the Snows" looks very like a confessional poem. Lowell and Sexton depicted themselves, not their mothers, in mental hospitals, but they followed Freud in looking to parents and nuclear families for first causes, for a muse and a music of unhealed wounds (often, as in Berryman, bound up with drinking). The adult Hass has some sympathy with confessional axioms: "the core of the self, we learn early, is where shame lives," he writes elsewhere in *Sun Under Wood* (1996). Sending his child self into the chapel, and his adult self into the poem, to answer his mother's alcoholism, Hass makes himself momentarily the child of Lowell, trying out the voice of the confessionals, and bringing that term (coined, for poetry, by M. L. Rosenthal) back to its literal Catholic roots.

But the young Hass is not going to confession; he is praying to the Virgin Mary, to a girlish, "unpainted" Mary, more virgin than mother, and he is trying to "bargain" for his own mother's salvation, as she will not bargain for herself. Hass's unobtrusive line breaks follow the syntax; they slow down, as if to make sure we could follow the boy, attach ourselves to his own loyal attachments.

So far, so pious, and so full of pity. But children in such situations do not only want to save their parents; they also—like so many healthier, more fortunate children—wish that they could escape to a place all their own. So did Hass, who modulates for the first time from what is literally true (the statue was really unpainted, the mother was really in the hospital, the candle did have a strong scent) into metaphor (Hass did not wish he could fly, but simply flew). The statue's face was a "day-moon" because it was white, like the moon, and because it was another world, invisible to adult mortals, like the dark side of the moon. And—again—the role that a watchful parent would take belongs here to somebody else, to the fictionally omnipotent Mother Mary: it is the statue and not the real mother (never named) who calls to the boy, "Come down!"

Hass could have arranged the third stanza in regular trimeters (like "bargain for us both") by breaking a line at "She'd call"; instead, he segregates the emphatic imagined voice of Mary from the explanatory inner monologue of the boy. That choice brings his cadence closer to the irregularity of the lines above; it also emphasizes the first rhyme, the childish "fly"-"high." "Getting high" in his imagination, in the early 1950s, Hass takes the tools of religion and uses them not to bind himself to his family or to the Catholic Church but to imagine a separation.

And that is what the adult Hass finds in "spirituality" (his term), and in poetry as opposed to organized religion: for Hass as for Allen Grossman, poetry and religion take the same impulse in opposite directions, the first toward heterogeneity and invention, the second toward conformity. Religion— etymologically, that which binds people together (the "lig-" in "religion" is the "lig-" in "ligament" and "ligature")—is one thing; spiritual experience, for Hass, is another. Both poetry and "spirituality," Hass has written, "had to do with negation," "saying no to the plausibly constructed world."

Yet without the church as a place of quiet refuge, without the side altar, without the "unpainted statue," the young Hass would not have attempted this psychologically important, exciting escape, not just from the family but from his growing body, into the "calm" of air, of stone. "I know we die, / and don't know what is at the end," Hass wrote near the end of *Sun Under Wood*. His own beliefs leave no room for another world. And yet Hass here follows up, pays ironic tribute to, shows his qualified respect for, the religious institutions of his childhood, the faith that could not save his mother from drink, but whose iconography let him "fly." If the poem concluded at "high," it would say so already—but it would also feel incomplete, leaving the young Hass in unsustainable and literally unbelievable reverie.

If only—the child thinks—he could become someone else, live someone else's life, even just the life of his older brother! Hass does not tell us in "Our Lady of the Snows" what happened next to his mother (who seems to have survived, still drinking, for years): he does not show her leaving any hospital ("a" implies more than one). Instead, his last stanza reminds us that despite the specific locale—one statue, one chapel—the poem evokes, Hass has been using the habitual mood (what Spanish speakers call the imperfect), remembering something that happened again and again. He concludes by remembering something else that happened again and again: "standing in my older brother's closet / studying the shirts."

Catholic faith, any organized religious faith, turned out to be like one of his brother's shirts: it was not durably his, it did not fit, it could not help in the way that adults might expect, but it became a stimulus to make things up. For much of the 1980s and some of the 1990s, Hass worked closely with the Polish Nobel laureate Czesław Miłosz, co-translating Miłosz's poetry into English. "Our Lady," responding to Hass's Catholic childhood, also echoes Miłosz's own Catholicism. The miraculous change a shirt might work on the boy (not just transformed but "absolutely transformed") is like the miracle of the snows, or like the miracles of the incarnation and the virgin birth, the fault-less mother, the perfect Son: important to imagine, but impossible for him to believe.

One thing will end up perfect in Hass's poem, though: his rhymes: "fly"-"high," "borrow"-"sorrow." The final stanza turns from remembered, pathetic desperation to something like diffidence, a colloquial shrug ("Though mostly"), and then to an understated generality, as if to apply to Hass the praise that Randall Jarrell (a sometime hero of Hass's; see Hass's poem "Old Dominion") intended for Elizabeth Bishop: "Instead of crying, with justice, 'This is a world in which no one can get along,' Miss Bishop's poems show that it is barely but perfectly possible—has been, that is, for her." Confessional poets often presented themselves as people who could not get along, who kept breaking down; Hass instead shows us a surprisingly calm adult, able to write that last line. Few single rhymes in English have done so much work.

"Navigable" also places the poem in other literary and Marian traditions: the Virgin is Stella Maris, patron of sailors, star of the sea. Here too Hass places himself in poetry's history. Before Lowell helped to invent confessional po-etry, he was a much-celebrated, complicated poet of rhyme and meter who combined tumultuous, Miltonic cadences with Catholic faith. One of Hass's earliest long essays (published in 1977) admired Lowell's long poem "The Quaker Graveyard in Nantucket" (1946), at that time widely thought dated. For Hass, though, Lowell's elegy for his drowned cousin remained alive, its drowned sailors and bloody whales presenting "an imagination of suffering and violence which it is the imperative of the poem to find release from, and each successive section of the poem is an attempt to discover a way out."

The young Hass of this poem, too, sought a "way out," and found it—as Lowell had—in nautical metaphors and in Marian symbols. "The Quaker Graveyard" also describes a famous English Catholic shrine, Our Lady of Walsingham, whose statue of the Blessed Virgin (as Lowell put it), "Expres-sionless, expresses God." Hass calls Lowell's version of the Virgin Mary "not the god of the sorrows"—that is, not the suffering Jesus Christ—"but the god-dess of an almost incomprehensible peace," the representative of some other realm, "the embodiment of what can't be embodied . . . She floats; everything else in the poem rises and breaks, relentlessly, like waves."

To read Hass on Lowell's Virgin Mary, the otherworldly, expressionless patron of sailors, is to see why the pale white hospital Mary of Hass's youth evokes sailing, why this image of Mary mattered to Hass so much later in his own life, and why a poet so temperamentally distant as Hass from Lowell would think (correctly) that reading Lowell could help later poets write poems. By the end of the poem Hass sounds nothing like Lowell, neither the stormy pentameter Lowell of "The Quaker Graveyard" nor the fractured Lowell of *Life Studies*, whom the first lines emulate. He is, instead, finally understated, almost self-confidently composed: not flying but sailing, however troubled, onward over the surface of this life, a boy and then an adult who (as the poet Liesl Olson later put it) "articulates the temptations and terrors of magnitude" without choosing to leave "this earth." Hass's calm, sad, invitingly general conclusion shows respect for the piety of orthodox adults, respect for the boy who stood in the closet, and respect for youthful escapism. It also implies that he has outgrown them all.

C. D. WRIGHT

Key Episodes from an Earthly Life

As surely as there are crumbs on the lips
of the blind   I came for a reason

I remember when the fields were no taller
than a pencil   do you remember that

I told him   I've got socks older than her
but he would not listen

You will starve out girl   they told her
but she did not listen

As surely as there is rice in the cuffs
of the priest   sex is a factor   not a fact

Everything I do is leaning   toward
what we came for   is that perfectly clear

I like your shoes your uncut hair
I like your use of space too

I wanted to knock her lights out
the air cut in and did us some good

One thing about my television set it has
a knob on it enabling me to switch channels

Now it is your turn   to shake or
provoke   or heal me   I won't say it again

Do you like your beets well-cooked and chilled
even if they make your gums itch

Those dark arkansas roads   that is the sound
I am after   the choiring of crickets

Around this time of year   especially evening
I love everything   I sold enough eggs

To buy a new dress   I watched him drink the juice
of our beets   And render the light liquid

I came to talk you into physical splendor
I do not wish to speak to your machine

Wright's history as a poet should not be separated from the literary history of
the places where she lived. Born in Mountain Home, Arkansas, she grew up
in the Ozarks, attended the University of Arkansas at Fayetteville, and came of
age as a writer there during the 1970s, alongside the improbably prolific and
visionary poet Frank Stanford, whose dreamlike—or nightmarish—images
give his work a following to this day. After Stanford's death in 1978, Wright
relocated to San Francisco, where she encountered the antilyrical asperity of
the language writers (especially Ron Silliman); she also became romanti-
cally involved with Forrest Gander, another young poet of Southern origins. The new couple lived in Mexico between 1981 and 1983 before settling
in Rhode Island, where Gander and Wright taught at Brown University,
already the home base of other, older experimental poets and translators such
as Keith and Rosmarie Waldrop.

   That experience made Wright, by the 1990s, one of the first poets to
integrate—inventively, intuitively, and successfully—the personal lyric of the
1960s and 1970s, the kind of poem that embodies the deepest feelings of an

imagined authentic self, with the features of fracture, disjunction, and self-critique that characterized the language writers and their allies. Her migrations among regions and among literary communities also left Wright uncommonly alert to her own sense of place. Wright's first full-length book, *Translation of the Gospel Back into Tongues* (1982), was a rain-soaked, blues-tinged, almost southern gothic memorial to Stanford; her second, *Further Adventures with You* (1986)—like her seventh, *Rising Falling Hovering* (2007)—reflected travels with Gander in Mexico. In between, she wrote about small towns in Georgia, prisons in Louisiana, and—above all—the Arkansas where she grew up.

In *Cooling Time*, her 2005 collection of poetic prose (much of it adapted or redacted from earlier writings), Wright imagined her ideal poem, "the poem I most want to write," as an elusive companion in an old Arkansas house: "It refuses to come forward, to stand still while I move to meet it, embrace and coax it to sit on the porch with me . . . The house smells like beets. For in this poem it is always Arkansas, summer, evening. But in truth the poem never sleeps unless I do." Wright also identified her own tastes and style thoroughly with her origins, and with "the division between urban and rural": "I like the sticks; I am, if you will, of the sticks." And yet, Wright added, New York could feel like "the sticks" too.

Wright avoids stereotypes—she keeps her places and people new—by making them canny, withholding information about them, keeping them unsettled: the characters in poems like this one inhabit a land, a home, and a life story that cannot be mistaken for anyone else's, but whose precise events remain hard to pin down. And in not quite becoming narrative, not quite resolving into familiar templates, "Key Episodes" also stands up for the intuitive, irresolvable power of feeling, of the body and its senses, especially those "lower" or more visceral senses—touch, taste, sexual arousal, proprioception—that keep us aware of our bodies, of what's near to hand.

Wright's poem may look back on a life, but it concludes with a passionate proposition: she—or the character for whom she speaks (a fictional character? a grandparent? a friend from home?) wants to do something with, or for, or to "you." What she wants begins with a promise, and with "crumbs on the lips of the blind": not sight but taste, not mere curiosity but bodily hunger, has brought her—where? To "you," perhaps to your house and to "what we came for": could it be sex? The poem lauds sensual pleasures and bodily features ("your shoes your uncut hair"). But "sex is a factor not a fact": sex could be just one form of the bodily intimacy, the life together, that the poet might propose. Apparently a former male lover has taken up with a younger woman, or a girl. "I've got socks older than her"; the insult is perfectly homely, and perfectly useless. But is the girl whom "they told . . . You will starve out" the same as the girl who is younger than the socks? If so, she seems brave rather than vulnerable. Could they be different women instead? What if the lines referred to different "episodes," different cruxes, years apart, in the same life?

Wright's title implies that the couplets represent separate days, or weeks, or hours, or years. At one point the poem might envision a marriage. "There is rice in the cuffs/of the priest" from all the weddings, and because he is slovenly. Other segments suggest revenge sex—*he* took up with *her,* so *I'll* pursue *you.* But the narrative situation—where it takes up a weekend, or takes forty years—is not the point. Instead the phrases revel, and they keep pausing in order to make sure that we can revel, in their sensory details, their earthy similes, their regional rhythms and their odd mouth feel: "leaning" (for "leading" or "tending"); "starve out" (for "starve"). The poem invites us to answer not the questions "What happened and to whom?" but the question "What was it like to be these people, in these bodies, in this place?"

Wright may be building up characters, but she is also coming very close to the strategy recommended by the language writer Lyn Hejinian, who has described her "compositional technique" of "building a work out of discrete intact units (in fact, I would like each sentence itself to be as nearly a complete poem as possible)." These sentences are not complete poems, but they come close: they accrete, they start and stop, they tell us what to notice in and near the spaces that the poet can present, and what we notice is regionally marked language (acoustically noteworthy) or else language tethered to some sense other than sight: crumbs on lips, rice in cuffs, touching (hair), feeling temperature and humidity (air—or possibly air-conditioning—on skin). The "knob enabling me to switch channels" takes us from the video image back to a thing we can touch; it also reminds us that this speaker likes to have some control over what she sees, until she gives it up—"it is your turn to shake or/provoke or heal me." That certainly sounds like some kind of sex.

Wright also shares food. Pickled beets are a regional specialty; "well-cooked and chilled," they pleased "him"—he made them transcendent, as well as translucent (liquid). Will they please "you"? The two couplets about delicious beets, taken one after another, would imply that "you" could not be "him": "I" hope "you" like beets at least as much as "he" does. They would tell us a story. But Wright does not want us to focus on the story alone, nor even to make it clear: instead she projects a place, a set of attitudes—angry, aroused, alert, expectant—and a set of goals for her own poems, which should feel like the Ozarks in the dark.

They feel like poverty too. Who sells eggs in order to buy a dress? Are they the ova of a graduate student, or the replaceable products of busy chickens? The context implies the latter, especially since hens—more than, say, goats and cattle—are sometimes the special province of young girls on farms. For whom did she buy the dress? For herself, to feel pretty in it? To look good for "him"? Can she make light of his appetites, or—as the phrase suggests—does she find the beets and the beet juice sublime? How can Wright make a single poem out of such various appetites—for local color, for vegetables, for sex?

In presenting a lover and a beloved who almost, but do not quite, set up a narrative—but who certainly give us an attitude and a place—Wright suggests that a present-tense self, a person defined by what's around her and how her body feels in that place, might offer a kind of freedom that the narrative self, stuck in chains of events, never gets. The poem about place, both regional and domestic, collecting "key episodes," becomes a kind of escape from the poem whose single tale could fix us in time. And proprioception, the sense of the self in experienced space, turns out to be inseparable from a sense of place, of what kind of place we are in, since both rely on intuition (as well as factual knowledge) to give us a sense of where we are. "Just as we are always with a body," writes the philosopher Edward Casey, "so, being bodily, we are always within a place as well. Thanks to our body, we are in that place and part of it."

Wright's lines are "with a body" indeed. They give us one person—and seek another, a lover—who sounds and feels organically, informally, coarsely, deliciously alive. Her ringing last lines resolve into regular iambic pentameter: if "PHYS-i-cal" could be read "PHYS-cal" they would constitute two lines of blank verse, a rhythm that Wright avoids until then (unless you count "Do you like your beets well-cooked and chilled"). That iambic conclusion allows Wright to end the poem with renewed confidence. Her kind of poem, her "talk," can indeed offer the "physical splendor" that speech and words do not normally reach.

Compared to a poem like this, an offer like that, other language is just an out-of-date television, an obsolescent answering machine. Poetry, for Wright—and not only in this poem—gives us back the intuitive, bodily knowledge, and the bodily delight, that other kinds of experience and other uses of language take away. That is why it should not become too clear—the intuitive mystery would slide out. Nor should it become too forbidding, too abstract. Instead, it has to come to us where we live.

Those goals are not only the goals these "Key Episodes" erect but the goals her other poems enunciate as well. In Wright's first book-length poem, *Just Whistle* (1993), the poet sketches the deeds of "the body," as if it had a will of its own: "The body takes off its jeans in the barn. Washes its face in webs and rain. The hair on its legs curled gold." "Wright's aesthetic," concludes the critic Lynn Keller, "combines the [language writers'] skepticism with faith in what she sees with her own eyes and experiences in her own female body." "The Ozark Odes," from *String Light* (1991), include the "total sales" from a "bait shop," folk rhymes ("sty sty leave my eye"), a list of evocative names of real "Arkansas Towns" ("Acorn / Back Gate / Bald Knob / Ben Hur / Biggers"), and a series of short poems devoted to "Lake Return": "Why I come here: need for a bottom, something to refer to; / where all things visible and invisible commence and swarm." The poet of "Key Episodes" immerses herself in this space ("I like your use of space"), in this cricket-clad night, as she earlier immersed herself in the lake.

Wright is hardly alone—nor is poetry alone—in trying to restore to the body, and to the "lower" senses, some of the power attributed to the soul. "If the body were not the soul, what is the soul?" asked Walt Whitman in 1856. In our own day George Lakoff and Mark Johnson use empirical data from cognitive psychology to argue that "we can only form concepts through the body. . . . Concepts and reason both derive from, and make use of, the sensorimotor system." "Because" and "although," "good" and "bad," like "one" and "two" and "in" and "out," arise from our brains' interactions with an irreducibly material world. You are your body, and have no experiences that are not part of it. As the anthropologist David Abram has put it, language is "a profoundly carnal phenomenon"; the "sensing body is not a programmed machine" but the source of all our feeling and thought.

Wright's unusual spacing and lineation, full of midline pauses and stops for air, emphasizes the process of breathing, the physicality of air in the pharynx and lungs (as do the otherwise quite different methods of Robert Creeley). For Abram as for Wright, the importance of breath and air to expression implies that the speaking body is also the soul. And that implication makes Wright's poem unusually, and self-consciously, alert to what she and other poets insist is a property of *poetic* language, against other ways of using words: it gives, or gives back, the immediacy of our bodies as part of a present, material, malleable, and unpredictable world. Prose is to sight as poetry is to taste and touch. And touch (to quote the German psychologist David Katz) requires contact: we experience things we see and hear "outside of our body and especially outside of our eyes," but "tactual phenomena" connect our own hands or skin to the things we describe.

To treat words as Wright can treat them is to try to give the words, the "talk," in the poem some of the powers we normally ascribed only to those "lower" senses, such as taste and touch, that require contact with the body: it is to try to make words show how bodies are real, as well as to situate them in a geographically specific place. Wright's distance from straightforward narrative—what she learned from the West Coast avant-garde—lets that attempt stand out, even as its details come from the Ozarks. This more embodied way of using language, one that pays equal attention to "lower" and "higher" senses and that prevents us from feeling like machines, is what Wright's lines promise both for "you," the beloved companion (whoever that may be), and for "you," the reader who takes in Wright's own words.

JUAN FELIPE HERRERA

Blood on the Wheel

Ezekiel saw the wheel,
way up in the middle of the air.
  Traditional Gospel Song

Blood on the night soil man en route to the country prison
Blood on the sullen chair, the one that holds you with its pleasure

Blood inside the quartz, the beauty watch, the eye of the guard
Blood on the slope of names & the tattoos hidden

Blood on the Virgin, behind the veils,
Behind—in the moon angel's gold oracle hair

      What blood is this, is it the blood of the worker rat?
      Is it the blood of the clone governor, the city maid?
      Why does it course in s's & z's?

Blood on the couch, made for viewing automobiles & face cream
Blood on the pin, this one going through you without any pain

Blood on the screen, the green torso queen of slavering hearts
Blood on the grandmother's wish, her tawdry stick of Texas

Blood on the daughter's breast who sews roses
Blood on the father, does anyone remember him, bluish?

      Blood from a kitchen fresco, in thick amber strokes
      Blood from the baby's right ear, from his ochre nose
      What blood is this?

Blood on the fender, in the sender's shoe, in his liquor sack
Blood on the street, call it Milagro Boulevard, Mercy Lanes #9
Blood on the alien, in the alligator jacket teen boy Juan

   There is blood, there, he says
   Blood here too, down here, she says
   Only blood, the Blood Mother sings

Blood driving miniature American queens stamped into rage
Blood driving rappers in Mercedes blackened & whitened in news
Blood driving the snare-eyed professor searching for her panties
Blood driving the championship husband bent in Extreme Unction

   Blood of the orphan weasel in heat, the Calvinist farmer in
      wheat
   Blood of the lettuce rebellion on the rise, the cannery worker's prize

Blood of the painted donkey forced into prostitute zebra,
Blood of the Tijuana tourist finally awake & forced into pimp sleep
   again

It is blood time, Sir Terminator says,
It is blood time, Sir Simpson winks,
It is blood time, Sir McVeigh weighs.

   Her nuclear blood watch soaked, will it dry?
   His whitish blood ring smoked, will it foam?
   My groin blood leather roped, will it marry?
   My wife's peasant blood spoked, will it ride again?

Blood in the tin, in the coffee bean, in the *maquila oración*
Blood in the language, in the wise text of the market sausage
Blood in the border web, the penal colony shed, in the bilingual yard

Crow blood blues perched on nothingness again
fly over my field, yellow-green & opal
Dog blood crawl & swish through my sheets

Who will eat this speckled corn?
Who shall be born on this Wednesday war bed?

Blood in the acid theater, again, in the box office smash hit
Blood in the Corvette tank, in the crack talk crank below

Blood boat Navy blood glove Army ventricle Marines
in the cookie sex jar, camouflaged rape whalers
Roam & rumble, investigate my Mexican hoodlum blood

Tiny blood behind my Cuban ear, wine colored & hushed
Tiny blood in the death row tool, in the middle-aged
    corset
Tiny blood sampler, tiny blood, you hush up again, so tiny

Blood in the Groove Shopping Center,
In blue Appalachia river, in Detroit harness spleen

Blood in the Groove Virus machine,
In low ocean tide, in Iowa soy bean

Blood in the Groove Lynch mob orchestra,
South of Herzegovina, south, I said

Blood marching for the Immigration Patrol, prized &
    arrogant
Blood spawning in the dawn break of African Blood Tribes,
    grimacing
& multiple—multiple, I said

Blood on the Macho Hat, the one used for proper genuflections
Blood on the faithful knee, the one readied for erotic negation
Blood on the willing nerve terminal, the one open for suicide

Blood at the age of seventeen
Blood at the age of one, dumped in a Greyhound bus

Blood mute & autistic & cauterized & smuggled Mayan
& burned in border smelter tar

    Could this be yours? Could this item belong to you?
    Could this ticket be what you ordered, could it?

Blood on the wheel, blood on the reel
Bronze dead gold & diamond deep. Blood be fast.

Herrera's effusive, energetic catalog of violent extremes may sound almost as if the poet improvised; its passionate leaps from scene to scene, noun phrase to noun phrase, react against the pervasive injustice that Herrera (named United States poet laureate in 2015) notices and envisions in the United States and beyond. And yet the same poem evokes puzzles and mysteries; it works both to see, and to see beyond, the grounds for outrage in a day's or a year's headline news. Like much of Herrera's work, it shows its roots in West Coast Chicano experience even while it exults in crossing national, regional, social, and linguistic boundaries; like all his best work, "Blood on the Wheel" uses its unruly textures and its array of rhetorical effects (some of them linked strongly to oral performance) to become at once public and hermetic, collective and yet idiosyncratic, on fire with a mission that we can follow but may never entirely grasp.

    Herrera began as a writer and performer, in Spanish and in blended Spanish and English, amid the West Coast Chicano/a movement of the early 1970s, joining "street theater groups that worked with musicians to do performance poetry," as he put it. That early work inflects his later verse. The live energy of performance infuses the couplets and lists of "Blood on the Wheel," propelled as it is by repetitions, catalogs, and syntax (or the absence of syntax) that does not require readers to double back, but lets listeners stay in the moment. The poem invites us to acknowledge the many ways in which it can be heard—as performance, as incantation, as sermon-like denunciation, as a series of riffs and antirealist takes on the interconnection of Detroit and Texas, poet and society, "the Groove Shopping Center" and the mysterious "Macho Hat." On one hand, it sprawls out in many directions, all over its imagined map; on the other, it holds itself together around the many implications of one complicated word.

That word, of course, is "blood," which comes to represent (among other things) violence, guilt (as in "blood on our hands"), life itself, vigor, a common humanity, and familial or communal loyalty ("blood ties"). Blood connects everything to everything, every body to every other body: we American readers (Anglo, Chicano or otherwise) might be connected by our culpable ignorance, by an outrageous and especially American devotion to violence, and by a kind of loyalty to one another that—if it does not destroy us—might save us instead.

Blood first is a sign of danger, pollution, and destruction, linked obscurely to "night soil" (feces) and then to "tattoos hidden," perhaps in prison, perhaps inked by gang members or ex-cons. Blood appears on the Virgin Mary, perhaps as a sign of modern American sin, perhaps instead as a promise of salvation; a nameless city runs with "the blood of the worker rat" or "the clone governor" or a maid, because all human blood, to the naked eye, looks the same. Blood can run in s's or in z's; it is no respecter of right and left, and does not pursue straight lines. Herrera goes on to find blood-guilt in gangster rap, "blackened and whitened in news," blood in the rape culture that blurs the lines between violence and ordinary sex, blood in the necessarily grueling struggle of agricultural workers (such as the lettuce pickers organized by Cesar Chavez) for better conditions and a living wage. There is blood, guilt, inescapable and sinful violence, in an America that rewards action movies such as *The Terminator*, a "box office smash hit"; that acquits O. J. Simpson; that generates the terrorist Timothy McVeigh, who blew up a federal office building in Oklahoma City in 1995. Such figures are our vicious, inverted nobility: we may as well call them, if we call anyone, "Sir."

Along with the traditions of protest poetry, denouncing injustice on behalf of a collective, Herrera also adopts devices from European and Latin American surrealism, with symbols that repudiate consistent sense. Why is there "blood on the couch"? (Is it bloody because we sit on the couch to watch television?) Is the "screen" a TV screen, or the screen in a confessional? What is "his whitish blood ring"? Why "dog blood . . . in my sheets"? We are not to know; we may never know.

Yet Herrera cannot stay away from characters, nor from ethical imperatives, for very long. "Blood from a kitchen fresco" extends the poem from prisons and televisions, symptoms of troubled nations, into a space where a family might feel at home; that family might include a grandmother, a daughter, and a father. It might also include "alligator jacket teen boy Juan," who sheds blood, or whose blood is shed, perhaps in a bowling alley: "Mercy Lanes #9."

Such attacks on an American culture of violence, on American macho and American capitalism, could be monotonous in other hands; Herrera avoids monotony by flipping through scene after scene, mixing vividly unambiguous phrases with sites where we might not know what exactly he wants us to see. These moments where symbols fly out of the grasp of semantics, where the poet's prophetic, denunciatory energy has propelled him away from the world of material things, retain our attention even as they tease, or repel, our interpretive skills.

"Blood" occurs most often as the first word in a line, the start of a repeated phrase: "Blood on the night . . . Blood on the sullen chair . . . Blood in the tin . . . Blood driving . . . Blood driving . . . Blood in the border web." Such initial repetitions, called anaphora, give the poem an organization easy to follow aloud, one that encourages lines, and whole poems, to stretch out, rather than driving them toward a predetermined end. Working against that expansion are moments of syntax, of completed sentences, or—more often—questions: these moments help Herrera make the poem seem open-ended without letting it fall apart. Anaphora in U.S. verse has strong associations with Walt Whitman, and with the young Allen Ginsberg, both precursors for Herrera's visionary-radical program. Herrera also uses epistrophe and mesostrophe, repetition at the end and in the middle of successive lines; such devices prevent monotony, keeping the poem organized as music is organized, invoking the call-and-response modes of gospel songs and spirituals, such as "Ezekiel Saw the Wheel."

That song and its words have many versions; some (such as Woody Guthrie's) attack corporations and profits in explicit terms. The oldest and most familiar versions of the song, however, describe Israelites "dressed in white" transported from Egypt, slaves delivered from bondage, and in the chorus (drawn from Ezekiel 1:14–28) a great divine wheel that turns as God has willed it, "way up in the middle of the air." This wheel—like capitalism, blood, or human nature—connects everything to everything else, and unlike capitalism it suggests a divine plan: in the biblical source, the floating wheel signifies "the likeness of the glory of the Lord."

Ezekiel's vision—like Jeremiah's, like Herrera's—rebukes a "rebellious nation" (Ezekiel 2:1) even while it foresees eventual redemption. The Americans in Herrera's poem, like the Israelites in Ezekiel, appear to have conquered themselves, to have succumbed to their own sinful, violent aspects: they also go out of their way to subjugate border crossers, to mistreat "African Blood Tribes" and indigenous (e.g., "Mayan") peoples. Herrera has said that Mexican heritage "is always connected to the indigenous history of the Americas"; those connections, which Anglos often ignore, provided an ideology for the Chicano movement of the 1970s, with its vision of Aztlán, the once and future indigenous and Mexican continent.

Herrera grew up in a Spanish-dominant household, and he has continued to mix English with Spanish within as well as between poems; though "Blood on the Wheel" does not use very much Spanish, it makes its Spanish count. *Maquila* (literally "mill") or *maquiladora* refers to a factory producing goods for export, and can connote "sweatshop"; a *maquila oración* would be a factory (or sweatshop) prayer. Such prayers might ascend from "my Mexican hoodlum blood," or from the "bilingual yard," or for that matter from "the Groove Shopping Center": in Herrera's Americas, where borders are for crossing, anybody can end up almost anywhere.

The distinguished critic Lauro Flores writes (in Spanish) that Herrera's work crosses and challenges the borders not only of nations but of genres, playing a "game of interaction with other artistic forms (music, painting, and theater)" while exceeding "limits imposed by the traditional notion of 'poetry'" (the translation is my own). Visions of excess and of interconnection, both shameful and saving, reach out across "Blood on the Wheel," across maps of the United States, Mexico, and other countries, as they reach out beyond this poem into the rest of the book where it first appeared. In *Border-Crosser with a Lamborghini Dream* (1999), "Blood on the Wheel" inaugurates a series of shorter texts with "blood" in their titles, about blood ties and the shedding of blood: the fierce "blood gang call" ("Calling all tomato pickers, the ones wearing death frowns instead of jackets"), the comic "blood mouse manifesto," "2pac blood," "aztec blood sample," and "ezekiel's blood," inspired by the vision of resurrection in Ezekiel 37: 1–14: "in that burial we found each other. We picked up / the bones."

Here, the resurrection has yet to come. His litany of sometimes fatal dangers runs from the exploitation of agricultural workers in Iowa and California to the breakup of Yugoslavia in the 1990s, domestic violence, and an apparent infanticide "in a Greyhound bus." Could all these sins have a common root, a common modern character? "Could all this be yours? Could this item belong to you? / Could this ticket be what you ordered, could it?" Those crucial late lines make up just one of two couplets without "blood": indeed, they ask whether the poem's "blood" belongs to "you." By participating in American consumer society, drinking the coffee we buy, eating things made from soybeans, accepting the protection of the state police and the "Army ventricle Marines," most of the people likely to read this poem have some blood on our hands, even if we carry some Mayan blood too. Herrera's vision of blood in circulation, of symphonic interdependence and interconnection, is also a vision of guilt and of contagion "in the Groove Virus Machine"; we readers must be at once oppressor and oppressed, infected vectors of a culture that plays like one big "mob orchestra." The crowd of the poem, the crowd that chants the poem, participates in its own indictment, in the indictment of a system we serve.

Can life, on either side of any border, become less harsh, get back on track? It can, Herrera suggests, but only if we attend to still more meanings for complex, common words. "Fast" equals "speedy," but also "durable," "hard to break or counteract." "Blood be fast" thus means not only that blood runs rapidly (when it is shed, as in action movies) but also that blood should give us durable connections to one another, as through extended families and family histories, past national borders. Blood links grandmother to daughter; blood can link farmers or workers in Iowa to their counterparts in California. And if our imaginations can become as capacious as Herrera's expansive poem attempts to make them, "blood" guilt can even do the work of "blood" inheritance. If we can feel our share in what goes wrong, in the damage our civilization can do, if we can envision those interconnections, we might work together to make it less wrong. It is a quick hope, but better than none, and a short, sharp conclusion to a poem whose very length contributes to its force.

CARTER REVARD

A Song That We Still Sing

On the way up from Oklahoma up to the Sun Dance
at Crow Dog's Paradise on the Rosebud Sioux Reservation,
                    they'd stopped a few minutes,
my Ponca cousins from Oklahoma—
                    they were way out there by some kind
            of ruins, on the August prairie,
                    some kind of fort it may
have been, they stopped
            to eat a little, get out and
stretch their legs, the van
            had got too little for
                    the kids and all.
                            And they were walking
not paying much attention and they heard
            the singing and then Casey said,
                    Listen, that's Ponca singing.
                Hear it? Where's it coming from?
They listened, and Mike said,
                    Sounds like it's over
            inside those walls or whatever
                    they may be, over there.
                        So they walked
            through the dry short grass
                    towards the raised earth walls
                and up on them and looked
inside that wide compound, and there
            was not a soul in sight.
That was a Wolf Song, Mike said.
            Yes, a Victory Song, Casey said.

When they told me later, we looked and
       decided that it was where the Cheyennes
and some of their allies had chased some troopers
       inside a fort and
        taunted them—

             after Sand Creek it was,
     that time the news got out of what
       had been done to Black Kettle and
        his people there beneath
   that big American flag which they'd been given
      in token that this peaceful band
        was not to be attacked,
    and then at dawn the Reverend Colonel
  Chivington and his men attacked and massacred
     some hundreds of men who could not escape—
       one small boy, running
    for refuge, was shot down at a hundred yards,
because, as Chivington had told his troops,
    Nits make lice. The women's breasts,
    sliced off, were made into
       tobacco pouches, as were the scrotums
of men. George Bent, a half-Cheyenne who was there,
        who'd been a Confederate soldier and
both wrote and spoke English and Cheyenne,
    has told about it in his letters—
      he saw White Antelope come out
    unarmed from his tepee, pointing up
  at Old Glory waving over the village there,
    then when the troopers kept on shooting,
he stood unmoved and sang, as they shot him down,
  the death-song he'd composed for such a time:

> *Nothing lives long*
> *except the earth and the mountains.*

So I asked Casey and Mike,
      what do you think you heard, inside that place?
  —*I guess,* Mike said, *up in Nebraska*
      there must have been some Poncas
          who joined the Cheyennes there and fought
     the soldiers till they chased them
             into that fort.
    Then Casey said,
       We recognized that song. It's one
        that we still sing.

What kind of poem, what kind of story, is "A Song That We Still Sing"? A demonstration of ease, of extended family connections; a memorial, and a horrifying history lesson, especially for listeners who do not know Cheyenne, Ponca, Osage, or Omaha culture; a ghost story; a revenge tale; a way to think about oral tradition and lore alongside the written record: Revard's poem is all those things, but it becomes, by the end, something else: an understated, and even playful victory ode.

The whole poem follows the narrative shape a-b-c-b-a, starting in the storyteller's present ("a"), diving into Mike and Casey's day ("b"), and then recalling historical events ("c") before returning, by stages, to the present day. Revard also repeats key words—"some kind . . . some kind," "a little . . . too little," "inside those walls . . . raised earth walls"—as if to suggest the return of ideas, people, ghosts, who come back as sounds, words, "songs," tenacious ideas, even when there is "not a soul in sight." His poem will testify to the powers in words, creating community and drawing "attention" even where nothing can be seen.

The 1864 Sand Creek massacre in eastern Colorado—Revard's "c" segment—"was the My Lai of its day," as the journalist Tony Horwitz writes. "It fueled decades of war on the Great Plains. And yet, over time, the massacre receded from white memory, to the point where even locals were unaware of what had happened in their own backyard." Cheyenne and other American Indians did not forget: the grounds (since 2014 a National Historic Site) have long held an annual memorial ceremony conducted by Cheyenne and Arapaho people. Sand Creek itself belongs to the historical record: George Bent's letters—along with dozens of other firsthand accounts—can be read today.

But this now destroyed fort (only earth walls remain) is no part of that record: its site gives Mike and Casey (real names for real people, the poet confirms), along with the Osage poet, reasons to tell a different story. In that story, whose echoes make up Revard's "b" segment, it is the troopers who were trapped "inside," not tortured (much less "massacred") but "taunted" (and then perhaps slain). That imagined skirmish, involving Ponca "allies," prefigures the pan-tribal goals of the American Indian Movement (AIM) in the 1970s. Casey's brothers (so Revard writes) were among the AIM activists who occupied Wounded Knee in 1973; the poet himself visited them there. One occupation leader, Leonard Crow Dog, lived at Crow Dog's Paradise, the site of an annual Sun Dance during the years when that ceremony was outlawed, and still the site of Sun Dances today.

Revard does not show us Crow Dog's Paradise; nor does he end the poem by depicting "troopers / inside a fort." Instead, he returns to the "a" segment, the conversation, where the real turnabout, the real victory, is this: the peoples and cultures that Colonel Chivington and his ilk attempted to erase did in fact survive, not only in generations that continue to live on midwestern land but also in a body of culture and song, one that recognizes tribal distinctions (Cheyenne is not Ponca) but allows for cooperation too. The physical continuance of generations ("kids and all"), the solidarity of cousins and other blood kin, also gives the lie to the bloody warrant of those mutilated genitalia: both culture and biology go on.

To say so is to push back against toxic stereotypes. As the novelist David Treuer has observed, "death [often] gives fictional Indians their power. And Indians in fiction [often] function as knowing ghosts whose presence alone speaks back in time to the crimes committed against them." For centuries Euro-American writers, and not only writers, have depicted Native peoples as groups who belong to the past, whose lifeways and cultures are destined to pass away. This very common way of thinking has been at worst an excuse for genocide, at best a mistake still made in plenty of grade schools, whose non-Indian charges come home believing that Indians, like dinosaurs, were beautiful and powerful and strange and walked the earth a long time ago.

Against this baleful cliché, Native American writers can insist on the contemporaneity of Osage and Ponca and Ojibwe and Diné (Navajo) and Cherokee lives, and on the continuity of their inherited cultures. The critic

Gerald Vizenor calls this insistence *survivance*, and Revard's poetry provides examples, without ever letting us mistake the poetry itself for the traditions whose continuation it honors. His poem praises the songs it contains, but it is not identical to those songs—not even formally much like them.

Like most of Revard's poems, "A Song" relies on complicated indentation. No two consecutive lines have the same left margin: that visual effect distinguishes the poem both from prose and from more compact, "squarer" sorts of poetry, aligning it faintly with ethnographic transcription and translation, but more clearly with oral storytelling, with the irregular pauses and emphases of a speaking voice. Yet the poem is no ethnographer's transcript: it is a story told by an individual who knows that he includes other people's accounts in his own, almost as Mike and Casey include the kids (more than they can fit comfortably; more than expected) in their van. The tabs serve as visual signs for that inclusion. The poem flows and changes as its story unfolds, but nobody could mistake it for a ceremony, a song, or a traditional oral form.

Instead, the verse looks conversational, casual, even formless, until its rhetorical and metrical figures emerge. Repeated single words lead up to the final repetition of "song" and "sing." Revard also uses his sharply enjambed verse norm (early lines break on "and" and "may" and "for") to make later self-sufficient lines stand out. "He stood unmoved and sang, as they shot him down, / the death-song he'd composed for such a time": two stately iambic pentameters (hearing "as they," with its medial sibilance, as one unstressed syllable). This dignified pairing introduces the death-song itself, another two-line unit, set off (unlike Chivington's cruel epigram) by white space.

That song stands at three removes from the conversational English Mike, Casey, and the contemporary poet share: the distich is a quotation (Revard's, of Bent) of a quotation (George Bent's, of White Antelope) of a translation (Bent's, from the Cheyenne). The song also looks like a climax and a culmination, something that could have provided the end of a less thoughtful poem: its elegiac sentiment, which is not and could not be a "Victory Song," commemorates all those defeated in war, and suggests (like more famous statements by other nineteenth-century Indian luminaries, such as Chief Seattle) that the tribe's decimation, if not quite "natural," can no more be resisted than death itself.

And that is why it cannot end the poem. Instead, Revard concludes with a neat reversal: individuals die, but the culture that Chivington wanted to kill off—the culture whose "inevitable" decline became an excuse for torture and murder—survives because present-day individuals choose to preserve it. "Nothing lives long," in geological perspective, and all people are going to die someday; and yet, considered in historical time—longer than one human life, but younger than mountains—the material of the Sun Dance and other collaborative ceremonial parts of Indian life is still here. White Antelope's death song has become part of some ceremonies: recordings exist online. Revard transcribes, into English verse, the death song, but he does not translate what Mike and Casey heard: that song, in the Siouan language Ponca (closely related to Osage and Omaha), might be reserved for people who hear it live.

For the critic and poet Dean Rader, "what distinguishes Native poetry from mainstream Euro-American poetry," generally, is its insistence on mixing "lyric and epic modes": Native poets, like earlier makers of epic, "transmit cultural traditions, they valorize deeds, they form national identities, and they preserve culturally specific linguistic patterns" within the much shorter scope, and the apparently personal voice, of a modern lyric poem. This blending of epic and lyric goals is not confined to Native writers' work, but it characterizes that work, at least in Rader's eyes: "A Song" makes a good example, even as it also blends family tale and historical record, commemoration and comedy. Revard could have printed the final, italicized sentence as one line of regular hexameter, in parallel with "he stood unmoved." Instead, he breaks it after the word "one," as if to emphasize the way the tradition moves forward, and also to show that Mike and Casey and their allies have other songs too. They do not—American Indian people do not—have only one song, or one thing, to say.

Nor do they have just one medium, or one literary genre, to use. "Comedy is worth more than tragedy any time that survival is at stake," Revard has written, though any Native history holds elements of tragedy as well. "A Song That We Still Sing" describes a bloody disaster, but by the end it is not just about that disaster. Where Glancy's poem of American Indian heritage stressed the ineffability of its quasi-sacred experience, Revard emphasizes transmission across generations, in the face of atrocity: he makes the commemoration of an atrocity and the almost comic celebration of present-day life, ritual, even tourism, parts of the same spoken act.

Revard has written repeatedly that "songs" (his term) hold groups of people together across space and time—they are not only individual utterance. "Music and song come down from way back in dinosaur time," he quips, "And ever since the first hisses got turned into whistling, the music has socialized the singers, has created communities." The poem as a whole represents his voice too: by embedding other people's speech and song in his own poem, Revard puts forward a text that is his own, but not his alone.

Nor are its sources and analogues Ponca alone, or American Indian alone. Revard, who is now professor emeritus at Washington University in St. Louis, has had a career, largely separate from his own poetry, as an eminent scholar of medieval literature. Medievalists know his claim to have identified the scribe who wrote much of Harley MS 2253 (itself a trove of polyglot, even "multi-cultural" French-English-Latin lyric). Revard has also adapted verse riddles from Old English, translating directly from Anglo-Saxon ("Swan") or applying the genre to new things (eagle feather; television set). "I want to show," Revard writes, "that this old Anglo-Saxon poetic form is still alive, will still blossom and fruit if planted deep and watered from Indian springs."

"A Song" also holds Anglo-Saxon cuttings and seeds. White Antelope's quoted distich recalls the refrain from another Old English poem, "Deor," a lament for position and honor lost: "Þæs ofereode, / þisses swa mæg"—"that changed" or "that was overcome"; "this might be too." Famously hard to translate, "Deor" has become itself a marker of the cultural and historical change that (on a smaller scale) its speaker laments; and yet "Deor," the poem itself, survives. When Revard mentions "some kind / of ruins," envisioning bare "earth walls," readers familiar with Old English might also bring to mind the poem called "The Ruin": that poem—extant only in fragments—contemplates a single standing wall or wall-stone (*wealstan*) where a prosperous castle, hall, or fortress ("some kind of fort," so to speak) once stood; that hall, its warriors, and their nation or clan were destroyed by war and disease (*woldaeg*), so only the *wealstan* survives.

The analogy to American Indian history should be clear, but Revard brings it up only to complicate it. Ponca (and Osage and Cheyenne) people, Revard's frame-story insists, can and should commemorate shattering losses, contemplate ruins, much as whoever composed "The Ruin" did. Yet unlike the native speakers of Old English, unlike the people who lived and died in "The Ruin," Native Americans who carry forward their cultures, and who do so as inventive individuals, are present, still singing, today.

ALLAN PETERSON

Epigraph

Within the epiphyte, the epigraph of a surviving oak
after hurricane Erin, I hear claws,
small ones you'd have to describe by scurry instead of climb,
caused by intention, by fear, caused by who knows what,
a patterned self-saving conclusion in the meat-ribbons,
neat as Vesalius, as a Japanese figure of strip-bamboo and grasses
standing on a hill overlooking Hokkaido,
clever and wistful in the eyes.
So much more of the world can fit in by looking down
the wrong end of the Bausch and Lombs,
and adding the one little wiggle before the s that means possession
at the end of every word. Accretion, flypaper, taking itself
as fact in the interconnection of all things,
brain meat mediating not greedily, but serene.
It is easy to dream or visit Disneyland, both synonymous
with surreal, and then write outlandishly.
There is plenty around in plain facts stuck to each other,
flying squirrels gliding and scrambling, each finger-needle
another idea for the bark, a little inward light as in August I dive in.
The ocean glows. I swim to the sandbar, a ladder of illumination,
self-healing lights, a scratchy quote above the waves.

Peterson has spent most of his life so far as a painter and as a teacher of painting:
from 1974 to 2005 he taught at Pensacola State College in northwest Florida,
where he directed the Switzer Center for Visual Arts. For most of that time
he was writing and rewriting poems: all his five full-length books came out
after 2000. These lines from his first collection, *Anonymous Or* (2001), serve
as a manifesto, an ars poetica, for the poems he had already written and those

he had yet to write: they say how he sees the world—literally how he sees it with his eyes, and also how he interprets the words, inscriptions, epigraphs that grow like epiphytes over and around and dependent on its nonverbal images. The same lines say how he interprets the further evidence of hearing and proprioception, and the theories that come to us from the natural sciences, which begin from observations like those Peterson makes on Florida's Gulf Coast.

The underlying action could not be much simpler: Peterson says what he saw and heard after August 3, 1995, when Hurricane Erin required the evacuation of Pensacola and surrounding counties. Then he goes for a swim. But its collection of facts and tropes seem complicated—perhaps awkwardly so. Peterson revels in facts whose relations would not have occurred to anyone else, and in deploying idiosyncratic (if you like it) or unidiomatic (if you don't) strings of words to relate them: "meat-ribbons"? Andreas Vesalius, the Renaissance anatomist? Contact lenses? The "inward light" of English Dissenting Christianity? Disneyland? Yet these things are all related, in Peterson's view: the poem will show you how. Peterson's style—much more subtly than the style of that other enthusiastic connection maker, Albert Goldbarth—emerges from the quietly enthusiastic way that he brings all these details together, while also respecting the way that they drift apart.

Epigraphs—not to be confused with epiphytes, epigrams, or epitaphs—may be anything written (Greek *graphein*) on or above something else, but the term usually denotes a brief quotation from another author that a writer reprints before the start of her own work. An epiphyte is a plant—such as a climbing vine, orchid, or bromeliad (common in this part of Florida)—that grows on or over another plant. An epigraph can conceal, or reveal, an elusive author's intention; an epiphyte can conceal something with claws, an animal whose "scurry" in search of prey or away from a predator may be said to have an intention (or not) about hunger or self-preservation ("self-saving"). Like A. R. Ammons, Peterson is a poet at home with the natural sciences, though Peterson's disposition favors not the models, graphs, and equations that non-scientists associate with physics and chemistry, but the ineluctably patient on-site noticings of the life sciences: ecology, organism-level biology, and the study of evolution.

The poem gets better, and does more for us, the more we learn about what the poet has noticed. Nocturnal southern flying squirrels (*Glaucomys volans*), native to Peterson's portion of Florida, can be both predator and prey: their claws and the teeth they are constantly sharpening (by chewing wood) makes them easy to hear, though hard to see. The scurry and the claws may be said to have a cause in evolution by natural selection, which works on organisms and parts thereof as traditional calligraphers work on Japanese scrolls, imperfectly but with elegance. The triangular leaves of some epiphytes (bromeliads, in particular) resemble bamboo leaves, which in turn resemble ink brushes; the roots and tendrils along the "surviving oak" resemble the muscles ("meat-ribbons") drawn by Vesalius in his famous illustrated catalog of all the bones, ligaments, muscles, nerves and other tissues in the human body. Both Vesalius and the unnamed "clever but wistful" Japanese painter give Peterson models for a naturalist's close looking.

Yet Peterson has written not just a teasingly intellectual, delightfully involuted observation but a critique of the way we tend to observe. What if the "self-saving conclusion" is not the behavior of whatever critter the poet has heard, but our own wish to find patterns we already know? Peterson never calls nature incomprehensible *tout court*, but his successive sentences and overlapping, sometimes baffling metaphors stress that there is always more for us to explain. If you look at the world the wrong way, you see "much more" of it, but you also make it—erroneously—your own, as if you had added the possessive *'s* to everything (rather than, like a good pluralist, a plain *s*). Even as it explains its observations—hearing the claws in the epiphyte and watching what turn out to be "flying squirrels"—"Epigraph" warns us against overexplaining: there is always "another idea." We should be like those flying squirrels, flitting from branch to branch, merely "clever and wistful" or even evasive, rather than overweeningly confident, as we try to make sense of this world before we "dive in."

Grounded in copious mental note-taking, ready for synthetic, tentative, and counterintuitive claims, "Epigraph" also—like a patient instructor—tells us deftly what we should not do. Peterson repudiates poetry that does not begin from something—no matter how tiny—observed in the external world; he does not want poems with no source outside one person's conscious or unconscious imagination. And, like many Floridians, he does not want to hear one more word about Disneyland or Walt Disney World, theme parks whose corporate, synthetic monoculture displaced, or squashed, a diverse organic environment.

Nor does he want to write about anyone's dreams: dreams, like theme parks, like doctrinaire surrealism, seem "outlandish" in a pejorative sense, literally taking us out of the land and the water, where the much more amazing, and less self-regarding, weirdness of nature and of earlier human accomplishments (e.g., scroll painting) resides. The critic Zach Pickard has shown at great length how the poet Elizabeth Bishop (who lived in Florida too, in the 1940s) repudiated surrealism and dream visions for what Bishop called "the always more successful surrealism of everyday life." "For the surrealist," writes Pickard, "emptying oneself of consciousness summons the unknown; for Bishop," however, artistic discovery came from a patient readiness (which she associated with Charles Darwin) "to observe the conscious world." Peterson sides here with Bishop and with Bishop's Darwin; he might even have had Bishop in mind.

But Peterson does not only refuse—almost jocularly—the antiscientific hubris of surrealists and theme parks: he also pokes a "finger-needle" at the hubris of some popular science. During the 1980s and 1990s, popular writing about biology and evolution featured recurring quarrels between ambitious thinkers from Harvard. The ant expert E. O. Wilson saw a close fit between genes and behavior, and a close fit between the natural sciences and other branches of human knowledge. He touted the discipline of sociobiology (which claimed that genes and natural selection could explain much of human behavior) along with the notion of "consilience," which meant that one unified mode of explanation (presumably mathematical and empirical) would eventually tell us all we wanted to know about everything from photons to philanthropists. Wilson's intellectual opponents Stephen Jay Gould and Richard Lewontin, while also committed to Darwinian evolution, stressed instead the unpredictability of still-evolving organisms and systems, the fact that one set of genes could produce many outcomes, and the truth that (so far) modes of explanation suited to the "plain facts" about one sort of object (photons, say) were not enough to help us explain another. Biology could not be reduced to physics, nor could philately or philology.

Peterson's poem considers these rival positions: he shows us "the interconnection of all things," as if to propose a consilient theory of everything, and a "ladder of illumination," seeing the whole of the coast from the sandbar. (Peterson's line breaks serve his sentences: the former emphasize the latter's qualifications and doubled-up shapes.) Those "self-healing lights" over waves also echo a more famous Florida poem, Wallace Stevens's "The Idea of Order at Key West," in which "the glassy lights . . . in the fishing boats . . . Mastered the night and portioned out the sea," like a single graph that could classify the whole world. Stevens's single idea, his graph of lights, fits a charismatic singer, who imposes her beautiful "idea of order," "fixing emblazoned zones and fiery poles" only temporarily upon the world. And Peterson's Gulf Coast after the hurricane is no fit subject for one big theory, but a mass of amazing, wiggling connections, fit for partial explanations, endless investigations, rebukes to the idea that we can explain everything: there is "plenty around" here, and always "another idea," as the poem itself keeps coming up with more and more sensory oddities, more and more things to see and touch and hear.

By the time the poem reaches the sandbar, Peterson's sentences have sided— wittily, wigglingly—with Lewontin and Gould. Stevens's "Idea of Order" (for a moment), Christian thinkers (for eternity), and proponents of consilience (such as Wilson) treat the world as if it were one poem with one author whose goals or meanings we could know, or as if it were an organism with one body, like one of the bodies sketched by the anatomical pioneer Vesalius, or like one giant tree. But Peterson's world isn't like that: it is more like a tree with other plants growing on it (epiphytes), or a text that includes words written by another author (epigraphs), or flypaper (which can collect many sorts of insects), or an evolving, unpredictable interface between water and land. "The organism is not specified by its genes," Lewontin insisted, "but is a unique outcome of an ontogenetic process that is contingent on the sequence of environments in which it occurs." "Evolution is . . . an historically contingent wandering pathway through the space of possibilities," and it is still taking place. Not only the vagaries of long-term uncertainty but random single events—a hurricane, say—can throw our models into a cocked hat.

That randomness enters Peterson's wobbly, almost jocular tone. The poet Annie Wyman, in a generally admiring review of Peterson's later book *Fragile Acts*, complained about his awkwardness of tone, his overenthusiasm for "snippets of popular science . . . There can be something a little gauche in the brick-a-brackery of Peterson's verse—something a little too wunderkammerisch, a little opportunistic or even tacky." We might indeed call his voice gauche, his enthusiasm for facts unmannerly, unsubtle ("tacky"), or (to use an adjective he might or might not welcome) geeky.

But the geeky enthusiasm, the awkward showing off, in these "plain facts stuck to each other" is part of the point. So is the lack of clear and consistent perspective ("the wrong end of the Bausch and Lombs," which the poet has identified as binoculars, though the company also makes eyeglasses and contact lenses). Peterson's poetry knows what it is about, and it differs from almost all other poetry written by living Americans (especially now that Ammons is no longer with us) in its power to encompass, and to admire, the oddity of facts and patterns of facts from the nonhuman world. Peterson treats these facts neither as symbols for something else human or divine, nor as parts of one big comprehensible pattern, nor as items that must be cordoned off from the meaning-making undertaken by human beings. Instead, they are still changing, still evolving, only partly understood: that is the glory in this view of life, which Peterson relishes as he listens to the streets, watches the flying squirrels, considers the mixed legacies of human civilizations, and swims out—albeit a short distance—away from it all.

RAE ARMANTROUT

Our Nature

The very flatness
of portraits
makes for nostalgia
in the connoisseur.

Here's the latest
little lip of wave
to flatten
and spread thin.

Let's say
it shows our recklessness,

our fast gun,

our self-consciousness
which was really

our infatuation
with our own fame,

our escapes,

the easy way
we'd blend in

with the peasantry,

our loyalty
to our old gang

from among whom
it was our nature

to be singled out

Look at an old picture of yourself—a candid group photo is best, but a posed head shot or even a painting will do. How would you have described yourself back then? Would you describe yourself the same way now? How much do you have in common with the person whose portrait you see? Did you want to stand out? Will you feel proud, special, melancholy, or just resigned when you realize how much you have grown up and changed? Armantrout pursues such questions in her characteristically terse, harsh style. An Armantrout poem can make no claim and pursue no query without trying to undermine its own terms: under the patient pressure of her short lines, key words in this poem, such as "nature" and even "latest," can seem to come apart from their usual meanings, even as we come apart from our previous selves.

Like most of her poems, "Our Nature" invites us to seek ironies and un-cover the dubious axioms under each phrase. It also stands out among those poems for the open pathos of its ending, which addresses the life of an ambitious artist, and perhaps also the afterlife of an art movement, such as the one to which she has belonged. Armantrout started to publish her poetry while living in the San Francisco Bay Area in the early 1970s; there she encountered Carla Harryman, Ron Silliman, Lyn Hejinian, and other language writers. "Our Nature" may also look back at them.

All pictures are "flat" compared to real life, though some revel in their flatness, while others disguise it; what could be flat, in particular, about a portrait, and why would that "flatness" provoke "nostalgia"? A portrait presents one moment in space and time: it is thus "flat" compared to the four-dimensional (in time and space) extent of a life, and looking back over that life might well prompt "nostalgia." But to be "flat" or two-dimensional is also to look unreal. Is all portraiture unrealistic, in words or in visual art? Are all our mental portraits "unrealistic" as well, turning evolving personalities into all too comprehensible objects, as if we could possess the people we knew?

Considered thoroughly enough, do our ideas about people dissolve, as a picture dissolves or loses focus when looked at for long?

The second stanza, like a second take or a second look at the same picture, enacts that dissolution, with help from puns, as when a "little lip" becomes the edge of a wave. Armantrout, who has always lived on the West Coast (in San Diego and in Northern California), once censured another poet for comparing the sea to beads, since "the ocean can resemble a vertical sequence of discrete, solid objects in almost no way imaginable." "Our Nature" seems to assert that we too are less like "discrete, solid objects" than our habits—and other poets' "portraits"—assume. Our impressions of the people we think we know are more like a series of low waves, coming at us and then, usually, falling away. That image of liquid succession ("the latest" impression, and then something later still) gains force and irony from its contrast with the self-contained, solid, "hard" stanza in which it rests.

If the poem ended there, it would be a cryptic rebuke, reminding us with a dry, uneasy authority that people always change. But Armantrout has more to say. "Let's say / it" becomes a hinge on which the poem turns, leaving the self-contained, pronounless quatrains behind. In their stead, we find one extended sentence, broken into one- and two-line bits, about a group of friends or allies who stuck together long enough to share adventures and to establish a "loyalty" later overruled, or contradicted, by the ambitions of its members. At the start Armantrout described everyone; now she speaks primarily of an "us," her generation, or her friends, or her political and artistic allies. The figure in Armantrout's poem, one of the people included in her pronoun "we," wants to show inner consistency as well as moral worth. But she is betrayed by her nature: "our nature," human nature, or the nature of art, which undermine whatever character they construct.

It is the nature of artists and their "gang" to strive for eminence, even at the cost of disconnection, as it is the nature of youthful "gangs" to grow apart. Outlaws of the Old West, quick on the draw, like the guerrilla movements of more recent decades, sometimes prided themselves on how they could "blend in // with the peasantry," escaping the law. Remembering their subterfuges, Armantrout also invokes bands of youth, in schools or in street gangs, whose loyalty to one another cannot last, since it conflicts with their members' desire to get ahead in the adult world.

It is hard to read "Our Nature," which comes from Armantrout's book *Veil* (2001), without thinking about how language writing, with its sometime promise of egoless investigation, of radical antisubjective critique, actually became (for better and worse) a name for a group of talented individuals. Armantrout collaborated with nine other language writers on *The Grand Piano* (2006–2010), "an experiment in collective autobiography" that tells the story of their West Coast scene. She seems, in retrospect, essential to that scene, though she did not publish prolifically in the early years, when she ran the reading series that gave *The Grand Piano* its name. And yet she admits, "I spent most of the 70s wondering whether I was in or out of the new nexus [of the Bay Area avant-garde]. (In that way it was a little bit like junior high.)" She remembers asking at that time, "What was this new poetics that later came to be known as 'language poetry' and was I part of it or not?"

For a writer of Armantrout's skeptical temperament, emerging from a shared movement or moment, the desire to stand out—though perhaps part of "our nature"—must have been especially vexed and vexing. Her poems remain ambivalent about ambition, as her halting manner—the matter of this self-critical poem, with its silenced "fast gun"—might imply. Yet they stay ambivalent about loyalty too, since loyalty can discourage critical thought. Hopes for group belonging, no less than aspirations to singularity, make Armantrout ask herself how she knows what she knows, and what her wishful thinking might conceal. "I do wonder," she asked in *The Grand Piano*, "how much we, 'language poets,' identify with and / or objectify one another."

Writing in the *New Yorker* in 2010, after Armantrout won the Pulitzer Prize, Dan Chiasson claimed that Armantrout "takes the basic premises of Language writing somewhere they were never intended to go: towards . . . a single individual's . . . uniquely broken heart." We may hear in this poem, with its rueful plural ("we," not "I"), anticipatory defenses against such praise. Yet Armantrout's lines in "Our Nature" do not fit just one movement or moment, nor do they confine themselves to one art. How can we all succeed together in an enterprise where individuality and unique achievement is held out as the goal and the prize? And what if that enterprise is not art but life?

Most of us want to be "singled out" or noticed in some way, even if we do not try to write new kinds of poems; most of us also want, or at one time wanted, to stand with our peers, to keep our friends, to stay close. We rarely get both; sometimes we get neither. That broader disappointment informs Armantrout's lines too: they end up with something like a tragic sense of how we grow up. Yet the word "nature," repeated in the penultimate line, should put us on alert, since Armantrout's poems so frequently (as she has put it) "examine claims to naturalness and objectivity carefully to find out what or who is being suppressed." Whose nature is ours? Was it always ours? Who are "we"?

Should we resign ourselves to the alienating consequence of our ambitions, as inevitable as waves on sand, or can we construct some better choice?

Armantrout elsewhere likens her poems' fitful movement to the mythical serpent ouroboros, which ate its own tail. Punning lines from her poem "Falling: I" warn us not to believe the stories we tell ourselves: "To swallow your own tail—// or tale—/ is no longer // an approved / form of transportation." She does not say what we should swallow, nor how we should transport ourselves, instead. Similarly, the ending of "Our Nature," having pointed out "our infatuation," leaves us with no clear place to stand, no more reliable substitute for the fallacies and hypocrisies, the cognitive and emotional mistakes, that Armantrout's melancholy juxtapositions diagnose. Instead, the idea of a person with one nature, capable of sitting for a unique portrait, falls down when we try to make it explain "our nature," to say why we do what we do.

Be true to yourself, be yourself, pursue your own nature: Armantrout's friable phrases cast some suspicion on those all-American instructions, whether or not we can learn to live without them. Her terrific, brief memoir *True* (1997) sets her desire to escape her cliché-ridden blue-collar childhood against her own suspicion about the stories of artists' escapes: "Somehow my life was leading me to the conclusion that received opinion was my enemy," she writes, adding, "I'm afraid, now, that I'm making my own myth." We may not be able to live without myths, but we should not let ourselves get trapped by them. Neither the myth of solidarity forever, the romance of the individual becoming herself at all costs, nor any heroic story of rebels defying old norms and creating great change in the arts survives the careful scrutiny of Armantrout's curt, melancholy, and chastened phrases, which ask instead how we remain, and how we became, the people that we and our friends think we are.

ELIZABETH ALEXANDER

Race

Sometimes I think about Great-Uncle Paul who left Tuskegee,
Alabama to become a forester in Oregon and in so doing
became fundamentally white for the rest of his life, except
when he traveled without his white wife to visit his siblings—
now in New York, now in Harlem, USA—just as pale-skinned,
as straight-haired, as blue-eyed as Paul, and black. Paul never told
     anyone
he was white, he just didn't say that he was black, and who could
     imagine,
an Oregon forester in 1930 as anything other than white?
The siblings in Harlem each morning ensured
no one confused them for anything other than what they were, black.
They were black! Brown-skinned spouses reduced confusion.
Many others have told, and not told, this tale.
When Paul came East alone he was as they were, their brother.

The poet invents heroic moments where the pale black ancestor
     stands up
on behalf of the race. The poet imagines Great-Uncle Paul
in cool, sagey groves counting rings in redwood trunks,
imagines pencil markings in a ledger book, classifications,
imagines a sidelong look from an ivory spouse who is learning
her husband's caesuras. She can see silent spaces
but not what they signify, graphite markings in a forester's code.

Many others have told, and not told, this tale.
The one time Great-Uncle Paul brought his wife to New York
he asked his siblings not to bring their spouses,
and that is where the story ends: ivory siblings who would not

see their brother without their telltale spouses.

What a strange things is "race," and family, stranger still.

Here a poem tells a story, a story about race.

Alexander has written a poem in three parts, with at least three intertwined topics: the first part stands—or could have stood—independently, the second complements and partially reverses the first, and the third completes and corrects the first two. As she concludes this particular "story about race," Alexander opens up larger questions about how we have learned to read any poem, as well as about how we make, and whether we can avoid, common assumptions about race and voice.

She begins unassumingly, with an anecdote whose emotional weight only later becomes clear. Great-Uncle Paul, "who left Tuskegee," decided to pass for white and "became fundamentally white"—if not in his sense of himself, then at least in how white Americans, and perhaps black strangers, treated him. That decision controlled how he treated his brothers and sisters, and it controlled how they chose to treat him: the final words of Alexander's first sentences—in order, "black," "white?" "black," "black!," "confusion," "tale," and "brother"—highlight his choice. Tuskegee is famous for the Tuskegee Institute, founded by Booker T. Washington in 1881. Washington wanted black Americans to excel at mechanical, agricultural, and other practical occupations, striving to avoid direct conflict over civil rights. A black man leaving Tuskegee, Alabama, in order to "become a forester" in 1930, perhaps with a forestry degree, would be in one sense following Washington's vision.

In another sense, of course, Paul was turning his back on Washington's (and almost every other) vision of racial uplift: in Oregon, the "pale-skinned," "straight-haired," "blue-eyed" Paul passed for white, as untold numbers of black Americans have done since the 1600s. Daniel J. Sharfstein's popular history *The Invisible Line* (2011) is one among several recent books to examine the phenomenon of "passing," which has (he writes) provided "occasions for articulating what it meant to be black and what it meant to be white." Whatever it means, it is not just about skin color or verifiable medical fact. Race, Sharfstein explains, "is not just a set of rules. It is also a set of stories that people have told themselves and one another over and over."

The ironies in such stories play off against the apparent artlessness, even the naïveté, in the first part of the poem, where Alexander adopts simplicity as a technique. She uses long lines, most of them broken at a natural pause, as if she were simply transcribing conversation; she repeats words ("siblings . . . siblings"; "confused . . . confusion"), rather than using variation through synonyms; her syntax and punctuation suggest the mild shock and amusement, the softened and habituated rue, of long-familiar history.

Alexander thus becomes a diffident, transparent conduit for just one of the many similar stories known to some readers: "Many others have told, and not told, this tale." Why is it so often told? Of what might Paul's tale, or tales of racial passing in general, furnish a good example? Do black poets have a responsibility to tell certain stories about black people ("heroic" ones, for example), and if they do, can Alexander fulfill it when she writes about Paul? A life of racial passing *might* be celebrated as an example of heroic philosophical inquiry, a demonstration that even such an overwhelmingly present, historically potent thing as race is without metaphysical foundation: the racial migrant, the once-black man living as white, might be a trickster, a double agent, a quester, having seen (like the apostle Paul) a new light, a new life. Or such a life might be an example of selfishness: the black-to-white migrant turns his back on his family, his natal home, and any larger black community.

Clare Kendry, the black-to-white migrant in Nella Larsen's *Passing* (1929), can be understood through either rubric—one reason this novel, nearly forgotten for decades, has acquired such a rich critical afterlife. The letter writer in Langston Hughes's short story "Passing" (1930) can be understood only as selfish: "That's the kind of thing that makes passing hard," he tells his mother, "having to deny your own family when you see them." He continues, "Since I've made up my mind to live in the white world, and have found my place in it (a good place), why think about race any more? I'm glad I don't have to." But of course he does think about it: "If any of my kids are born dark," he continues, "I'll swear they aren't mine. I won't get caught in the mire of color again. Not me. I'm free, Ma, free!"

Most of us would not want to imagine our own family capable of such sentiments, and so Alexander uses her powers of invention to construct a "heroic" story instead. Though living as white in a white state, with an "ivory spouse," Paul's attention to detail, his meticulously and mysteriously coded forestry manuals, are a kind of sub rosa rebellion. He practices a double-voiced writing, with his black or blackened "graphite markings" and "silent spaces" equally telling a story about oppression, independence, and the arbitrariness of social categories for those (black) readers who are able to read them.

African American thinkers have a strong tradition around such coded sto-ries, from W. E. B. Du Bois's records of "double-consciousness" to Henry Louis Gates's model of literary "signifying," from oral performance to intensely writerly art. Alexander's great-Uncle Paul also wrote books, "ledgers," records of trees. As Alexander links him to literary tradition, her poem becomes self-consciously literary too. Words such as "cool," "sagey," and other adjectives come to the fore; nature becomes sublime (redwoods); and the verse paragraph ends by describing itself, as well as Paul's putative work, in slightly highfa-lutin ways: "graphite markings in a forester's code."

This second part of the poem—from "the poet" to "code"—amounts to a gloss on part one, a reinterpretation that the poet herself understands as fic-tion (she uses "invents," and then "imagines," three times in four lines). There is no evidence that Paul saw his job as a coded rebellion against race, and plenty of evidence that Alexander prefers a black art that is identifiably black. Her collection of essays, *The Black Interior* (2004), praises Robert Hayden, who "insisted that, when it came to his writing, he was a poet first and black, second," but it implies that she feels closer to Gwendolyn Brooks, who altered her early, elaborate style in an attempt to get closer to black readers' needs. "It's presumptuous to think that all black artists . . . are part of the same large and bumptious family," Alexander says, "but I'm a weird sister ever-searching for her strange black artist brothers." Being a black artist is like being part of a family: not all black artists are her sisters and brothers, but all her full sisters and brothers (according to this line of thought) must be black.

Yet "Race" does not indict Great-Uncle Paul. Alexander refrains from using the rhetoric of black nationalism, or treason and loyalty; she doesn't even use the words "pass" or "passing." Alexander might not want to give Paul a label he did not choose, or perhaps the label does not quite fit, since he "never told anyone / he was white." Rather, he became "fundamentally white" because he was pale-skinned and blue-eyed, and because in Oregon in 1930 such people were simply assumed to be white (until 1926, Oregon's constitution banned "free Negroes" from settling in the state).

The first part of "Race" "tells a story," and the second provides one way to interpret it, however implausible. The third verse-paragraph gives us another view, one that is neither tragic nor comic, neither condemnatory nor "heroic"; its wry restraint is an achievement. The Harlem brothers and sisters refused, choosing spouse over sibling, the family they made over the family into which they were born. Great-Uncle Paul had already made the same choice. The siblings seem admirable, while Paul may not, but the poet concludes with less judgmental terms: race is "strange," family even "stranger"—indeed, strange in many of the same ways.

Staying calm without sounding cold, rejecting stereotypes, acknowledging each side, Alexander shows how she can see both Paul and his siblings as part of *her* family. From the slightly high-flown, unsustainable language of the second part, Alexander returns to the calm demotic of the first: if "heroic" diction was the wrong way to make a story into a poem, this third part might demonstrate a right way, by drawing respectful conclusions in balanced apothegms (out of seven lines, three are one-line sentences) that do not say more than the story itself can show. And what that story shows is strange enough: consideration of race can cause members of the same family to treat one another almost as "strangers," and a story about race that can do justice to a family such as Alexander's, indeed to any family at all, turns out to be one that can present race *as* a story, that is, as a sequence of decisions and impressions, related by cause and effect, by economics and politics and geography, and by the inner lives of the characters in it. Race is neither biological fact nor dismissible fiction, but an unwieldy set of narratives that Americans live inside.

So the poem ends, with a story of how we read race. It also leaves us with unanswered questions—if not unfinished stories—about how we read poems. Readers of "Race" will likely assume, even if they know nothing else about her, that Elizabeth Alexander is black and identifies herself as black, and has family members who do so too. They will be right; they may have seen her on TV, since she wrote and recited, before a crowd of millions, a poem at President Obama's first inauguration. Yet her poem "Race" offers a gentle caution about what we assume when we read poems. Do all poems "tell a story about race," or just this one? All the time, or (the first word of this poem) just "sometimes"? Do readers—black, white, both, neither—expect that all black poets, or all their poems, should bear marks or stories of race (as Paul tried not to do)? Do readers make the same demand of white—or apparently white—poets and their poems? Does Alexander's last line hint that any poem can be made— if only through "silent spaces" like those in Paul's ledgers—to speak about race? Can black writers evade that demand? Can white—or "white"—writers address it too?

LIZ WALDNER

A / ppeal A / pple A / dam A / dream

It was too hot. I put the fan in the window and me in the bed
And the linen sheet only to cover my ribs.

When I woke, I heard some bird had turned the sky
To water in its probably lavender throat.

I'd dreamed I'd had a hose and walked, watering
A lawn.

Some had come to me for the water I was.
One I never saw went with me watering the lawn.

Next, you sent me a letter; sorry it's been so long
But I'm moving the buttons on the coat I bought you.

A strange shape of cloth like a blue tomato carefully pinned
In a gray tissue came with it. What is it?

I unpinned pins until I saw the wrapper bore pictures of pins
In the places they'd been.

When I put them back in, I woke. When I woke I wore that coat
You knew how to fit instead of my skin.

Friend, come button me in.

"A / ppeal" comes at the start of Waldner's 2004 collection *Dark Would (the
missing person*) for good reason: it's a consistent, sparkling—and, for some

readers, sexy—introduction to a poet whose verbal surfaces can seem volatile, even fissile. Waldner's couplets about a couple, herself and her "you," pursue the visceral quests and the satisfactions, the mysteries and the delights, of summertime naps, of childish waterplay, and of specifically sexual experience: it works hard to have adult fun. The more-than-sonnet-sized poem to a lover or friend or friend-turned-lover pursues a contemporary interest in queer symbolism, in phallic substitutes, in dreams of female masculinity, in role-switching. It's full of modern paraphernalia too: an electric fan, and a modern garden hose (invented, along with lawnmowers, in the 1870s).

It's also a poem whose concrete nouns make more sense, do more work, if we take them on a detour through up-to-date (or at least through vintage 1980s) theories about sex, gender, and the unconscious. Though friends and lovers, women and men, have shared and mended clothes and fabrics for millennia, the "strange shape of cloth," and the adjusted buttons, suggest modern do-it-yourself traditions that celebrate noncommercial fabrication, from William Morris's handmade objects to 1960s commune life (Waldner has said that she wrote, or at least began, this poem in the 1980s). The poem takes up much older traditions too: it is, among other things, a poem about the story of Adam and Eve, about Adam's rib and our first parents' first clothes, about a fall into experience that—for Waldner as for William Blake—can leave us happier than we were before.

If you are already familiar with the second, third, and fourth chapters of Genesis, and with *Paradise Lost*, you can skip this paragraph. If not, you'll find parts of a story that all literate—and many illiterate—speakers of English once knew. In Genesis 2, after creating the world, with Adam in it, God tells Adam to tend his garden. Then—saying, "It is not good that man should be alone"—God sends Adam "into a deep sleep," extracts "one of his ribs," and creates Eve, "and they were both naked, the man and his wife, and they were not ashamed" (Genesis 2:25). In *Paradise Lost* (8:460–467) Adam dreams that God is creating Eve for him even while God does so: John Keats could thus propose, 150 years later, that "the imagination is like Adam's dream: he awoke and found it truth." The serpent, later called Satan, entices Eve to eat fruit from the tree of the knowledge of good and evil, and Adam eats too: "And the eyes of them both were opened, and they knew they were naked, and they sewed fig leaves together, and made themselves aprons" (Genesis 3:7). Aware of themselves as adults, as sinners, Adam and Eve must leave the Garden and discover physical labor, painful childbirth, and death.

One Christian tradition has it that the Fall was a good thing after all (a "fortunate fall," *felix culpa*) because it allowed human beings to be redeemed by Christ. A later antinomian, or blasphemous, or sex-positive, or humanist, tradition (the adjective you prefer says a lot about your ideas), embraced by William Blake and by science fiction and fantasy writers such as Philip Pullman and Raphael Carter, makes the Fall a good thing in itself, later corrupted by grown-ups or priests or authorities who tell us we should be ashamed. (Milton's own Adam and Eve experience sexual pleasure before the fall, as do his gender-fluid angels: see *Paradise Lost* I:423–425.)

Waldner joins Blake, Pullman, and C. D. Wright in rewriting the story of Eden to favor sexual pleasure and human solidarity, deemphasizing authority and sin. And like Carter (see Carter's novel *The Fortunate Fall*), she does so in a gender-fluid way: the poet's dreamed hose is, as Megan Bayles has written, a "queer phallus," hard and limp, difficult and easy, masculinized and feminized at once, a wet phallic substitute that might require "A/dam" or "a dam" (also an old spelling for "dame"). (Waldner's other poems—in this book and in her earlier volume *Homing Devices*—make explicit reference to same-sex love.) Waldner rewrites the story more drastically, and in her own richly echoic, playful language, than a simple list of its queer-positive aspects suggests. This possibly female Adam wakes to her partner after she meets the serpent-like hose, in a scrambled set of events, puns, and invitations that tie into knots the chronology of the original tale.

The opening could not be more casual. Why not sleep naked (nothing but linen "to cover my ribs") on a hot day? Why not, in a fertile summer, wake to the watery warbling of "some bird"? Adam's original task involved naming all animals: this "A/dam" has not learned the right names for them yet. Birds that coo and warble could be pigeons, or more compact, tree-bound songbirds (Waldner, in bed, does not see them: hence "probably"). The lines manifest a five-beat, dactylic norm—they set us up to expect ten to fifteen syllables, dominated by rhythms like "PRObably," "LAVender," and "FAN in the."

"A lawn"—just two syllables, one whole line—thus feels like an interruption: it brings us up short. The Freudian entendre should be clear: a phallic hose brings control over urination, fertility, and reproduction. Full bladders can generate such dreams as well. "Primal man," Freud himself speculated, "had the habit, when he came in contact with fire, of satisfying an infantile desire . . . by putting it out in a stream of urine"; primal woman had no such luck. But Waldner dreams otherwise: in her dream it is not clear who owns fertility, who controls wetness, who gets engulfed by "the water I was." Such confusion makes the poet's dream-self not grotesque, not abject, but attractive to unseen companions (like T. S. Eliot's "third who always walks beside me" in "The Waste Land," like a secret admirer, like the Holy Ghost).

It also puts into slippery, euphonious, even palindromic practice (saw-was, some-come) the reversals imagined by feminist psychoanalysts and philosophers such as Elizabeth Grosz, who seeks models and metaphors for "an active and explicitly sexual female desire." In our all too familiar Freudian and pre-Freudian axioms, Grosz continues, "Woman is man minus the phallus, and thus without the benefit of its consequences: she lacks the capacity to initiate, to activate." Must woman adopt her own hose? Should it work like a man's? Can it be more flexible? Can it replace the phallus with something fluid, open, or not penetrative?

Grosz and many other theorists argue that male authority, male control over sexuality and society, involves control over who gets to speak, even over how and what words can mean. That problem, bound up in the very word "authority," is what Jacques Derrida called phallogocentrism, the phallus as the assumed or imagined center of the divine or human Word. To that problem Waldner's dream-vision proposes at least a few symbols for a solution. She imagines herself at once owning "the phallus" and making it into something equally powerful but capaciously fluid, wearable, in some ways feminine—not just the apple or the tomato, but its recuperated, sheltering "peel." Phallic and fabric, penetrating and enclosing, devices merge even before the poet wakes up from her dream. That dream moves from a lawn and a hose to a letter, a fabric (a textile, as in "text") that she can alter, opening its "strange shape of cloth" to reveal something even more mysterious, something whose color looks like nothing in nature. Ever seen a blue tomato?

Adam's dream revealed Eve: the dream in "A/dam" gets part of its "A/ppeal" from the way it rewrites, or peels, or repeals, the story of the "A/pple" so that what its Adam and its Eve discover is something new, an artificial fruit that might resolve the riddles of sexual difference, bringing a long-awaiting "letter" that looks like an invitation to lie under a sheet together, to open up—as well as to share—remade clothes. Other parts of *Dark Would* use more clearly sexual language, often in gender-scrambling contexts. Waldner has called herself, in correspondence, "not gender neutral but gender fertile." A poem called "Os/Tensorium" ("os" meaning "bone") reads, in part, "can't finger slide/my little into your dark." The beautiful quatrain "Wood (First Daughter)" praises "your hipbone, your shoulderbone, soon," asks "to do it with you," and concludes, "I would be content that we might procreate like trees."

It may seem awkward to view "A/ppeal," which holds almost no abstract nouns, through abstract ideas about sex and gender roles—and it is almost always awkward to speak at length, without scientific cover, about bodies and fluids and sex. But that is the kind of speech the poem provokes: it yields, among other things, remakes of Eden, in which the new fruit and the new woven garment revoke the shame, and the authority, of the old. The punctured, penetrated fruit is like a pincushion, no worse for being pierced. The coat, altered by hand and by both parties, stands not for shame but for individuality (clothes are altered to fit the wearer). This awakening into sexual self-consciousness, into pairs and suggestive invitations, into self-conscious and sexual roles, is not a matter of falling into set scripts (masculine and feminine, for example) but a form of freedom: we sleep to wake refreshed, and soon we may not sleep alone.

"An explanation," Waldner has also written, "is/only a likeness/only like another Thing." To follow the likeness and the resemblances among the literal things (hoses, pincushions, buttons) in this inviting poem is to construct a fortunate fall, a future of what Blake himself called "the lineaments of gratified desire." Waldner's "A/dam" wakes to a second self that—if she, or he, or they, will come to bed, will "come button me in"—inaugurates a time of better desires, a summer that is not "too hot" but rather enwraps its couple in their best coat. You, reader, could be part of such a couple too: so Waldner's closure suggests.

This story of Adam and Eve is less a story of breaks and departures and falls—even fortunate falls—than it is a set of echoes, almost like a child's nonsense speech, repeating monosyllables, seeking rhymes, playing on the simplest of words (and finding there double entendres), as in "button" and "pin." Its sound play can—I hope it does—delight readers who do not care to interpret it at all. Few poets come up with such unpredictable arrangements for so many near-rhymes, so many of what linguists call minimal pairs ("some" and "come," but also "long" and "lawn"), so many densely packed similar sounds—though the arrangements also, as I have tried to show, do intellectual work. And it goes on, ends up playful rather than ponderous, because its theoretical heavy lifting gets done by such small, domesticated words. Read the poem once, and it might be baffling; twice, and its sexual invitations, along with its Edenic story and its scrambled gender roles, grow clear; three or four times, and you might simply enjoy the density with which certain sounds, rhymes and near rhymes, race and thread through repeated small words—"saw"-"saw," "came"-"come," "woke"-"woke"; "pins," "been," "skin," "button," "in."

KARI EDWARDS

>> > >> > >> PLEASE FORWARD & > >>

no realLy. Call me a front lawn stiff. > >>call me excelling† "or
a") as some may in mAIlboxes . . . the real porcupine > >> "What
if I'm knitting legs of tape. boxes Of jinks? a public service-. true
blUe tubers?> It's > the too ma[n]y >>the >.a a>a other prime
time Subject†:†: it's whose "A Mystery": it's whosss a collabOration, who's the merely > >> whose Fro†:†:"))))" > >> > who will
step over the accom[p]animent>> who will stop the> \- be a ma-
niac land- fill >> whose broad band could be the :: > >> even the
most fruitful -----ot really. Call me the path alla mimICkin / a >
the >too many>two slashes > three marks and a later >

you / ve got a > >>high pitched? infinitely regressice? rigressive,
()&resistan{cP{e+*&future progressive& Standard Superintendent? coming in loud an##%!`~~ ~ at > >> as a > in time for > full
> prolific, reproductive magic mutiplied by ,-o===oo –take
warNing > >> †:†Fwd: Fast Fwd: yellow †.† Leg of cal-me-a-sort-
a-[of] (pick-me-up)-dropme off --- part of the Original Message
Follows--- > >> forwarded) > >> no choice >> two slashes > >>
>>> "full tiMe anxiety" " > >> I've heard > >> behind the Sub-
ject†:† IN the Subject I found them As > _____ > lovers quarrel
> Subject{S}†:†: t> >>professional as a parrot > >>>>> I found
them† stilts in the erratic >. . . . >>; following me the Subject. / \\\
Calling me Subject.//> _----// Calling me ishmael?

turn(ed} to feel___ it was surely a / the more / of- the big—o-
switcherroo. sOmeone please told me hold me&> in their >>
Personality switch to, (*&^^%"Which is why they're, we,
someone—R, only a thouGht, (*) (_(that big mistake. a It were,

to follow, has followed, in its but who knew and nevermind{ed}
the > >> -†300000000+ times slot?† in one time of > many >>
since—Goodbye, > >> > >> christ. did All occult ME meorabilia
an the place, > >> the everlast- ing The leftbehind ?:? has made
me.† again thisTSt > >> To†:† hotmail.com@@@ moloch.com >
grond brushing - me. alwayS you do))(& I'm yellow. I'm knitting
curi- ous millionS@.com, >edge) > twittering something "" ___

kari edwards appears to have been the first significant poet in English to identify in public as transgender. (Because she sometimes critiqued the very idea
of binary gender, sympathetic critics refer to edwards both as she / her / hers
and sie / hir / hirs; here I use she / her, the pronouns chosen by those who knew
her best.) When edwards signed books she would normally draw a horizontal
line through her own name and then write, beside it, "NO GENDER"; *No
Gender: kari edwards* became the title for a volume of posthumous responses
to her work.

She was also dyslexic; her differences and dissonances from prose sense and
from verse conventions reflect her own experience of a language that would
never become transparent, that could not point to unquestioned, consistent
truths, that would not fit her life unless she wrestled with it and rearranged it
radically first—maybe not even then. The poet—who assembled hard-to-
classify prose and verse texts throughout her career—began writing at length
and for publication in 1997 while taking classes at the Naropa Institute in Colorado, where she had hoped to study with Allen Ginsberg, though he died before they could work together. Instead, edwards found allies and models in the
so-called New Narrative writers, such as Kevin Killian, Bruce Boone, and
the late Kathy Acker, Bay Area creators (almost all of them LGBTQ) whose
prose works tore up, inverted, turned into collage, or otherwise altered almost
beyond recognition the characters, plots, settings, and descriptive language of
the realist novel. Her verse and prose texts (like Acker's fiction) can also be read
as attacks on identity, and on categories, semantics, and consecutive or logical
sense as such, with gender as one category among them.

Those texts make language itself not only an alphanumeric or aural phenomenon, but a set of mysterious—or flirtatious, or frustratingly or joyfully
bizarre—physical objects on a page. "PLEASE FORWARD" belongs among
edwards's most aggressive experiments in visual text: we cannot even reproduce

the full extent of its oddities in this book, since—like every other poem in verse or prose in edwards's *Iduna* (2003)—it appears on a page with a backdrop of oversize grayscale letters, words and nonwords ("also alse ar ko ta to oino"), with running headers or footers composed of other words, some of them printed upside down ("area under pact ages test fire limo comb").

We can, however, reproduce the most distinctive visual aspect of this particular page: its resemblance to the error messages, misformatted texts, and other non-user-friendly output of a computer from the early 2000s. The writer's own sense of self, her own experience, fits standard English—so the jarring format implies—no better and no worse than standard English rules of reading, writing, and comprehension fit this cluttered, counterintuitive computer script. "I think now that computers can do so much with text and images that not to use these tools in the creation of a piece of art seems like not using all the tools available," edwards said in 2003. Used in this way, those tools make us slow down, make the text obviously harder to read, less like conventional prose or poetry: they make it into something that most of us have to work extra hard to understand. That strange and disturbing work, on the verge of nonsense, also reflects the kind of work that severe dyslexics such as edwards herself had to do in order to write and read anything at all. Such work, "PLEASE FORWARD" implies, is more than worth it; it may prove essential for the survival of our unstable, incomprehensible selves.

The opening phrases of "PLEASE FORWARD" ask what it would mean to put such a self "forward": would it be like sending an email, or mailing a letter, or sending someone something spiky and disturbing, like finding a live porcupine in the mail? Would it be a "real lie"? Would that means of representing an identity seem too aggressive, "too ma[n]y," a typographical neologism that means "may" and "many" and "manly"? What if identity, speech, voice, expression are not just "A Mystery" but "a collabororation" (both "collaboration" and "oration"), a speech from multiple voices, without one source?

Perhaps edwards's way of being in the world is like the alternate paths electronic signals can take through cords and machines. Perhaps the language of her self is to the language of secure cisgender (non-trans) selves as the language of a garbled email, too many times forwarded or "Fast Forwarded," is to clear newspaper prose. Only "part of the Original Message Follows." But to portray oneself as a garbled email, as a result of malfunctioning systems (the system of gender, the system of electronic messaging) is to portray oneself as a passive victim—not a portrayal that edwards can accept. Nor will she speak as a "professional parrot," reproducing the discourse she receives. She would rather see herself as someone who is moving forward, someone who is greater than (">") what she had been ("a greater than a"), a survivor from the ship-wreck of convention, a stiltwalker, an Ishmael, someone who will no longer make the "big mistake" of following a conventional order, whether in religion or in typography.

If that social order is the order of the Abrahamic religions, the Christianity whose symbol is † or the Islam whose crescent symbols resemble (and ?, whose one God is like a "Standard Superintendent" or an omnipresent sysadmin, well, then, the poet would rather be a devil, writing from a hot place (Hotmail), from "ground" level, from "moloch.com." For her the biblical command to be heterosexual, to "be fruitful and multiply" (Genesis 9:7), has to be mis-read, misspelled ("mutiplied"). She will be multiple, rather than muted and plied, not one subject but "Subject{S}": her name is "Leg" or legion, like the devils in Luke 8:29–30, like millionS@.com (which could not be a real domain name), weaving or knitting texts together, "curious," "twittering something."

This mode of language use is at once an experiment, an urgent expression of an unfixed experience, and a kind of occult practice, a magic whose symbols edwards borrows from computers to make her own. That practice (like other modern occult practices) might be sexual too. It might involve orgasm ("the big o"), erotic intimacy ("someone please told me hold me"), or even multiple *o*'s ("300000000"). The climactic phrases imagine a specifically trans kind of intimacy, in which to be held is to be seen rightly after a "switcheroo." The disruptive joy that edwards wants to imagine looks more like a magical summoning than like anything that fits into any familiar bodily "slot."

"My own gender doesn't make sense," edwards told the poet Ellen Redbird, "so I can see that other things don't make sense." Asked if her work was "a critique of systems," edwards responded, "Yes, and I so see those systems— family, capitalism, the corporal restraints of gender and time—as violence against the subject." Every aspect of "PLEASE FORWARD" joins that critique. As Trace Peterson has argued, edwards worked "to deviate from normative syntax and grammar as a gesture toward what is outside signification, what is liberated not just from grammar but somehow also from gender."

Most trans women and trans men, of course, do not view our own lives as parts of a radical struggle to overturn all binary symbolic orders. Many of us feel, more simply, like people whose sense of ourselves, sometimes or all the time, does not match the gender we were assigned at birth. The still emerging set of self-identified trans poets—identified and collected, apparently for the first time, in Peterson and TC Tolbert's 2013 anthology *Troubling the Line*—includes writers such as Joy Ladin, who remain at home with clearer lyric modes. But much of the action in *Troubling the Line* comes closer to edwards: many of its poets try to reflect trans experience by overturning or undermining the idea that we must see ourselves accurately within the discrete categories (gender among them) that our upbringing or our society gives.

"Poetry and, as far as I am concerned, writing in general needs to cut the linear language in half, create a new syntax," edwards promised in 2001. That cutting, that creation, involves attacks not only on pronouns ("he," "she") but also on typography, on nouns and verbs, and on semantics. It requires a poetry that goes to (if not over) the edge of comprehensible writing and speech. It asks us to treat the English language as strange, as something we need to rewrite, as something more like computer code: the younger trans poet Cody-Rose Clevidence, who identifies as neither male nor female, has used computer languages and typography for a book-length treatment of that kind.

Some of it looks, of course, like nonsense. But on the other side of that nonsense—these writings promise—comes a better sense. "Future progressive"—a halting and uncertain promise—refers both to a possibly better future, and to the grammatical tense and mood of "will be happening," "will be reading," for something that has not happened yet. "PLEASE FORWARD" thus looks forward to a future with poets such as Clevidence, as it anticipates collaborative, evolving, participatory media such as Twitter, founded in 2006—not by coincidence a medium more democratic, more obviously open to more writers (including trans activists, but also noxious harassers) than older media such as printed books. "PLEASE FORWARD" thus speaks, even more than other early electronic poems composed by trained programmers, to the work of self-making and self-revising that so many of us now undertake on the Web. (Many of those other electronic poems, such as Brian Kim Stefans's and Nick Montfort's, cannot be adequately reproduced on a printed page; you can find Montfort's at http://nickm.com/poems.)

Beyond its computer-speak, and more than almost any other text by almost any other author of those years, "PLEASE FORWARD" embodies an aspiration to make everything new, to oppose old systems, to be "radical" and "resistant," while showing how strange and difficult and halting and fragmentary and frustrating such resistance can seem for people who want to practice—or even to understand—it fully. It is one thing to advocate the undermining of familiar categories and symbols and ways of reading and hierarchies; it is another to really, or "realLy," undertake it. This writer undertook it; this text—like her other texts—shows how exhilarating, and how tough, it could be.

AGHA SHAHID ALI

Tonight

Pale hands I loved beside the Shalimar
  —Lawrence Hope

Where are you now? Who lies beneath your spell tonight?
Whom else from rapture's road will you expel tonight?

Those "Fabrics of Cashmere—" "to make Me beautiful—"
"Trinket"—to gem—"Me to adorn—How tell"—tonight?

I beg for haven: Prisons, let open your gates—
A refugee from Belief seeks a cell tonight.

God's vintage loneliness has turned to vinegar—
All the archangels—their wings frozen—fell tonight.

Lord, cried out the idols, *Don't let us be broken;*
Only we can convert the infidel tonight.

Mughal ceilings, let your mirrored convexities
multiply me at once under your spell tonight.

He's freed some fire from ice in pity for Heaven.
He's left open—for God—the doors of Hell tonight.

In the heart's veined temple, all statues have been smashed.
No priest in saffron's left to toll its knell tonight.

God, limit these punishments, there's still Judgment Day—
I'm a mere sinner, I'm no infidel tonight.

Executioners near the woman at the window.
Damn you, Elijah, I'll bless Jezebel tonight.

The hunt is over, and I hear the Call to Prayer
fade into that of the wounded gazelle tonight.

My rivals for your love—you've invited them all?
This is mere insult, this is no farewell tonight.

And I, Shahid, only am escaped to tell thee—
God sobs in my arms. Call me Ishmael tonight.

There are no instant classics, but Agha Shahid Ali's ghazal "Tonight" comes close: appearing in four versions between 1996 and 2003, this version, which is the poem's last and longest incarnation, gave its title to Ali's posthumously published *Call Me Ishmael Tonight: A Book of Ghazals*. By that time ghazals were frequent and easy to recognize in American poetry, thanks in large part to Ali's poems, essays, and lectures, which sometimes used "Tonight" as a test case. It is a poem about lost love and loneliness, about Islamic and Western religious inheritance, and—in characteristically evasive ghazal style—about Ali's life between cultures, languages, and continents, first within and then away from his native Kashmir. It is an exemplary ghazal meant to show Americans how and why we should think about the form. And it is a poem given to blasphemous rebellion against religious dogma—a rebellion that itself belongs to the international, multilingual, thousand-year-old tradition of the ghazal.

What is a ghazal? The term (pronounced "guzzle") originated in Arabic, where it denoted a topic: early Arabic ghazals were lyric poems about erotic love, and like other Arabic poems they used monorhyme (all the lines end on the same sound). Poets of medieval Persia codified the form by employing couplets of uniform meter and length, with the same word or phrase, the *radif*, at the end of each couplet. A rhyme—the *qafia*—also appeared in each couplet, twice in the first and once, just before the *radif*, in all others. All the couplets had to be complete and independent in sense and syntax, almost as if they were separate poems. The final couplet also contained a name (usually the poet's own name or his pen name, the *takhallus*). Like other kinds of classical Persian poetry, ghazals had stock phrases and comparisons, shared freely among writers; sometimes the poets cited earlier ghazals directly, or quoted Islamic sacred texts. The form encompassed secular, erotic longing and (as in the work of the poet Rumi) mysticism, in which the beloved is God. Persian ghazal form spread throughout and beyond the Islamic world, from Indonesia to Sweden. Mirza Ghalib (1797–1869) and the revolutionary leftist Faiz Ahmed Faiz (1911–1984) were masters of the modern Urdu form; contemporary Urdu singers, especially Begum Akhtar (1914–1974), gained broad fame for recordings of classic ghazals.

Faiz and Begum were Ali's family friends. Ali grew up in Kashmir, the violently disputed territory (once an independent state) between India and Pakistan; he and his family lived in the part of Kashmir controlled since 1947 by India. Most Kashmiris are Muslim, which is one source of friction with India's large Hindu majority. The poet grew up bilingual in English and Urdu, attending English-language Catholic schools. He came to the United States in 1975 as a graduate student in literature, then built his reputation as a poet during the 1980s and 1990s, often writing about his homeland. Peaceful for much of Ali's childhood, Kashmir turned bloody in 1989, when the Indian army put down an armed rebellion. The continuing violence informed Ali's 1997 collection *The Country Without a Post Office,* where an earlier, shorter version of "Tonight" appeared.

Ali devoted his last years to the ghazal. He assembled an anthology (*Ravishing DisUnities: Real Ghazals in English* [2000]) and wrote an enormous variety of ghazals himself. The real ghazal, Ali liked to insist, derives its unity from its formal properties of length, rhyme, refrain, and the rest; as for a subject, it ought to be hard to pin down. "Tonight" may seem hard to pin down—the poet Kazim Ali called it an ars poetica of the ghazal, and its independent, colliding fragments serve that purpose. So do its impieties, its religious allusions, and its overlapping figures of national exile, homelessness, religious disillusionment, and hopeless love, each of which comes to stand for all the rest in a kind of playfully flighty lament, a sorrowfully circuitous game. However playful, the ghazal does end up with something to say: about Ali's own place among and between religions, nations, and languages; about lost love; and (as the poet Raza Ali Hasan suggests) about Kashmir.

The games begin with the epigraph, the first line of "Kashmiri Song," by Laurence Hope (pseudonym of Adela Nicolson), whose melodramatic quatrains each conclude with the word "farewell." Set to music in 1902,

"Kashmiri Song" became wildly popular in Britain and in the United States. The epigraph amounts to both tribute and insult, thanking the English writer for her interest and then promising to show what a real Kashmiri song (a real ghazal) by a real Kashmiri can do. "You" are the beloved, but also the listener: are "you" Kashmiri? American? Whoever you are, the poet must now live without whatever pleasure or shelter "you" once gave him. ("You," never "he" or "she"; in the traditional Urdu ghazal the beloved is always grammatically male, while Persian has no grammatical gender.) "You" might also be Kashmir itself, the land that had alienated the émigré author, though other Kashmiris (some of them religious militants) now hear its "spell." If "you" are a human beloved, then Ali must be lonely, but if "you" are God, or religion, then Ali must consider the loss of religious belief.

Older poems suffuse "Tonight," and not only ghazals. The second couplet quotes a writer who lived (like Ali) in Amherst, Massachusetts. "Where Thou art—that—is Home / Cashmere—or Calvary—the same," Emily Dickinson wrote, in a poem that Ali quotes elsewhere. The soul, she suggests, can never be without a country, or else it is always already without a country, always in a condition of internal exile. The Dickinson poem that Ali quotes here (not the same one) begins, "I am ashamed—I hide—/ What right have I—to be a Bride." "Fabrics of Cashmere" are glamorous, too rich for her. But she will marry nonetheless, "no more ashamed" (her poem concludes) of her "dowerless" lack of material wealth.

Ali cannot manage such confidence. Instead he seeks "haven": "prisons" should open their gates, not to let prisoners out but to take him in. (Both Ghalib and Faiz were really imprisoned.) To love and be loved in return, to dwell within and be a citizen of a nation, and to find oneself at home within a set of religious beliefs are for Ali attractive forms of confinement, but forms impossible for him.

What if that impression were shared in Heaven? What if all organized worship (Islam, Christianity, Hinduism, and all others) came to seem unbelievable or pointless, not only to human beings but to God? Such a God would be lonely, and sour too: he might turn against his archangels, freezing them out. So Ali's fourth couplet suggests. It is also the first couplet without a personal pronoun, and the first to diagnose not Ali's own malaise but a wider problem in "Western" or "Eastern" culture, or in both. What problem? Perhaps the modern loss of religious faith; perhaps, instead, the tendency of religions to harden into brittle and mutually incompatible doctrines. Hindu shrines often have statues of heroes and deities (Shiva, Vishnu, and many more); by contrast, Islam, like Judaism, insists that any pictures of God are "idols," like the idols that Abraham destroys in the Koran and in the Jewish Talmud. Ali's mischievous fifth couplet, in which the idols talk back, reminds us that anti-iconic faiths rely on the very pictures they attack: without them iconoclasts would have no way to prove their commitment. (During the 1990s the Kashmiri conflict destroyed many temples and shrines, most famously the Charar-e-Sharif shrine to a Sufi saint.)

If the fifth couplet rules out religion, what remains? Art, and tradition pursued for the sake of tradition: "mirrored convexities," as in the architecture and poetry of the Muslim Mughals, whose empire included diverse Kashmir. To be under the "spell" of these mirrors is to love and be loved by art. But it is also to enter a mirror, to become double or multiple, as Shahid Ali, a Kashmiri American living within and yet outside Islamic traditions, working in English while thinking of Urdu, was double (or triple, or more) throughout his career. To be ornate, multiple, and hard to pin down—in Ali, as in his friend James Merrill—is almost always a good thing, and the ghazal itself, with its disconnected couplets, renders its poet multiple too. But to be split up in that way, within this poem, is also to live in disorienting freedom: "He's left open—for God—the doors of Hell tonight." We may pity ourselves because we have lost our belief, or pity a God whose heaven and hell seem interchangeable, since neither exists. (We may also, if we are angry enough at religious fundamentalists, want to consign their false God to hell.)

At this point we are deep into the religious dimension of the ghazal heritage, in which love and heartbreak stand for doubt and faith. But Ali will not remain trapped in that dimension, nor in any dimension, of his rotating allegory. The eighth couplet reverses the vehicle and the tenor, making the smashed idols stand for erotic abandonment. The lover's heart is an idolatrous temple itself, wrecked and empty when the beloved proves unworthy; a temple looks empty whenever it lacks a "priest," here a Hindu or else a Buddhist cleric with saffron robes—Ali does not confine his impiety to the Abrahamic faiths.

And yet it is those faiths he contravenes. Elijah, a prophet in the Hebrew Bible (the Old Testament) and in the Koran, denounced Israel's wicked King Ahab and his wife, the promiscuous, pagan Jezebel. To damn Elijah and bless Jezebel is to defy God. Yet it is also to join traditions of antinomian worship, as in some strains of Sufi Islam, in which what sounds like blasphemy (e.g.,

Rumi's praise for wine) expresses intense faith, "drunk" on God): another one of the doubles and disunities that comprise the poem.

Urdu ghazals have meters based on quantity (syllable length) rather than stress (as in English): Ali insisted that "real ghazals" use constant line length, and indeed all the lines in "Tonight" have twelve syllables. They do not, however, have constant meter: the first couplet is perfectly iambic, the third a mouthful of triplets (*pri*-sons, let *o*-pen your *gates*), the sixth with its "mirrored convexities" ametrical. Moreover, Ali rhymes stressed with unstressed syllables: "spell" and "expel" with "infidel" and "Ishmael." Both the rhymes and the syllabics encourage us to ignore the stress accent of English, to emphasize syllables in other ways: the voice may rise in pitch, for example, as it finds the *qafia* and the *radif*. And in doing so it may suggest, at least to many American ears, the variability in pitch and pace that distinguishes the fluent English of South Asia. Ali is thus (to quote the critic Aamir Mufti) "writing Urdu poetry in English," learning from his other mother tongue not just in imagery but in sound.

Gazelles are traditional images for an evasive beloved, and here they also make a bilingual pun, "gazelle" and "ghazal." Is the poet the wounded, dying, captured animal? Or is he the pursuing lover, the hunter (as in so many Petrarchan sonnets) who may never catch his prey? The hunt ends at dusk, with the last of the Islamic calls to prayer. Dusk is also when the poet's "rivals" assemble, called together by the beloved, who thereby reveals herself as cruel or unchaste. Such an assembly is also traditional in the Persian and Urdu ghazal. If the beloved is God, the rivals might be other, orthodox forms of worship; if the beloved is the land of Kashmir, the rivals might be the members of militant factions, terrorists, or national armies whose "love" for their homelands has kept Ali away. And now the poem—already a maze of mirrored self-description—describes its own end: "This is mere insult, this is no farewell tonight." Yet "farewell" is indeed a farewell.

Exclaiming, "And I, Shahid, only am escaped to tell thee," the poet declares himself a refugee again: he has "escaped," as an agnostic or an apostate, from the catastrophe of belief, but also "escaped" from the country that he still calls home. The penultimate line adapts Job 1:15–19. "Shahid," as another of Ali's ghazals reminds us, means "'The Beloved' in Persian, 'witness' in Arabic." Witnessing the clash of orthodoxies (Christian, Muslim, Jewish, Hindu, and so on) throughout history, God Himself might fret. But of course an omniscient, omnipotent, and incorporeal God would not "sob": the last line is blasphemy in the context of Job (whose God is always right), and also a sidelong reference to the Christian pietà. Will Ali cast himself as Jesus? As Mary? No, his pen name will be Ishmael, the son whom Abraham exiles in Genesis (Genesis 21:14) but the chosen one in the Koran (sura 37, "As-Saffat [Those Who Set the Ranks"], also the sura in which Abraham rejects idols). Ali affiliates himself decisively with Islamic tradition, though not with belief. He also performs a virtuosic formal move, since the last line—while it must contain both a final *qafia* and a name—does not require that the name *be* the *qafia*.

And here again Ali is tricky, doubly allusive, as well as international: "Call me Ishmael" is of course the first sentence of that other story about exile, blasphemy, and international travel, *Moby-Dick*. To reread "Tonight" is to catch more such references, perhaps political, certainly religious, literary, polyglot, intercontinental. Some references will emerge for any careful reader, but others might emerge only for those who know more about Ali's own home region, or for readers familiar with the Urdu, Persian, Turkish, and Arabic verse whose intricate resources Ali began to open up for Americans through this tormented yet playful paragon of ghazal form.

D. A. POWELL

[when he comes he is neither sun nor shade: a china doll]

a second song of John the Divine, as at the end

when he comes he is neither sun nor shade: a china doll
a perfect orb.   when he comes he speaks upon the sea

when he speaks his voice is an island to rest upon.   he sings
[he sings like france joli: *come to me, and I will comfort you.*   when he comes]

when he comes I receive him in my apartment: messy, yes
but he blinds himself for my sake   [no, he would trip, wouldn't he?]

he blinds *me* for *his* sake.   yes, this actually happens
so that the world with its coins with its poodles does not startle

I am not special: have lied stolen fought.   have been unkind
when I await him in the dark I'm not without lascivious thoughts

and yet he comes to me in dreams: "I would not let you marry"
he says: "for I did love you so and kept you for my own"

his exhalation is a little sour.   his clothes a bit dingy
he is not golden and robed in light and he smells a bit

but he comes.   and the furnace grows dim.   the devil and the neighbors
and traffic along market street: all go silent.   the disease

and all he has given me he takes back.   laying his sturdy bones
on top of me: a cloak an ache a thief in the night.   he comes

"when he comes" is not the most complicated nor the deepest poem by D. A. Powell, but it may be the best introduction to his powers. It's also the final poem in his third book, *Cocktails*, whose title denotes after-dinner drinks (hence sociability and dates); the drugs that keep HIV-positive people alive; and stories (tales) about sex with men (people with cocks). *Cocktails* concludes with a sheaf of poems reimagining Jesus Christ and His apostles from sex-positive, antinomian, or scandalous perspectives, "writing the spiritual self through sexuality," as Powell has said. This messianic "he," the prophetic lover who may or may not be the risen Christ, comes (arrives) and comes (ejaculates), and then does it again (the Second Coming): he is, in a way, the spirit of desire itself, both satisfied and unsatisfied, a vision of the miraculous fulfillment that some of us seek in bodily (for example, sexual) experience and some of us get from imagination alone. The poem belongs to a tradition of fulfilled visions (compare Lucille Clifton's) whose supernatural visitors bring the poet verbal power. Here that visit becomes both comic and sexy. The power to imagine "messy" gay sex, even to seek it out, is the same as the power to create this poem, and all those powers push back against—render bearable—the difficulties of this life, not least the terrors and the inconveniences, at the end of the 1990s, of living with HIV.

When is there "neither sun nor shade"? At night, of course: this prophet, whose words calm ocean waters, comes at night (we might say he makes booty calls). He is substantial, in the flesh (not just a ghost or a "shade") and his words—or Powell's words about him—have an almost mantra-like repetition. "He comes," "he comes," "he sings," "he sings," "he comes." The phrase "he comes" recurs five times, suggesting unusual sexual prowess: the repetition itself suggests the repetitions of disco beats. France Joli's signature song "Come to Me" (1979), recorded in three versions on the eponymous album, is a sugary, torchy, propulsive disco track, with harp, trumpet, bells, congas, and Syndrums. Its promise of full acceptance and sheltering love fits the sexy redeemer Powell envisions, the Christ figure who belongs at the end of a book that Powell has called "my *Paradiso*." A Christ who sang like France Joli would sing alto or high tenor—he would be sexy, but also sexually ambiguous: he might be a disco queen. The "china doll" and "perfect orb" whose "voice is an island" suggests the perfection of the world to come, while his "orb" could be a disco ball.

But this Christ does not come to a disco: he comes to a home. Sexually voracious divinities have blinded their human hosts since the story of Danaë, but if the spirit of another, better world and its great sex were to visit Powell at his place in San Francisco (near "market street," perhaps in the historically gay Castro neighborhood), that spirit might have to "blind himself" so that Powell's lousy housekeeping would not distract him. This savior, instead, would help the poet cut himself temporarily off from the secular "world with its coins and poodles," joining the tradition of love poets who find the whole world in one another's arms, and who find Christian metaphors for it too (in John Donne's "The Good Morrow," for instance).

Powell's confession "I am not special" both echoes the collective admissions in Jewish and Christian prayers (Daniel 9:5, for example, and Psalm 106) and suggests the self-abasement of a sexual bottom. Whether or not we are bottoms (and, of course, whether or not we are gay men), we are "not without lascivious thoughts": here as throughout *Cocktails* Powell preaches salvation as open to all who come. That salvation means sexual satisfaction as well as spiritual and physical health: this savior will take upon himself the sins and the diseases of the world, and also undo the association between gay sex and illness that long predates (and that during the 1980s impeded official response to) HIV. Even without that association, without sexually transmitted diseases of any sort, without homophobia, sex (between men, between women, between men and women) might still involve an element of abjection, of humiliation, of *nostalgie de la boue*. That's part of the sex appeal this Christ figure possesses, just as in Powell's other poems (for example, his sonnet "dogs and boys can treat you like trash. and dogs do love trash," earlier in *Cocktails*). This poem even conjectures as to *why* our sexual longings should so often fasten on people that seem "a bit dingy," "a little sour." Because sexual fulfillment (for Powell) is a redemptive act, it ought to be open to everybody, and at its best it shows that it is for everybody, by violating some boundary or taboo that keeps people apart.

Those arguments are hardly Powell's alone. The literary theorist and science fiction writer Samuel R. Delany, in *Times Square Red, Times Square Blue* (1999), defended the anonymous hookups and casual gay sex that he found in 1970s and 1980s New York as a way that gay men could experience firsthand a liberation from social barriers. Delany imagined these sexual encounters—sometimes the basis for lasting friendships—as a kind of secular communion: "in a democratic city," Delany wrote, reasonably enough, "it is imperative that we speak to strangers, live next to them, and learn how to relate to them on many levels, including the sexual."

Powell's Christ figure who comes in the night differs from the anonymous partners of Delany's utopias not least because this figure may not really come:

he may be a never-present messianic fantasy, or a kind of wet dream. Powell's vision of paradisal messy sex at home with a mysterious visitor may be just that, a vision, the sort of thing that happens only in porn. It may also be a vision that has as much to do with infection as with ecstasy: the dream-savior who "takes back" "the disease" may be the figure who brought "the disease" in the first place, either the partner who infected Powell, or the God who decreed that there should be HIV.

Powell has named as sources for the religious scenes in *Cocktails* not only the Song of Solomon but "the odes that are attributed to Simon of Cyrene," early Christian poems that appear to express a homoerotic attraction to Christ as Savior: in Willis Barnstone's translation from one ode, "The Son is the cup / and he who was milked is the Father / and he who milked him is the Holy Ghost." Another source here is the Book of Revelation, or Apocalypse, attributed to John of Patmos or John the Divine. Powell's first "song of John the Divine" concerns the "holy prepuce," the foreskin left after Jesus's circumcision ("strange flower in my hands porphyry shell clipped wool"); this "second song" gives us the whole man, at once intensely embodied and "perfect," as if from another world. Almost every part of the poem that does not echo disco hits draws on biblical elements or on New Testament language: in 2 Peter, which denounces "the lusts of the flesh," "the day of the Lord will come as a thief in the night" (2 Peter 2:18, 3:10). John of Patmos beholds "one like unto the Son of man," who says "I am he that liveth, and was dead" (Revelation 1:13, 18).

That sense of resurrection—of something brought back and made whole *again*—animates Powell's unusually long, end-stopped lines. Powell said that he developed the characteristic, and even longer, lines of his first book, *Tea* (1998), by "turning the paper sideways." The poems in *Tea* were longer than they were tall, and like this one, they usually doubled titles as first lines. This very long line lets Powell get readers used to multiple midline stops; it therefore lets him sound excited, or nervous, when he manages a line with no internal stops at all ("when I await him in the dark I'm not without lascivious thoughts," for example). The long and meterless line also lets Powell place repeated phrases in varying positions within a line: "he comes" comes one syllable after the start of a line (three times), two syllables after ("and yet he comes"), and twice at line end, as in the fulfillment of a promise: as it was in the beginning, so it shall be when he, the sexy stranger, the savior, comes again.

Like much of *Cocktails*, this lyric explores one way of being Christian. But it is also a way to fight back against other ways of being Christian, ways that deny the humanity, or the legitimacy, of gay desires. Powell grew up in California's Central Valley, and before that in Tennessee, with very religious family members: he has said that his aunt wrote a "thousand-page treatise . . . on the Revelation of John." A savior who says (echoing Mark 12:25) "I would not let you marry, for I did love you so and kept you for my own" seems more plausible than a deity who permits sex only in heterosexual marriage. Powell's Messiah—unlike religious conservatives' mistaken versions of Christ—will let us live in our bodies, in our "bones": he will make even our sour breath, our remembered faults, seem acceptable and sweet. And then he will come.

ANGIE ESTES

Sans Serif

It's the opposite of
Baroque, so I want
none of it—clean
and spare, like Cassius
it has that lean
and hungry look, Mercury's
clipped heels, the rag
of the body without
breath. A chorus of
alleluias, on the other
hand, is not only opulent
but copious, a cornucopia
of opinion which concludes
that opera is work, the *haute* gold
opus of the soprano, which does not
oppress yet presses against
her chest like the green glass *flacon*
de l'opéra held between
her breasts to keep the cognac
warm. Her notes hop
from hope to hope
like the layers of *l'opéra*
cake: Steeped in coffee syrup,
buttercream and *ganache* rising
in between, and a thin
chocolate coat slipped
over all, its name is scrolled
in glaze across the top—*l'opéra*

finished with a lick
of gold leaf.

Estes's splendid, almost decadent poem amounts to a brief manifesto in favor
of the style she calls Baroque, associated with France and with French culture; with ornaments of all kinds, in all the arts; with operatic grandeur, and
with a flourish, though also with the ornately miniature (less Baroque, in art
historical terms, than rococo); with excess, but also with brevity; and with
dessert. Defending unmoralized pleasure against utility, Estes describes, and
defends, her own verse style. In doing so she ends up defending the feminine—and attacking sexism among tastemakers—as well.

Estes begins by telling us what she rejects. Sans serif font first appeared in
1816 but became popular a century ago, starting with Akzidenz Grotesk (1898),
when modernists—in type design as in poetry and architecture—tried to
sweep away the prettier clutter of earlier eras. It is that ornament, and its he-
donistic or permissive spirit, that Estes defends, at first through counterattack.
Spare tastes and ascetic dispositions have long associations with moral goodness, from the medieval poem "Cleanness" to Boy Scout bromides about clean
living; Estes turns those associations around, connecting austerity with Cassius from Shakespeare's *Julius Caesar*, "lean / and hungry" for power.

Spareness suggests efficiency, clean lines, and high velocity. Estes attacks
those associations too: to cut the serifs from the "feet" of a letterform would
be to clip the diminutive wings from the heels of Mercury, god of messengers
and speed. Serifs and ornaments on a letterform also resemble the breath that
comes up from a living body (visible, as steam, on a cold day). To lack ornament is to lose one's breath, to be dead; to embrace it is to place oneself amid
a lot of breath, amid collective song, as at a Baroque oratorio—say, Handel's
Messiah with its "Hallelujah" chorus. Start by opposing ornament, Estes's
string of comparisons implies, and you will end by opposing life itself.

Support ornament, on the other hand, and you will be rewarded by a cascade of beautiful sound effects, the euphonies and consonances that Estes
builds into her lines, where almost every syllable makes half a rhyme with
almost every other. Consider the overlapping *n*'s, *o*'s, and *p*'s in "not only opulent / but copious," a phrase that describes itself and describes what will follow:
"a cornucopia / of opinion which concludes / that opera is work." The poem has
held rhymes all along—"clean" and "lean," for instance—but only when it
moves from riposte to encomium does it display the full density of sonic pat-

tern that Estes can produce: she has said that the poem arose from her fascination with "the sound of 'op,'" along with a cake she ate in Paris and a flacon that she found in a shop in Virginia.

Heinrich Wölfflin's influential book *Renaissance and Baroque* (1888) disparaged the very Baroque that it helped to define. "Baroque," Wölfflin wrote, originally meant "absurd," bizarre, or irregular, and "carried a suggestion of repugnance and abnormality." Seventeenth-century High Baroque art was grand, unbalanced, even histrionic; eighteenth-century or late Baroque could be decorative, confectionery-like, self-conscious about illusion, a style also called rococo. "Baroque forms are full, opulent, and curled over in round and generous whorls," Wölfflin generalized, with "irregular distribution of ornament" and "overlapping forms and motifs," akin to Estes's overlapping rhymes. Baroque ornament implies excess and duplication, including the sonic near duplications of rhyme; it instantiates the medieval rhetoricians' *copia*, meaning more of a good thing. The same Latin term yields English "copious" and "copy" (which echoes "coffee"), as well as "cornucopia," the plentiful horn. To her own sonic richness Estes adds the bilingual puns that her work often favors: "opera" means work in Latin, the plural of *opus*, akin to French *oeuvre*.

Such work is always also play. To the present-day art critic Stephen Calloway, Baroque represents the "extravagant and whimsical" throughout Western history; "more than just color and opulence and . . . decoration," it is "an attitude towards life and art" that Calloway discovers in Art Deco, in the films of Tim Burton, and in the fashion designs of Elsa Schiaparelli, to whom Estes devotes another poem.

Artists and art historians also associate the Baroque with color, as against Renaissance emphasis on line: the art historian Charles A. Riley II writes that the practice of "dividing painters into two groups" this way goes back to Wölfflin. In such divisions, the valorized, "classical" terms—line, structure, balance, permanence, black and white, logic—usually seem male, while their "baroque" opposites—color, texture, curves, mutability, emotion—belong to women. (Edward Johnston developed the sans serif font of the London Tube after a manager requested "something 'straightforward and manly.'") Where some modernists contrast real (masculine) work on structure against mere (feminine) surface frivolity, Estes is keen to point out that ornament and "finish" are hard work too. The soprano's song is a work of art, worthy of honor, and so is the ganache; so is the small flask, the *flacon de l'opéra*, between her breasts; so are the making of cognac, and type design with its picas and serifs, and the fashioning of a décolletage.

So is poetry; so is Estes's poetry, which she presents as a form of profound decoration, its texture as rich as coloratura song. Structure is texture here; the ornaments and the chromatic parts become the main event—without them we have no line, no key, no poem. And rather than claiming heroic, manly independence for one singer, one aspect, or even one work, the poem presents a kind of collaboration, a heavily worked surface that requires all its parts.

Estes's defense of women's work, of collaboration, and of Baroque style, in poetry and in life, finds a logical terminus in its defense of the sweet at the end of a meal. Desserts are "decorative arts, like jewelry making or fine cabinetry," writes the food historian Michael Krondl. "A gorgeous dessert also has something of a virtuoso musical performance, perfectly crafted but also impermanent and fleeting." For the great pâtissiers, he continues, "confectionary was as much a branch of the decorative arts as it was of cuisine." We admire the artistry on the surface of a cake, even as we dig in. "Finished" (completed) "with a lick" (a flourish, or a serif), the cake is also "finished" (completely consumed) with a diner's last "lick" (morsel, bite). Opera cake emerged in the mid-nineteenth century, when French *salons de thé* created rectangular pastries for "just one customer at a time." These customers were usually women, newly free to roam the city and spend money without the approval of men; still today, as the patissier Pierre Hermé tells Krondl, "patisserie carries values that are decidedly feminine."

Estes's poem carries those values as well, not least in its canny arrangements of pronouns. Lean and spare, sans serif fits the word "it," used three times in the first sentence (and echoed by "it" in "opposite"); Baroque ornament and cooperative luxury, on the other hand, fit the word "her," as pronoun and possessive adjective, used three times in the middle of the poem. "He," "him" and "his" do not occur at all. As for colors, none turn up until the singer, whose sound is gold, whose flask is green, whose cake is chocolate, gold, and buttercream. A defense of the Baroque becomes not only a defense of women's work, of the female, but a defense of the feminine, of everything disparaged or dismissed as girly, pointless, frivolous, weak.

In such things Estes finds a source of strength. The aesthetic appears, for Estes, at its best not in ambitious structure and heroic projects but in small things, single lines, single pages or "leaves," bits of music or parts of letterforms that go beyond what our mere survival requires. Likewise dessert, writes Krondl, exists apart from "basic human needs"; in that respect it is like opera, like cognac, like rhyme. And here Krondl, and Estes, recall *King Lear*: "O reason not the need! . . . Allow not nature more than nature needs, / Man's life is cheap as beast's." There is something of that spirit, if not that world-altering passion, in Estes's protest against all austere regimens: we have to understand her poetry generally (which often defends the effete, the ornamental) not as a defense of existing privilege but as a claim that privilege, ornament, and aesthetic experience more generally deserve to be widely shared. (Estes's other poems make clear that her defenses of rich living, of some elite tastes, do not represent her own, apparently Appalachian, background.)

To advocate the Baroque or the rococo against the sans serif, to defend opera cake and opera glasses, is to defend decoration (in any art) as valuable, meaningful work, the sort of work that—in the home, far from kings—has been the underappreciated work of women since the bourgeois household came to be; it is (in Julia Serano's phrase) to "empower femininity," as well as to defend the taste and effort of individual women. And an ode to ornament and decoration, an implicit defense of women's work and women's tastes and temperaments, Estes's poem also becomes an homage to interdependence: to the collaboration that creates any art, the "cornucopia" of workers that come together at the opera, for example, or to serve dessert in a restaurant; to the particular art forms, such as Handel's *Messiah*, that require many people to play and sing in time; to the collaboration between writer and reader involved in the making of any poem; and even to the collaboration of sorts between Estes's uneven, persistently enjambed, and hence syntactically interdependent lines, whose grammar and wealth of near rhymes require us to take them three or five or twenty-nine at a time. Her lines have no wish to go naked, to stand alone. Instead they clothe one another with shared sounds as they describe what she likes, what her poems are like, what she gives us permission to like: first the "chorus" as "cornucopia," and then the "hop / from hope to hope."

W. S. MERWIN

To the Wires Overhead

This is the year
when the swallows did not come back

you have not noticed

now all spring
the evening messages
are no longer passing through
the feet of swallows
lined up in a row
holding you
under the high
strung sparks of their voices

with the notes of that
music changing
as once more they would go
sailing out and once more
singly or in pairs or
several together
across the long light they would
skim low over the gardens
and down the steep pastures
and over the river
and would come back to their places
to go on telling
what was there while it was there

you do not hear
what is missing

Much of W. S. Merwin's poetry laments the damage that human beings have done to the nonhuman world; much of the rest looks back at the past, his own and other people's, and wonders nostalgically at our distance from it. This poem accomplishes both tasks, sadly and—until the abrupt conclusion—smoothly, in a way that typifies Merwin's mature style, with a sharp pair of twists at the end. It responds, grimly if gently, to our changing environment, our changing climate, to what scientists and activists have taught us to call the Anthropocene, in which birds, fish, and other animals have their migrations disrupted, and many of them go extinct. Yet it also enters a tradition much older than climate science, and older than English, in which poets use their verse to seek a tranquil, sustainable attitude toward the fact that we all die.

All the poems in Merwin's 2005 volume *Present Company* address something or someone ("To the Face in the Mirror," "To Impatience," "To My Teeth"): they fit, if they do not parody, the literary theorist Jonathan Culler's notion that lyric poems essentially or primordially address entities that will not or cannot reply (God, the dead, lost loves, or, in this case, wires). Merwin's poetic lines, conduits of imaginative "power," compete with the literal electrical energy, the transmission of power, in the cables "overhead." Merwin speaks; the wires "do not hear." You might think that Merwin addressed industrial civilization, wire-building civilization, though in fact he may be talking past it. You might think that Merwin imagined he could talk to the wires, or thought that the wires could answer him, or expected us to regret that they could not. In another kind of poem, the poet might indeed be troubled by the fact that his addressee—his lost lover, his dead friend, a star—cannot answer.

Here, though, the wires trouble Merwin not because they won't respond but because they are present, and swallows are not: the means of secular human communication, the version of secular, practical, electrical power and power generation, that the wires represent have driven away the cyclical, nonhuman, organic kinds of communication, and the kinds of life, that the poet prefers. Once cables and swallows coexisted; now only bare wires loom "overhead," like the denuded branches represented as "bare ruined choirs" in Shakespeare's Sonnet 73. Instead of the birds and their variously combined paths, "singly or in pairs or / several together," we have only human-made parallel lines, the lines of the wires and the lines of a poem.

Those lines would be recognizable as Merwin's to anyone who had read almost any of Merwin's thirty-odd books. Since the mid-1960s the poet has eschewed not only conventional meter but most punctuation: his verse depends on cadence and on sense to tell us where the syntactic divisions should go. The resulting tones are softer, sadder, sometimes more ambiguous or polysemous (that is, they carry more meanings) than normal punctuation would permit. Merwin's style encourages us to treat any line end that *could* be the end of a phrase or a sentence as if it *were* the end of a phrase or a sentence, so that (for example) "Once more they would go," and "over the gardens," and "over the river," and "go on telling," each attain a plangent finality. "Messages / are no longer passing through" could be a sentence in itself, evoking the gospel song ("This world is not my home / I'm just passing through"), but the wires are also "no longer passing through / the feet of swallows" who used to stand on them.

"To the Wires Overhead" belongs to an American tradition in which absent birds and silent seasons mark a wrongheaded civilization: as the scholar and poet Angela Sorby has shown, such poems in the late 1800s (notably Henry Wadsworth Longfellow's "The Birds of Killingworth") helped to turn public opinion against the fashion for plumed hats, and hence saved some actual species of birds from extinction. But Merwin does not expect to make the kind of practical difference that Longfellow made: indeed, he seems to have given up on the kind of practicalities implied by telephone or telegraph "wires," by timely, topical communication. The absence of swallows comes to Merwin as a kind of news (one can imagine an article in a local newspaper about it), but Merwin's poem does with that news what the critic Jahan Ramazani says that poetry tries to do with news, folding it into an "inwardly recurring ritual," so that its "present-mindedness is tethered to the deep or mythical past."

Many older lyric poems contrast the seasonal cycle—death in winter and rebirth in spring—with the one-way trajectories of human lives. And some of those older lyric poems focused on swallows: Gustavo Adolfo Bécquer's often translated "Volverán las oscuras golondrinas" ("The dark swallows will return") insists that the swallows will come back each year, but the poet's love, once gone, will never return (Robert Lowell's loose translation concludes "Don't fool yourself, you'll not be loved like that"). Becquer's may be the most famous Spanish poem of the nineteenth century, and Merwin would surely know it; he began his career as a translator, lived in Spain and Mallorca, and has translated hundreds of poems, many of them from Spanish. Abandoned by the once-reliable swallows, Merwin is like the lover abandoned by Bécquer: the music and magic are gone. Merwin must also have in mind John Keats's "To Autumn," which includes glimpses of human industry (cider making, harvested "stubble plains") that does not harm its raw materials, and which concludes as "gathering swallows twitter in the skies." Keats's swallows, like Becquer's, will come back. In Merwin, however, the birds disappear, abandoning in particular the "steep pastures"—symbols of human stewardship—from which pastoral poetry got its name.

Other poets lament the fragility or death of a wild nature, an ecosystem that once worked without us. That is not Merwin's brief here. Migratory swallows (introduced to the United States from Europe at the end of the nineteenth century) normally thrive among human settlements, as they once thrived in this now stark locale. The horizontal power lines and the vertical "feet of swallows" once made a beautiful grid, one that each summer extended itself into a kind of net, traced by the swallows as they "would / skim low over the gardens" before departing for the fall. These graceful migrations (Merwin gave the title *Migration* to his 2007 new-and-selected poems) imitated the travels of human beings, who like to bring one another news. But now the news, the "notes," the "telling" are all gone: this evening is like the last evening on earth.

As much as it relies on the ghosts of absent punctuation marks, Merwin's mature style depends at least as often on repeated, common words—here, "telling," "places," "messages," even "feet"; to reread the poem is to gather them up and watch their many potential meanings unfold. The "evening messages" that the absence of swallows bring stand in elegiac contrast to the songs of the swallows themselves, but also to the songs of earlier poets, who could rely on the birds to return, who knew "their places" each year. Their recurrence, their "telling," like the "telling" of tribal songs, of Homeric epic, implied a continuing order in the human as well as the nonhuman lifeworld. But no more; we are left with the wires, the otherwise empty sky,

Merwin developed his sad, smooth, effortful style in the 1960s as he tried to write poems appropriate to other international catastrophes—the clear-cutting of tropical forests, for example, and the war in Vietnam; in his most famous book, *The Lice* (1967), a poem called "The Asians Dying" begins, "When the forests have been destroyed their darkness remains." Merwin's twenty-first-century poetry—calmer, usually, than *The Lice*—adapts that style to the slow-motion tragedy of the Anthropocene, visible in temperate North America as well as in East Asia or Hawai'i (where Merwin lives). And—unlike *The Lice*—"To the Wires Overhead" does not exactly ask us to do anything. The ending says that the wires do not hear Merwin, but also that we, "you," the reader, do not hear the swallows (they are "what is missing"). It says too that "you," the reader, do not hear Merwin, do not hear anybody or anything: if we had heard them, if we could hear them, we—meaning all of Western civilization—would have made different choices some time ago.

Merwin thus enacts in a suburban or urban space the realization that writers such as Roy Scranton bring back from expeditions to the clear-cut tropics or, in Scranton's case, the melting Arctic. "We live today in a world in which we've been struck low, perhaps lower than ever before," Scranton concludes; "we find ourselves reduced to something less than human, lacking even the dumb instinct for survival we attribute to plants. . . . On a geological time scale, we're just another rock." We can try to do something about it, if we like, but we must also learn to live with the sense in which, at this point in our lives, in the life of humanity, nothing can be done. Our voices, too, will sooner or later go "missing"; no one will "go on telling / what was there."

What could have been a jeremiad, or a simple lament about the end of life, thus becomes both (in part) and neither (as a whole): the poem challenges us (as did the last stanza of James Merrill's "Self-Portrait in Tyvek™ Windbreaker") to supply "what is missing" if we can, to respond as we will, to face the fact of the swallows' nonreturn. In the same few words it challenges us to face the fact that at some point we and our language and our music and our culture will go away too; those outside it may not notice when it has gone. Merwin's halting style—"the notes of that / music changing"—replaces the older assurance of older forms, the promise of immortality in other poetry, almost as silence replaces the swallows' song this year. We may try "to go on telling," but "you do not hear"; at some point, perhaps soon, you too will be gone.

BERNADETTE MAYER

On Sleep

I have a book full of beds but I'm not scared
Now I won't write the poem about sleeplessness since
I can't sleep again even with Dash who sleeps so well
& I won't write about dreaming that sleep is 1 / 3rd Egg St.
Or about dreaming I finally got some sleep, I won't write:
Sleep, I can't come tonight
Or, I can't get to first base with sleep, oh restlessness
Or, Oh elusive sleep where art thou gone thou fuck
Sleep is you oh hops tea youngly and safely hopping about
          so healthily
Sleep is an illusion in the beginning of sleep
Why do I want you to be a certain way, sleep
& why am I so afraid you'll never come back
Especially since this weekend was so fucking hot
Too hot to make love to sleep, too hot to feel air in lungs
You could only feel the air like cold's envelope
          surrounding the body like sleep
Sleep is the lion in the bed who scares me by coming close
But I know how to act, I never get killed
Sleep is the stealing of beds inside and outside
And the simple finding of them
Sleep is my favorite thing to do, Sophia said. What was yours?
Sleep is the train my father saw in the sea during the tornado
We're in the last car, it's a spacious sleeping & dining car
Sleep is a lot like the $21.50 taxi ride I took to my dentist
          in my dreams
I steal the beds inside of sleep again & see the buildings
     & jewels that sometimes begin sleep
I can't sleep, I can't sleep with you

I do not know how to write commercially though some commercial
    writers who are quite successful also cannot sleep I'll bet
    sleep means something, look it up in Skeats Etymological
    Dictionary. Let me tell you what I'm worried about, my
    unbent block of wood under rails, my slipping sinking
    gliding dormant soul of myself, I am worried about these
    things (and then I will get back to the subject of rigid
    sleep with unbent pots of teas, potent mixtures that make
    you sleep perhaps if you are lucky): I am worried that
    the New College of California will never pay me the
    thousand dollars they owe me for my Walt Whitman
    lectures, that therefore I won't be able to go back to the
    dentist (or that they will pay me and I will be able to go
    to the dentist), that I won't have enough money to get
    through the summer, that I won't be able to proofread
    two books and edit two books by a week from Monday,
    that in order to do that I'll have to deny myself sleep
    or even the attempt to sleep, that Dash won't love me
    because it's hot in New York and my front tooth is
    crooked, that I might die even sooner than my parents
    did cause I spent most of my life troubling my heart
    about them, not to even speak of inheriting their physical
    falsities, that I am a complete idiot, that I am lacking in
    courage, that my fears and hatreds of dentists and school
    principals and doctors will ultimately do me in, that I will
    become a bitter person, that I am so unrealistic as to be
    surprised about what happens in nuclear power plants
    and NYC public schools, plus something I can't say here
    about love.
I dream I am in a museum with Dash. He leads me though a small
    space to an ice cave. At first I'm scared & have to listen
    to the voice of god saying, "Lead with your backpack."
    Then the space opens up. We go to see the paintings of

somebody named Johnson through fancy panelled halls
& stairs.

Another thing I worry about is all my writing that is unfinished and
how there is so little time for it and how there might
never be & how who cares? like, what's so special about
that?

I dream there is a broken plant in my bed. A (named with names I
can't say here) character is sitting at the foot of the bed
laughing at me because I cannot move properly and I
have broken the plant myself. Then a lion hand-puppet
comes floating unattached through the room and I notice
it's pouring out.

I know how to attend to the moment of the text and all this writing
about oneself, this is not to the point. I worry about that.
Maybe if you went to Harvard it's o.k. Besides not going
to Harvard I worry about the other mistakes I've made in
my life, I won't trouble you with a list.

It was easy enough for Gertrude Stein, she has some cash. I guess we
have to think of ourselves as being like Catulluses these
days. We might live longer than he did but we won't
write much more cause we have to spend so much time
earning a living. & then we can't really expect to have
our works like his lost for a thousand years & then found
again because there might not be any more world by
then, at least not here

I worry about why the masses sort of love disasters

I worry that my own heart and the hearts of others beat too fast all the
time these days, though sometimes on the street or in the
subways you see somebody skipping about lithely and
you know then you are replaceable

I thought of a new capitalist method of falling asleep: you say to
yourself: I have the ownership of sleep, sleep is mine.
This is called the proprietary or entrepreneurial or

landlord method. The first time I tried this I fell asleep
right away, almost magically, and woke again soon with
a start, my heart pounding, having dreamt that my
blankets were made of darts

You can also think of sleep as being "with" the moon, that sometimes
works. Or you can try the 20th century t.v.-ish marriage
method and say to sleep: "Sleep, compromise." Or, a
variation on that, cross-cultural: "Sleep, my comrade,
compromise."

Another method of falling asleep is the negative or Aristotelian mode.
You say to yourself: though the water in my apartment is
always rusty and roily, nevertheless I am still entitled as a
human being to sleep. You don't even need an apartment
to sleep, much less one on the Lower East Side of NYC
where sleeping conditions are so bad

After all if they want us all to move to the suburbs or to the country
where it's much quieter and cooler, there's plenty of
other nuclear power plants there we could live near so
we could still worry homeopathically, which concept in
medicine is based on the notion of the hair of the dog
that bit you, as you know

When you wake up in the middle of the night and that or the number
of warheads on each missile worries you, always write
down your thoughts about sleep. In the morning you
might find that they are dreamlike enough to reassure
you that you got more sleep than you thought

This is a work in progress. I invite you to contribute to it. A railroad
tie is called a sleeper, that's why we sometimes sleep like
logs

A word of warning: Vodka is not a cure for radiation or sleeplessness.
As far as I can tell it only wakes you up and its glow is
not conducive to the most artless lambency necessary
for a really famous night's sleep in a world where the

reclining reviewing of the day's and night's positions is
perhaps more welcomed. But this is a question of good
luck too, and now good evening.

Mayer's longer and longer lines might make her seem the friendliest of
poets—but they might also strike you as rambling or repetitive if you are used
to reading obviously well-crafted, conventionally or traditionally organized
poems. Mayer's writings, in all stages of her unusual career, take place in conscious opposition to the idea of the clearly bounded, well-constructed, freestanding poem—though "conscious" may be the wrong word for a poet who
has claimed that our waking hours may not be "any different from our non-
waking state." Her interest in sleep and dreams, in sources for involuntary
inspiration, take part in her larger ongoing search for open-ended and spontaneous ways to make art.

Mayer began making verbal art works in downtown New York in the 1960s
and 1970s; her early writings, like her famous workshops at the Poetry Project
at St. Mark's Church in the Bowery, emphasized procedure and innovation
over any entirely personal expression. Yet she did so in a scene that also had
room for the self-expression of hippies, performance-oriented writers, and
proto-punk-rock provocateurs, many of whom might have taken to heart
Mayer's famous advice (from "Experiments"): "Work your ass off to change
the language & don't ever get famous." Mayer's later work—often in
collaboration—continues to pursue goals associated with St. Mark's, and with
the so-called second generation New York School: it has an aesthetic of intimacy, of intentional disorganization, attacking the boundaries between the
conscious and the unconscious, between the sayable and the unsayable, between "prose" and "poetry," between deliberate and improvised creation. A
poem in *Scarlet Tanager* (2005) begins: "Recently I've been writing down in
prose,/whatever is floating around in my mind & then/turning the prose into
a poem." And Mayer continues: "I recorded a dream that if I did this I
could/reach everybody to write poetry."

That is a dream of equality, as well as a dream of liberation, of utopia, found
in ways that thwart self-conscious, consecutive, critical thought. Mayer's book
Utopia (1984) begins with a poem to sleep: "in sleep each night/each of
you/one of us is/brilliant." Her attempt to bring sleep into poetry, to cross
its border, is also an attempt at radical democracy. Not only do her poems

disarm and disable our critical apparatus, our "adult" attempts to decide what works and to connect all the relevant dots, but they also invite us into a dream state, or a state a bit like babyhood, where we live in the moment and take the experience as it comes.

Yet "On Sleep," for all its length, describes an invitation the poet cannot quite accept. It is also—for all its innovation, for all its post-1960s attitude— quite traditional: poets since Petrarch and Philip Sidney have found occasions for poetry in bedtime loneliness or insomnia. Until the end of the poem Mayer does not herself attain the sleep and dreams she seeks. Instead she is stuck with the waking world, its practical demands, its bad politics, and its money economy. "On Sleep" consists of free associations, riffs, and memories on the idea of sleep, but it also tracks whatever else occupies her mind as she tries and—for a while—fails to find the state the title names. It begins with the rhetorical figure called paralipsis (for another example in this book, see Albert Goldbarth), saying you won't do something and thereby doing it: she has, in fact, written "the poem about sleeplessness," and she has written down her dream of "Egg St."

Poetic notions about the power of sleep go back a long way—to the Book of Genesis and to Adam's dream (also important to Liz Waldner). Many of them figure sleep and dreams as creative: without them we would be unable to conceive of anything new. "Sleep is common, public, a vulnerability we all share," writes Siobhan Phillips, "even as sleep also brackets the sleeper in the most impenetrable of privacies." Sleep is your own: you are the boss of sleep. Yet sleep can also be something we share, not only in the sense in which people "sleeping together" may do more than sleep (Mayer is "sleeping together" with Dash, whose nickname connotes connection) but also because sleep is something we have in common; it is something we all know we need.

When you can't sleep, what else to do but think about sleep? Mayer will even tell sex jokes about sleep: she can't sleep with sleep, as it were—she can't even "get to first base with" it. Tea made from hops is an herbal sleep aid. Sophia is apparently a child, which makes "Sleep is my favorite thing to do" cute rather than sad. But Mayer's real daughter Sophia was born in the late 1970s (she figures in Mayer's great 1982 long poem *Midwinter Day*). Perhaps she uttered this sentence, perhaps Mayer started to write the poem, years ago. In any case, Mayer aspires to the ingenuousness of a child's inquiry. For a child, sleep is free. But for adults, sleep can feel costly (it might cost $21.50 per unit of time); it means not doing other, worldly things. By placing her worries about money, in their prosaic detail, right into the longest "line" or segment of the poem, Mayer finds another way to break down the wall between poem and nonpoem, so that whatever enters the poet's life (even her finances) should find its way into her art.

By the time of "On Sleep" Mayer had become an authority to poets who disliked the idea of authority, a model for poets who wanted to break all molds. Her process of composition, with its "under-punctuated, slippery syntax and run on sentence structure," its "underspecified pronouns" (as Gillian White has put it) presents a conscious example of unbounded spontaneity, showing others "how to attend to the moment of the text." Can it still do so after she has been practicing it for a few decades? Any writer who has evolved a recognizable style might worry about such things, and it is no wonder that for Mayer—who values organic spontaneity so highly—such worries might keep her awake.

The poet Nada Gordon, herself a downtown New York figure, explains that for Mayer, "the process of writing (as incorporated into a life) holds sway over product (the poem considered as a constant, sterile object)." That model arises from Mayer's temperament, but also from her radical democratic politics, opposed to any "proprietary or entrepreneurial or landlord method." Worse yet would be "Aristotelian . . . entitlement." "The whole cause and effect idea comes from Aristotle," Mayer has claimed; "it's a whole way of thinking that people in the western world have adopted. It does nothing but harm." The last parts of the poem tell off, ward off, refuse, the kinds of inauthentic safety associated (for Mayer) at once with secure sleep, with capitalism, and with nuclear power.

Perhaps it is even immoral to sleep well inside a society that depends on such things, or in a society run, hierarchically, from Harvard. Gertrude Stein (who did go to Harvard) gave Mayer her most important model early in Mayer's career: Stein's writings, like Mayer's, insist on an ongoing, anti-hierarchical present—they do not tell stories in any conventional sense, sometimes ramble, and do not resolve. But Stein was never her sole model. Mayer (like Frank Bidart) translated and adapted Catullus in the late 1980s, and the ancient Roman poet's scandalously personal, passionate poetry gives her a model for literary survival that has little to do with institutional authority, and even less to do with the society we have now.

The long loose lines, the openness, and the sense that anything can enter the poem all help Mayer, and help us, imagine a better alternative to that society, whether or not we could really live there. And she says so: "I invite you to contribute to it." That invitation issued, she can relax into a pun: she can play with words and admit "we sometimes sleep like logs." Wordplay and the creation of verbal communities can help Mayer get to sleep, and help her wake up ready to share words. (Phrases such as "artless lambency," for example: her informality need not confine itself to common terms.) Mayer's style, the ending suggests, will help us sleep well—it will work even better than alcohol, that common and famous sleep aid; her style will help us think, as vodka would not. Mayer even slips in the joking suggestion that this sort of ongoing poem might well put us to sleep. Above that self-deprecating suggestion, though, comes the serious sense (as in much of her work) that a less deliberate, less organized, less formal, and friendlier—but no less intelligent—way of writing than the ones we grew up reading might improve our way of living, might grant a better evening to us all.

Mayer had a stroke in 1994. She then had to relearn the physical process of writing, having lost the use of one hand; "people who don't know me can't tell/that it's hard to talk," she wrote in the late 1990s. That years-long recovery, which required attention to motor skills that were once automatic, has reinforced—as Maggie Nelson put it—Mayer's "ongoing commitment to transcribing the minutiae of liminal consciousness," from hypnagogic imagery and dreamt words to the "shifting colors in her field of vision." That commitment informs this poem too.

"It seems to me that every thing in the light and air ought to be happy," Walt Whitman announced in his poem "The Sleepers": "Whoever is not in his coffin and the dark grave let him know he has enough." Mayer does not exactly tell us to be happy, nor tell herself to be happy, simply because we can breathe and have not died. But she does speak to herself, reassure herself, say "I'm not scared"; as she tries to go to sleep (and perhaps succeeds) she gives herself, and us, tactics for calming down, cheering up, accepting the weirdness and the limits and the frustrations of the world she seems to love to share with Sophia, with Dash, with the Lower East Side, and with hand puppets, though not with nuclear reactors. She is a poet devoted to experiment and to the present moment, but above all she devotes herself to openness, to open-endedness, to making a poetry that will let anything and anyone in—including, with your permission, you.

DONALD REVELL

Moab

Where the later kids grow tall
The talk is colors.
Avert your eyes, nary a vowel,
Avert your eyes.
Dying, like dirt reading a magazine, neither laughs nor cries.

I heard a hissing in the sun at sunrise.
Oh my Savior, this very morning
You must step out of the sun,
Colored in no color at all
But in the sound of grass stains

Waking the snowfields,
Waking even the crags and caverns
Whose simple pleasures are my destruction,
Against whose arrows my sons have nothing to oppose.

Revell's title denotes both the biblical land of Moab and the town in Utah closest to Arches National Park; his confident, rapturous sonnet-sized poem testifies at once to his ecstatic Christian faith and to his experience of the desert and mountain West. It also reverses courses in a dramatic, even visionary way. The long, confident sentence that constitutes the second half of the poem asks us (as do many of Revell's later poems) to live in an eternal, joyous present, to surrender and be "destroyed" by a generous "Savior." Yet the poem does not begin in that present: it starts by imploring us to do the opposite, to look away from the attractions of a natural, present-tense world. Revell swerves powerfully from commands into prayers, concisely giving—or at least trying to give—us the enthusiastic experience (both of the park, and of God) that animates him.

Why would "later kids grow tall" in Moab? Why would they talk about colors, and why would a grown-up ask them, or himself, or you, to "avert your eyes"? If the title denotes the national park, the answers could be simple: "later kids"—children younger than other children; younger brothers and sisters; adolescents—show how tall they have grown by hiking and climbing over the sights of the park, famous for its red rock formations, columns, spikes, arches, mesas, and overhangs. You might "avert your eyes" so as not to look right at the sun; given the splendor of land and sky, you might have to tell yourself twice to "avert your eyes." Revell emphasize the warning not just by repeating it but by framing it with line breaks.

If you "avert your eyes" from the landscape, though, you may not be able to read it, to decipher the signs it presents. But are the signs real? Nature—rocks, sunlight, "dirt"—is not a human language and cannot be read in the way that we read magazines; "dirt," rocks, land, sky, and sun are inanimate, fit subjects not for theology or psychology but for the natural sciences. Or so you might think: that modern secular notion dominates much modern poetry, from Wallace Stevens's "The Snow Man" (in which trees and weather signify "nothing" on their own) to the science-friendly meditations of A. R. Ammons.

It is a notion that Revell's later poetry strives to oppose. His is an animate nature, nothing like Stevens's, something like Henry David Thoreau's and something like Gerard Manley Hopkins's, a nature that sings with evidence of creation, of immanent salvation in the visible world. If we try to "read" this nature, we will have to imagine it not as illiterate, emotionless, dead "dirt" but as the work of a Creator who is, and who lets us stay, deeply alive.

That imagination, or discovery, begins in Revell's second stanza, whose "hissing" suggests both the evaporation of what little dew a desert landscape receives and the coming of Satan, the future serpent, to Eden. Yet in Revell's cosmology it is the divinity who invites us to look at nature, at the nonhuman world, and Satan who asks us to turn away from it, and so Revell prays—"Oh my Savior"—that the sunrise will deliver a vision of animate nature, of "snowfields," "crags and caverns" already awake. ("Snowfields" would be rare around Moab, Utah, but possible: the arid town, given to temperature extremes, gets about seven inches of snow per year.)

Revell prays for a vision of animate nature, for firsthand experience of what theologians call panentheism (roughly, the sense that God permeates everything). And he gets what he prays for. Parallel participles ("waking," "waking"), balance the earlier imperatives ("Avert," "avert"), making the Savior's visit seem as urgently real as the earlier, dangerous sun. The parts of the landscape, in shade and in sun, really are "waking," presenting their real, divinely animated selves. Their simple pleasures, their arrows, which are also sunbeams, ought—like the arrows of Cupid; like William Blake's "arrows of desire"—to strike us, and make us more alive. These "arrows" strike both kids and adults; they give us a revelation that lies beyond argument and cannot be opposed, canceling time, and doubt, and death.

"It is simply natural," Revell states in *The Art of Attention* (2007), "that plain attention is a piety and that the unaggressive articulation of attention in poems may be a form of prayer, an instance of worship, a forwarding of peace." Merely to describe what one sees is to give evidence, in Revell's mind, for a Creator: "I know that there are atheists," he has written more recently, "but I cannot for the life of me find them, not even one." Such declarations—and "Moab" is another—present themselves both as descriptions, as claims that are already true, and as performances, ways to call that truth into being, ways to deliver Revell's Good News. Thus he writes of the places he sees as if they were heaven; he has done so about Mississippi, and about Maine, and even about the Bronx of his youth (in elegies for his father and his mother).

He originated this mode, though, in and for the desert West, whose majestic extremes suit his temperament. The environmental writer and scholar SueEllen Campbell writes that the American Southwest shows her "light so intense that at evening I feel sunblasted," light that projects a "home space, huge and open, [that] lets me see a long way . . . on a mountaintop, or at the bottom of a canyon." Such light, coming through the arches that name the park, frames the sun in "Moab," suggesting Christ's entry (i.e., the Incarnation) into the material world—though, when we set him within human history, he brings not peace but a sword (Matthew 10:34). That kind of epiphany would connect not only our earth (the place we live) to other places, but our time to other times past, present, and future, making all those times one and the same, almost as Revell makes verb tense and mood—imperative ("You must") and indicative ("heard"), perfective (one-time action) and imperfective (general or repeated action), present and past—join up, treating them as if they were all one: "you must" has the same force as "is."

Revell has not always written or felt so ecstatically. During the 1980s, he portrayed an articulate, wrung-out disillusion with life and with the built-up industrial Northeast, where the Bronx-born poet spent his youth: at the end of "The Northeast Corridor" (1990), apparently set in an Amtrak station, "The television / crumples into a white dot as the last / train of the evening, my train, is announced. / I lived in one place. I want to die in another." His poems from the 1990s distanced themselves from prose sense, erecting hermetic alternatives to this world: the first poem from *There Are Three* (1998), for example, declares, "the soul catches the wind / between numerals. Once / I was eager to remain outside / forever, and I did."

Since then his poetry has reversed course dramatically, reflecting the poet's confidence—as his own prose says over and over; as "Moab," in its last long sentence, also says—that the visible world declares God's presence for us. Revell taught at the University of Denver from 1985 to 1994, at the University of Utah in Salt Lake City from 1994 to 2008, and then at the University of Nevada–Las Vegas, living with his family (the poet Claudia Keelan and their son and daughter) a few miles outside Las Vegas's urban core. Though Revell is not and never has been Mormon (denominational references in his writings suggest that he is eagerly Episcopalian), his move west tracks the history of the Latter-Day Saints, whose belief in a new, American revelation echoes Revell's. Old Testament place names in Utah, Moab among them, reflect the Mormon settlement there.

But what about the original, biblical Moab? Mentioned in Exodus 15, the Israelites' praise song for deliverance from Egypt, the Moab of the Hebrew Bible is a land occupied by the Israelites' enemies. In Numbers 22–24, Balak, the king of Moab, invites his prophet Balaam to look out from "an high place" over the Israelites and curse them. But God moves Balaam to bless them instead: "How shall I curse, whom God hath not cursed? Or how shall I defy, whom the LORD hath not defied? For from the top of the rocks I see him, and from the hills I behold him . . . Let me die the death of the righteous, and let my last end be like his!" When Balak rebukes him, Balaam responds: "Must I not take heed to speak that which the LORD hath put in my mouth?" (Numbers 23:8–13). Something like Balaam's experience informs Revell's poem: looking out from a high place over children, "the later kids," he can only bless them; he is overcome.

Yet Balaam is not the only biblical figure to climb a mountain in Moab: Moses dies there, on Mount Nebo, after seeing the whole of the land that will belong only to subsequent generations ("later kids," one might say). "Thou shalt see the land before thee," the Lord tells Moses, "but thou shalt not go thither" (Deuteronomy 32:52). Revell's vision of the Son "waking even the crags and caverns" enables him to see, and to love, the idea of a world that will persist beyond his own death, a world that belongs instead to his literal and figurative "sons."

Revell's epiphanic lyric therefore doubles as a father's prayer. Its relatively simple vocabulary invites readers—including very young readers—into the time and place that it discovers, above civilization, outside history. That time and place seem initially like a haven for riddles, or a place apart from this world, the kind of cave that appealed to ascetics and mystics, such as the desert-dwelling Essenes who wrote the Dead Sea Scrolls. Members of such sects might accustom themselves to "dying," or encourage one another to "avert your eyes." But the poem then moves into an evocation of real space, of morning light and "snowfields," and into synesthesia, hearing the grass. Revell's quasi sonnet (three segments, fourteen lines) finally invites us not to avert our eyes but to delight in what they reveal. If this world and the landscapes in it are "my destruction," or yours, or everyone's, it is a kind of destruction—a dissolution into immanence, into this world and the next, and a kind of peace—that introduces something better to come.

TERRANCE HAYES

The Blue Terrance

If you subtract the minor losses,
you can return to your childhood too:
the blackboard chalked with crosses,

the math teacher's toe ring. You
can be the black boy not even the buck-
toothed girls took a liking to:

this match box, these bones in their funk
machine, this thumb worn smooth
as the belly of a shovel. Thump. Thump.

Thump. Everything I hold takes root.
I remember what the world was like before
I heard the tide humping the shore smooth,

and the lyrics asking: *How long has your door
been closed?* I remember a garter belt wrung
like a snake around a thigh in the shadows

of a wedding gown before it was flung
out into the bluest part of the night.
Suppose you were nothing but a song

in a busted speaker? Suppose you had to wipe
sweat from the brow of a righteous woman,
but all you owned was a dirty rag? That's why

the blues will never go out of fashion:
their half rotten aroma, their bloodshot octaves of
consequence: that's why when they call, Boy, you're in

trouble. Especially if you love as I love
falling to the earth. Especially if you're a little bit
high strung and a little bit gutted balloon. I love

watching the sky regret nothing but its
self, though only my lover knows it to be so,
and only after watching me sit

and stare off past Heaven. I love the word *No*
for its prudence, but I love the romantic
who submits finally to sex in a burning row-

house more. That's why nothing's more romantic
than working your teeth through
the muscle. Nothing's more romantic

than the way good love can take leave of you.
That's why I'm so doggone lonesome, Baby,
yes, I'm lonesome and I'm blue.

Moving between the poles of story and song, of one heartbreak story and anyone's heartbreak, Hayes brings together in a bravura way European and African American technique. He also brings identifiably African American
strands of musical culture together with one another. The cultural critic Craig
Werner has argued that black American music has a blues strain (about lonely
endurance and the presence of the past), a jazz strain (about the future, devoted to individual invention), and a gospel strain (all about hope and collective improvement), and Hayes's terza rima acknowledges them all, making for
a lyric that is unusually capacious—and emotionally volatile, and, by the end,

wrenching. Hayes's modulations show how a poem addressed to somebody can also address anybody, how the "I" of a poem can be at once the poet himself and the reader who takes it up, and it leaves room not just for multiple voicings, but for an unusually broad range of emotions: if it's about one thing, then it's about how those emotions, at one moment, conflict and co-exist—how we contain contradictions, not just in our opinions and our identities, but in our hearts. It might be the only poem in American English that sounds at once jaunty and frustrated, crushed by vicissitude and yet eager to sing.

Though they make up a freestanding poem, these sixty-nine lines also belong to a larger set of "Blue" poems in Hayes's 2006 volume *Wind in a Box*. Three are called "The Blue Terrance"; in most of the rest Hayes addresses or adopts the voices of historical characters—Dr. Seuss, the poet and activist Amiri Baraka, the rapper Kool Keith, the segregationist senator Strom Thurmond. "Some of us be best friends / or fried fiends, but all of us be / floundering interiors, be all these things / at once, America. Why you be?" asks "The Blue Baraka." Those three poems each entitled "The Blue Terrance" appear to describe the poet's own life, though we cannot assume that every incident happened to the real Terrance Hayes: the poet confirms in interviews that much, but not all, of his apparently autobiographical work reflects literal truth.

All of it, though, reflects thoughts and feelings the poet has had, that we might have too: "you can return to your childhood too," and ask whether its difficulties were like Hayes's own. A "blackboard chalked with crosses" could be a set of addition problems, or something else vexing, a set of "crosses" to bear; a child tired of staring at a blackboard might cast his eyes down to the floor, to the math teacher's toes. A toe ring, with its "o" sound and its O shape, plus crosses or X's, suggest tic-tac-toe, a game in which (when it's played right) nobody wins. The lonely "black boy" in Hayes's second stanza feels lost and lonely in his own body, a "funk / machine" not in the sense that it makes him want to get up and dance, but in the older sense (from which "funk," the musical term, derives) of shameful dirt and odor—someone who smells funky ought to get clean.

Instead he digs himself deeper into a dirty hole like a grave: a row of white crosses could represent a cemetery, and the child in the poem, remembering "what the world was like" before some sort of loss, could be in mourning. (Hayes's mother, the father who raised him, and his biological father were in 2006, and 2015, all quite alive, but Hayes as a child never met his biological father; that absence gives Hayes a clear subject for other poems.)

Hayes fuses terza rima—the *aba bcb cdc* . . . rhyme scheme invented by Dante Alighieri, who used it to depict hell, purgatory, and paradise—with American blues. In Hayes's version of rhyme, which matches vowels but not always consonants, *buck* rhymes with *funk* and with *thump*, *night* with *wipe* and *why*. The form suggests a chain or sequence that pulls reader and characters along in an almost predestined journey, like the journey of Dante's pilgrim, lost in the woods in the middle of life's way. The journey takes Hayes to the shore, and then into the ocean of adolescent sexual awakening, bringing frustrations of another, comical kind. A teen who thinks about sex all the time might well see the tide on the shore as a form of "humping"; he may have been "humping" somebody recently, or maybe he wishes he could, but he found her door closed. There is no well-known blues song with the lyric "How long has your door / been closed?" but there could be: the feeling of being left out, of waiting too long, of continual letdown, is part of the essence of blues, if not the essence of adolescence. The garter, thrown out at the end of a wedding, also signals sexual frustration—it's a tease, and this young person did not catch it: he feels unworthy, inadequate, as well as left out, inferior, treated unfairly, morally suspect, left holding "a dirty rag."

By this point "The Blue Terrance" has certainly shown us the blues: it has shown us persistent sorrow and a persistent wish to share it, to expand the voice and diminish the body, until you are "nothing but a song." Hayes also remember the roots of acoustic blues in rural poverty, in men and women of the Mississippi Delta who had to live by agricultural labor and who owned little or nothing, not even their songs. "The blues will never go out of fashion" because human life will always include sorrow and pain: the emotions—loneliness, dejection, sexual frustration—that give rise to the blues are as much a permanent part of human capacity (so Hayes suggests) as the law given to Adam and Eve in Genesis 3:19, "By the sweat of your brow you will eat your food" (the King James Version has, instead, "In the sweat of thy face"). Blues speaks to the Fall (as in "falling to the earth"), to the "call" from God to Adam in Genesis 3:9–10, when God, in effect, finds Adam and says "You're in trouble": it speaks to what does not change in the human condition, what both Dante and Big Mama Thornton might have felt. Those earthy, bluesy feelings animate Hayes's poem—they may also be familiar to "you."

But Hayes's poem of the earth is also a poem of the sky. Its stargazer considers the human capacity for the new, for invention, for taking imaginative risks and testing extremes, the capacity Werner (among others) identifies with jazz: Hayes's unpredictable not-quite-pentameters partake of the syncopated, improvisational ongoingness of jazz, of the rhythmic invention that has been the special province of jazz from Jelly Roll Morton to Flying Lotus. Hayes's later poem "Liner Notes for an Imaginary Playlist" begins with "Wind Solo" by the Felonious Monks, "from the album *Silense*, 1956": "1945, after everyone got hip to the blues, this is the code / The hipsters devised." Neither the band nor the album exists, but the principle of invention certainly does: that poem, like this one, seeks a breath of fresh air.

Yet that quest for novelty—the soul of improvisation, perhaps the soul of poetry—is itself nothing new: it is as old as lust, as old as dissatisfaction, older than the fantastic tales originally designated by "romance" and "romantic," a word that Hayes repeats where a "pure" terza rima would find rhymes. That repetition borrows from classic blues form, which repeats entire lines; and (like most classic blues) it suggests frustration. To watch your lover engage in intellectual speculation, to watch him as he enters his own world, is to lose touch with him, at least temporarily: a lover "watching me sit / and stare off past Heaven" is a lover who has less than Hayes's full attention. These lovers may not stay together for long.

For all the attention it pays to sights and sound, "The Blue Terrance" also pursues its frustrations, its dissatisfactions, through senses closer to the body: through touch, tongue, teeth. The literary scholar Denise Gigante has described "the creative power of taste as a trope for aesthetic judgment." For her, aesthetic taste (supposedly a function of the mind and soul) cannot be fully untangled from gustatory taste (a product, at least in part, of tongue, teeth, mouth, nose, body), at least not since the late eighteenth century. Nor, for Hayes, can either kind of taste be fully separate from the contradictions of sexual appetite. The physical power, the effort, required to taste meat— "working your teeth through the muscle"—stands for the wrenching emotions of having been jilted, or dumped, as well as for the strength required to make those emotions into an art both personal and putatively universal, an art form that comes from the body, an art like the blues.

That is the kind of art Hayes's poem tries to become: like many of the other poems in this book, "The Blue Terrance" turns into an ars poetica, a claim about what poetry ought to be. It ought to seem both new and old; it can integrate disparate techniques (like terza rima and the blues) and disparate impulses (like blues and jazz). It can cry out to you, or cry for you, on your behalf. And it should take in both body and spirit, earth and sky, becoming a kind of "wind in a box," live spirit that comes from dead matter, immaterial aspiration contained in material, verbal form. Art draws us together that way; it shows us higher things. That's what Werner would call the gospel impulse, and Hayes acknowledges it too.

Then he comes back down to earth. Hayes's last stanza is the only one in the poem that could be a blues lyric; it uses the shortest sentences, the most colloquial words, and the near clichés ("good love," "doggone lonesome") that Hayes has kept out of the rest of the poem. Becoming almost generic in its language, leaving behind the visual details ("gutted balloon," "toe ring") in earlier stanzas, this one relies for novelty almost wholly on rhythm and on its surprising informality. Here is Hayes at his jauntiest, at his most "musical," the point at which he could almost be singing: here, too, is Hayes at his lowest, admitting that he does not "love / falling to the earth," does not want to feel the way he feels.

At this point, in other words, Hayes is both flaunting his own contradictions, and singing the blues. And in doing so, he speaks both to "you," and for "you"; he speaks, as so many disaffected blues singers, torch singers, rock singer, and other singers have spoken, both to whoever has left him and for whoever feels the way he feels. His blues terza rima—perhaps the first poem ever to combine the forms—has become overtly what so many lyric poems try to become, albeit tacitly, and to do what John Ashbery's and Killarney Clary's poems in this book told us that they could do: reach out from the poet to "you," to you as an individual, to people like you, to entire categories of people (in "The Blue Terrance" that includes blues fans, teenage guys, former teenage guys, and black southerners), and yet it appears to speak, in solitude, to you alone.

Hayes plays the piano, as a serious amateur, and he paints (most of his book covers show his paintings): he told one interviewer "Though I studied painting growing up, I also studied, in a less academic sense, music. . . . One reason I chose poetry over painting or music has to do with poetry's capacity to reflect, if not embody, all other art forms." Hayes's poetry sometimes seems to reflect, if not to embody, all other kinds of poetry as well: it represents not a compromise among them but a way to say and do and be many things at once—a wise grown man and a sullen teen, an heir of Dante and an inheritor of specifically black folk traditions. ("I like Amiri Baraka, I like Stanley Kunitz," Hayes has also said, "two poets who couldn't be more different. I'm interested in bringing all these styles together.") And in being many things at once, Hayes remains himself, an heir to the plural mantles of lyric: he also, like it or not, stays blue.

JORIE GRAHAM

Futures

Midwinter. Dead of. I own you says my mind. Own what, own
whom. I look up. Own the looking at us
say the cuttlefish branchings, lichen-black, moist. Also
the seeing, which wants to feel more than it sees.
Also, in the glance, the feeling of owning, accordioning out and up,
seafanning,
& there is cloud on blue ground up there, & wind which the eye loves so deeply it
would spill itself out and liquefy
to pay for it—
& the push of owning is thrilling, is spring before it
is—is that swelling—is the imagined fragrance as one
bends, before the thing is close enough—wide-
eyed leaning—although none of this can make you
happy—
because, looking up, the sky makes you hear it, you know why we have come it
blues, you know the trouble at the heart, blue, blue, what
pandemonium, blur of spears roots cries leaves master & slave, the crop destroyed,
water everywhere not
drinkable, & radioactive waste in it, & human bodily
waste, & what,
says the eye-thinking heart, is the last color seen, the last word
heard—someone left behind, then no behind—
is there a skin of the I own which can be scoured from inside the
glance—no,

cannot—& always

someone walking by whistling a

little tune, that's

life he says, smiling, there, that was life—& the heart branches with its

wild arteries—I own my self, I own my

leaving—the falcon watching from the tree—I shall torch the crop that no one else

have it whispers the air—

& someone's swinging from a rope, his rope—the eye

throbbing—day a noose looking for a neck—

the fire spidery but fast—& the idea of

friends, what was that, & the day, in winter, your lower back

started acting up again, & they pluck out the eyes at the end for

food, & don't forget

the meeting at 6, your child's teacher

wishes to speak to you

about his future, & if there is no food and the rain is everywhere switching-on as expected,

& you try to think of music and the blue of Giotto,

& if they have to eat the arms he will feel no pain at least, & there is a

sequence in which feeding takes

place—the body is owned by the hungry—one is waiting

one's turn—one wants to own one's

turn—and standing there,

don't do it now but you might remember kisses—how you kissed his arm in the sun

and

tasted the sun, & this is your

address now, your home address—& the strings are cut no one

looks up any longer

—or out—no—&

one day a swan appeared out of nowhere on the drying river,

it

was sick, but it floated, and the eye felt the pain of rising to take it in—I own you

      said the old feeling, I want

      to begin counting

again, I will count what is mine, it is moving quickly now, I will begin this

      message "I"—I feel the

smile, put my hand up to be sure, yes on my lips—the yes—I touch it again, I

      begin counting, I say *one* to the swan, *one,*

do not be angry with me o my god, I have begun the action of beauty again, on

      the burning river I have started the catalogue,

      your world,

I your speck tremble remembering money, its dry touch, sweet strange

      smell, it's a long time, the smell of it like lily of the valley

sometimes, and pondwater, and how

      one could bend down close to it

and drink.

Graham looks at a tree in a field on a sunny winter day and imagines the end of human civilization. That's what happens in the outside world in the course of this poem: the rest of it takes place inside Graham's mind. To like her late verse is to want to visit that mind, whose intricacies connect the delights of minute perception to the somberest, scariest, and at this point best-supported scientific predictions about the future of the Earth.

To meet her where she is now, it helps to see how she got there. Graham became one of America's most influential—and most imitated—poets before she turned forty; the beautifully observed, determinedly irregular free verse of *Erosion* (1983) and the longer, stranger work in *The End of Beauty* (1987), with its self-interruptions and very long lines, paid uncommon attention to the moment-by-moment fluctuations of thought and perception. Graham (who grew up trilingual in English, French, and Italian) drew not only on American and European poetic technique but also on the history of painting and the theory of cinema. Those early books examined not just the process of perception but the ethical tangles involved: poems such as "Salmon" and "Imperialism" (in which a young Graham, half paralyzed by thought, contemplated the filthy, holy Ganges) asked whether the human (or Western) drive toward closure, the wish to "own," master and understand our experience from "one deep-driven / nail point of view," could ever be separated from a culpable Western drive to master other countries, other cultures, and to use up the resources of the physical world. Her later career since then—seven more books, including a 2015 new-and-selected—may be seen as a set of efforts to build on those earlier philosophical and cinematic discoveries: to represent the flux of perception, the tumult of thought, and the accumulated guilt of our civilization in ever stranger or more urgent styles, without repeating herself.

And yet "Futures" opens on a scene that repeats itself throughout the history of poetry, if not the history of plant life on earth. Bare trees and strong wind in "midwinter" suggest the nadir of the agricultural cycle, the "dead" moment before life can be renewed. Poets from Percy Bysshe Shelley to Christina Rossetti ("In the bleak midwinter") and William Carlos Williams have found in such scenes symbols for rebirth (those scenes, and poems, come up in Charles Wright's poem earlier in this book). They can stand both for one poet's mind—depressed or worn out, needing reassurance in nature—and for the renewals promised by political movements or by religion.

But to see it that way, to impose a narrative on the dead landscape, is for Graham an attempt to "own" it, and hence to repeat the process by which Western culture has engaged the land in irreversible processes, exhausting the soil of the Great Plains, for example, and taking uranium, oil, and coal from the ground. "We used to think that shape, a finished thing, was a corpse / that would sprout from the ground, Easter in every heart," Graham recalled twenty-five years ago, in "Pollock and Canvas"; "what do we / think // now?" Graham's characteristically long and violently enjambed lines—no pattern will let us predict where the next one will end—mimic the tug-of-war between the part of her mind that wants to tell a story, that cannot help giving a shape to what she sees, and the part that objects to the imposition. Is the impulse to make a metaphor, to possess a story—to see bare trees, for example, as inverted "cuttlefish," or as seaweeds—so far from the impulse to "own" other human beings?

Nobody could seriously believe that making metaphors about fallow fields is morally equivalent to owning slaves. Graham instead recognizes a common drive to "own," to impose our own individual, dominant will, both in the microperceptions (some might call them microaggressions) of poetic figuration and in the macroaggressions of modern world history. That history means "trouble at the heart" of a land with a legacy of "master & slave," of "crop destroyed," of "radioactive waste in it, & human bodily / waste," as in Iowa's hog lagoons. Once we believe that nonhuman nature is ours, we might end up doing whatever we wish with it; once we believe that our acts and perceptions are there to serve our purposes, our "ends" (as in that title *The End of Beauty*), we might use other people and other parts of the earth as means to those ends, till they're gone. Indeed, we are already doing so, through unsustainable agriculture, and through global climate change. And yet Graham's temperament (not to mention her intellect) cannot stop interpreting: not for her the quasi-Buddhist or Quaker striving toward silence before the land that other poets (Gary Snyder or W. S. Merwin) affect.

Instead, Graham turns her habit of scrutiny inward on herself, on her "eye-thinking heart," an awkward figure for that inward turn. It would be good to "scour" (both to examine closely and to scrub completely) the inward self, that "skin of the I own," without imposing ourselves on some external nature, without even taking up other people's time; but we live among other people, speak to other people, cannot bear to cut ourselves off from them. Such onrushing phrases (as Calvin Bedient says) record Graham's "urge . . . to say that something 'is,'" that it exists for her at a particular moment, "despite time's instant self-dissolution." That sense that something else exists and that she has seen it authorizes, in turn, her sense that she is real, that she remains herself. Yet to write about the self, about the guilt of being a self, the guilt of privilege, the process of self-scrutiny, is to write about being a self among other people, stuck in an endangered nonhuman world.

Most poets are not so affected as Graham by guilt about Western civilization, nor by the idea that the world as we know it will end. Opposing her seemingly endless, one-way sentence to the tradition of shorter poems that see in the bleak midwinter annual renewal, Graham also opposes herself to a blasé pedestrian "whistling a / little tune, that's life." "That *was* life," she corrects him silently; she knows, as he doesn't, that spring may not come back. Graham's ongoing lines track the consuming anxiety of someone who believes she, her privilege, and the history that has produced them (along with "radioactive waste") are part of the problem. The (presumably American) land here bears in its past a "blur of spears roots cries leaves master & slave." The branches (as in famous earlier poems and songs) stand clearly for lynchings, so the sun it-self, setting, suggests a noose. After such history, what comes next? How to imagine a future, let alone "futures"?

Graham has taken the setting for a Christmas poem and turned it into something like Easter without the Resurrection: a scene of collective guilt, absence, and death. Crows "pluck out the eyes"; "seafans" look like Christmas trees underwater, upside down. This later tree is not so much the cross of Jesus as the crosses on which thieves were killed beside him: crows "pluck out the eyes at the end for / food." That line break, like others, does a great deal of work: who wouldn't want food? Don't crows have a right to food, just as human beings have a right to food, the food for which modern agribusiness has seized the land? Capitalism, America, and the bourgeois West have built what we have around speculation, around "futures." But what if we have no futures, "if there is no food"? If we no longer trust "futures" in the sense of investment vehicles (the original "futures" were bets on the price of grain) because we no longer trust the climate or the free market, can we trust that there is a "future" for kids? (Graham's poem was first published in 2007; it anticipates the economic crisis of 2008 and beyond, rather than reacting to it.) A line break itself is a "turn," and a poet can "own" it. But individual human beings cannot ordinarily "own," cannot control, weather ("the rain is everywhere"), or entire societies and their markets, or "sequence," the passage of time.

Graham could have ended the poem by repeating "turn." Instead, she cuts away to romantic memory ("how you kissed his arm in the sun," though by now there is rain) and then to another scene, an approaching swan. If Gra-ham's opening invokes many poems, her ending points to one: William Butler Yeats's "The Wild Swans at Coole." Yeats counts swans every year at the same lake ("The nineteenth autumn has come upon me / Since first I made my count"); discovers an odd number ("nine and fifty"); and compares their ma-jestic annual return ("Their hearts have not grown old") to the one-way journey that is his own life. Once in "your world"—the swan's world, or Yeats's—Graham feels at home, released from her anxious detachment. And yet the idea that we are poisoning the world, that we who kiss and we who educate have no future, remains: you would not want to drink standing water, "pond-water," nor would you want to eat anything in close contact with the highly poisonous lily of the valley. Once we imagine a post-civilized life, a future where money is only something we "remember," can we still partake of worldly beauty?

We can understand swans: we can see where they begin and end. We can understand branches, and perhaps our own bodies ("I own myself"), and we can understand "The Wild Swans at Coole." But can we understand, or imagine, or try to visualize, the end of the world? What about the global financial system, or the progress of a geological epoch, or the mechanisms of climate change? Such entities are what the literary scholar Timothy Morton calls "hyperobjects," "massively distributed across Earth," so that "we find ourselves inside them": they are too complicated for single metaphors, too big and too challenging to grasp at once. "Hyperobjects are so huge, temporally and spatially, that they cannot directly be seen. Yet they manifest as rain or drought, in the case of global warming, or as frogs and daffodils in the case of evolution." When we try to understand them in their "vast nonlocal configuration," we struggle with our assumptions about time and space. But we had better try: they are "incomparably vaster and more powerful than us." Our troubles with hyperobjects began in one sense with the steam engine, with the economy of fossil fuels, but in another (as Morton insists) it started with agriculture, when human beings first began to feed one another with crops that we put in the ground. "This is the historical moment," Morton insists, "at which hyperobjects become visible by humans" (it may be the "post glacial" moment of dg nanouk okpik's poem in this book too).

We can see Graham's recent style—the style of "Futures" (as opposed to the style of *The End of Beauty*)—as a way to reflect that visibility. The uncanny, scary, incomplete perception and cognition of (for example) global warming and soil exhaustion, hyperobjects defined by their casual relationships with smaller things too numerous for us to count (with every atom of carbon in the air, each nitrate ion acidifying the soil), inform the uncanny, unbalanced, insistently unfinished (both "unpolished" and "never-ending") lines in Graham's late work. And that work tries, as Morton says that other artists have tried, "to think ourselves out of a ten-thousand-year-old structure" and to throw outward into our sense of the language "the weird contradiction between being and appearance that hyperobjects force us to see in all things."

Collective guilt cannot, after all, foreclose all beauty. We are so made as to admire, try to admire, or like what we see: we are so made as to live in the world, to perceive it, to "begin the action of beauty again," to find reasons to like being alive. We live, we continue to live, in time as in a river, as the swan floats or swims on its river, even though the river appears to be "burning." We may be moved (we ought to be moved) to take some sort of political action (however unlikely its goals) about the dooms we face. But we may also permit ourselves to see and to feel, to admire and to appreciate the phenomena of the guilty, burning world.

LAURA KASISCHKE

Miss Weariness

At first she looked like all the other girls, but then

the chipped fingernail, and then

she sat down in a folding chair
and let the other girls pass by

in their ballgowns, in their bathing suits, in their
beatific smiles, but she

had tossed her heels aside.

Enough of industry, enough
of goals and troubles, looking ahead, grooming and dreaming
and anything that ended
in *i-n-g* in this
life ever again, she said.

O, enough, even, of the simple stuff:

The will-o'-the-wisp, the rain on a lake, all
those goldfish in their plastic
baggies at the fair. To them

it must have been
as if the world were divided
into small warped dreams, nowhere

to get to, and nothing to do but swim.

"Miss Weariness" comes in the middle of Kasischke's 2007 book *Lilies Without*, one of seven poems about unlikely entrants in an impossible pageant. The first is "Miss Congeniality," who "sang" and delivered a "speech . . . about peace, in praise of the war"; the last is "Miss Consolation for Emotional Damages," who began as a moth from a fairy-tale Europe but "woke / one morning as a careless / American girl, mouth / stuffed with pink / fluff." Though Kasischke also writes novels, and though her other poems often have elements of realistic autobiography, the people in the "Miss" poems are not realistic characters: they stand for what their names say they should be.

That means that they look back to the genre called allegory. The most famous allegories show us how to be good: in John Bunyan's *Pilgrim's Progress* (1678) Christian must avoid Mr. Worldly Wiseman, listen to Faithful and Goodwill, and find the Celestial City. Edmund Spenser's complicated allegorical poem *The Faerie Queene* (1596) includes an enchantress named Duessa ("doubleness") and knights who represent temperance, friendship, and justice. Contestants in real beauty pageants, who represent ideals or locales ("Miss Congeniality," "Miss Maryland"), replicate the structure of Christian allegory, along with its promise of rewards for being good: their famous cheerfulness and their well-scripted behavior suggest that life's big problems can be solved, or even that cheerful demeanor plus beauty can solve them.

For Kasischke's Misses—and for this one in particular—life does not work that way. Shifting from what Miss Weariness does, as if seen from the outside, to what she thinks and what she might have said, Kasischke's clever and terrifying portrait, built up out of common American material—a folding chair, a county fair—portrays (without offering resolution) the particular problems of girls and women in a society that feminism has not yet transformed, along with the enduring problem, for any gender, of finding purpose in this world.

Time pressure, "busyness," overscheduling, the achievement trap: journalists and social scientists identify this problem, by all those names, as a chief source of stress in American life, especially in the lives of women with children. The journalist Brigid Schulte calls it "the overwhelm." It has many sources, from labor-intensive standards of feminine beauty to the well-documented phenomenon that Arlie Hochschild named "the second shift," whereby mothers in the paid labor force never get to relax once they come home. Schulte summarizes research on "contaminated time," supposedly free time when women in fact keep getting interrupted; on multitasking ("women report feeling more frustrated, irritated and stressed by it"); and on busyness as a "social norm." The sociologist Liah Greenfeld, in an essay called "Busyness in Contemporary American Society," has described the way that even "leisure" activities seem to eat up free time: "holidays, birthdays, anniversaries, celebrations of achievement, and all the shopping, and cooking" add up to an "exhausting job of being joyful." Despite our affluence as a society, Greenfield concludes, "we are veritably torn into pieces by all these simultaneous and necessarily conflicting demands." These demands come on top of the pressure for women—and teenage girls—to look sharp, to dress for the role they want.

"Miss Weariness" looks like a poem about these pressures, about the overwhelm, with attention to its sources in teenage life: pushed (by herself and others) to become the perfect pageant girl, Kasischke's heroine grows up—or expects to grow up—into a role where time pressure will be even more intense. No wonder she can't take it. But Kasischke's poem gets stranger and sadder than that. Social critics who offer solutions to the overwhelm—solutions that individuals, not just employers and governments, can carry out—usually ask us to reflect, to set priorities, to push away other people in favor of "me time," and to pay attention to simple things; they ask us, in other words, to do what literature in general and lyric poetry in particular is frequently supposed to help us do. Schulte quotes the very popular poet Mary Oliver as she asks us to get off the clock, to seek "the time of the 'right moment,' the eternal now." "Life will be over quickly." Seize the day.

It's not bad advice. But for Miss Weariness, it hasn't helped: she feels let down and fed up, "even" with the sort of experience that for so many other observers serves as a remedy. Not just the American dream, but all the dreams, feel "small," feel "warped": the dreams of subversion, rebellion, independence—pursued, and embodied, by other sorts of poetry—might not be much more than "be yourself as long as your true self [is] really cool." (I quote the journalists Kara Jesella and Marisa Meltzer, writing about teen magazines.) Miss Weariness's malady—it might be better to say her personality—has something in common not just with the problems of the second shift, of contemporary social roles, and of stressed-out teens, but with the older problems of ennui, or *acedia*, the state in which there is nothing we want to do. In Christian theology *acedia* is a sin; in nineteenth- and twentieth-century writing it becomes ennui, or boredom, failure to care for what the world can provide. It also becomes—as in Herman Melville's "Bartleby the Scrivener"—a mark of individuality.

Miss Weariness individuates herself—no longer resembles "all the other girls"—not because of anything she does but because of what she refuses to do: she will not prepare "in this / life" for any future goal, not even the goal of self-realization. She thus belongs in a line of literary refusals from Satan to Bartleby to Doris Lessing's ultimately suicidal Susan Rawling ("To Room Nineteen"), characters who cannot and will not take approved routes to success. If the poem is an allegory, she stands for that refusal, for wrong turns, for saying no. But if her life is a wrong answer, there is no right one: not in this poem, which feels less allegorical as it goes on and its startling sonic effects emerge.

The first sentence takes us to the end of the pageant, first stopping short ("then / the chipped fingernail," as if to introduce a verb) and then going on and on, as the parade of more hopeful girls goes on ("in their . . . in their . . . in their"). Other girls stand. Miss Weariness sits, amid vowel rhymes such as "pass by . . . aside," while "chair" rhymes exactly with "air," and later with "fair." This former contestant, refusing to act, has given up verbs (action words) and participles (the root is the same as "participate") in favor of exclamations. The overlap between the *-ing* in "anything" and the gerundive or participial *-ing* let Kasischke suggest what she has given up: not just every kind of teenage planning ("looking ahead, grooming and dreaming") but every kind of thing.

For the modern sufferer of ennui, not only is there nothing we want to do but there is nothing we want to become, or to be. And that version of ennui, or acedia, or weariness, might apply with special force to the young women, or "girls," in Kasischke's pageant, allegorically on their way not just to a destination offstage or to an awards ceremony (which Miss Weariness cannot bring herself to attend) but to a social position in adult life. In parallel with adults'—with mothers'—"overwhelm," there is the busyness of bourgeois teenage life, the resumé-building of teens who play three instruments, volunteer at two homeless shelters, take twelve APs, excel in soccer and swimming, and fret constantly about that other competitive pageant, college admissions. One of many teens in one of many newspaper pieces on this problem (admittedly one that comes with privilege) complained that her peers "are not teenagers . . . We are lifeless bodies in a system that breeds competition [and] hatred."

That bourgeois problem and the problem of the overwhelmed (not necessarily bourgeois) mother and the problem of the beauty myth, where too much primping is never enough, look to Kasischke's Miss Weariness like the same problem: we go through life preparing and preparing, setting "goals" and striving to meet them, using our hopes about the future and our sense of obligation to others as fuel until we have used them up. The cheerleaders in

Kasischke's novel *Boy Heaven* tire of their roles too, always anticipating, always practicing, and always expected to smile: their coach says sarcastically near the end of a workout, "Maybe *tomorrow* morning you'll be a bit *peppier*," at which point "a groan rose from the bleachers. A groan of infinite weariness. A chain gang of cheerleaders in hell being told they'd be pushing a rock up the side of a hill for all of eternity." In *Boy Heaven*, the narrator and her risky friend begin "sneaking out of camp in my car," with disastrous results. But Miss Weariness can only escape to the fair, which is no fair: its leisure replicates the traditional, adult-sanctioned contests that she has already seen at school, or at home, or onstage.

As we are to the poet, as the poet is to her pageant contestant (or former contestant), so is Miss Weariness to her unfortunate fish, the prize that she no longer wants. Goal-oriented, future-directed "industry," cosmetic or academic, will get her nothing more valuable than a bag of goldfish at the county fair. "Miss Weariness" makes dizzyingly effective the novelistic device of shifting perspective: Kasischke moves from the viewpoint called third-person limited, in which we see and know (from the outside) just what Miss Weariness sees and knows, into free indirect discourse, where we read Miss Weariness's thoughts as if they were Kasischke's own: "Enough."

That sentiment makes the girl feel like a goldfish herself: the shift in perspective comes as a shock, and it does far more work than the clichés ("rat race," for example) that Kasischke's metaphor echoes. Nothing of lasting importance can be added to the already watery worlds where those fish live— that is why their lives are like "rain on a lake," figures both for excess and for futility. The isolated fish are nonetheless, so to speak, all in the same boat, with "nowhere / to get to," though they keep moving. They look as busy as Schulte's Americans feel. Compared to the fish, though, Miss Weariness has one choice: she can stop moving. "She / had tossed her heels aside." That minimal gesture of resistance—that stop—fits the sudden stops, the jagged enjambments, in Kasischke's lines: "Enough of industry, enough . . . O, enough." That hard stop, that repetition, replaces a narrative that will not take her anywhere: it supports a kind of sit-down strike.

So do her sounds. Kasischke pairs very irregularly enjambed lines (they have no length norm and could break anywhere) with unpredictable but prominent rhyme. That pair is her aural signature and her invention (other poets who use it now are sometimes copying her). "Swim" has no full rhyme anywhere, though it matches the *m* in "them" and "dreams" and the vowel in "been." It feels like the end, but it might also feel disappointing: the poem has nowhere else that it can go. Nor does the girl in the poem. On the other hand, her feeling now has a name ("weariness") and a poem all about it. If she is a goldfish, she is not the only goldfish—they cannot communicate directly (each in its own bag), but they can see one another, each stuck in a "small warped dream." In the same way, Miss Weariness, her peers, and her readers can at least complain: here they can see an astonishingly articulate allegory for a too often dismissed (and, not by coincidence, feminized) complaint. They can imagine that they are complaining together: they can present, in this array of almost rhyming phrases, a persistent, familiar, and frightening common cause.

FRANK BIDART

Song of the Mortar and Pestle

The desire to approach obliteration
preexists each metaphysic justifying it. Watch him
fucked want to get fucked hard. Christianity

allowed the flagellants

light, for even Jesus found release from flesh requires
mortification of the flesh. From the ends of
the earth the song is, *Grind me into dust.*

Why would you want to obliterate yourself, whip yourself (as the medieval flagellants did), not only "get fucked" but "get fucked hard," get ground into dust? And why would you identify that experience not only with sexual pleasure but with deliverance into a heavenly "light"? The psychoanalyst Jessica Benjamin suggests one reason: "The masochist's wish to be reached, penetrated, found, released—a wish that can be expressed in the metaphor of violence as well as in metaphors of redemption—is the other side of the sadist's wish to discover the other," she writes. "The masochist's wish to experience his authentic, inner reality in the company of another parallels the sadist's wish to get outside the self." You might want to approach obliteration, find pleasure in being ground into dust, because you do not want to be alive, but you might also do it to prove—to yourself and to others—that you can reveal your deepest self, and still survive.

It isn't something you can do alone. Sadist and masochist, or penetrator and receiver, go together in Bidart's title like mortar and pestle, and what they "grind" is the soul, which disappears into fine powder and thereby (like a pharmaceutical ground and mixed by an apothecary) does what it was always meant to do. Get penetrated, fucked hard, ground into dust, Benjamin suggests, and you will, simply by having survived the extreme experience, understand that you exist, that there is something to "you" besides the vulnerable, penetrable flesh, and that somebody else can make "you" come alive.

But there is no "you" in Bidart's haunting and fragmentary poem, which combines its shocking BDSM language with several unlikely formal goals. These seven lines (eight if you count the resonant title) bring together grating, clashing levels of discourse, from the phrase "fucked hard" to words that would fit textbooks in Continental philosophy. It is not in any obvious sense a "song," though it does speak, or sing, for its pair of objects: it is the poem the objects would write, if they could write, and its shape on the page—a small, jagged thing (every line break is enjambed) caught between two larger things—suggests the grinding that mortar and pestle can do.

In fastening disparate, often abstract, kinds of language together to make a compact point about the core of the soul, the poem represents Bidart's style as well as any one poem could. And yet the poems that first got him widely admired were far longer than this poem, and generically unlike it: they were dramatic monologues and narratives about people overmastered by violent desires. "Herbert White" put words in the mouth of a necrophile serial killer; "Ellen West" dramatized the last months and days of a historically documented suicidal anorexic. "The Second Hour of the Night" retold the Greek myth of Myrrha, a king's daughter cursed to lust after her father, who deludes himself into having sex with her: he is "not free not to desire," Bidart writes, as "no creature is free to choose what / allows it its most powerful, and most secret release."

Bidart's imagination, it should be clear, responds to destructive sexual extremes. But what does he do with those extremes, and why? Put another way, how does he use the resources of poetry—its range of words, its line breaks, its ability to isolate and place sustained scrutiny on single pieces of language—to embody and to investigate extreme or dangerous or (as we say now) kinky sex? And why does he emphasize (as, for example, D. A. Powell—who writes on sex even more often—does not usually emphasize) domination, subordination, difficulty, or pain?

If what struck you first in "Song of the Mortar and Pestle" was the sharp divide in kinds of language—metaphysical justification here, "get fucked hard" there—what might have struck you second was Bidart's confidence that he could make connections between them, that these slices could add up to a whole. And that whole has to do with the self *as* a whole, the sense that we are, that we can be, that we want to be, something metaphysical, something other than flesh, embodiment, "dust." That claim is the exact opposite of the claim in (for example) C. D. Wright that we are, and should realize we are, and should try to revel in, our physical bodies. Bidart's protagonists, singly and en masse, push or stretch or take the flesh as far as it can go.

He finds a distant model in Catullus. Bidart has translated the same two-line Latin poem, Catullus's poem number 85, three times: the first, from 1990, reads "I hate and love. Ignorant fish, who even / wants the fly while writhing." The second, from *Desire* (1997), entitled "Catullus: Excrucior," runs *"I hate and—love.* The sleepless body hammering a nail nails / itself, hanging—crucified." The third comes right before "Song of the Mortar and Pestle" in Bidart's book *Watching the Spring Festival*: "What I hate I love. Ask the crucified hand that holds / the nail that now is driven into itself, why." Bidart's Catullus hates and loves not a particular beloved but the human body in general and his own human body in particular, which becomes both a required tool for pleasure, or ecstasy, or self-fulfillment, and an object that must be destroyed.

Sexual desire for Bidart seems inseparable from self-destruction, self-abasement, and self-sacrifice, as in the sacrifice that Christ made on the cross. And desire, in turn, becomes a means for metaphysical inquiry: it lets us find out (by experiment) what's real, whether anything exists beyond the mortal body, whether anything can survive it. Every sex act involving bondage and discipline, or sadism and masochism, in this sense recapitulates—or blasphemously parodies, or pays homage to—the Christ who died on the Cross, and did not die.

"Mortification" means, etymologically, "killing," but literally it refers to the practices (not only whipping but wearing of hair shirts, intentional undereating or eating bad food, going barefoot) by which monks could show disdain for this life. The historical "flagellants" whipped and beat themselves, or caused themselves to be whipped and beaten, in public, in Catholic Europe from the eleventh century onward. Some were condemned as heretics, although their practices (including public self-whipping) continued in some parts of Renaissance Europe, and continue today in the Philippines. Jesus had nothing to say about whipping yourself, though the flagellants thought they imitated his ordeals. "Release from flesh requires / mortification of the flesh" could mean that Jesus suffered so we could be saved. Applied to sex, however, it means that intensely shameful ("mortifying") or violating acts can make some of us come (bringing sexual "release").

Likening sex at once to penetration and to destruction, to "grinding" (as in the website Grindr, launched after the publication of the poem), Bidart's guilty pleasure also suggests the ambivalence described by Leo Bersani in his famous essay about HIV / AIDS and AIDS-phobia in the 1980s, "Is the Rectum a Grave?" Bersani opined that "gay men" pose a threat to heterosexual masculinity "not because of the parodistic distance that they take from that identity, but rather because, from within their nearly mad identification with it, they never cease to feel the appeal of its being violated." The gay male body is—in Bersani's vision—at once mortar and pestle, unified and cleaving, attracted to the very masculine "hard" strength and integrity that anal sex (for Bersani, the paradigmatic gay male sex act) violates.

Both the integrity of the body and the religious prohibition against men lying with men are violated by desire in general (which breaks down barriers between human beings) and by a penetrative, or grinding, mortar-and-pestle-like sex act in particular. And one of the partners (if not both) in that act experiences that violation as punishment, the punishment that social and religious rules already tell him that he deserves. If you grow up in a culture with such rules, then being punished, feeling guilty, becomes part of the turn-on: if it doesn't make you feel guilty, it can't feel sexy. That feedback loop (which affects nongay men, and women, too) enters Bidart's poem, as it enters Powell's, and that is one reason that Jesus, who carries away our sins, enters both poems too. Bidart is trying to acknowledge the weird, endless loop of guilt, submission, and fetishistic desire, and to come up with another, less shaming vocabulary for it, all in the space of six uneven lines.

For Bersani, sex—which he identifies, somewhat parochially, with penetration—promises a "radical disintegration and humiliation of the self"; sexual experience should not merge a person with another person, or let them get off on each other, so much as it should pulverize or obliterate the self as such. Fuck me so hard that I will forget who I am. No wonder both English (the Renaissance "die") and French (*la petite mort*) have phrases that describe orgasm as death: and to be pulverized, reduced to dust, is to die in a with Christian overtones—ashes to ashes, dust to dust. (Bidart even has a much earlier poem called "Guilty of Dust," whose title quotes "Love (3)," by the Church of England priest and poet George Herbert: "Love bade me welcome, yet my soul drew back, / Guilty of dust and sin.")

"Song of the Mortar and Pestle" dramatizes rough sex and religious devotion, using one as a metaphor for the other, but it is also an argument about what they share. And it is the kind of argument that the great critic Eve Sedgwick—like Bersani a founder of what we now call "queer theory"—would have called "universalizing," since it shows what desirers have in common, rather than what sets some people apart. It is not just that some metaphysics, some religions, some sexual practices, "approach obliteration," and indeed none of those practices ever quite gets there (the word "approach" is important; so is the word "watch"). Rather, from your own bedroom to "the ends of/the earth," whatever turns you on, whatever you believe, you are part of a "desire" that also lies behind, and helps support, and yet also violates, all sorts of metaphysical systems: the desire to take the body outside of the body, to make a song of that destructive trip, to pulverize the self, and thereby make it live.

ROBYN SCHIFF

Lustron: The House America Has Been Waiting For

Room for all our sons. Time
saver. Put away your hammer. Four
rooms with the last
room on the left facing the side yard for which an extension is already planned. Times
change, so should your house. Tomorrow is prefabricated. It's coming on the bed of
        a truck. It has a living
room in another dimension, an opening in the crowded continuum with
room for overnight guests. Some of them won't want to come. They won't be
        missed. A vigilante highwayman is pulling onto the exit ramp. He
spent his last quarter at the tollbooth at the end of the past. The future is coming. It
spends its time, the new money, on golf courses and gardening. It has four
rooms and an eat-in kitchen. It's a straight shot here and when your new
life pulls up it will resemble a train car that jumped the tracks to avoid the heroine
        who's been tied there her whole
life and now has a chance to

live in a house with four
rooms and a sun porch. Its name is Lustron: luster on steel, the luster is porcelain.
        The future
lives in a porcelain-reinforced four-room house with a doily under every vase like
        the clean white shadow grace would cast were it not the source of light itself.
        It's so safe here, porcelain flowers
live forever in a porcelain-reinforced

saferoom, luster on steel like

living in the barrel of a mythic Glock. Imagine a whole

life that feels like the satisfaction of passing through security with undetectable
weaponry in your carry-on. The future is in the overhead compartment and it
won't be long until it's safe to turn it on. It

changes a man to know it's near. I left some

change in the giant putty-colored bed pan into which I emptied my

life; why don't you get yourself some gum to chew while you gossip about my past in
the airport lounge unless you've already

spent so much backyard dynamite preparing your lot for your new house that you're
wading in the curls of

spent firecracker wrappers contemplating the boundless footfalls you

spent mounting the backstairs of Victorian

life while the future parked around the corner was ready to pull up to your curb and
deliver the dreams you earned on the battlefield where you

spent your body. I think you heard the engine idle and thought it was your
neighbor's television's poltergeist

spending its broadband on satellite coverage of a black hole pulling nothing. I've
heard the control

room monitors broadcasting the activity of every grave and it breaks my heart to
learn Mrs. Winchester and I were both wrong about eternal revenge. Not one
soul has ever returned—they all go forward with their anger to

spend deep in the future. In fact, they

save it up, adjust for inflation, and always back both sides comparably in the name
of perpetuation. Lustron has a no-nonsense Westchester model house, which

I like to think of as a Winchester Mystery House for a Western Destiny already

won. See how fast the past slips into the future; it's a matter of a few letters and

a notary public to change your

spent cartridge and you're ready to aim again. It

changes a man to start over. It

changes his perspective—but it doesn't

change the future, the future is a prefabricated four-room house with nowhere to

run. This is what I mean when I tell you to

spend the day reading in bed, maybe

spend some time in the tub, or watch a made-for-television movie. You can't

change your

life so why not enjoy it safe in the knowledge you already live in the porcelain-

enameled mythical Glock everyone's always talking about smuggling into the

cockpit.

Change seemed to be in the air when the privacy curtain dividing cockpit from cabin

changed to a locked door, but Glock first manufactured plastic curtain rods, and the

future was always sliding open in its name. It slips into the shower with you, and

though radio-sheer, you sensed it pulsing near the radio-opaque cuticle scissors

you exchanged for your ticket at the last security check. The past is a hangar of

manicure scissors at Newark International Airport; the future grows claws.

Rumor has it the future stationed air marshals at Denny's to listen for certain words

to be spoken, like the pool of monkeys forced to type until the name of God

appears, and once uttered a sting like a rapture will be triggered. The word is

Lustron. Luster on steel. Four

rooms and a bomb shelter. A porcelain in- and exterior. Let the chosen disappear

and stay a few more minutes here on Earth with me. The museums are empty

and free and I want to run my hand along the underside of the porcelain
        patroness Madame Pompadour's desk to find the hidden drawer where she kept
        her Glock. She
changed her will and left it to us. Imagine a house so poised you can live in its
        teacups. Four rooms and a creamer. They survive revolutions. Some of them are
        virgins. The future is a Louis XVI teacup
saving itself for you. The tea is Paul Ceylon, popular with those who sometimes
        orders take and sometimes afternoon tea with something savory to tide them
        over until probate passes. The Pope sanctioned it and the future

saved you a seat at the Lustron corporate anniversary party. The cake is a simple
        one-level sheet shaped like a Lustron House, which is to say, the cardboard box
        a mythical Glock shipped in. Through transubstantiation it tastes like blood.
        Everything
changes
save the Glock.
Save a piece in your freezer; it's the wedding cake for your commitment to the future.
        Four rooms and a bride who
spends everything but
saves box tops to redeem a year later for what she gave up. Throw things to the river,
        but
save the Glock; you can take it with you.
Life is a series of exchanges; everything valued escalates; the luster is porcelain, even in
        the next
life. Trade is the mother of beauty. Heaven will be knowing no one can
save up. There are four
rooms in eternal salvation. Four
rooms and a motherless Glock.

Introduced in 1947 and manufactured for only three years, Lustron homes (like their more famous round rival Dymaxion) were prefabricated housing intended for the families of returning G.I.'s: the houses' outer walls used not wood but rather porcelain and steel. The Lustron company failed for many reasons, but one of them seems to have involved federal loan fraud: "Seldom has there occurred a like mixture of idealism, greed, efficiency, stupidity, potential social good, and political evil," recalled one employee. Of the 2,500-odd houses manufactured, about 1,500 survive; you can see some at www.lustronpreservation .org. (The poem's subtitle is a slogan from the advertisements.) Several Lustron houses attract tourists in and around Iowa City, where Schiff and her own family live.

The Lustron house and the postwar years help Schiff explore a nervous ambivalence about safety and security, war and technology. They also let her address the events of September 11, 2001, indirectly, by examining that day's long-term consequences: reinforced cockpit doors on passenger airplanes, changes in travel security and in gun culture, the rise of the surveillance state. Schiff also likens the technology of housing, surveillance, and weaponry to her own poetic technique. How much does the maker control the work and the form, and how much does the form control the maker? Do the answers to those questions, or the way we feel about them, change with the form?

Schiff updates a challenging medieval form called the *canzone*, used by Dante Alighieri and others, in which each stanza reuses the same end words. Schiff's five stanzas ostentatiously discard the metrical requirements—her lines can get so long they sound like prose, or contract to single words. As with most of Schiff's work, the combination of elaborate pattern, frequent enjambment, and absence of meter owes something to the modernist poet Marianne Moore. Schiff also moves the required repetitions from the ends to the beginnings of every line: "room," "save," "life" / "live," "spent" / "spend," and "change." As if Schiff had not challenged herself enough, some of the line endings also recycle words, especially in the final stanza: "Glock," "four," "but," "change."

Schiff's poetic "technology" thus repackages an old concept of the stanza (Italian for "room") so that it sounds contemporary (to us). The Lustron had four rooms and could be iterated (manufactured) indefinitely, just as Schiff's new canzone stanzas, each with five key terms, can be rolled out again and again. Yet how new is the stanza, really, compared to old versions?

What new expressions does it permit, or prevent? Can it liberate, or shelter, or confine?

Schiff is not the first poet to bring Moore's elaborations into our own time: her nearly Baroque style has parallels now in Angie Estes, and in the talents of Amy Clampitt, rightly praised during the 1980s, who compared her own poetic lines to rhizomes and roots: in a typical Clampitt sentence, "the strawberry's // red skeins crisscross the gravel / with such rigor you might suppose / it knew the habitat to be untenable / unless tied down." Like those poets, Schiff's elaborate work likens poetic technique to plant cultivation, to craft skills (woodworking, welding, weaving, glassblowing, interior design), and to the making-do, the triage and the bricolage, of household life.

Yet Schiff is self-suspicious in a way that those earlier poets rarely are: she insists that each new technique has a potential for violence, if not for "political evil," and her elaborations speak to the spying and lying, as well as the concealed weaponry, that for Schiff characterize both the post–World War II bourgeois American settlement and our post-9 / 11 society. Is technology to blame? To what extent does it let us do what we wanted to do anyway, and to what extent do its affordances—the things it lets us do, the ways it allows us to live—shape our wishes? "Each technological gadget in her book *Revolver*," Schiff has said, "including the rhetorical turns, has the capacity to make and to destroy." Schiff, in other words, pursues in poetry the analogy between the forms of verse, the forms of rooms inside a house (or an airport), the forms of technology (gun parts, for example), and the forms of social life (its rituals, its expectations, its calendars, and so on) recently explored by the scholar Caroline Levine in a book called *Form*. What do forms let us do? What do they ask us to do?

You can ask such questions in any poetic form, about any kind of dwelling space, but they seem especially sharp when the house is prefab, the forms unmistakably artificial, organized on assembly-line models analogous to, and perhaps learned from, the assembly of guns (a motif throughout *Revolver*). The Winchester Mystery House, now a tourist attraction in San Jose, has its own gun connection: the famously confounding, labyrinthine structure was built over decades by and for Sarah Winchester, the wealthy widow of the man who invented the buffalo-killing Winchester rifle. When do we decide—and when has the form of our society quietly decided for us—how we should live, or when we should go to war, and whom to shoot? Will our rhetoric and our available technology let us build houses, poems, families that we can live in, without seeking (after World War II, after 9/11) eternal military vigilance, or "eternal revenge"? Schiff repeats such questions as we spiral deeper into the poem, which starts with a flurry of slogans about the future: the personal future of a returning G.I., a future or current father, who can put down his hammer and enjoy his new "side yard." As the lines get longer—so long that they grow ungainly—the future turns ominous: will it include vigilantes? Will it, like a greedy fifties wife, spend the "new money" on "golf courses and gardening," or spend money a man doesn't have? Is the Lustron house, like the "porcelain flowers," like suburban life, like the prize in Laura Kasischke's "Miss Weariness," a false reward that patriarchy says we must accept? Is it an empty form?

Those "porcelain flowers" belong in a "porcelain-reinforced/saferoom," a delightfully barbed line break and a compound word that negates its own implication: if you need a saferoom, you're not really safe, or else the people around you don't feel safe. To live inside such a safe room might feel like "living in the barrel of a mythical Glock." Schiff is not so much critiquing that easy target, the suburban 1950s, as enjoying 1950s slogans while critiquing the United States after 2001. In our day, going to airports means "passing through security," a physical motion that is more like moving the barrel of a gun than any physical trip (even through a steel prefab house) a 1950s mom or dad would likely make.

By this point Schiff has stopped echoing the cheery language of Lustron sales and real estate agents and opened up a kind of satirical fantasy. Someone's life has been emptied into a bedpan; someone's "past" (sexual? military?) makes them unfit for 1950s purity, or perhaps unfit to fly. The patriarchal porcelain-insulated suburb of the Lustron house, of homeland security, is a "black hole" into which television pulls everything and nothing: the underworld of the Victorian and Cold War past sucks into itself anything that might represent change or movement in the present. There is no such thing as progress, Schiff's third stanza implies, only a set of military expeditions— each with its own technological innovation—into an underworld of endless war.

So it seemed during the Second Iraq War, during the presidency of George W. Bush, when Schiff wrote the poem; so it may seem, after so many drone strikes, even today. And those wars, like the Cold War, perhaps only extend (as Jorie Graham's "Futures," earlier in this book, suggests) a "Western

Destiny" already woven into American culture and language, visible in the built environment and the cleared spaces of the Midwest, where "it / changes a man to start over" but "it doesn't / change the future." New poetic forms, like new houses, like new western territory, can represent a fresh start: that is the myth of the "American Adam," as the critic R. W. B. Lewis put it. But what looks like formal and technical novelty—here as throughout Schiff's insistent poem—actually represents a trap, or a maze, like the Winchester house, and continues the deadly violence of the past. "The future is a prefabricated four-room house with nowhere to run," and new technology cannot make us more secure.

So what can? We could "spend the day reading in bed," an invitation (to her husband, the poet and filmmaker Nick Twemlow) that Schiff's other poems repeat. But it is also an invitation to despair about changing anything else in this world, much like Blaise Pascal's admission (also quoted by Elizabeth Bishop) that we could avoid all the troubles of this life if we could just sit quietly in our separate rooms. Technology, human invention, human curiosity—whatever takes us out of our own rooms—remains a marvel, but reveals itself as a menace: "the future grows claws."

Not the Lustron but the Glock is the form that succeeds, the form that stands for our America. As Paul Barrett explained in *Glock: The Rise of America's Gun*, the real Glock—introduced in the early 1980s—stood out for its "light, resilient, injection-molded plastic" components, and for its ease of manufacture (since, like the Lustron, it could bypass older, slower methods of fabrication). Both powerful and portable, the gun acquired a (false) reputation in the 1980s for being able to bypass airport security; it also became "the handgun of choice for cops," a symbol of "modernism and efficiency" that stood for "law and security, but also menace, danger and fear." The "plastic curtain rods" that were the Austrian Glock company's original product make a physical link between the safety of the household and the violence abroad; the fictional, undetectable porcelain Glock (introduced in the movie *Die Hard 2*) links the romantic violence of American mythology to the real violence sent abroad in America's name.

For whose "future" is that "Louis XVI teacup / saving itself"? What other future might it occlude? What will happen when (like the regime of Louis XVI) it breaks? Schiff's sense of history goes back before Louis XVI, to Alexander Pope and his 1717 poem *The Rape of the Lock*, where Queen Anne at her Hampton Court palace "Dost sometimes Counsel take—and sometimes Tea."

(She, too, attends to trivial matters while more consequential, more violent ones pass by: a few lines later in that same poem, "the Hanging-judges soon the Sentence sign / And Wretches hang that Jury-men may dine.") To "take orders" is both to follow orders, and to become a priest; Ceylon (now Sri Lanka) produces high-quality tea, but Paul Celan (1920–1970) produced dense, challenging, much-admired modernist poetry; critics often connect Celan's poetry to the Holocaust, in which his family died.

Celan probably would not have enjoyed "the Lustron corporate anniversary party," nor the familial shelter of the Lustron house, nor the Winchester house, nor the affluent suburbs of Westchester County, New York (where Schiff went to college). He might, however, have understood the bleak claim about history. "Everything / changes / save the Glock": as we move from the 1710s to the 1780s, the 1950s, the 2000s, what does not change is the sense that history grows out of the barrel of a gun. Worse yet, if history is not a series of episodes united by nothing but violence, it might just be "a series of exchanges" involving bad economic assumptions, flimsy tokens ("box tops"), false promises, and the ever-present threat of force. "Trade is the mother of beauty" riffs on Wallace Stevens's line "Death is the mother of beauty," from Stevens's "Sunday Morning," a poem (like this one) about not believing in heaven or God. But Stevens's poem really believes in evanescent beauty; in what, if anything, does Schiff believe? If her Lustron house and her poem about it contain nothing but a historicist nihilism, why doesn't the poem feel or sound bloody, or angry, or even very resigned? Why does it seem, at least in part, so inviting?

Schiff does not deprive her poetic technique (its repeated words, its overextended sentences) of its power to please, even while she makes it stand for the violence of American individualism, and of American revenge. She also makes her sallies against domesticity oblique enough that we can continue to admire the house: most of her readers are not going to give up on getting married, or eating cake, or living in America, nor is she. Like Schiff's other poems (the most recent involve her young child), the Lustron house shows us how to recognize the precariousness of bourgeois safety, the presence of violence, without arguing that we must give up all that we own. Temporary safety, companionship, housing, are not "eternal salvation," but they are nothing to sneeze at. Nor is the wish that a loved one "stay a few more minutes here on Earth with me." Nor is beautiful technique, the kind that makes you want to run your hand along it. On the other hand, those things are not as compatible as they seem with the vision of maternity, security, and peace that lay behind the Lustron in the first place: nothing, not even porcelain and steel, lasts forever, there is no "eternal salvation," and you cannot put off death or trade it away forever, not even with the finest gun.

MARY JO BANG

Q Is for the Quick

"The quick brown fox jumps
Over the lazy dog." It was a little bedtime story
And it was only told us if we would "be quiet."
But quiet was a difficult thing to be.
The heart makes a jump-start sound

Each time someone comes up the steps.
A foot gives off the white grate of shoe leather
As it meets a stair. They wanted us also to "be happy,"
Which was even more difficult
In view of the sad fact

That happiness is part of a pair called a "Smug Set"—
Happiness plus some other benignly self-satisfied state.
The story, once we "deserved" it, began,
"Shh, be quiet,"
Just as the quick baby was about to leap.

The story had various endings, each a variation
On the theme of danger that came from caution
Being thrown to the wind. Each ending was equally nefarious,
With the kit inevitably falling
Into the lazy dog's mouth—

The rust color of one, a fox, becoming one
With the cause of the other, a dog.
The idea of gore being nothing but a simple aside.
The endings were all perfect formulations, equal parts
Plaintive whine and equal parts plausible excuse.

"The quick brown fox jumps over the lazy dog" is a famous sentence for reasons that have nothing to do with poetry: supposedly the shortest standard English sentence containing all twenty-six letters, it proved helpful for a century in testing manual typewriters, and it comes to Bang—along with the alphabet itself—as a kind of herald for all the arbitrary orders that children learn, for what Continental philosophers and psychoanalysts such as Jacques Lacan and Julia Kristeva call the symbolic order, and for what educators call, simply, discipline. Bang's dry style works against that discipline: its dissonances, its attacks on smug, too-easy happiness, show what gets left out, who is not served, and how children are sad when adults treat the order we know as the best we can have.

The poems in part one of Bang's 2009 volume *The Bride of E* occur in alphabetical order, from "ABC Plus E: Cosmic Aloneness Is the Bride of Existence" to "Z Stands for Zero Hour"; part two, also alphabet-themed, comprises five prose poems. The alphabet thus functions throughout the volume as (among other things) a reminder of the arbitrary orders that both constrain our lives and make them comprehensible. We may read Bang's poem (like Laura Kasischke's "Miss Weariness") as a protest against those orders, a defense of the girls and boys, men and women and others, who do not fit into them.

But Bang's poem is stranger and bitterer than that. The "story" the poem brings its children has no satisfying ending, and it cuts off, makes impossible, whatever other stories and other sounds the children were sharing before the adults, with their white shoes, arrived: as to the ends *those* stories could have had, who knows? (In *The Bride of E* the poem appears with a full stop after "sound" and none after "steps": the poet herself has corrected the error for the present volume.) Bang's poem, with its literally multiple levels ("stories"), its connecting stairs, imagines and then rejects a story about maturation where questions are answered and goals are met; a story about education where children learn that the world is just and has places for them; and, not least, a story about the alphabet itself in which B comes after A, and U follows Q. These stories do not do what the children would like them to do; instead, the "sad fact" is that they are primarily, or only, means of social control.

The literary scholar Patricia Crain has studied the "individual, social and institutional practices surrounding the internalization of the alphabet, the first step in literacy training," at home or at school. For Crain, modern attention to the alphabet, from the *New England Primer* on, has served as an entry into "a form of literacy in which the self is both mirrored and created through silent, solitary reading." Not to learn language, or, later, not to learn writing, not to be able to say and perform "ABCDEFG," is to stand outside family, culture, and civilization, to live as a kind of speechless orphan; but to learn them, to listen to the people (mostly adults) who impart them, is to take into oneself, to agree to imprint on one's very being, a set of arbitrary rules.

If the process goes smoothly, a child becomes herself, becomes the person that her family and her society would like her to be, by learning to be quiet, obeying grown-ups, and taking their rules as her own, from the order of letters in the Roman alphabet to the right way to eat with a knife and fork, and thenceforward to wedding etiquette, standardized test-taking, and heterosexual, procreative monogamy. But the process is never entirely smooth: we may notice it and accept, or object, or resist. We may feel less like the children of fathers or mothers—well tended by the guardians of the alphabet—than like children in a boarding school or an orphanage, supervised by something impersonal (as impersonal as capitalism or language), though unlike the orphans in famous tales and musicals (*Annie*, for example) we cannot expect parent substitutes to show up and meet our needs at the end.

"Quick" can mean both "speedy" and "alive," and "the quick and the dead" is a proverbial opposition: a baby too quick to be tended might become dead, but an authority too intent on keeping babies safe might prevent them from feeling fully alive. For Bang, we can never "be quiet," can never wholly empty our prior experience in order to accept authority, because our bodies are always telling us something, whether or not we listen to what they say: the "jump-start" of our own heartbeats distracts us, though (unlike a jump-started automobile) it cannot really let us get away. We are therefore trapped—in Bang's scenario—in a space where we have to get what we "deserve," and it is a space that, according to Bang's black humor, puts babies in danger each night: the stories her alphabetical authority generates are not fairy tales from the French (or the Disney) traditions, in which mistreated girls get princely rewards, but cautionary tales such as those in *Struwwelpeter*, where children who take risks get hurt.

Bang's language chafes against that kind of regulation—not only against the rules the white-shoe adults promulgate but against the rules of creative writing ("show, don't tell"). She gets startlingly abstract, almost sarcastic: after the slivers of vividness early on, the white shoe on the orphanage stairs, the poet concentrates on her ideas, or rather on rejecting other people's mistaken ideas, about what we can grow up to be. When concrete nouns come back, they present fables' animals, with the fables' morals reversed: who ever heard of a "quick" fox (young foxes are called kits) being eaten by a lazy dog? Not

Aesop; perhaps Kafka, or Samuel Beckett, or the biblical Ecclesiastes: "The race is not to the swift, nor the battle to the strong, nor yet bread to the wise" (Ecclesiastes 9:1). This fractured fairy tale—the counterpoem within the poem, the provocation to which Bang's own poem reacts—becomes not only a means to enforce obedience, to prevent kids from telling their own stories, but a parable of the arbitrary, mixing up not just right and wrong but prudence and recklessness, cause and effect, tame and wild, abstract and concrete, as the rust-colored fox becomes "one / With the cause of" a dog.

What causes a dog? Other dogs, through procreation? Human beings, by categorizing a dog as a dog? Or God, the final cause (in scholastic philosophy) of all created things? If you do believe in an omnipotent and benevolent God, then you might have to view "gore" as a "simple aside"; the injustice and the carnage in this world are a sidelight or necessary imposition beside the goodness that God, the ultimate adult authority, has placed all around us, a goodness we cannot comprehend.

Bang isn't buying it. Her guarded and resentful children reject—though in vain, since the poem and the story end anyway—the very idea that stories can have hopeful endings: every night, she implies, they hear what is effectively the same story, with the same incredible "endings" (notice the plural). Bang turns up the consonance, the alliteration, and the repetition to give her final lines a sonic satisfaction their sense belies: nothing is "perfect," and only excuses are "plausible," but at least the p's and q's line up: we go to bed with nothing but formal closure, nothing but arbitrary order, to enjoy.

We might say that Bang picks up and translates into a more easily followed, more narrative-friendly vocabulary the goals of such challenging writers as John Yau or Bang's own early teacher Paul Hoover (whose poems can play similar games with stories and forms). In our century, as the critic Brian Reed has explained, those skeptical goals inform poems that take forms from the alphabet, and from other patterns that "offer blueprints for composition without instantly and appreciably burdening poets with the weight of the [poetic] past." We are orphans with respect to the traditions of Milton and Tennyson, as well as with respect to the metaphysical consolations that some of those poets could accept. Instead, we contemporary poets live in the orphanage of arbitrary or elementary prose forms, like the order of the alphabet.

But to see "Q Is for the Quick" as a poem about poetry, about the traditions of poetry, is to ignore its sullen, peculiar, perhaps heartbreaking charge: it is a poem about children without adults, and about adults who cannot reach children. In the books Crain examines, "mothers are meant to counter the anatomizing potential of alphabetization by asserting a connection between the alphabet, the world and the mother's voice." That does not happen here: the people who alphabetize, who discipline, are only a "they." Somebody who refuses to accept stories, who will not respond to the offer of any reward, who will not buy into any system, might be a feisty child, but she might also be, as we say now, depressed.

"From a linguistic point of view," Kristeva writes, "depression is characterized by a disavowal of the symbolic. 'Language means nothing to me; I am indifferent to what you say; I am different from the rest of you; I want to withdraw' "—so (in Kristeva's view) a depressed child might say. So the orphans, the "we," in Bang's poem seem to say as they complain—quietly— to one another and to themselves. "Q Is for the Quick" becomes, viewed through this lens, a poem about ineradicable sadness, a poem about being someone—a representative someone, a set of someones, a plural, a "we"— that no symbolic consolation can mollify. If Michael Palmer discovered during the 1980s how to use avant-garde techniques, refusals and diversions of prose meaning, to present visionary or transcendent experience, Bang figured out in the 2000s how to use some of those same techniques, in the spirit of Samuel Beckett, to describe sadness, bitterness, and a more than ironic awareness that nothing good lasts; that is her stylistic signature.

All of us have something to cry about, some reason—at school, at home, in an imaginary replay of *Annie*—to reject what the smug adults say; all of us have some reason (whether or not we believe it) to think the world unjust. But Bang has also had reasons of her own. *The Bride of E*—a book pervaded by symbols of childhood, from *Alice in Wonderland* to *Annie*—is Bang's sixth; her much-admired fifth book, *Elegy* (2007), responds at devastating length directly to the sudden death of her adult son. Orphans and other children in institutions can imagine surrogate parents; readers of children's stories, especially child readers, can imagine that we are orphans, waiting to be rescued by the real parents who will give us a happier life. Yet such stories, Bang's phrases propose, are how we deceive ourselves: "the idea of gore," the fact of the mortal body, is not peripheral but central, and any other story is at best a "plausible excuse."

LUCIA PERILLO

Viagra

Let the dance begin.

In magazine-land, you two are dancing—
though a moment ago you were engaged
in some activity like stringing fenceline
or baling hay—why else the work gloves
sticking up from your back pockets?
In a whirlwind of pollen, you-the-man
have seized you-the-woman to your breast
—his breast, her breast, tenderly, tenderly—
now you turn away and shyly grin.
Oh you possessors of youthful haircuts
& attractive active wear from L.L. Bean,
you whose buttocks are still small enough
to permit the rearview photograph:
don't you already have enough silver coinage
pouring from life's slot? But no, you also want
the river's silver surge when its bed drops off,
you want the namesake in all its glory—*Niagara*:
even the barge of animals teetering on its lip.
This ploy was wrought by some 19th-century huckster,
the honeymooners gathered on the shore's high bank
to watch the barge drop as creature-cries* rise up . . .
before all the couples re-bungalow themselves
to do what, then what, it's hard to imagine
after so much death. I always thought *Tigers*
until I read the barge was full of dogs and cats—
one baby camel, a demented old monkey,
la petite mort, that little French whimper

given up by the ordinary before it breaks into splinters.
The widow Taylor straps herself in a barrel
and rides it safely over the century's cusp,
& Maud Willard imbarrels herself with her dog
who'll leap from the busted staves alone.
Still, wouldn't the ride be worth that one live leap—
doesn't part of us *want* to be broken to bits?
After all, our bodies are what cage us,
what keep us, while, outside, the river
says more, wants more, is more: the *R*
(*grrrr, argh, graa . . .) in all its variegated coats.
A sound always coming, always smashing, always spoken
by the silver teeth and tongue that guard the river's open throat.

Perillo's chatty, funny poem gets its title from pharmaceutical branding, begins with a joke about a once inescapable advertisement ("Let the dance begin" was Viagra's initial slogan), and ends with an image of death, which devours all things. The same image merges the "mouth" of Niagara Falls, with its endless spikes of silver spray, and the monstrous *vagina dentata* of Freudian imagination, the toothed nightmare that devours men. How does Perillo get from here to there, from light stabs at popular culture and its unrealistic worship of fertile youth to serious speculation about the meaning of orgasm and the denial of death?

One answer lies in Perillo's temperament, which speaks to her body's story. Perillo was diagnosed with multiple sclerosis in 1990 and now uses a wheelchair; some of her other poems address her disability directly. Before she pursued a career as a poet, and long before her MS diagnosis, Perillo worked for the U.S. Fish and Wildlife Service in the Pacific Northwest. "How do you manage to stay in the moment," an interviewer asked her in 2014, "and not fall into despair?" "I've already fallen," Perillo answered. "This is the voice from the swamp. The trick is to make it interesting." Few poets have developed such comedic skills, so many ways to bring into serious poetry the tactics of light entertainment, from puns to Internet memes to icebreaker anecdotes; few poets come back so consistently to entropy and bodily decay, and few poets show such a supple sense of what we have in common with other animals. Our bodies, like theirs, require clean air, food, water; like theirs, our bodies can break down.

Human beings, however, try to deny it. What Perillo finds delightful yet ridiculous, worthy of mockery, in advertisements for Viagra, which tend to show middle-aged couples outdoors, is their insistence that we can refuse to get old. Perillo also pokes fun at Robert Frost, who insisted in "Two Tramps in Mud Time" that both poetry and farm labor should be "my avocation and my vocation": certainly she's having fun with sexual symbols— gloves like condoms, pollen like sperm. The Viagra ad that Perillo envisions portrays the sort of middle-aged affluent couple you might find on a dude ranch, and they haven't (yet) grown too fat, too thin, or too ill to fit their costly "activewear." But they do not believe they have enough: they want consistent, conventionally successful (doubly orgasmic) penetrative heterosexual sex: "you-the-man" giving his "silver coinage" to "you-the-woman," filling "life's slot."

Perillo's poem does not oppose the existence of a drug that helps men get erections. It does, however, find in the demand for such a drug, and in the glossy promotions for it, people who want to have their cake and eat it too: to deny time entropy and death, even while pursuing the very pleasure most bound up with time and change, with one-way progress, chaos and release. What to do with an advertisement averring not just that Viagra works but that life is a dance that need never end?

Make fun of it, of course; and make fun of the drug's name, which must have come about, as most drug names do, from strenuous professionals (often English majors) playing with word associations. (The doctor and science writer Suzanne Koven notes that "Viagra" might come from Latin *vir*, man, as in "virile," and *agra*, farm, suggesting "fertile"; she does not imagine the pun on the falls.) The drug is a stunt even when it performs as advertised, just as the fake Noah's Ark for nineteenth-century "honeymooners" was a stunt (though the animals really went over the edge). Here the poem's satirical energy relies not just on its double entendres but on the wacky diction in which Perillo's best poems specialize: "re-bungalow," "imbarrels." As usual in Perillo, the humorous surface allows her to entertain herself, and to entertain us, as spectators at the falls were entertained, while admitting the harshest of truths: the human desire to entertain and to be entertained, the wish to kill time, and the sex drive end up not just similar to each other, as if they all came from a single source, but similar to—perhaps inseparable from—Freud's *thanatos*, the wish to lose oneself, or to die. We go over the falls, we watch animals go over the falls, we seek orgasms, for adventure, because we want to escape our bodies and our lives: "doesn't part of us *want* to be broken to bits?"

Frank Bidart's poem in this volume certainly says so, but he does not try to make that part funny, nor to see it from a deflating remove: Perillo does. Publicity-seeking daredevils really have gone "over the falls in a barrel," as the saying goes; Annie Edson Taylor, for example, survived the stunt in 1901. Perillo imagines herself and her readers, present and future consumers of Viagra, and their partners and wives at once as the "dogs and cats," as the human barrel-riders, and as the barrel or the cage. Falling bodies, bodies immersed in water, bodies having sex, and bodies dying—all these, for Perillo, resemble one another, and the similarities among them (each one going "over the edge," or "going down," as the idiom has it) can make orgasm look sad or mortality look ridiculous, as well as making them both look like Niagara Falls. Walt Whitman, who visited the Falls twice, played on the same associations: "Something for us is pouring now more than Niagara pouring," he wrote of urban life, "Torrents of men, (sources and rills of the Northwest are you indeed inexhaustible?) / What, to pavements and homesteads here, what were those storms of the mountains and sea?"

Like Bidart, Perillo suggests that desire involves self-surrender. Like D. A. Powell, she considers human bodies not just as vulnerable but as already ill. And like Liz Waldner, she can't stop thinking about water. More than any of these poets, though, Perillo has been trying to turn our attention away from idealized, supposedly typical bodies and to the greater variety—the whole ark, as it were—of bodies that real people actually have. Embodiment itself is what human beings have in common with other animals, such as the animals on Noah's (or "some 19th-century huckster's") ark; embodiment is also something that visibly disabled people share with the nondisabled, and to fully acknowledge anyone's body, we have to acknowledge sexuality too.

Other poets, such as Jillian Weise (see her 2006 book *The Amputee's Guide to Sex*) have turned these arguments into crisp lyric and incisive verse essays. But Perillo—whose poems can note her disability but do not often begin with it—seems to have got there first. In an essay called "Sick Fuck," Perillo addressed the changing relationship among her sense of her body, her sex life, and her MS: though a therapist "felt that my giving up on hope [for a cure] had darkened my outlook, I think hope shackled me to my body as it dropped like dead weight to the floor of the sea. And surrendering hope has left me feeling unburdened, lighter, strangely giddy as I float." Perillo finds "an erotic component to this surrender—it comes from the self relinquishing control, throwing itself away. Then the body is offered to whatever seizes possession of it—whether the seizer be disease or time or a human lover." The pursuit and the enjoyment of sexual ecstasy is a kind of release, for Perillo as for many other writers, from the dry single separateness that afflicts most human bodies, ill or well: though health is a matter of bodily integrity, "when it comes to sex . . . what we want is leakage: for the essence of self to get through to some-body else somehow."

For Perillo to want sex is to want to go "over the edge," to get out of the body somehow. For the men in her poem, to want Viagra is to want to get out of the body doubly, to overcome both the cage of embodiment generally and more specifically the cage of erectile dysfunction (which, in the ads, is caused by age): they want their penises to be more like barrels. But when you go over the falls, your barrel might break. These men are, so to speak, bad readers, bad travelers, like tourists who visit the falls but can't see what's in front of them. "The operating assumption in our culture," writes Mira Bellwether, "is that only hard penises can have sex, that soft penises can't have sex and aren't sexy. This is deeply, deeply incorrect." (If that strikes you as a confusing sen-tence, you may have a narrow definition of "sex.") Women and men with other, less commercially celebrated kinds of sexuality—women and men not fixated on the penises (reliably hard as barrels) that the Viagra ads tell us to want—can have a sexuality that is, so to speak, ours, or *r*'s.

Perillo's sometimes exuberant lines—her lines that go, so to speak, over the top, and over the line breaks themselves—never tells us to stop wanting such things, if we want them. Rather, Perillo's light mockery reminds us that there are things more important than what we want, and that we will not, in the end, get what we want—time passes, the river of time flows only one way. In the deep background of Perillo's themes and tones moves such gentle satire on sexual mores as Alexander Pope's *The Rape of the Lock*; behind her images, we might see the Hudson River School painters, especially Thomas Cole, with his famous allegorical canvases showing the one-way River of Life.

More than most poets in our day, Perillo makes fun of what she may also believe. And more than most poets, Perillo shows the pleasure she takes in sound, along with a pleasure (like Albert Goldbarth's) in collecting facts. The "shy . . . grin" of the ad's mark matches the pleasure of saying, inside a poem, "grrrr, argh, graaa," and the pleasure of placing inside a poem facts that no poem has held before. Her slightly talky metrics, her free verse a bit ampler than iambic pentameter, give the impression that she's lengthened the stan-dard conversational line of English verse in order to squeeze those facts in.

(Other poems in the same collection, *Inseminating the Elephant*, show light-ning striking an Allman Brothers reunion; Elvis Presley impersonators, or "Elvi"; and an old science fiction cartoon vehicle called "Amphicar.") Here the fun serves a question about the Freudian death wish (for Freud, as for many later commentators, inseparable from its opposite, the drive to create new life).

It also serves a feminist end, as the poem redirects the power in sexual sym-bols toward hungry women, away from manly men. The river runs over the falls, and after the falls, and around the falls it makes lots of noise; the absurd onomatopoeia of the end that connects the river's sounds to the doomed "creature-cries" also connects both to the noises of sex. The river thus sounds like it's "always coming." But what it says will not comfort the drug compa-nies who named their penis pills after a tourist attraction and a waterfall. If sex—as our sex-obsessed culture keeps on saying—contains the instructions for a happy life, those instructions may lie less in men's back pockets than in what can be "spoken," from your mouth to somebody's ear. Sexual, erotic, ro-mantic, or bodily fulfillment—if it comes at all—must also come with lis-tening skills, with an openness to our imperfect, real bodies (especially but not only if those bodies have visible disabilities), and with a sense that men's needs are not the only needs around. The closing tableau of the river, with its powerful waters, speaks for women's bodies, not men's: though there is nothing brutal about the Viagra ad, it is still a drug for cisgender men's bodies, and Perillo scores neat points against our conceptions of heterosexual sex by relo-cating its powers in what women do. She also relocates sexuality, at the very end, flirtatiously, provocatively, at high volume, away from the anal ("back pockets," "buttocks") to the oral, "the silver teeth and tongue," the "open throat."

MELISSA RANGE

The Workhorse

His every hair and shred
sheds two uses, or more, for our daily bread.

Good sidekick, stock stand-by,
he helps us tear the ground and haul the rye.

Too much sweetgrass made him lame,
or we did; too much bridle made him tame,

which we did. Nails in his foot
mean he's not good-for-naught;

disease in the hoof, he's a no-shoe
no-show on the field. It's a no-go,

when he founders on the clock:
he'll go free, barefooted, to the block.

Bring me the workhorse; bring me
the pack-mule, the breeder, the gee-

upped whip-smart; I'll end their agony.
Bring me the betted-out racehorse, the pony,

petted and stunted, that made money on the bit,
stumping round a ring. Bring me the unfit,

the falterer, the one who wouldn't take
the halter, the bucker none could break.

Bring me the tons of shoe-iron,
and may the miners leave the mine;

bring me the saddles and the reins,
and may the cattle keep their skins.

Workhorse, pale horse, ghosthorse dead to striving,
bring me the toil of the living

that never rests, that after death still labors—
bones fixing glitter onto shiny paper.

Like Richard Wilbur—but more than twenty years and at least two generations later—Range uses inherited versions of rhyme and meter to describe a
horse. Her horse, too, offers figures both for ethical obligation and for the craft
of verse, and like Wilbur's it stands for labor. In fact, Range's "workhorse"
has already spent his life performing unglamorous labor; that workhorse is
now a dead horse (as in the idiom "beating a dead horse"). He is also an ar-
chetypal horse, an any-horse, the sort of horse that has been and will be rendered, bones and skin used for gelatin, food additives, glue. (Though not all
real glue comes from horses, the making of horses into glue has long been proverbial for slaughter.)

Like Wilbur, Range writes with the conscious goal of perpetuating, of
proving still viable—for her it may feel like reviving—old, elegant form: not
just rhyme and meter as such but the especially difficult, or dated, challenge
of full rhyme in couplets. The poet and scholar David Caplan goes so far as
to call the closed pentameter couplet "the ugly stepsister" at the contemporary
formalists' ball. Yet Range never sounds like a poet of Wilbur's generation,
nor of any prior era: her slangy, speedy staccato delivery could belong to no
earlier writer. She also takes up, as a Christian believer would, the vocabulary
of the contemporary Christian left.

Range's workhorse pulls along with its doomed carriage the variety of people
and things, experiences and tones, scraps, discards—the apparently unlovely
parts of life and language that may seem not to fit a well-ordered society or
an elegant line: these are, as Jesus put it, the rejected stones that become the

cornerstone (Psalms 118:22; Matthew 21:42). Both the making of poems and the functioning of a modern industrial democracy—so Range suggests, while lamenting her own suggestion—are all too similar kinds of furious exercise, testing and winnowing, creating winners and losers, in unceasing labors and endless competition, in which most experiences, most lives, and most points of view are ground down, silenced, used up.

But Range takes a while to get there. She opens instead with syncopated optimism, speaking for the people who are going to consume "our daily bread," giving thanks—as a conventional prayer before meals would—both to the animal involved and to whoever else brought them to our table. Nobody eats horsehair, but she thanks the horse for his hair as well, for all the other ways that he proves useful. Her next couplet continues in that vein, giving thanks for the labor, the man-hours and the horsepower, of animals and people; she sounds grateful, too—satisfied and self-contained.

Then the poet changes gears. Range's first book, *Horse and Rider*, from which this poem comes, mixes poems about the upland South, its agriculture and its folkways, with poems about symbolic horses, shields, grenades, and other symbols of ancient (even Homeric) and modern war. This workhorse is not a warhorse, nor is he a show horse (another proverbial opposition). We might expect to celebrate his peaceful contributions. Instead we've killed him: the repeated syncopated "or we did . . . which we did," following the full rhymes, makes us, the fortunate, the people who simply eat "our daily bread," responsible for the troubles of those who sow the grain and bake the bread.

Literally Range's poem says in its first twelve lines that workhorses work until they cannot follow directions, or until their feet fail. Our society, her society, takes laboring horses, strips them of dignity, and then works them to death, so that the only "freedom" they attain comes when they are too exhausted to use it. How much better do we treat laboring people? Range's apparently playful and closely set rhymes—"foot," "not," "naught," "shoe," "show," "go"—set off the bleakness in her prose meaning. This workhorse, unshod, might put you in mind of John Henry; his fate would not make you recall the Statue of Liberty, except that the American promise of freedom for immigrants, as well as the famous sonnet by Emma Lazarus, enter the poem through loud allusion. "Bring me the workhorse," someone or something says; Lazarus has the statue say "Bring me your tired, your poor, / Your huddled masses yearning to breathe free." Good luck with that. (Range has said that the title and the refrain "Bring me the workhorse" first came to her in a song called "Workhorse," by the singer Shara Worden, who records as My Brightest Diamond.)

Who is speaking in Range's couplets now? Range has begun to use first person plural, the collective voice of her efficient, deceptive, country. Not just the workhorse but the "pack-mule" and the "gee- / upped whip-smart" (a horse that has been whipped so that it will keep moving) all find the same promise here: "I'll end their agony." So do "the unfit" (a rhyme with "bit"); so do the apparently untamable, the horse too tough for cowboys, "the bucker none could break." What fate do we promise such horses? We will kill them.

When Range shifts her grammatical speaker from "we" to "me," her mood from indicative to imperative ("Bring me"), her poem begins to speak for the slaughterhouse, for the rendering plant, for the resources that turn worn-out living bodies and the material attached to them (saddles, for example) into material fit for new use or resale. Kill the worn-out horse and you can use his saddle elsewhere; take off the horseshoes and you can use their iron again. Turn the workhorse (who will die, sooner or later, in any event) into a "ghosthorse dead to striving," render the pieces, and you will be able to avoid waste, save labor, make the horse useful even in death, by (among other products) manufacturing glue.

That glue will in turn find new use in schoolchildren's projects, "fixing glitter onto shiny paper"; their sparkly pages are a diminished, down-to-earth version of the heaven of constellations into which ancient epic heroes ascend after they die. Everything that glitters, Range's poem says, conceals—if it does not reveal—a history of unglamorous effort, and of exploited human and non-human animals. Walter Benjamin's famous remark about civilization ("every document of human civilization is also a document of barbarism") backs her up. Range speeds the language up, makes it disconcertingly elegant, as she speaks for the America that she envisions as (among other things) an abattoir.

Yet it would be wrong to see here nothing except protest (and probably wrong to see the poem as a primer for, or against, vegetarianism). *Horse and Rider* is a left-wing book, a southern book, an antiwar book, a sparkling book that revels in its rhymed and metered forms, but it is also a Christian book: Range holds a graduate degree from Emory University in theology, and many of her poems use tales from the Bible or terms drawn from Christian belief. The horse that works itself to death for the farm, like Shel Silverstein's terrifying Giving Tree, is also a type of Christ, giving up its body over and over for unworthy human beings like you and me.

The workhorse "that after death still labors," whose sacrifice lets "the miners leave the mine," escaping from underground, is also Christ, who entered hell to rescue condemned souls (Ephesians 4:9, and the noncanonical Gospel of Nicodemus). Christ gives believers, through communion, "holy bread." That bread, in turn, has "two uses," as does Christ himself, being flesh and grain, God and man; and Christ on the Cross, of course, had "nails in his foot," the implements of his death becoming the means of human salvation, the ultimate "good." The same rhyming couplets that constitute a sharp protest against a secular society—one that works people and horses to death—celebrate Christian belief. The Statue of Liberty cannot save all "the unfit." But Jesus—Range's version of Jesus—can.

Should the poem's Christian dimension remove its ironies? Can it be theologically orthodox and still object to the way that Americans treat nonhuman animals, or assembly line workers, or home health care aides? Of course it can: we should not have to envision death as the only end of labor, comfort as something we find only in the next world. If the horse is Christ, then "we made him tame" by ignoring the social justice in the Gospels, the Christ who asks the rich to work for the poor. (A horse who "goes free" but ends up on a "block," especially in a poem by a southern poet, suggests nineteenth-century slave auctions, given the abolitionist trope in which Christ is like a black slave.) In the Christian vision of "The Workhorse," human workers (not to mention workhorses) should not have to depend for respite, for justice, *only* on the paper heaven of that final line.

To see the protest—and the solidarity with an American Christian left—in "The Workhorse" is to see where Range gets the righteous energy that propels its metrical lines. But she has not written an uncomplicated call to arms. Range's protest against modern late capitalism is also a promise of death. Her metrical elegance, and her sometime sarcasm, reinforce the self-awareness, the intelligent doubts about her own position, that distinguish this outraged and frustrated poem from the simpler political poetry that we may call (pejoratively) propaganda.

"Bring me," joined by the antiphonal "and may," suggests petitionary prayer: may we have the products of civilization without the barbarism, saddles without skins? Such prayers are not often answered. But Range does not say that she, or we, will leave civilization for some wild country where all horses run free: she concludes in an angry ambivalence. Her meter reflects that ambivalence too. Range has made it "gee-up": though her norm is iambic pentameter ("or WE did. TOO much BRI-dle MADE him TAME"), almost none of her lines hew entirely to that norm—some have only three iambic feet, and many gallop into triple substitutions ("BRING me the," "PET-ted and"). Having begun in syncopations, the poem slows down to end in two almost perfectly regular, uncommonly forceful eleven-syllable lines. The last one envisions "bones in glitter on shiny paper": a constellation, a school project using school glue, but also that glittering, page-based thing, a poem, which represents but cannot fix the injustice its working animals suffer, no more than it can make a horse immortal, or bring the ways of heaven to earth.

JOSEPH MASSEY

Prescription

To think through
each word's
particular weather.

To stand
just far enough
outside of the page.

A field drapes
the eye
in limitless revision.

How shadows
that fill the gap
between two stones

imply the sky's weight.

Most of Massey's poems are as short as this one, or else comprise short, potentially stand-alone parts; most of them present, or re-present, what he can
see. I chose this one because it shows how to read the others. In a poem that
begins as a set of instructions, Massey uses his careful, dry sentence fragments
(further slowed by a line break after each phrase) to tell himself how to write
and what to notice; his poem also helps us think about how we see, how
we combine our intuitions and our experience in order to figure out where
we stand, what we know and who we are. That investigation, in turn, can
stabilize us, both literally and emotionally: in knowing where we are and
what we see in front of us, we can address our anxieties, our anomie, our self-
absorption, "just far enough."

Reading a Massey poem can feel like bringing binoculars into focus, or like trying—successfully—to discern the shape and the identity of an object far away. It might even feel like getting new glasses: the world gets sharper, more interesting, in ways you could not have predicted before you attached your-self to this new (verbal) frame. Massey promises to fit sound and association, what's audible or notable on the page ("each word's / particular weather"), to what's outside it, within the "field" of the eye.

In other ways the experience of a Massey poem is not like getting new glasses: for one thing, it does not happen all at once. Poetry uses language and takes place in time: so does our process of figuring out what it is we have seen and where we are. But this process ordinarily moves quite fast, and without conscious thought—it doesn't take long between the moment you see two wings, a beak, and a tail and the moment you think "bird." Massey's poetry, with its uneven, slow-moving short lines, attempts to slow down the process of perception to the point where we can experience—can think and feel—what are ordinarily intuitive, subconscious impressions and "revisions." Those impressions have their own modes of operation, modes that poetic language can imitate, or contravene, or simply note.

The neuroscientist Jennifer Groh has explained the variety of intuitive or unconscious "rules that your brain uses to construct visual space, the recipe for converting a two-dimensional data set" (what the eye alone sees) "into a rich mental model of a three-dimensional world." Those rules allow us to check our eyes against each other, against our prior information about the scene we face, and against the evidence of our other senses: for example, we decide whether something is concave or convex (a rule called "space to shading") according to our intuition about the location of a light source. We decide how far away something appears to be (where it belongs in our imagined "frame") according to our expectations about how big that thing is (for example, a toddler and a skyscraper might occupy the same percentage of our visual field; we would expect the toddler to be much closer).

"Every iota of spatial information detected by your brain," Groh continues, "whether visual, auditory or body related, must be defined with respect to some reference point," and that definition brings in not just sense data but conscious, emotionally freighted expectations: "your sunglasses might simultaneously be on your head, in the garage, in the United States and even in the Milky Way." To read Massey's poetry is to notice how all those definitions work together, how they all apply to you. Massey's poetry tries to slow perception down and to isolate its elements so as to demonstrate how far is "just far enough," how we learn what the work of perception implies.

How to frame this work of vision? How to "stand" outside one's own continuous observation, put things (and people) in the right frames, and admire—even find awe in—that unending perceptual process, without letting it close up too fast? They are questions bruited by earlier poets, among them the austere and self-conscious George Oppen (1908–1984), whose phrases' "unresolved, lacunary quality," its anti-egotistical "syntactical openness and hesitancy" (I quote the Oppen scholar Peter Nicholls) stand behind Massey's tones. And these questions do not occur only to poets and neuroscientists: they define certain strands of Continental philosophy, notably the phenomenology of the French thinker Maurice Merleau-Ponty, who insisted that we cannot get outside or beyond our environments and the means by which we perceive. Instead, we should realize that we think by means of them, and that we are remade by them, in "a process" (as Merleau-Ponty implied) "of limitless revision." Those same questions have also driven the art of photography at least since the 1920s, when modernist photographers such as Alfred Stieglitz rejected the earlier "pictorialists" who took their cues from nineteenth-century painting. Stieglitz and his peers, in turn, inspired (and were inspired by) American modernist poets, especially William Carlos Williams, by far the greatest influence on Massey (his other influences—Oppen, Lorine Niedecker, Robert Creeley, Larry Eigner—took lessons from Williams in turn).

Massey's other short, semiphotographic poems follow Williams and Oppen in their attraction to subjects other writers would not consider significant or beautiful. "Notice," for example, begins "By the parking lot / of a house / emptied after foreclosure," though it ends with a wasp on "a half-opened fuchsia." Williams insisted that poets should try to stay local, to reflect a particular place, and Massey has done the same, in this case for the light and shadows of Humboldt County, California, which at first struck the East Coast native as "utterly foreign . . . The landscape is open—gapingly so—ocean on one side, mountains and hills on the other—and perpetually shifting in its timbre, in its quality of light." Massey wrote most of *At the Point*, the 2011 book that includes "Prescription," in Humboldt County, though he lives in western Massachusetts now.

Massey does not imitate a particular photograph. But his stanzas—a series of "fields," a series of frames, divorced from premodern technique as modern photography divorced itself from painting—might feel like photographs, or like meditations on what photography can do. They show how we frame (and cannot help framing) what we see, whether the "frame" is an abstract preconception, the literal limits of sight, a metal rectangle, or a rectangular page. Massey's poems, with their many breaks, show us negative space—the sky, gaps, shadows—and they show us how negative space, absence, and implication matter as much as positive things seen and named: the gaps between his stanzas can even evoke the "gaps" where shadows fell. The poem itself is something like a shadow, an object produced when the external world acts upon our intellect and our eyesight. (The poem by Robert Creeley elsewhere in this volume does similar work with the unsaid, with negative space on the page, or silence between lines.)

Massey also shows what poems can do that photographs (of any sort) cannot. The poet's temporal art can "think through / each word"; it can not only stimulate but mimic thought, including second thoughts and the mental process of "limitless revision." The brevity here serves that purpose too: a longer poem would not be able to slow down as much, would not ask us to place so much weight on each word. And a verbal and temporal art form—unlike a visual, instantaneous one—can try to evoke synesthesia, turning sight into "weight." It can change the pace at which we imagine, by changing the shape of its line breaks. And it can work as an explicit set of instructions, telling us what to do, or what we can do.

Any sympathetic reader will find in Massey's poetry of careful eyesight, of landscape, location, and atmosphere, a worthy heir to Williams's (and Stieglitz's) projects. Yet Massey stands apart from his sources, not just in self-consciousness about what the poet must "think through" in order to see but also in the emotional "weight" and in the sort of person his poems ultimately project. Massey's laconic lines investigate stances and masses, shadows and gravity, not least because their impersonality, their way of fixing a body in place, provides emotional ballast. The poet who stands behind this poem needs accuracy, needs revision, as if they alone could let him keep his head: he ties himself to the rocks, to the ground, so to speak, so that he does not fly off the handle or float away into vague space. And that is why Massey at his best depicts at once a form of calm and a kind of anxiety. His poetics of intensely revised and carefully arranged perceptions may take us out of ourselves, allow us to bear an otherwise intolerable weight, and calm us down.

Massey calls his poem "Prescription," a word applied not just to drugs but to opticians' lenses, without which we could not see clearly: he describes not something he wants but something medically required, something we might need too. In another of Massey's many poems about the northern

California coast, sand dunes and detritus represent his states of mind: as the tide goes out, "The panic / that would // pull me / under // somehow / recedes." "Prescription," too, reflects a held-off panic, an inner necessity to get the visible world just right, and that necessity carries "weight," a word that suggests the technical process of color saturation, the density of ink on a printed "page." It also suggests the weight of the sky that the giant Atlas, in Greek mythology, must hold up, on his own, until the end of time. The "limitless" work of that unfortunate titan resembles the moment-by-moment, restless, endless work of putting the perceptual world together, of turning that 2-D retinal picture into a 3-D world. Both kinds of work resemble the emotional work of keeping the self together, of taking each day's responsibilities as they come.

That present day, in turn, may look like a gap between two grinding stones: the best navigators could find the line in between. In Massey's gaze, even the smallest hint, the blandest object, itself becomes a kind of line to follow, an escape or a remedy (the smaller the better, perhaps) for a personality that wants, or needs, to be taken out of itself. The poet, for a while, becomes his eye, and leaves his troubles in the white space that surrounds the page. The eye cannot stop revising; the giant cannot rest from holding the sky; the poet cannot stop trying to correct his vision, though eventually the poem must end. And when we see someone (poet or not) so insistent, so perfectionist, about a minuscule process, we might wonder what he or she is leaving out: what happens in the "shadows," in the rest of his life, in the space outside the frame.

DG NANOUK OKPIK

Date: Post Glacial

A fern curls and drinks   water next   to the Chena River;
she / I engrave / s   with drill bows   the tattoos

      layered   on the backside of a gray whale,
polish   with cotton in circles   to bring out the design.

Over the sea black-whales   arch and span,
      while four-sided sabers   guard the processing

        barge—a city atop the sea.

Pollen lands   where the air is good.   Dig for chert bone.

Find an antler.   Reel in the velvet   make a map for trade.

Small wooden faces   flat   with skin-lined splinters ask:
      Should we prune   *more trees or tag and replant?*
We   the Red Stone people
     keep our millwork central.
In the New Stone Age   don't let the paddlewheel rust.

Around our chins   tie the knitted   musk oxen hat
with ivory toggles   firm and fixed.

Kiln powder in beveled pools   on beetle rust greens.
   The talc settles   no rain in seventeen days.

Invent a fan to blow   the north wind   to cool the ivory
                                                                   bone etch.

The tall grass

calls bent birch   snowshoes to make tracks. *Do we run*

a tap dry of soot   and sludge to forge roots?

How many drink   wild tea, dip blubber in seal oil?
From the horizon   she / I watch / es fire opals   come from

molten rain,   the clay mass   returns to
                          full grass baskets.

You might expect a contemporary poem about the changing global climate,
about the future of Inuit traditions (based as they are on Arctic and subarctic
ecology), and about whales and whaling to sound pessimistic: to become a
jeremiad, a protest or a lament. And okpik—"Inupiat, Inuit, raised by an Irish
and German family in Anchorage," as her first volume says—has written laments, poems against corporate oil drilling, poems that speak for whales and
other animals sacred to Inupiat culture past and present and endangered by
contemporary life. But this poem is not one of those laments: instead, it envisions a happier period, what geologists call the postglacial or the Holocene,
not exactly as a paradise lost, but as an ideal to which we might someday
return. Her "post glacial" people follow traditions and exemplify sustainable
lives, but they are also surprisingly intimate with what either is or else resembles modern technology: they are not just a distant past but a near future that
the First Peoples of the American and Canadian North might live to see.

The poet (who spells her name without capital letters) invokes that future
first by invoking the water cycle: her "fern curls and drinks," as a human being
would. "She / I" refers not to the fern but to the composite persona, both poet
and animal (usually poet and whale) that okpik inhabits through her book
Corpse Whale: the virgule and conjoined pronoun, though awkward in recitation, remind us that okpik does not want to see herself wholly apart from the
nonhuman world. "She / I" seems to be tattooing a whale! Is she making a

model whale? No: the "black whales" "over the sea" must be real ones, since they swim there ("arch and span"). The poet writes (in correspondence) that the whales' tattoos suggest those which Inuit women traditionally receive on "face and cheeks"; she adds that her "brother is a whaling captain in Kaktovik, AK" who practices traditional (and legally protected) whale hunts. A "processing // barge," however, protected by "four-sided sabers" (a brand of powerboat), belongs to the principally Japanese practice of nontraditional, industrial whaling: it looks like a threat to older forms of life, for Inuit people and for whales.

In the near future, however, things could be otherwise. A barge that resembles "a city atop the sea" could be turned into housing, and de-militarized; it could become part of a sustainable economy, one big enough to include new small cities, and big enough for arboriculture, big enough and literate enough for the question "tag or replant?" These phrases envision a space and time appropriate for such questions, "where the air is good"; okpik offers neither a protest against the bad present, nor a look back at a traditional past, so much as a near-future ecotopia. "New Stone Age" translates "neolithic," the period in human history when agriculture began, but this New Stone Age has paddlewheels that can rust. It may lie in our future, not—or not just—in our past.

Yet it draws, of course, on traditional crafts. Ivisaaq, "red stone," is a form of hematite commonly used as an ochre pigment or glaze; "red stone people" might be named for it. Arctic cotton, or eriophorum, grows in traditional Inupiat lands; the Chena River, near present-day Fairbanks, flows into the Yukon River and does not reach the sea (there is a Redstone River in Alaska too, but it is nowhere near the Chena). Chert bone, or bone chert, is not a bone but a chalky or bonelike form of the rock called chert, noted for its sharp edges and therefore suitable for making knives and spears. The poet, who uses Inupiat words copiously elsewhere in her poetry, avoids them here, perhaps to make this future seem available to us all: a future designed along Inuit traditions might have room for people from other backgrounds, whereas the future we will have if we continue to drill for oil has room for no one.

This tableau obviously draws on the postglacial period in the sense that archaeologists use the term: the time when the glaciers receded and many peoples, including those that would become today's Inuit, made new ways of life in the north. But it might also be "post glacial" in another sense, in that okpik works to imagine a way of life that could persist and flourish when glaciers are gone: a traditional society, in other words, with norms drawn from cold-weather Inuit culture, fit for a warm, flooded earth. She has not ruled out snow and ice—people use snowshoes for something—but she has not depicted them directly: her poem strives for a double exposure, a way to see the past and future, a postglacial (Holocene) traditional life and a postglacial (Anthropocene) life with a light burden of technology, together.

What about those "fire opals," that "molten rain"? We may be watching a sunset, but the language applies more readily to a volcano, or a manmade disaster—one she sees from far away, almost as the poet of this safe space can watch the demise of a civilization that she does not need, one that does not belong to her. "Come from" uses the simple present tense of events that only take place once (what Slavic languages call the perfective), but "returns" suggests the continuous present, for events that take place over and over: even volcanoes are part of a natural process, spewing up earth and returning it to the earth.

Like C. D. Wright, okpik attends to all the bodily senses, letting us hear each phrase as if in isolation, envisioning each thing before we move on to the next. Her lines run out to the margins of the page, as if to notice the entire environment, horizon to horizon, but without filling it up (she leaves white space inside). By the time okpik begins to tell us what to do, or to ask us questions ("How many?") about what we see, we have had time to imagine that we are there. Her style, in other words, fits the task called world-building, commonly undertaken by writers of science fiction and fantasy, who have to make credible places and societies that cannot or do not exist. "Date: Post Glacial" treats this place and its people that way, placing okpik momentarily among them ("we") but largely adopting a kind of observer status, showing us a safe, sustainable space, where problems seem local and can be solved: there may be a drought, but there are still "full grass baskets," and the water table permits the cutting and sculpting of clay.

If the date in "Date: Post Glacial" is both past and future, then the poem participates in a project now undertaken by authors of prose, indigenous and otherwise: the project of imagining a future in which human beings might live less destructively than we do now. Science fiction writers such as Geoff Ryman and Kim Stanley Robinson attempt to find, or stoke, hopes for preserving what we call civilization; cultural critics and novelists such as Paul Kingsnorth, who view industrial civilization as wholly doomed, use the techniques of fiction to imagine what might replace it. "Date: Post Glacial" might conceivably belong in either camp. and it belongs to a third category, one historically linked to poetry rather than prose: it is not just a utopia but a pastoral cornucopia, one whose "full grass baskets" imagine a space in which we have satisfied our basic human needs. "We the Red Stone People" then discover the leisure to make art, whether that art consists in tattoos and carved stones or in a set of English-language poems.

The journalist Charles Wohlforth, who lived with climate scientists and with Inupiat people in Alaska, has compared our current challenges to those of the Medieval Warm Period, the time from about 800 to 1200 CE when "warming made the entire north a rich, open frontier for development based on whaling," and the people who would become modern Inupiat and Inuit spread out from what is now Alaska to Greenland. Today's climate change, Wohlforth (writing in 2004) continued, could "return us in a circle to the Medieval Warm Period," but it could also produce a planet "beyond the scope of human experience." History is no cause for complacency, even if it alleviates despair. Nor can we look back to history: we have to imagine the future with the help of the past, and that is what okpik's set of indigenous terms, her vision of "post glacial" Inupiat lifeways, attempts.

ROSA ALCALÁ

Class

It's not work
just because
you can get it.

It's the luck
of the hem
and the heel

a perfectly turned
drinking clause
made readable.

What some call
internal dialogue
my dad would have called

brandy.
It's not work
if you can spell

it. A union line
hemmed against
cold weather

gives Poles
and Spaniards
little to talk about:

pre-printed placards
struggle to rhyme
equality with anything

And Jersey
keeps me rubbernecking
like free verse

can cure
some poor fuck's
lung cancer.

Today, students
are working out
class schedules

and I propose a course
objective of carrying
paint drums

across the length
of my office
until someone gives.

Since the 1950s, many—perhaps most—well-known American poets have taught in universities, pursuing a familiar American promise: that the study of culture, and within it literature, even poetry, can be made fairly available to all. But universities also show how America can be unfair. The people who clean the classrooms are not the people who teach in those classrooms. The students whose sports and clubs meet three evenings each week are not usually the students whose full-time jobs pay for their books, and the latter group is less likely than the former to study poetry. Social class, and the limits of working-class life, can thus trouble or undermine the goals of the classes—for example, the literature classes—that a university holds.

That pun on "class" is where Alcalá's tersely frustrated poem begins. Alcalá also pursues questions much older than modern universities: Is poetry "work"? Is it a craft to be learned, a kind of labor measured in years, days, hours? Is it like other kinds of labor, and if so, what kinds? Or is it, instead, a luxury, a product of what Latin authors called *otium*, nonwork, a privilege? Alcalá raises those questions (which are also Virgil's questions, and John Milton's) without letting go of the historical moment and the economic position that she herself occupies; she also points to the changes in higher education that have made the study of poetry and the pursuit of a college degree less leisurely than they once were.

Alcalá's mother and father held blue-collar jobs in New Jersey; her father worked in a dye house (a plant for dyeing fabric), where he belonged to a labor union. Her first book, *Undocumentaries* (2010), reflects her research into labor history and into her own family background. "As a first-year tenure track assistant professor," she remembers, "I knew no one who worked in a factory, even though almost every adult I knew growing up, including my parents, were factory workers." "Factory is something not heard / but written in degrees / as breath. It never signs off," begins her poem "Autobiography." As such dense lines suggest, Alcalá has tried to reflect on class injustice, as well as on Chican@, Latin@, and Puerto Rican heritage, without writing poems that could be mistaken for memoir. Her own advanced training—at Brown University and the State University of New York at Buffalo in the 1990s and 2000s—would have placed her among writers deeply opposed to memoir-like, confessional, first-person poetry; by the time she wrote "Class," first published in 2007, Alcalá taught in a graduate program at the University of Texas–El Paso, one of very few that support creative writing in both English and Spanish.

What does it mean to read a poem and say you "get it"? Alcalá's first stanza opens up several meanings; maybe the kind of poem where you "get it" (i.e., understand and sympathize intuitively) isn't the kind of poem that counts as "work" (i.e., a literary work; i.e., intellectual effort, worthy of a college class). A poet with democratic aspirations would more likely satirize such a claim than endorse it. But "work" can also mean "paid employment"; "get" can mean "obtain," not "comprehend." Read the stanza that way, and it might represent a blue-collar parent rebuking a studious child: what you got (a literary education) might not get you a job.

Alcalá's opening stanza juxtaposes literary "work" ("John Milton wrote three long poems and many other works") with paid employment ("How long have you been out of work?"), and both with the effortful interpretation ("Reading Milton can be a lot of work") for which professors and critics get paid. Those critics (myself, for example) may work hard, but we have also had some "luck" on the way to our literary jobs. Some of us grew up financially secure enough that we could study whatever we wanted; some of us dressed (chose hem and heel) for success, or dressed to impress. Some of us found the right people to go out drinking with, people who helped us find literary careers, or (in a less mercenary vein) people who steered us toward poetry we loved.

Can a class-conscious poetry work to make these connections, these pre-conditions for literary success, "readable"? It can, but success in that goal will not make class injustice melt away. Poems, like brandy, can certainly "spell" (relieve, reduce pressure on; also ensorcel or enthrall) people who enjoy them, though poetry, unlike brandy, sets out to make us think. It may also set out to denounce exploitation. Yet the best "union lines"—lines of argument about unions, or catchphrases that make unions stronger—do not necessarily make the best poetry. "Union lines," as in picket lines, must unify people of varying taste and literacy. They should also unify speakers of multiple languages, as they did in the heyday of the U.S. labor movement, from the 1930s through the 1960s, when unions supported many white "ethnic" workers—from "Poles" to "Spaniards"—even while brown and black people were turned away.

Alcalá has been separated from unionized "Poles / and Spaniards" by, so to speak, a Jersey barrier: to look closely at labor disputes now, to look at factory workers from the perspective of a full-time college teacher, is to look at harm from one remove, like the "rubberneckers" on New Jersey's highways. Her careful poetry may not speak for them, any more than it can cure "some poor fuck's / lung cancer." Words are not the medicine he needs. The expletive testifies to Alcalá's frustration, and not to hers alone (other contemporary poets, among them Mark Nowak and Rodrigo Toscano, have made entirely separate careers as labor organizers, though Nowak is now a university teacher too).

Alcalá's clipped lines suggest frustration with poetry but also with labor activism. "Work," "class," and "lines" have multiple meanings, and all of them point to things that are hard to change. The actual histories of the U.S. labor movement, "placards" for pickets and marches that have already occurred, testify only to partial success: nothing matches (rhymes with) the dream of full equality, and though the labor movement has its own history in poetry, chronicled by scholars such as Cary Nelson, neither old (rhyming) nor new ("free") forms of poetry seem able to liberate blue-collar workers in Alcalá's twenty-first century, when picket lines are a less common sight. If poetry, in twenty-first-century America, cannot fix large economic injustices, it can at least give us ways to think about them, and it can alert privileged readers (like me) to experiences that we have not had. It can also give pleasure, and it can make us more versatile, more flexible, stronger users of words in language, exercising ("working out") our cognitive, verbal capacities. But the poet's students are not necessarily "working out" either their verbal skills or their abs; they are "working out / class schedules," even as she is stating "course / objectives" for the benefit of an educational bureaucracy.

Even as Alcalá distills her own working-class past, she speaks to the annoyances—intellectual and practical—of her academic present; they pop out when she addresses her students, as the word in the title reappears within the poem. The critic Jennifer Ashton has argued—against its left-wing, avant-garde detractors—that "lyric," that is, poetry "equated with the expression of a self," can serve the cause of social and political equality: it can push back against "the widening reach of markets into every aspect of daily life," as well against recent changes in higher education that make teachers and students of literature feel more like bureaucratized drones. "My university doesn't really care if I finish my second book," Ashton quips; instead, she's supposed "to fill . . . classrooms as tightly as possible." In such a climate, poetry can help her and her students make figurative space. Institutions require teachers like Ashton, like Alcalá, to speak neither in the clipped language of cold picket lines nor in the challenging language of modern poems but in the cant of educational bureaucracy, where each course must have "course / objectives." What is your "objective" when you reread a book you love? Though Alcalá seems to be writing about university teaching, her difficulties with institutional goals could also describe what middle and high school language arts teachers have had to face in the age of the Common Core.

Seeing the gap between avant-garde poetry that claims to address injustice and words that most victims of that injustice would understand, and seeing the other gap between bureaucratic educators' "objectives" (which must be measured) and the goals of poetry (which cannot), Alcalá wonders whether a few hours of carrying paint drums would bring privileged students or oblivious administrators to their senses. Her parodic "course" looks more like an obstacle course or a course in physical training than a college class, but it would teach students who did not know such things how physically challenging—and how mentally draining—the labor of a factory floor can get. Her proposal might not make them all "get it," but it could make them more generous (more likely to "give"), less complacent, or less closed off to experience not their own; it could, on the other hand, just make them fall down ("give way") or give up (on the physical task), even more exhausted than a classroom teacher at the end of the day.

Like Robyn Schiff in her canzone or Liam Rector in "Saxophone," Alcalá has constructed her poem around the multiple, sometimes conflicting, emotion-laden meanings of common words: "class," "work," "line," "get," "give," "course," "spell," "call," "free" (as in "cancer-free"). These words, together, point to her discomfort (and not hers alone) at the intellectual and social distance between many classrooms and many factory floors, as well as the distance between the ideal classroom (a space for democratic inquiry) and the real one (a space where bureaucracy impinges and social privilege gets reinforced). It's not only that this one teacher feels out of place—the poem works hard to avoid becoming mere autobiography, one person's story, and uses "I" and "me" only once apiece. Nor is it just that other students from working-class backgrounds might also feel out of place. Rather, Alcalá's poem attacks, scrapes against, line by line, the intellectual and geographic separation of the academy from other, less chatty, less theorized places of work, pointing to more generous views of "class," of "work," of labor. Its sarcastic epigrams (what "is not work," and who says?) let us inhabit her persistent sense, somewhere between an educator's beleagueredness and an activist's outrage, that the U. S. class system, the U. S. academic system, and the U. S. labor market, must not continue as they are.

GABBY BESS

Oversized T-Shirts

What if I'm actually boring and I only know
how to communicate with people [men]
via a hyper-sexualized version of myself?
I'm posting this inquiry
to the conspiracy theory message boards.

Sitting on your couch in my best underwear,
with my hair up and your old shirt on,
I am a small boy swallowed by his
father's clothing
Proud & Smiling.

LOOK WHAT I'VE DONE, DAD.

Last night, our naked asses touched
and that is what we were:
Two Naked Asses Touching

We weren't supposed to do this
We weren't supposed to get naked
like this and then leave our bodies
to look down on ourselves, aerially,
viewing the shapes that our spines
could make together

Now I sit on your couch and project an image
of the word BORING onto your forehead as
if your thoughts were showing through

your skin.
Our fingers,

fractions away
from holding hands,
remain heavy islands

(There is probably a mathematical equation
for figuring out the amount of time spent
staring at empty hands in the average lifespan

For the amount of time that is spent walking past couples
and laughing

For the number of times I have wanted to scream out to them,
to those filthy hand-holders:

YOU ARE FUCKED UP

And the number of times that I simply continued to walk,
turning
like an unsteady sniper trying
to carefully discern
which pair of hands
could be loosened to fit
mine between them)

You look straight ahead, unflinching,
as I look at you, projecting
more words onto your forehead. Our spines create
shapes unnamable and our faces look sad
but I think that is just the way our faces are.

"Alt-lit"—a term coined around 2010—denoted verse, prose, fiction, memoir, long blog posts, and an unstable mix of all those forms, created by, for, and about young writers (many under twenty-five) and tightly connected to their presence online. Alt-lit makers characteristically saw no bright line between curated periodicals and Tumblrs or blogs, between proper books and PDFs or other large files, between recognizably literary genres—short stories, stand-alone poems, published essays—and supposedly ephemeral, character-istically digital forms. Their wide-eyed "post-ironic" or ingenuous stances com-plement a deliberate—or naive—disregard of institutional, social, generic, and technical boundaries between art forms. The same disregard marked such widely noticed authors, artists, filmmakers, and showrunners of the early 2010s as Miranda July, Sheila Heti, Tao Lin, and Lena Dunham, with their hybrids of comedy and documentary realism, their novels that felt like blogs. (All are older than Bess, and only Lin published in self-declared alt-lit venues.)

As with bloggers and fanzines—and Beats and confessional poets before them—these writers were drawn to parts of life too abject or embarrassing or too bound up with ephemeral popular culture to fit into more sophisticated, older frames; detractors point out that the writing lacks familiar signs of technical competence, while proponents argue that it has techniques of its own. Like Dunham, Bess pursues an ambivalent, push-and-pull relationship to the confessional and to celebrity, along with a clear commitment to the femi-nist project of making previously untold, previously shameful, gendered expe-rience clear. "What's remarkable, and often enviable, about Lena Dunham," Bess has written, "is her ability to view herself as a case study." "Oversized T-shirts" looks like a way for Bess to present her own sadness as a case study, along with her skepticism about whether she can be more than that, whether she can hold other people's interest. Its desperate divagations, its unstable tone—exhibitionist, or evasive?—and its incorporated slogans also explore how friendship and romance change when they are conducted largely online.

Bess opens with a blizzard of inappropriateness, in tones (flighty, self-conscious, chatty), terms, and even typography (square brackets, "hyper-sexualized," Internet slang, "asses") that would have seemed awkward, un-dignified, or baffling in almost all earlier poems. Poetry has for centuries changed (or "progressed") as poets let previously prohibited tones and forms of language into their art, from the "language really used by men" in Wordsworth to T. S. Eliot's "etherized" to the blow jobs in Allen Ginsberg and John Wieners. It's easy to see Bess's unsexy deshabille, her disheveled bodies and hypercasual language, as the next link in that long chain. But she feels like a weak link: she sounds insecure as well as naive, like someone dressed up in clothes too large for her, the "small boy" her third and fourth sentences describe.

She is not a boy, and her friend or lover or friend with benefits, whose naked ass touched hers, is not her father: her metaphor heightens the awkwardness, the inappropriateness, that the poem has set out to address. How *should* she see herself? How should we see her, whether we are in the same room with her or reading her writings and art online as strangers? And how can she present herself at once as an apostle of sharing, of openness, as someone who has chosen to make herself an example (as Bess says that Dunham has done), and still convey her fear that she's out of control?

She can do so through her next two figures: out-of-body experience and the party game Forehead Detective, in which players write words on one another's foreheads, then try to guess what's on their own. The first figure ("leave our bodies / to look down on ourselves") speaks to the detachment that comes with inappropriate, almost involuntary sexualization ("you are responding to my body, not to me; I feel as if I did not live in my body") as well as to mortality (she sees herself from above, as if she's deceased). The second figure speaks to the goal that lyric poets have long pursued: we use words to make explicit, to make available to other people, an otherwise unknowable inner "me." Forehead Detective, in Bess's hesitant verse, acts out, almost travesties, that serious literary project. Ascribing to other people the qualities that we fear in ourselves (boringness, for example), we speak to the sense of isolation, the sense that we are stuck with our flawed, separate selves, that lyric poets set out to assuage. "Yes! in the sea of life enisled," wrote the Victorian poet Matthew Arnold, "we mortal millions live alone." (He, too, felt like a heavy island, as well as feeling sexually unsatisfied.)

The more isolated you feel, for Bess, the more expression you crave, and the less good it does you. "Oversized T-shirts" ends up describing the solitude of the single person inside the T-shirt, the difficulty she has in touching anyone else. Such feelings are hardly specific to a digital generation (as Arnold's verse proves), though the informal sociolect of our time gives Bess new ways to make those feelings vivid. Alone, or "alone with other people" (the title of Bess's 2013 book), we see couples on the street and feel jealous of them—we may want to come between them, or to destroy them, or to join them and make a third. (Marjorie Garber has written that it's "very common, especially for adolescents and others inexperienced in love," to "fall in love with a couple . . . they have, after all, succeeded in winning that most desirable of objects, each other.") Bess remembers those sights in an awkward and talky nonsentence, as if embarrassed by the aggression and the unruly desire ("like an unsteady sniper") that her own wish implies. When she looks back "at you," she sees words, as if reading a screen.

Bess gets her technique and her audience from the Internet, and it's tempting to say that she gets a great subject there too: here are two people intricately dependent on digital media wondering whether their dependence on media has cut them off from some more authentic—or less "hyper-sexualized," or truer—version of themselves. What sort of poet begins by wondering whether she can be reduced to her image online, whether she's nothing more than a name on a message board (a "conspiracy theory message board," devoted to dubious connections), and ends by suggesting that she will always look sad? This sort of poet, of course: a post-confessional poet, one whose poems build up and then distort a sense of unmediated, Internet-age self-disclosure. Life online—so we are told (so Bess must have been told)—destroys traditional boundaries between private and public language, appropriate and inappropriate speech, since anything that can be thought can now be said, written, or read somewhere. These vaults let some alt-lit writers try to construct a new tone, at once vulnerable and defiant.

In doing so they might be liberating themselves and their readers (especially young female readers) from a patriarchal double bind. The alt-lit poet Ana Carrete, for example, entitles one poem "i feel tired and google all my sentences" and another "Freudian clit": in the latter, "the stress that we release is the product / of not being allowed / to feel okay / while being honest." Another new poet of the 2010s, Patricia Lockwood (check out her volume *Motherland Fatherland Homelandsexuals*), owes her sudden fame to her real talents in verse, but also to her raunchy, comedic presence on Twitter, and to the popularity of her important prose poem "Rape Joke," which has been shared online tens of thousands of times. Online presence and openness about sex (both pleasurable and traumatic), in Lockwood, in Bess, in Carrete, and indeed in culture, are related: the habits encouraged by one make the other possible. Transformed by online communities, new modes of poetry create a space, perhaps the only space, where we can feel at once honest and okay.

Bess's poem calls more skeptically on similar effects. Faces don't touch in this poem, only "Naked Asses," in a line whose capitals suggest a catchphrase (something like Rainer Maria Rilke's definition of love, "two solitudes," parodied). Maybe expressions, emotions, felt needs, are real, but they do not point, in the way that previous generations of writers believed they did, to consistent, unchanging souls or selves. Or maybe they do point to souls, to selves—but that pointing, that "projecting," feels different now that privacy feels different, on Facebook and Twitter and Instagram. Bess has written a poem that examines—is not just a symptom of but a take on—how we "read" each other online and in person, what privacy and intimacy now mean. But she has also written a poem about one troubled romance, about two people who "get naked," end up looking down on themselves, and do not like what they have become.

Some social critics call Bess's generation "digital natives," always already confident online. But the sociologist danah boyd, who has studied teens' online lives, considers the term misleading. Instead, boyd says, social life online—in blogs and tweets, on sites such as Facebook, and elsewhere—has three distinguishing features: "persistent content" (the ephemeral is now archived), "invisible audiences" (you don't know who will read your posts), and "collapsing contexts," as when people who know you from school or from your family discover posts meant for people who know you from work or through your drag king alter ego. These features bring fleeting social interactions, blog posts, and bits of conversation closer to the status already enjoyed (at least in aspiration) by works of literary art, which (their authors hope) persist through time and get read by strangers, who make sense of them in divergent ways.

Conversely, the constant exchange of emotion-rich texts online might make the boundaries of literature—of finished artwork—seem beside the point: the jagged lines and exclamations ask what sort of text we have been reading, whether it counts as performance art, monologue, a script for performance, or an unconventional poem. The poem itself faces collapsed contexts, uncertain bounds, as Bess's raw style reveals—even though it concludes with a familiar disappointment, a resignation and a twist, and a pair of lines that are nearly blank verse ("that is just the way our faces are"). Our wish for experience shaped, for a poem that feels closed, like the almost reflexive tropism of so much spoken English toward the pentameter, stays with us, and with Bess still, even as she hovers above her former self, a creature from the future, in midair.

Besides her own writing (poetry, short fiction, reviews, and personal essays) and her video art (available online), Bess edits *Illuminati Girl Gang*, an all-women, youth-oriented, mostly online journal of poetry, fiction, and visual art. Bess's interviews and essays, as well as her Black Dot series of visual poems (available as of early 2016 at http://theblackdotseries.files.wordpress.com/2012

/o2/theblackdotseries.pdf), situate her in between new and old media, between performance and written text, close to a line of performance artists and "confessional" gallery artists such as Tracey Emin.

They also make clear her feminist goals. "Learn to reclaim your body," Bess writes in "How to be a female artist." "Know that if you are a woman, your body is intimately linked to your work. Resent this." That reclamation may be the part of alt-lit that survives. In 2015 several alt-lit venues, among them the popular website HTMLGiant, shut down; several male alt-lit authors and editors (Lin among them) faced accusations of sexual misconduct. *Illuminati Girl Gang*, however, continues: one of the website Gawker's stories on the alt-lit implosion read "Alt-Lit Is Dead and Its Women Writers Are Creating Their Own Scene."

Bess's consistent wit sets her apart from her peers, but her sensibility—her sense that she can have listeners and readers, both visible and "invisible audiences," even for language that seems and sounds ephemeral—sets her among those peers, apart from earlier poets with similar goals. Yet Bess is not the first poet to envision words on other people's foreheads. In 1972 Hannah Weiner, a poet and performance artist associated with the St. Mark's Poetry Project, began to see "words in the air, on every available surface, on people, on the page before she wrote them, and on her forehead from within," in the scholar Judith Goldman's summary. Weiner then developed her "clair style," in which several fonts and type styles differentiate the "seen" words from the others: her dense and challenging clair-style texts withdraw from the kind of social or gossipy exchanges that define poetry such as Bess writes, in favor of dense, almost unintelligible challenges, pointing to Weiner's mental illness, or to a spirit world, or—as Goldman argues—to the slippery externality of language.

In Weiner, writes Goldman, "words no longer promise that they will do what we want them to do, whether we mean to limit them to instrumental, informational, or representational functions. They propose instead that we may do only what they . . . desire." The ill-fitting messages and the refracted slogans ("LOOK WHAT I'VE DONE," "YOU ARE FUCKED UP") in Bess's far more legible poem ask whether words can fare much better for her. Must we do only as our words, or our webcams, or our generations allow? Yet Bess's poetry stands out not least for its immediacy, its way of reaching out to imagined readers, and for the yearning in its affect: urgent, frustrated, ready to be heard, energetic, and almost desperate to put into the networked world whatever she has to say.

BRENDA SHAUGHNESSY

Hide-and-Seek with God

There are no hiding places left, Cal.
Every dark space isn't really dark
but pinkish black, flesh and oblivion,
filled with me, with us, deathly
and breathless and holding on, skin
about to split and give us away.

Is it better to run? Run down
the street—the floating red hand
that means *don't walk* looks
like a heart. But I'm too afraid.
If we just close our eyes truly enough,
believing hard, no peeking, we can
be invisible. Don't let him find
us, Cal. Don't let him find us again.

The winsome, naive or faux-naive language that Shaughnessy's title introduces, and the simplicity of the phrases that follow, make room for—you
might say they get out of the way of—the overwhelming emotion the poem
presents. The size and approximate shape of a sonnet, unrhymed, with its
sestet and its octave reversed, the poem pretends to be (but could not literally be) a mother's speech to her not-yet-born child. Speeches to not-yet-
born children have been a minor lyric genre for hundreds of years (take
Sylvia Plath's "Child," or Anna Letitia Barbauld's "To an Invisible Being
Expected Soon to Become Visible"). Such poems tend to imagine children
as risky, scary, endangered beings of nearly infinite potential: Barbauld's
coming child, for example, will "grasp at all the claims the Almighty wrought!"
Plath's newborn child's "clear eye is the one absolutely beautiful thing," despite her own "wringing of hands."

Shaughnessy's child, however, cannot stand for infinite potential, nor for a putative deity's putative bounty: Cal has already been born, and—as the other poems in Shaughnessy's collection *Our Andromeda* make very clear—he has serious disabilities that affect both communication and motion, and which probably mean he will not walk or run. Shaughnessy's simplified language fits her imagined communication with a young child—in fact, a child too young to speak—but they also fit the rawness of her animus against a creator God who did not play fair, who already caught, as it were, and injured her son. Few last words in few poems have ever had the force of Shaughnessy's "again": the word makes her God the exact opposite of any benevolent creator, anyone we could trust or believe.

It seems absurd, even insulting, to approach a poem with this topic and this affect by using the ordinary analytic tools of literary criticism: would it be better to love it, share it, cry, and then leave it alone? For some readers it might. And yet *not* to examine a poem so raw, so memorable, a poem about motherhood and loyalty and the messy emotions around life with any new-born, a poem that also addresses severe disability—not to use, with such a poem, the same lenses and gauges that we use with poems about hockey, or about falling leaves—would be to collude with the sexist, ableist social conventions that have made childbirth, motherhood, disability, and negative emotions around them unspeakable, unseemly, invisible. It is better to write poems about them, if they are your subjects, and better for critics to make available, when the poems work, hypotheses about how and why they work.

This one works (as did Plath's) with raw, frightening materials, in rhetorically sophisticated ways. The first stanza describes the initial unity and safety of the womb, whose "oblivion" has inspired male poets—Sophocles, for example, and Ben Jonson—to wonder if it would be better not to have been born. Shaughnessy's close-up mimesis of the birthing process, in a poem whose "breathless" pace suggests childbirth and labor, owes less to that classical tradition than to the poets of the 1970s and 1980s, such as Sharon Olds, who worked intently and demotically to put women's physicality onto the page.

Once that physicality has been recorded, once Shaughnessy has remembered it, she moves on, asking in all seriousness (with Sophocles) whether it would have been better not to enter this world: we enter an allegorical dimension of streets and stoplights, leaving the warmer, literal space of the flesh. Does the "don't walk" sign, the "red hand," invite the exhausted new mother to retreat into herself, to block out the rest of the world, to curse God? Shaughnessy cannot be sure: "I'm too afraid." If you believe in an omniscient God, then there is no sense running or hiding, and if you don't—and Shaughnessy is not, elsewhere, a poet of religious dogma—then what you can't "close your eyes" to avoid, what you can't run away from, is the empirical, present-tense world, the world with its walk / don't walk signs and with its many children who cannot walk, because they are infants or because they have disabilities (or both).

That same world holds many distraught mothers, many of whom have children with disabilities, though only one of them could have written this poem. In one way as specific as poetry gets—it's addressed to one child with one first name—the poem also works toward generality: it could *almost* be recited, reused, quoted, spoken by any birth mother who fears for her child's well-being. The simplicity of its diction, the easy availability of its double meanings and its images (who, in developed nations, has never seen walk / don't walk signs?), strains to make the poem available as a resource, as shared experience, for other parents, especially mothers, given the womb and the birth with which it begins. Shaughnessy shares the poem with them, with us, because she cannot wholly share it with Cal.

Poetry seeks the impossible: it originates in lack, in things the poet cannot have in the world outside the poem, or cannot say in denotative prose. "If an emotion eludes me," Shaughnessy has written, "a dream, a yearning for my child's good health, certainty, adventure, and all the possibilities—I write about those things precisely because I can't have them." The literary theorist Jonathan Culler argues that all lyric poetry represents speech to an absent or impossible listener: if you are speaking to your copilot or your stage manager and she is in the room and you know what you want her to do, you can simply use prose, but only poetry can speak to God, or to a Grecian urn, or anyone else who cannot respond (Culler's claim came up earlier in this book when W. S. Merwin addressed bare wires.) "Hide-and-Seek with God" turns out to do what Culler thinks all poems do, not because it speaks to God, but because it speaks to Cal, who is unlikely to answer in comprehensible words, even when he is past infancy; it also, of course, imagines that the child and his mother could "run" ("run? Run" the poem reads) even though God has sent him the awful signal "don't walk." The glowing, disembodied palm on the pedestrian sign is the deity's hindering hand, making mere human regulation (what the law says) into physical impossibility (what God decrees).

It is a play on words, and a grotesque visual pun, that only the child's mother or father could make. Shaughnessy and her husband, the poet and critic Craig Morgan Teicher, have also written in prose about their son, who turned five in the year *Our Andromeda* appeared: diagnosed with "a catastrophic brain injury at delivery," Cal "has severe cerebral palsy. He's nonambulatory, nonverbal, and has a smile that lights up a room like nothing else. Yes, we've been through hell, but we've had this angelic, loving, marvelous child with us the whole time." "Hide-and-Seek with God" does not undermine the sentiments of the essay (entitled "Enduring Discovery: Marriage, Parenthood and Poetry"), but it gives voice to stranger, more frightening feelings, among them the feeling that the visible world is so dangerous and so cruel—so cruel to Cal—that it would be better to live elsewhere, in the dark.

The much longer title poem of *Our Andromeda* imagines another planet, another dimension, in which medical problems and human disasters can be solved: "People still get sick / in Andromeda," but "everybody knows what they // need to know / Even doctors, / even patients. Even, yes, insurance / companies . . . You'll learn to read so much more easily there." But there is no Andromeda, no private darkness intense enough: mother and child, poet and Cal, are what they are, what they will be—they are already "found."

Found by God, or malign fate, or chance, but also found by loving, attentive parents and benign caregivers. People with disabilities have long been hard to find—even "invisible"—in other ways: those who could pass for nondisabled often did so, and those who could not pass, or who could not perform all the tasks expected of typical children or adults, were not supposed to be seen or heard. The United States, like many countries, has a shameful history (and it is not over yet) of badly run or deceptive institutions designed to hide disabled children from normally abled adults and kids, and a parallel history of taboos against speaking and writing about disability: that is a way to be "invisible" that Shaughnessy's poetry pushes back hard against.

It also pushes back hard against former taboos around discussions of motherhood, around negative maternal feelings: Shaughnessy—along with Rachel Zucker, Elizabeth Treadwell, Arielle Greenberg, Erika Meitner, and other poets without much else in common—belongs to a generation of women poets who have made being pregnant, becoming mothers, and raising children some of their principal topics, finding ways to bring awkward, extreme, messy, or socially disapproved feelings about motherhood into the craft of verse (you can find more of those poets in Rebecca Wolff's 2007 anthology *Not for Mothers Only,* also mentioned earlier in this book in connection with Linda Gregerson). To believe that mothers can have unmixed feelings or that mothers can simply face facts is to indulge in a kind of disbelief as willful—and much less sympathetic—than the disbelief near the end of this poem, "if we just close our eyes truly enough," which also recalls the prayer for fairies near the end of *Peter Pan,* the last in a line of echoes from writings for children, along with the language for children ("no peeking") that Shaughnessy uses throughout the poem.

Such language almost dares sophisticates to hate it, and then says to those sophisticates, "This poem is for Cal and for me: I don't care what you think." But we should care what Shaughnessy thinks: her intense, frightening poem of maternal love and cosmic resentment is also a memorable arrangement of language, a poem as well made, as perfect for its situation, as any we have.

CLAUDIA RANKINE

You and your partner go to see the film *The House We Live In*. You ask a friend to pick up your child from school. On your way home your phone rings. Your neighbor tells you he is standing at his window watching a menacing black guy casing both your homes. The guy is walking back and forth talking to himself and seems disturbed.

You tell your neighbor that your friend, whom he has met, is baby-sitting. He says, no, it's not him. He's met your friend and this isn't that nice young man. Anyway, he wants you to know, he's called the police.

Your partner calls your friend and asks him if there's a guy walking back and forth in front of your home. Your friend says that if anyone were outside he would see him because he is standing outside. You hear the sirens through the speakerphone.

Your friend is speaking to your neighbor when you arrive home. The four police cars are gone. Your neighbor has apologized to your friend and is now apologizing to you. Feeling somewhat responsible for the actions of your neighbor, you clumsily tell your friend that the next time he wants to talk on the phone he should just go in the backyard. He looks at you a long minute before saying he can speak on the phone wherever he wants. Yes, of course, you say. Yes, of course.

Likely no book of poetry—no book designated as poetry—in the United States in the twenty-first century has received as much attention, discussion, and debate as Rankine's *Citizen: An American Lyric* (2014), from which these paragraphs come. They occupy exactly one page of the meticulously designed book, which includes other anecdotes like this one; sparse pronouncements and queries in verse ("How to care for the injured body, // the kind of body that can't hold / the content it is living?"); evocative, more conventionally lyrical blocks of prose; essays on racial stereotypes in sports, such as those that vex Serena Williams; and multipage "scripts" for short videos, co-created with Rankine's husband John Lucas, about instance of deadly racial injustice: Trayvon Martin, Hurricane Katrina, the Jena Six. Printed (like museum catalogues) on glossy, photography-friendly paper, *Citizen* also incorporates visual elements: a two-page work of graphic art by Glenn Ligon, whose text repeats Zora Neale Hurston's apothegm "I FEEL MOST COLORED WHEN I AM THROWN AGAINST A SHARP WHITE BACK-GROUND": a color photograph of the 2007 Rutgers University women's basketball team; J. M. W. Turner's painting "The Slave Ship" (with which the book ends).

These elements—and the near (though not total) absence of self-contained units in verse—trouble the bounds of the category "poetry," to which its author and publisher say that *Citizen* belongs. Yet *Citizen* was a finalist in poetry for the National Book Award, the Los Angeles Times Book Prize, and in Britain the Forward Prize and the T. S. Eliot Prize. The National Book Critics' Circle nominated the book in two categories, poetry and criticism. Rankine won the Forward Prize, the L. A. Times Prize, and the NBCC award in poetry, as well as the PEN Open Book award and the NAACP's Hurston / Wright Legacy Award in poetry, as well as several other awards. And very sensibly so, if "poetry" means a text that brings together the many aspects of language in order to explore someone's, or anyone's, interior life, to challenge the transparency of common language, and to do something that mere exposition or narrative could never do. Rankine's wary, exasperated, outraged book, taken all in all, asks (and gives no one answer) how she and other people ought to respond to stereotypes and assumptions around race, the overt violence, the tacit self-regulation, the assumptions and attitudes and awkwardness, from thoughtless snubs to hate crimes, that race and "anti-black racism" (the term Rankine uses in interviews) can produce.

The book appeared at a horrifyingly appropriate moment. Completed after the shooting of Trayvon Martin and the acquittal of his killer, the book was published just before the deaths of Michael Brown in Ferguson, Missouri, Tamir Rice in Cleveland, Eric Garner in Staten Island, and Freddie Gray in Baltimore; the protests in Ferguson; and the sudden national attention, in white-controlled mass media, to black men's deaths at the hands of police. All the parts of *Citizen* ask how and whether a black person, or a person whom others identify as black, can live as a citizen, equal to other citizens, protected by custom and law: much of the book explores the common assumption that a black person in a historically white, privileged space—Wimbledon's tennis courts, or a suburban street—amounts to a dangerous anomaly. That idea helped kill Trayvon Martin. What else does it do to the people who harbor it? What kinds of contradictions, nervousness, wariness, expectations of anger, passivity, self-defense, or violence does it entail? How often do white people perpetuate racism without realizing it? Can poetry help them realize it? Should this dark-skinned Jamaican American poet care? Can poetic language speak to what Rankine has called her "visceral disappointment . . . in the sense that no amount of visibility will alter the ways in which one is perceived"?

Citizen raises all those questions at once: it does so with particular elegance in its most self-contained segments, the short prose anecdotes about microaggressions, moments when—so it seems on first reading—the poet has been treated differently and unjustly, or seen someone else treated badly, for reasons of race. But Rankine puts these anecdotes in the second person: only prior knowledge about her can lead us to envision "you" as black, and sometimes that version of "you" would be wrong. It is no accident that these parts of *Citizen* have no first-person pronoun, only "you" and "he" and "she": they describe what happens when you do not have an "I" apart from others, when you cannot get wholly outside the way in which other people construct "you" (though who can?). Their constructions depend on what they think they see. And "you," in the central paragraphs of this four-paragraph anecdote, have nothing to see: you have to rely, unfortunately, on words, which rely in turn on their users' assumptions. When those assumptions conflict—when you realize that the "menacing black guy . . . walking back and forth" is in fact the "nice young man . . . standing outside"—the police are already on the scene.

This story of a black man in suburbia becomes a horrible parody of a classic problem for introductory courses in philosophy: are the morning star and the evening star "the same," since the terms point to the same object, the planet Venus, seen at different times or by different observers? It's an academic question about the night sky, but it can be a life-or-death question if the subject is a black man on a lawn. "You" could not see him over the phone, but neither could the neighbor who called the police; that neighbor saw "a menacing black man."

Rankine's poem shows—among many things—how where you are, where you think you are, and where other people can say that you are affects who you think you are: it is a bitter demonstration of what we might call the social phenomenology of place. To feel at home in your body, confident in your identity, well recognized, you might have to feel literally at home in your home: "bodies are shaped by their dwellings," writes the philosopher Sara Ahmed, and "the skin of the social might be affected by the comings and goings of different bodies." The white suburb reveals its residents' expectations about safety, exclusion, and whiteness—the first, in their minds, depends on the second and third—once a visible black body comes to town.

Why are so few black bodies already in town? *The House We Live In* could help us answer: the film is the third of three documentaries aired on PBS in 2003, collectively called *Race: The Power of an Illusion*. Much of *The House We Live In* tells the story of American residential segregation in the twentieth century, from de jure racial barriers to redlining, white flight, and the modern disparity in wealth between white Anglo and black families, much of which comes, still today, from the worth of their homes. The harm of racism, in the account that the film and the poem presents, is not only harm done on purpose by racists. Injustice is all around us, often without any ill-meaning person or institution we can isolate or subdue. Nor is there any authoritative party who could hear a cri de coeur as if from outside. That absence helps explain Rankine's spare, grim affect, her absence of detail: she doesn't need to make this situation vivid for us. We already know, or should know, or should have known.

Rankine's prose style can approximate the clipped, depressive temperament of certain present-day fiction writers (Lydia Davis, for example), or even the depressive realism, described elsewhere in this book, of Louise Glück. In Rankine's 2004 prose work *Don't Let Me Be Lonely* (like *Citizen* subtitled *An American Lyric*), the poet diagnosed in herself "a deepening personality flaw: IMH, the inability to maintain hope, which translates into no innate trust in the supreme laws that govern us." Why would you trust the laws—how could "you" feel like a fully empowered citizen—in the land of Travyon Martin and Freddie Gray?

Rankine's panoply of short prose and verse forms in *Citizen*—including this anecdotal second-person form—can feel like ways to get around that "personality flaw," ways to look outside a frustrated self. They are also ways to depict a systemic problem, one that cannot be presented rightly unless you can somehow see around your one "I." No more "poetic" poem (Rankine implies), and certainly nothing presented as fiction, would do. Against the power of stereotypes to block out sight, the poet deploys not the counterpressure of any rich, self-consciously poetic image-making language, but a dry style that performs what W. H. Auden maintained ought to be poetry's only ethical goal: "to disenchant and disintoxicate."

Here Rankine's "you" lets you, the reader, ask what you would do, or why you did what you have already done. Why did you feel "responsible" for your neighbor? Why did you tell "your friend" not to talk in the front yard next time? If he should have known that his visibility, as a black man in suburbia, "walking back and forth talking," would bring the police, shouldn't you have known that "your neighbor" was talking about your friend? How could you be so insensitive as to give your friend such victim-blaming advice? On the other hand, isn't it good advice? Surely it's up to him, not up to "you," where and when your friend chooses to place a call; but what would you do if you were he?

If you're not from a group that gets racially profiled—not visibly black, for example—you can never know. Rankine describes on another page a "friend" who "argues that Americans battle between the 'historical self' and the 'self self,'" the former racially marked ("her white self and your black self, or your white self and her black self"), the latter somehow free from race. We probably think that other friend is white: why? A person of color would likely know better, would know how hard or how ridiculous it is to imagine that we are not marked by the illusion, or the imaginative construction, called race. "The perception that race is not an active part of existence," Rankine told an interviewer, "allows people to make the mistakes that they make against each other." "From that which is systemic we try to detach ourselves," she wrote in an earlier book-length poem, *Plot* (2001). "But some of us have drowned and coughed ourselves up."

If you are used to the idea that you can present yourself however you like, walk wherever you choose, apparently unaffected by race, then you might be white. And if part of being white is not having to think about being white, another part is having your whiteness pointed out through the reactions, the comments, or the mere presence of people who are not white. All of us have been shaped by what we call "race," but white people—white writers—often don't know it. "Yes, of course" could be the sound of a white person knowing it.

Except that it isn't. Rankine distilled the anecdotes in *Citizen* from stories that she solicited from friends. As she revealed in a radio interview, though, her source for this particular page was herself—this "you" could have been "I." Her grammatical choices show how the same situations look and feel different to speakers with differing background—different versions of "you," different values for that variable—even as they ask you to see yourself in her place. Such questions, addressed to readers of many colors, propel her editorial work too. While she was finishing *Citizen* Rankine coedited an anthology of essays, *The Racial Imaginary: Writers on Race in the Life of the Mind*; its introduction, which she cowrote, invites "white artists" to "examine the interior landscape that wishes to speak of rights, that wishes to move freely and unbounded across time, space and lines of power." Such wishes—she hopes we will see—cannot come true. Both *Citizen* and *The Racial Imaginary* reflect, sotto voce, a public dispute in 2011 between Rankine and her former colleague in Houston, the poet Tony Hoagland, about race and racial privilege in one of his poems; the two poets' "open letters" to each other about that dispute were later posted on the Academy of American Poets website. Some of the sentences there reappear in *Citizen*, whose anecdotes and verse and photographs, taken together, show how you, or "you," can't—alas—get entirely outside the systems by which other people see you.

Citizen in general, and this reflective, narrative page in particular, keep on panning out, breaking the frame, showing how around each domain, each picture, each idea of "you" and "I" there are larger, unacknowledged assumptions and systems in play, and not only about race. It may be that poetry, or poetic language, wants to give us the right to speak "wherever," to make us heard as if from everywhere and nowhere, as if superior to our mortal, frail, and socially classified bodies. But poetic language (as Rankine's argument with Hoagland made clear) does not always get what it seems to want, does not always work as a poet intends. And even if we could write or read poetry that way (and it is by no means clear that we can), we cannot speak as if from nowhere, live as if disembodied, from day to day, as we pick up our kids, mow our lawns, or talk on our phones. If your listeners cannot stop seeing you as a "menacing black man," then everything you say will be connected, willy-nilly, to your blackness, or your manhood, or your potential menace, or the surprising absence of any of those things; nothing you say will *not* be racially marked. And if that is true for black speakers, for black bodies, why should it not be true for white speakers as well? If you have not seen a picture of me or heard my voice, how do you think I look? Do you think I am white, black, Taiwanese American, or all three? Male or female or both? What if you learned you were wrong?

BRANDON SOM

Oulipo

So then me and you come
You assured led by the tongue
Dark fall a winding wind
A detour circles song

Drum din when the rain comes
Erasure the song sung
Details wandering in a wren
Ditto cuckoo song

Truth bends when you hum
Jig lure reel rig seine
Bird calls wander heavens
The fall circles round

Often we were conned
Trees were things wrens sung
Too tall wild in midair
Falsettos so soon hamstrung

Kerplunk plans mean you've come
Be sure these songs swim
Phonecall frogmen when
Tempos spiral down

Bunkbeds wing me across
Secure belonging's bobbin
Seawalls make waves mist
Tiptoe tidal flats

Trouble the sea for a son
Feel sure you don't belong
You don't write what men say
Sea tales consume song

Trundled nights of a nun
Fissures between rival tongs
You sell wontons here
Detuned doo-wop songs

Backhand within each psalm
Young girl in a tea-stained sarong
Make-do the long nightmare
Lingo miscues song

Just in sweet meat buns
Insure deeds with alms
Doorbells wane once you're in
Dark clouds sluice down shrubs

Strum then strings you've strung
Speech chirrs inside tongues
You sell wrong names here
Data research shows

Trunks fend off wind that comes
Leeward they have swung
So long waiting here
This talk cites coos wrong

A monk lends me his car
Bugs chirr sovereign songs
Clouds shawl a wan mien
A junco suitor calls

Drunk wren between me and dawn
Expert far-flung tongue
Forestall the fading path
Burrow straight through song

Translate dreams in sons
Be sure to tear shit up
Due to wagers made here
Pray tell absurd sounds

Dressed in tight ass funds
He sure street fought some
Shut out wrong men here
All told buckles song

Trumped again add up sums
Leave sure you've had your fun
Dutiful sons wandered here
Laid down bicycles in the sun

Locket syrinx in a palm
Procure mahjongg songs
Judo bygone rift rafts
Echoes pseudo song

"Oulipo" is a serious, ambitious poem about language and immigration, propelled by frustration, befuddlement, and fascination with the ways in which
culture and language are and are not handed down, with the ways in which
America has and has not changed, and with paradoxes around Chinese
American—and, more generally, second- and third-generation immigrant—
identity. It's also a playful, bravura performance of syllable-by-syllable
not-quite-free association, an homage to the few, equally virtuosic poems in
English that it remotely resembles, as well as to Tang dynasty poetic form.
    On top of all that, it is a homophonic translation, a literary form in which
the new version matches the original not meaning for meaning, but sound

for sound. More accurately, it comprises eighteen homophonic translations from the same original. These eighteen quatrains of "pseudo-song" comprise (as Som's note explains) eighteen attempts to emulate in English the sounds of a famous lyric by the Tang dynasty poet Li Po, as recited in "northern Chinese, Peking dialect" (aka Beijing Mandarin) by Lo Kung-yuan on a Smithsonian Folkways LP released in 1963. The LP sleeve comes with a translation (no translator credited): "In front of my bed the moonlight falls. / I wonder whether there's frost on the ground. / I raise my head to look at the bright moon, / Then lower my head, thinking of my native home." Other, less idiomatic translations—all with moonlight, bed, and homesickness—abound: the scholar André Lévy, writing in 1991, called it "perhaps the most popular poem in Chinese literature—at the very least, the most popular among the overseas Chinese" (something like Robert Frost's "Stopping by Woods on a Snowy Evening" in the United States).

Li Po's original presents nostalgia, exile, a man far from home. Som's "Oulipo" does so too, though it might take a while to see how and why, because Som's compact quatrains incorporate so many other projects. Some of those projects are puns. "Oulipo"—pseudo-French for "Where is Li Po?"—also denotes OULIPO, or Ouvroir de Littérature Potentielle ("workshop for potential literature"), an invitation-only society of poets, novelists, and other writers founded in Paris in 1960 and claiming among its members Italo Calvino, Georges Perec, and Raymond Queneau. Oulipo promoted gamelike invented forms, hoping to downplay authenticity and tradition and to encourage creativity. One Oulipian technique involves using only proper subsets of the alphabet: Christian Bök's *Eunoia* (2001), for example, uses only one vowel for each of its several-page sections: "A law as harsh as a *fatwa* bans all paragraphs that lack an A as a standard hallmark."

Homophonic translation is an Oulipo practice too, though the most extravagant, best-known homophonic translation in U.S. poetry is the version of Catullus published in 1969 by Louis and Celia Zukofsky: in it, Catullus's Latin "Nulli se dicit mulier mea nubere malle / quam mihi, non si se Iuppiter ipse petat" became "Newly say dickered my love air my own would marry me all / whom but me, none see say Jupiter if she petted." Beside such examples Som's quatrains might seem positively transparent: they might also look like the quatrains in Harryette Mullen's *Muse & Drudge* (discussed earlier in this book), which also combine resistance to prose sense, attention to sound play, and an interest in ethnic stereotypes.

Yet if we come to them with the right expectations, Som's quatrains do not resist prose sense very much: they invoke Chinese people who "come" to Amer-

ica, the Chinese poetry that they bring with them, and the tasks assumed, or
the fights picked, by their descendants. "Me and you come"; you are "led by
the tongue." A traveler who speaks the English "tongue" might lead the way
for travelers who do not; to be led by the tongue is also to have mouths to
feed, to become an economic migrant. A poet adapting Li Po is "led by the
tongue" (i.e., Mandarin) in which the poem is heard. The adaptation "circles
song" in the sense that it orbits, without quite zeroing in on, the sounds that
Li Po's own poem could have made: those sounds indeed resemble most of
the English words that Som derives from them, though English of course
cannot reproduce Chinese tones.

Som's poem thus becomes an "erasure" of the original "song sung" in Chinese by Li Po or Lo Kung-yuan, as well as a "cuckoo song," an imitation. As
a Chinese American descendant of immigrants, writing in English, is the poet
a "cuckoo," depriving Li Po's Chinese-language heirs of the attention they
should get instead? Is all poetry, all rendering of experience into sonic art, necessarily inexact, a free adaption, since "Truth bends when you hum"?

Som's playful meditation on authenticity turns more serious as it reflects
the difficult lives of actual immigrants: "Often we were conned." Urban Chi-
natowns had little greenery: "Trees were things wrens sung." Newcomers, like
seafarers and detained persons, slept in "bunkbeds" and had difficulty securing
their "belongings." During the Chinese exclusion period (1882–1943) U.S. law
made it difficult or impossible for Chinese people to come to America legally,
or to reenter once they had left. One workaround (addressed in Som's other
poems) involved taking a "paper-name," pretending to be the son or brother
of someone already legally in the United States; such identities could be
purchased ("you sell wrong names here"), and the "coaching papers," used to
learn the fake identity, thrown in the sea before the ship reached the United
States. An immigrant arriving in this way might "trouble the sea for a son," or
"feel sure you don't belong." So might the poet of a later generation wondering
where, in any poetic tradition—American, English, "experimental," "autobiographical," "Asian"—*he* belonged.

"Oulipo" revisits questions that have come up throughout this book. Who
is the "I" in a poem? Is it the poet, or you, or anybody, or the representative of
a particular group, such as graduate students, or Oulipo fans, or Chinese
Americans? Can it be, or attempt to be, all of these? How does the "I" in a
given poem find, or conjure into being, its "you"? A poet writing in Chinese
would not "write what men say," since written Chinese uses ideograms, with
no direct links to how the language sounds. But contemporary American

writers of experimental poetry would not "write what men say" in another sense, since they would not stick to "the ordinary language of men," which William Wordsworth identified (in 1799) as the language of genuine poems (some of those poems might even—like Samuel Taylor Coleridge's "Rhyme of the Ancient Mariner," written with Wordsworth's assistance—let "sea tales consume song").

Som thinks not just about the theory of poetry but about its history: how much has poetry—what "poetry" means and does—changed since Wordsworth and Coleridge? Since Li Po? How much has Chinese American identity changed? Have models of poetry as conceptual exploration, resistant to speech, or perpetual experiment replaced or displaced models of poetry as "lyric," or rendered it obsolete, as the eminent critic Marjorie Perloff and many others have argued since the 1980s? (Perloff now teaches at the University of Southern California, where Som is earning a graduate degree; USC also has poets famous for teaching, such as David St. John, who remain committed to lyric modes.) Using words (or letters or sounds) as if they were game pieces moved in accordance with rules, Oulipian techniques can work against the idea that literature expresses the clear thoughts and feelings of a single self: Perloff argues that Oulipo's emphasis on "the nontranslatability and irreducibility of poetic language," its "constraint . . . that forces the poet to give up an illusory artistic 'freedom,'" "has as its corollary the elimination of ego." Yet the same techniques can also show how ego, the sense of an interior self (me myself, you yourself, your grandmother's self, or anybody's self), arises within (and by means of) social, linguistic, and even biological systems ("inside tongues"). As the systems change the "I" changes too; but it's still there, like a "syrinx in a palm." The difficulties of the present-day poet refract the difficulties his ancestors faced, from Li Po to Wordsworth and beyond: they are not the same difficulties, not the same lives, but they are strangely present in the same short strings of words, each of which is the same and not the same as a similar-sounding source in Chinese.

Som's quatrains also emulate Li Po's quatrain form, with syllable counts of five to seven per line, two of which rhyme (Chinese classical rules would not permit six-syllable lines). Som's English has fewer connectives and fewer articles ("Shut out wrong men here") than English in general does: if (as experts often say) John Milton tried to write English as if it were Latin, Som writes American English as if it were Chinese. His riffs on Chinese sounds also produce frequent end rhymes, sometimes on syllables that sound "Chinese" in English ("sung"-"strung," "tongs"-"songs"-"belong"). These aural effects tend to hold the poem together aurally, where halting syntax might otherwise split it apart.

But the poem never feels split up: instead, it accretes not only similar sounds but overlapping details from tough immigrant lives, or from clichés about those lives—gang wars in Chinatown, "fissures between rival tongs"; misunderstandings, where "lingo miscues song"; jobs in restaurants or bakeries ("sweet meat buns"). Looking back through distorting mirrors, or trapped in the restricted opportunities of a classic Chinatown, the immigrants would prefer to be birds, juncos or wrens, wanting—like Li Po himself—to escape their "wan mien." But they cannot: denied their own dreams, immigrant parents "translate dreams in sons." Those sons might prefer to "tear shit up," refusing to honor their parents' or grandparents' debts. Though some sons fight ("He sure street fought some"), others are "dutiful," even if, as they prosper, they give up their frugal bicycles in favor of American cars.

Som has much to say about fathers and "sons": for mothers, we should look to other poems. But the images in the final quatrain could apply to daughters and to sons: a keepsake, a "locket," perhaps holding hair, feels like a reed instrument ("syrinx") that can play only "mahjongg songs," frivolous lyrical work for the old. Rather than continue to play such things, Som will "judo bygone rift rafts," using poetic technique to overturn what once floated, what once came here over the seas, at once honoring and attacking the "sea tale" of assimilation and social mobility.

Addressing immigrants' histories through modernist techniques, "Oulipo" reclaims, for contemporary Chinese American poets, effects of "Chineseness" that white Anglo modernists had tried to make their own. Li Po's verse, along with that of his peers, often works by implication, presenting images without explicit connections, letting readers who know the contexts infer the ideas. That sometime reliance on parataxis, along with the novelty of ideograms, encouraged Euro-American modernists (especially Ezra Pound) to derive new verse techniques from their sense of "Chinese." It's a neat kind of justice for Som to apply later modernist techniques in order to make a poem about bilingualism, about estrangement, and about people who are—or whose grandparents were—really from that nation.

Some of those grandparents were incarcerated in the United States. From 1910 to 1940 most of the Chinese people who entered America came through Angel Island Immigration Station, in San Francisco Bay, where more than 100,000 of them were detained. Another poem from Som's collection *The Tribute Horse*, "Bows & Resonators," takes place at Angel Island, imagining conversations among detainees. "The Chinese experience on Angel Island," write the historians Erika Lee and Judy Yung, "became a contest of wills and wits": immigrants endured physical humiliation and confinement while trying to defeat laws meant to keep them out. As with immigration today, observers—and appellate courts—could find the initial screening process arbitrary, or cruel, or bizarre. Some would-be immigrants were detained for months or even years.

Some of those immigrants wrote and recited poems. In the "crowded, noisy, unsanitary and sparsely furnished" quarters of Angel Island, as Lee and Yung explain, detainees carved hundreds of poems into the walls: classical Chinese poems that they had memorized, and also poems that the immigrants composed. Almost all the Angel Island graffiti poems (both original and remembered) use "classical" form: five or seven syllables, four or eight lines, *xaxa* rhyme. This form gave the detainees links to their homeland and language even as they waited to enter what would become (if they were not deported) their daughters' and grandsons' country. There Chinese American identity— like Som's eighteen successive quatrains, like "poetry" itself—would be the same and not the same as being Chinese, continually retranslated from an ever more distant original, reflecting the stress and the chances of a new place. These symbols of Chinese Americanness (for so they have become) also look now like signs that what we call lyric poetry endures: it is not just a product of one era nor of one culture, but responds to a widespread human need. "The majority of the poems" at Angel Island (Lee and Yung explain) "were undated and unsigned, probably for fear of retribution"; both men and women wrote poems, though only the poems from the men's barracks survive. The detainees' poems (in Chinese and in English translation) have become a staple of Asian American literature classes and modern poetry anthologies; Angel Island (like Ellis Island) is now open for visitors, and Li Po's own poem—as Som's note informs us—can be read today on the walls of room 105.

ROSS GAY

Weeping

I'm thinking here of the proto-Indo-European root
which means the precise sound of a flower bud

unwrapping, and the tiny racket a seed makes
cracking open in the dark, which has evolved

in a handful of Latinate languages to mean the sound
of lovers exiting each other, implying as well the space

between them which usage is seen first in Dante
in the fourteenth century, elbowing it for good into our mouths

and minds, and of course the sweet bead of sugar
imperceptibly moseying from the fig's tiny eye precisely

unlike sorrow which the assembly of insects sipping there
will tell you, when I tell you my niece, without fit or wail,

knowing her friend Emma had left and not said goodbye,
having spent the better part of the day resting on her finger,

sometimes opening her wings, which were lustrous brown
with gold spots, to steady herself at the child-made

gale, or when she was tossed into the air while my niece
took her turn at pick-up sticks until calling Emma

by holding her finger in the air to which Emma would wobble down,
and Mikayla said *Deal us in* when we broke out the dominoes

at which they made a formidable duo, whispering to each other
instructions, and while the adults babbled our various dooms

Mikayla and Emma went into the bedroom where they sang
and danced and I think I heard Mikayla reading Emma

her favorite book, both of them slapping their thighs, leaning
into each other, and at bedtime Mikayla put on her PJs

carefully, first the left arm through while Emma teetered
on the right, then the other, and in the dark Mikayla whispered to
    Emma,

who had threaded her many legs into the band of Mikayla's sleeve,
while she drifted, watching Emma's wings slowly open

and close, and Emma must have flown away for good, judging
from the not brutal silence at breakfast, as Mikayla chewed

the waffle goofily with her one front tooth gone, and weakly smiled,
looking into the corners of her room for her friend, for Emma,

who had left without saying goodbye, the tears easily
rolling from her eyes, when I say she was weeping,

when I say she wept.

How old is poetry? what about "lyric poetry"? what about "lament"? Perhaps
quite old: in weeping for "her friend Emma" who has "flown away for good,"
Mikayla joins a line of incantatory and memorable elegy that goes back all
the way to Gilgamesh's lament for Enkidu: by completing this poem, Ross
Gay has joined it too. How old is Mikayla? Not very: the distance between
the very old and very young, the very sophisticated and the apparently naïve,

drives the poem, along with the distance between past and present, made-up
and literally real—and each of those kinds of distance will close up, or diminish drastically, between the beginning of Gay's extraordinarily long sentence and its sudden end. The closing-up of that emotional distance—bringing
together adult and child, delight and distress, the ancient and the contemporary
and the childish—seems to Gay, and not only to Gay, like some of the most
important work that contemporary poetry can do. It also seems—within the
poem—like something poets of Gay's sort cannot help but do, almost as many
children of Mikayla's approximate age cannot help but make, or summon,
imaginary friends.

That does not mean that everybody will like them, or get to know them, or
believe in them. With such a long sentence, and such explicit investment in
Mikayla's joys and regrets, Gay offers a poem that will seem, to some readers, too
simple, or just "too much": those readers, having come to the end of this book in
which (if I've done it right) the recondite and the demotic, the accessible and the
challenging, mingle, will find Gay's poem outrageously sentimental, so open
to excess of feeling—to childish feeling—as to rule nuance and innovation out.
Other readers—and I am one of them—will take Gay's poem as a heartbreaking
and entirely successful manifesto. Gay may sound loose and informal, as his
sometimes redundant or even self-mocking adverbs—"precise," "tiny"—imply.
At the same time, he lets us relish virtuosity in his syntax: this one-sentence
poems sweeps a few millennia, and then a day and a night, between two parts
of an dependent clause. Capaciously learned, or mock-learned, yet domestic
and even homely, Gay has used his couplets to make at once an homage to his
inventive niece and a claim about why poetry exists, and what that poetry—or
at least some kinds of it—shares with the recent and distant past.

Poetry of this kind—"Weeping" implies—exists to show grief, to protest,
but also to give us new terms for our experience, to honor the new and the
young (buds, or children), to protect reverie, to appreciate solitude, to exult,
and to befriend. What Emma could do for Mikayla, poems (or at least some
kinds of poem) do for us. Poems emerge from the kind of counterfactuals,
and from the kind of play, we associate with children. They seem excessive,
uncouth, even embarrassing, when they are at their best; they try—and fail—
to make up for death and loss, loneliness and time and change. And that kind
of imaginative compensation, embedded in all poetic uses of words, works
(when it does work) in similar ways, whether we are a sophisticated contemporary writer, or a young child sad at the loss of a friend who is actually a
butterfly, and who probably does not literally exist.

Nor do the almost impossibly specialized terms Gay evokes in his first few couplets exist. There is no "precise" word for the flower's budding in English, nor in proto-Indo-European, a language that historical linguists have to reconstruct through speculation, much as adults speculate about young children's minds. Nor is there a single word for "the sound / of lovers exiting each other" (having acknowledged adult sexuality, the poet will not return to it in this poem); nor for the single drop of fructose-rich water at the end of a fig (which might nourish a butterfly). Instead, if we want to evoke these things, we have to make up new sounds, or phrases, or poems.

Or at least we have to try. Allen Grossman called poems, in general, "hermeneutic friends," able to keep us company when real friends cannot; poems in this sense (though their memorability, their verbal nuance, still sets them apart) resemble children's imaginary friends, who may be other children or talking hymenoptera. And young children—as the psychologist Alison Gopnik has shown—tend to know, even when they refuse to acknowledge, the line between things imagined, and things in real life: "preschool children spend hours pretending," she writes, "but they *know* that they are pretending." Rather than not knowing the difference between the literal and the figurative, the imagined and the actual, "children may seem confused because they are such expressive and emotional pretenders. They can have real reactions to entirely imaginary things." So can you, if you are a reader (or writer) of imaginative literature: that may be one of the reasons you read. And one definition of "growing up" (though there are many, more hopeful, others) is as a process by which children are forced to acknowledge the difference between the real and the unreal, to regard more and more of what they imagined or wished into being as unimportant, or nonexistent, or gone without saying goodbye.

Weeping for Emma, who never said goodbye, Mikayla is weeping for her own diminished ability to regard imagination as equal to reality: that ability, and not a real butterfly whose "wings . . . were lustrous brown / with gold spots," is what has gone, or else what is going, away. (Even if a real brown-and-gold moth or butterfly had "spent the better part of the day" on Mikayla's finger, as few flying insects would do, it probably would not "thread . . . its many legs into the band of Mikayla's sleeve"; one real butterfly with that lustrous pattern, by the way, is called the Question Mark.) As if to heighten the pathos, or dare us further to call the scene sentimental, Gay shows Mikayla weeping while smiling through her front teeth, one of which also does not exist.

The gap in her front teeth is like the space between lovers, but also like gaps between one day and the next, or between one event and the next, the moments of suspended time that lyric poetry strives to create. (I have been writing about poetry and lyric poetry almost interchangeably, because for Gay—as for most of the poets in this book—they are interchangeable, but that "most," and that "almost," are important: there are poets, and poems, and theories of poetry, now as in 1800 and in antiquity, that have no truck with Grossman's, or Gay's, fundamentally lyric goals.) The lyric poet, Gay implies, lives partly outside time, and has not wholly grown up: he can enter not only into Mikayla's world of talking, companionate butterflies, but also into an imaginary history of language. That language does not so much re- place as supplement the real one, as Emma supplements Mikayla's human family—and as poetic language supplements, rather than replacing, the kind of language we use to greet our friends in person, or to tell kids it's bedtime.

Poetic language is in this sense irretrievably "sentimental," as well as im- practical (and therefore, according to a long and sexist tradition, childish or feminine): anything you can defend as the essence of poetry, another reader can attack as excessive or needless, as language where (to quote Elizabeth Bishop) "emotion too far exceeds its cause." The poet and essayist Mary Ruefle has explored, in typically quirky fashion, the association between poetry it- self—or perhaps lyric poetry—and sentimentality: "When the late American novelist John Gardner defined sentimentality as 'causeless emotion,'" Ruefle quips, "he must have been thinking about kittens. But it seems to me the ef- fect of an image in a poem often acts like a kitten: we are expected to go 'ah' deep down in our interior sphere, and to slightly elevate ourselves in relation to the world, as if the soul were a beach ball." Or a butterfly.

"If your teachers suggest that your poems are sentimental," Ruefle proposes, they "probably need to be even *more* sentimental," since "expressions are al- ways inadequate, often pitiful . . . Poetry is sentimental to begin with." For Gay as for Ruefle there is no bright line—maybe no line at all—between the expressively adequate and the over-the-top, the irretrievably sentimental: what matters is whether the language holds our attention, whether we find it per- suasive, and whether we care. There is, as well, no bright line that human be- ings can draw between ludic and the poetic; between a child's and an adult's creativity; between language shared (with adults, with a kid, with a butterfly) and language savored alone. One reader might try (as Gay has tried) for sym- pathy with Mikayla's generous consciousness; another might notice the skill with which Gay manipulates his story about her, modulating in and out of it through these long lines, almost like lines of dominoes. Sometimes those lines "wobble"; at others, they seem to fly. This poem about imagination thus becomes an ode to unlikely technique: Gay and other adults notice how Mikayla has learned to put on her PJs, a not inconsiderable skill for a young child, while Mikayla notices the delicacy with which Emma "has threaded her many legs" (like the many lines, or nouns, in Gay's poem) "into the band of Mikayla's sleeve."

Weeping for the loss of her almost certainly imaginary Emma, Mikayla is of course weeping (like Gerard Manley Hopkins's Marguerite in "Spring and Fall") for time and change and loss in general. Gay's poem almost joins her. That last line, with its five monosyllables, stands in sharp contrast to every other line and every other line break in the poem. But Gay does not say that he weeps, and he points out (even before introducing anything else about his niece) that she has no "fit or wail"—she will not throw a temper tantrum; she even smiles. And Gay smiles back: seeking images and terms that seem "precisely / unlike sorrow" (the second use of "precise" in this poem) he seeks, amid loss, gratitude, if not joy. In doing so Gay participates in the same Romantic enterprise as Wordsworth and Hopkins and Keats, who sought in the language they shared with other human beings some kind of compensation for maturity as well as for mortality.

Gay also participates, here and throughout *Catalog of Unabashed Gratitude* (2015), in an intuitive enterprise of his own. The relatively short and much-admired book—most of which uses much shorter lines, though similarly long sentences—works very hard to find reasons to like this world, to appreciate life as it is, and in particular to appreciate the embarrassing, awkward, indelicate, or even icky parts. *Catalog* holds an homage to feet, beginning "mine are ugly feet"; an "ode to sleeping in my clothes"; an ode to the armpit; and an ode "to my best friend's big sister," who once gave the poet, at poolside, a comically "thoughtful critique / of my just / pubescent physique." Gay has also written about the pleasures of urban gardening, of literally getting one's hands dirty in an effort to make something grow: it is an enterprise that requires diligence and patience as well as attention to roots and weeds, and it rewards neither anger nor irony.

The poet Kyla Marshell asked Gay in an interview what it meant for him to have written "a book about flowers by a black man," adding "even though you do talk about race, I wonder if perhaps you were resisting all the things you could talk about." Gay belongs to a twenty-first-century flowering of African-American poetics, one that relies on institutions (such as the Cave Canem workshop) built during the 1990s. But the Gay of *Catalog* also belongs in a line of explicitly, riskily "sentimental" or excessive poets with U. S. and

Latin American precursors, poets who set out to defend the strongest feelings they can represent: Larry Levis and Gerald Stern (a teacher of Gay's at Sarah Lawrence) stand for this line in the 1980s and 1990s, as Gay and such well-informed yet faux-naïve poets as Dorothea Lasky—the author of a wonderful, polemical pamphlet called "Poetry Is Not a Project"—stand for it now.

"His heart's really out there," Gay has said of Stern. "And that's something you don't really learn how to do, necessarily, if you're a man, or brought up in sort of a male way, or even if you're an American." Gay's heart is really out there, too: he has evolved a style meant to put it out there, to defy adult expectations about decorum or compression, in the name (as another poem says) of "loving / what every second goes away." Gay's current work could never be mistaken for Lasky's, nor for Stern's, nor for Pablo Neruda's, but like them he sees passion, compassion, and aesthetic success as tightly interfused, excess (of feeling, of grammar, of devotion, of enthusiasm, of belief) as just enough. And this view, too, goes back surprisingly far: to write a long lyric poem in praise of weeping is to align oneself, if distantly, with the seventeenth-century Catholic poet Richard Crashaw, whose poems of extreme emotion ("The Weeper," for example, about Mary Magdalene) used to be commonly cited as examples of bad writing, of sentimental, or feminine, excess. Gay's look at a modern day child's lost butterfly thus points forward to that child's next smile, but also backward into the English Baroque, as well as to English Romantics like Wordsworth; to demotic American late Romantics of the 1970s and 1980s, like Stern; and even to Elizabeth Bishop, who imagined in "The Man-Moth" that the titular figure, if treated gently, would give us his tear, "cool as if from underground springs and pure enough to drink."

These precedents align with one another, like the spots on Emma's wings, and together they make a claim, if not for poetry in general, than for the kind of poetry that Gay has chosen to write. This kind of poetry lets readers (adult and otherwise) move from "thinking" (the second word in the poem) to feeling: it gives us the ability to cry for others, without being overcome by it; it counteracts the callousness of adulthood, and lets us notice—and feel for—the smallest things (the drop on the fig; Emma's threadlike legs; a tear). To dismiss this sort of weeping, to walk away from it, is to walk away from feeling, or from the numinous, or from poetry itself, or even from other human beings. To attend to it—to care for it, to care about it, to represent it tenderly and attentively, whatever its supposed cause—is, conversely, to keep the language (all the way back to its "proto-Indo-European roots") alive, and to be able to represent joy.

A little girl weeps because she has lost her butterfly: the subject seems more appropriate for a minor Victorian, or for a contemporary amateur, than for a serious poet of Gay's prowess. And that is part of why it matters. Mikayla's tears, as a topic for modern poetry, might (before you had read this poem) strike you as an occasion for kitsch: "sentimental, trivial stereotypical, and therefore contrary to the values of true art," in the poet and scholar Daniel Tiffany's formulation. We might see Gay as rescuing real child-hood, real wonder, and genuine feeling (new and different each time) from commercial, too-simple facsimiles. Or we might see Gay as (in Tiffany's terms) a radical who wants to defend it all: "if radicalism in the arts implies—at least in part—reorienting the viewer towards whatever appears to be . . . trifling, indulgent or worthless" (such as an imaginary butterfly) "then kitsch still marks an elusive frontier." *Catalog of Unbashed Gratitude* does not sound like much of the contemporary poetry that Tiffany prefers, but it might well be called radical—it goes, so to speak, to the roots—in its pursuit of senti-ment: to enter into the melancholy, belated imagination of this gap-toothed child, the morning after Emma has gone, is to reject, at least temporarily, most kinds of distance, most sorts of irony; it is to see all feelings, all psyches, as worthy of consideration, and as real.

Gay told Marshell that he had not made "a book against anything; it's a book imagining, or advocating, for something . . . I want to express a sort of wild love." He advocates, among other things, attachment: his attachment to his niece, and to her family, and to the American English that belongs to him, just as much as Florentine Italian belonged to Dante; attachment both to literary history, and to a kind of human expression possible for young children, prior to any self-conscious literary history; attachment to growing things (figs and fig trees are a motif throughout *Catalog*); and, finally, his niece's attach-ment to her imaginary, diminutive friend, the butterfly that represents (as it did for the ancient Greeks) *psyche*, the soul. If we want to defend, or to cherish, or to delight in, any of those attachments—so Gay's thirty-seven-line sentence suggests—we should know how it might feel to defend them all.

Sources

These pages give sources for poems; first publication for poems where first publication affects the order for this book's table of contents or comes up in an essay; and sources for almost all text quoted in essays. I do not give sources for private correspondence, nor for quoted text that is easily available online in multiple reliable editions, in the public domain, and not subject to relevant textual controversy, such as quotations from the Authorized Version (King James Bible).

INTRODUCTION

W. H. Auden, *The Dyer's Hand* (New York: Random House, 1962)
Jonathan Culler, *Theory of the Lyric* (Cambridge, MA: Harvard University
    Press, 2015)
Northrop Frye, *The Bush Garden: Essays on the Canadian Imagination* (1971;
    Toronto: House of Anansi, 1995)
William Fuller, *Playtime* (Chicago: Flood, 2015)
Noah Eli Gordon, "An Interview with Dawn Lundy Martin," *Denver Quarterly*
    44, no. 4 (2009), repr. in *The Volta*, www.thevolta.org/tremolo-issue3
    -dlmartin-p1.html, accessed March 23, 2016
Juan Felipe Herrera, *Notes on the Assemblage* (San Francisco: City Lights, 2015)
Randall Jarrell, *Poetry and the Age* (1953; Gainesville: University Press of Florida,
    2001)
Douglas Kearney, *Mess and Mess and* (Las Cruces, NM: Noemi, 2016)
Marianne Moore, *Selected Poems* (London: Faber and Faber, 1935)
Rick Snyder, "The New Pandemonium: An Overview of Flarf," *Jacket* 31
    (2006), http://jacketmagazine.com/31/snyder-flarf.html, accessed
    March 23, 2016
Stephen Voyce, *Poetic Community: Avant-Garde Activism and Cold War Culture*
    (Toronto: University of Toronto Press, 2014)

JOHN ASHBERY, "PARADOXES AND OXYMORONS"

Poem from *Shadow Train* (New York: Viking, 1981)

Sources of Quotations

Michael Clune, "Strong Opinions," *Twentieth Century Literature* 58, no. 1
    (2012): 141–149
Bonnie Costello, "John Ashbery and the Idea of the Reader," *Contemporary
    Literature* 23, no. 4 (1982): 493–514
T. S. Eliot, *The Sacred Wood* (1920; London: Faber and Faber, 1997)
Susan Schultz, ed., *The Tribe of John: Ashbery and Contemporary Poetry* (Tusca-
    loosa: University of Alabama Press, 1995)

TATO LAVIERA, "TITO MADERA SMITH"

Poem from *Bendición* (Houston: Arte Público, 2014); first book publication:
    Enclave (Houston: Arte Público, 1981)

Sources of Quotations

Juan Flores, *Divided Borders: Essays on Puerto Rican Identity* (Houston: Arte
    Público, 1993)
Juan Flores, *From Bomba to Hip-Hop: Puerto Rican Culture and Latino Identity*
    (New York: Columbia University Press, 2000)
Carmen Dolores Hernandez, ed., *Puerto Rican Voices in English* (Westport, CT:
    Greenwood, 1997)
Urayoán Noel, *In Visible Movement: Nuyorican Poetry from the Sixties to Slam*
    (Iowa City: University of Iowa Press, 2014)

RICHARD WILBUR, "THE RIDE"

Poem from *New and Collected Poems* (New York: Harcourt, 1988); first publica-
    tion, *Ploughshares* 8, nos. 2–3 (1982)

Sources of Quotations

James Longenbach, *Modern Poetry after Modernism* (New York: Oxford
    University Press, 1997)
W. S. Merwin, *Collected Poems 1952–1993*, ed. J. D. McClatchy (New York:
    Library of America, 2013)
Bruce Michelson, *Wilbur's Poetry: Music in a Scattering Time* (Amherst:
    University of Massachusetts Press, 1991)

LUCILLE CLIFTON, "MY DREAM ABOUT THE SECOND COMING"

Poem from *The Collected Poems of Lucille Clifton 1965–2010,* ed. Kevin Young
    and Michael S. Glaser (Rochester, NY: BOA, 2012); first publication (as

"my dream about the inevitability of the second coming"): *Virginia Quarterly Review* 58, no. 4 (autumn 1982)

Sources of Quotations

Elizabeth Alexander, "Remembering Lucille Clifton," *New Yorker*, February 17, 2010

Rita Dove, *The Yellow House on the Corner* (Pittsburgh: Carnegie Mellon University Press, 1980)

Rachel Harding, "Authority, History and Everyday Mysticism in the Poetry of Lucille Clifton: A Woman's View," *Meridians* 12 (2014): 36–57

Hilary Holladay, *Wild Blessings: The Poetry of Lucille Clifton* (Baton Rouge: Louisiana State University Press, 2004)

CARLA HARRYMAN, "POSSESSION"

Poem from *Property* (Berkeley, CA: Tuumba, 1982)

Sources of Quotations

Lyn Hejinian and Barrett Watten, eds., *A Guide to Poetics Journal: Writing in the Expanded Field* (Middletown, CT: Wesleyan University Press, 2013)

Ron Silliman, *The New Sentence* (New York: Roof, 1995)

JOHN HOLLANDER, "SONGS & SONNETS"

Poem from *Powers of Thirteen* (New York: Atheneum, 1983)

Sources of Quotations

Anne Ferry, *The Title to the Poem* (Stanford, CA: Stanford University Press, 1996)

John Hollander, *The Figure of Echo* (Berkeley: University of California Press, 1981)

John Hollander, *Vision and Resonance* (New Haven, CT: Yale University Press, 1985)

John Hollander, *The Work of Poetry* (New York: Columbia University Press, 1997)

CARL DENNIS, "MORE MUSIC"

Poem from *The Near World* (New York: William Morrow, 1985); first publication: *New Yorker*, September 10, 1984

Sources of Quotations

Carl Dennis, "Two Lives," *New Yorker*, April 18, 2016

Carl Dennis, *Poetry as Persuasion* (Athens: University of Georgia Press, 2001)

John Gardner, *The Art of Fiction* (New York: Vintage, 1985)

Earl Ingersoll, Judith Kitchen, and Stan Sanvel Rubin, *The Post-Confessionals: Conversations with American Poets of the Eighties* (Cranbury, NJ: SUNY Press / Associated University Presses, 1989)

Randall Jarrell, *Complete Poems* (New York: Farrar, Straus and Giroux, 1969)

Thornton Wilder, *Our Town* (1938; New York: Harper Perennial, 2003)

LIAM RECTOR, "SAXOPHONE"

Poem from *The Sorrow of Architecture* (Port Townsend, WA: Dragon Gate, 1984)

Sources of Quotations

Georg Simmel, *The Philosophy of Money*, ed. David Frisby, trans. Tom Bottomore, David Frisby, and Kaethe Mengelberg (New York: Routledge, 1990)

CZESŁAW MIŁOSZ, TRANS. ROBERT PINSKY AND CZESŁAW MIŁOSZ, "INCANTATION"

Poem from Robert Pinsky, *The Figured Wheel* (New York: Farrar, Straus and Giroux, 1996); first book publication: Miłosz, *The Separate Notebooks*, trans. Robert Hass and Robert Pinsky (New York: Ecco, 1984)

Sources of Quotations

Clare Cavanagh, *Lyric Poetry and Modern Politics* (New Haven, CT: Yale University Press, 2009)

Seamus Heaney, *Finders Keepers: Selected Prose 1971–2001* (New York: Farrar, Straus and Giroux, 2002)

Seamus Heaney, "Poetry's Power against Intolerance," *New York Times*, August 26, 2001

Czesław Miłosz, *Native Realm*, trans. Catherine Leach (1968; New York: Farrar, Straus and Giroux, 2002)

Czesław Miłosz, *New and Collected Poems* (New York: Ecco, 2003)

J. R. R. Tolkien, *The Monsters and the Critics and Other Essays*, ed. Christopher Tolkien (1983; New York: HarperCollins, 2007)

ROBERT GRENIER, "SHOE FROM THE WAVES"

Poem from *A Day at the Beach* (New York: Roof Books, 1984)

Sources of Quotations

Jonathan Culler, *Theory of the Lyric* (Cambridge, MA: Harvard University Press, 2015)

Robert Grenier, "Attention" (1985), repr. http://eclipsearchive.org/projects /ATTENTION/html/pictures, accessed February 25, 2016

Martin Heidegger, *Being and Time*, trans. John Macquarrie and Edward Robinson (1927; New York: Harper Perennial, 2008)

Kevin Opstedal, "A Literary History of the San Andreas Fault: Bolinas Section," *Jack* 3 (2001), www.jackmagazine.com/issue3/renhist.html, accessed February 25, 2016

Bob Perelman, *The Marginalization of Poetry: Language Writing and Literary History* (Princeton, NJ: Princeton University Press, 1996)

RITA DOVE, "LIGHTNIN' BLUES"

Poem from *Thomas and Beulah* (Pittsburgh: Carnegie-Mellon University Press, 1986)

Sources of Quotations

Earl Ingersoll, ed., *Conversations with Rita Dove* (Jackson: University Press of Mississippi, 2003)

Malin Pereira, *Rita Dove's Cosmopolitanism* (Urbana: University of Illinois Press, 2003)

Pat Righelato, *Understanding Rita Dove* (Columbia: University of South Carolina Press, 2006)

A. R. AMMONS, "TARGET"

Poem from *Sumerian Vistas* (New York: Norton, 1987)

Sources of Quotations

M. H. Abrams, "The Correspondent Breeze: A Romantic Metaphor," *Kenyon Review* 19, no. 1 (1957): 113–130

Roger Gilbert, "Footprints from a Poet's Path: The A. R. Ammons Collection at East Carolina University," *A. R. Ammons's Poetry and Art* (Greenville, NC: East Carolina University, 2008), n.p.

YUSEF KOMUNYAKAA, "FACING IT"

Poem from *Dien Cai Dau* (Middletown, CT: Wesleyan University Press, 1988); first publication: *The Made Thing: An Anthology of Contemporary Southern Poetry*, ed. Leon Stokesbury (Fayetteville: University of Arkansas Press, 1987)

Sources of Quotations

Subarno Chattarji, *Memories of a Lost War: American Poetic Responses to the Vietnam War* (New York: Oxford University Press, 2001)

Paul de Man, "Autobiography as De-Facement," *MLN* 94, no. 5 (1979): 919–930

Robin Ekiss, "Poem Guide: Facing It," Poetry Foundation, www .poetryfoundation.org/learning/guide/237896#guide, accessed February 20, 2016

Elizabeth Wolfson, "The 'Black Gash of Shame': Revisiting the Vietnam Veterans Memorial Controversy," *Art 21* (2015), www.art21.org/texts/the -culture-wars-redux/essay-the-black-gash-of-shame-revisiting-the-vietnam -veterans-memorial-, accessed March 23, 2016

DIANE GLANCY, "HAMATAWK"

Poem from *Lone Dog's Winter Count* (Albuquerque, NM: West End Press, 1991); included in MFA thesis, Iowa Writers' Workshop, 1988

Sources of Quotations

Diane Glancy, *Designs of the Night Sky* (Lincoln: University of Nebraska Press, 2002)

Diane Glancy, *In-Between Places* (Tucson: University of Arizona Press, 2005)

Gabriel Gudding, *Literature for Nonhumans* (Boise, ID: Ahsahta, 2015)

LUCIE BROCK-BROIDO, "DOMESTIC MYSTICISM"

Poem from *A Hunger* (New York: Knopf, 1988)

Sources of Quotations

Lucie Brock-Broido, "Myself a Kangaroo Among the Beauties," in *By Herself: Women Reclaim Poetry,* ed. Molly McQuade (St. Paul, MN: Graywolf, 2000), 192–195

Alicia Eler and Kate Durbin, "The Teen-Girl Tumblr Aesthetic," *Hyperallergic,* March 1, 2013, http://hyperallergic.com/66038/the-teen-girl-tumblr -aesthetic, accessed February 20, 2016

James Longenbach, *The Virtues of Poetry* (Minneapolis, MN: Graywolf, 2013)

KILLARNEY CLARY, "ABOVE THE INLAND EMPIRE TODAY"

Poem from *Who Whispered Near Me* (New York: Farrar, Straus and Giroux, 1989)

Sources of Quotations

Killarney Clary, *Shadow of a Cloud but No Cloud* (Chicago: University of Chicago Press, 2014)

Steven Monte, *Invisible Fences: Prose Poetry as a Genre in French and American Literature* (Lincoln: University of Nebraska Press, 2000)

Barbara Herrnstein Smith, *Poetic Closure: A Study of How Poems End* (Chicago: University of Chicago Press, 1968)

JOHN YAU, "MODERN LOVE"

Poem from *Radiant Silhouette: New & Selected Work* (Santa Rosa, CA: Black Sparrow, 1989)

Sources of Quotations

Dorothy Wang, *Thinking Its Presence: Form, Race, and Subjectivity in Contemporary Asian American Poetry* (Stanford, CA: Stanford University Press, 2014)

John Yau, *The Passionate Spectator: Essays on Art and Poetry* (Ann Arbor: University of Michigan Press, 2006)

Timothy Yu, "Form and Identity in Language Poetry and Asian American Poetry," *Contemporary Literature* 41, no. 3 (2000): 422–461

ROBERT CREELEY, "OH"

Poem from *Windows* (New York: New Directions, 1990)

Sources of Quotations

Robert Creeley, *Selected Poems: 1945–2005* (Berkeley: University of California Press, 2008)

Robert Creeley, *Tales Out of School* (Ann Arbor: University of Michigan Press, 1993)

Ben Friedlander, "On Robert Creeley: 'Reading in Pieces,'" *Jacket* 31 (2006), http://jacket2.org/commentary/ben-friedlander-robert-creeley-reading-pieces, accessed March 23, 2016

Charles Olson, "Projective Verse" (1950), repr. *The New American Poetry 1945–1960*, ed. Donald Allen (1960; Berkeley: University of California Press, 1999), 386–397

Mark Scroggins, *Intricate Thicket: Reading Late Modernist Poetries* (Tuscaloosa: University of Alabama Press, 2015)

CHARLES WRIGHT, "DECEMBER JOURNAL"

Poem from *The World of the Ten Thousand Things: Poems 1980–1990* (New York: Farrar, Straus and Giroux, 1990)

Sources of Quotations

Charles Altieri, *Enlarging the Temple: New Directions in American Poetry During the 1960s* (Lewisburg, PA: Bucknell University Press, 1979)

St. Augustine, *Of True Religion*, trans. J. H. S. Burleigh (New York: Regnery, 1966)

Peter Brown, *Augustine of Hippo: A Biography* (Berkeley: University of California Press, 1969)

Robert Denham, *The Early Poetry of Charles Wright: A Companion 1960–1990* (Jefferson, NC: McFarland, 2009)

Peter Stitt, *Uncertainty and Plenitude: Five Contemporary Poets* (Iowa City: University of Iowa Press, 1997)

Helen Vendler, *The Ocean, the Bird, and the Scholar* (Cambridge, MA: Harvard University Press, 2015)

Charles Wright, *Quarter Notes* (Ann Arbor: University of Michigan Press, 1995)

ALLEN GROSSMAN, "THE PIANO PLAYER EXPLAINS HIMSELF"

Poem from *The Ether Dome and Other Poems: New and Selected, 1979–1991* (New York: New Directions, 1991)

Sources of Quotations

Harold Bloom and David Lehman, eds., *The Best of the Best American Poetry 1988–1997* (New York: Scribner, 1998)

Allen Grossman, *The Long Schoolroom* (Ann Arbor: University of Michigan Press, 1997)

Allen Grossman, *True-Love: Essays on Poetry and Valuing* (Chicago: University of Chicago Press, 2009)

Allen Grossman with Mark Halliday, *The Sighted Singer* (Baltimore: Johns Hopkins University Press, 1992)

Geoffrey Hartman, *Wordsworth's Poetry 1787–1814* (New Haven, CT: Yale University Press, 1964)

Jamey Hecht, "The Piano Player Explains Himself," *Sagetrieb* 19, nos. 1–2 (2004): 59–67

François Noudelmann, *The Philosopher's Touch: Sartre, Nietzsche, and Barthes at the Piano* (New York: Columbia University Press, 2012)

Jeremy Siepmann, *The Piano* (New York: Knopf, 1997)

ADRIENNE RICH, "AN ATLAS OF THE DIFFICULT WORLD XIII (DEDICATIONS)"

Poem from *An Atlas of the Difficult World* (New York: Norton, 1991)

Sources of Quotations
Piotr Gwiazda, *US Poetry in the Age of Empire* (New York: Palgrave, 2014)
Jahan Ramazani, *Poetry and Its Others* (Chicago: University of Chicago Press, 2013)
Adrienne Rich, *A Human Eye* (New York: Norton, 2009)
Adrienne Rich, *Arts of the Possible* (New York: Norton, 2001)

LOUISE GLÜCK, "LAMIUM"

Poem from *The Wild Iris* (Hopewell, NJ: Ecco, 1992)

Sources of Quotations
Joanne Feit Diehl, ed., *On Louise Glück: Change What You See* (Ann Arbor: University of Michigan Press, 2005)
Louise Glück, *Proofs & Theories* (Hopewell, NJ: Ecco, 1994)
Alice Robb, "The Three Most Important Traits of the People Who Make the World Work" (review of David Zweig, *The Invisibles*), *New Republic*, June 1, 2014
Helen Vendler, *The Given and the Made* (Cambridge, MA: Harvard University Press, 1995)

JAMES MERRILL, "SELF-PORTRAIT IN TYVEK™ WINDBREAKER"

Poem from *Collected Poems*, ed. J. D. McClatchy and Stephen Yenser (New York: Knopf, 2001); first publication: *New Yorker*, February 24, 1992

Sources of Quotations
Elizabeth Bishop, *Poems, Prose, and Letters*, ed. Lloyd Schwartz (New York: Library of America, 2008)
Josh Glenn, "Camp, Kitsch and Cheese," *Hermenaut* 11–12 (1997), repr. *Hilobrow*, http://hilobrow.com/2010/06/05/camp-kitsch-cheese, accessed March 23, 2016
Langdon Hammer, *James Merrill: Life and Art* (New York: Knopf, 2015)
Robert Pogue Harrison, *Juvenescence* (Chicago: University of Chicago Press, 2014)
James Merrill, *Recitative* (San Francisco: North Point, 1986)
Helen Vendler, *Last Looks, Last Books* (Princeton: Princeton University Press, 2010)

Carl Wilson, *Let's Talk about Love: A Journey to the End of Taste* (2007; New York: Bloomsbury, 2013)

LINDA GREGERSON, "SALT"

Poem from *The Woman Who Died in Her Sleep: Poems* (Boston: Houghton Mifflin, 1996); first publication, *Colorado Review* 20, no. 1 (spring 1993)

Sources of Quotations
Dan Chiasson, "Form and Function," *New Yorker*, August 31, 2015
Linda Gregerson, "*The Faerie Queene* (1590)," in *The Oxford Handbook of Edmund Spenser*, ed. Richard McCabe (Oxford: Oxford University Press, 2010), 198–217
Linda Gregerson, *Negative Capability: Contemporary American Poetry* (Ann Arbor: University of Michigan Press, 2001)

KAY RYAN, "EMPTINESS"

Poem from *The Best of It* (New York: Grove, 2010); first publication: *Atlantic Monthly,* vol. 272, no. 2, August 1993

Sources of Quotations
Gary Saul Morson, *The Long and Short of It: From Aphorism to Novel* (Stanford, CA: Stanford University Press, 2012)
Alan Williamson, *Westernness* (Charlottesville: University of Virginia Press, 2006)

ALBERT GOLDBARTH, " 'A WOODEN EYE. AN 1884 SILVER DOLLAR . . .' "

Poem from *The Kitchen Sink* (St. Paul, MN: Graywolf, 2007); first publication: *Poetry*, vol. 166, no. 2, May 1995

Sources of Quotations
Albert Goldbarth, *Pieces of Payne* (St. Paul, MN: Graywolf, 2003)
Mark Halliday, "Gabfest," *Parnassus* 26, no. 2 (2002): 203–215

HARRYETTE MULLEN, "HONEY JARS OF HAIR"

Poem from *Recyclopedia: Trimmings, S*PeRM**K*T, and Muse & Drudge* (St. Paul, MN: Graywolf, 2006); first book publication, *Muse & Drudge* (Philadelphia: Singing Horse, 1995)

Sources of Quotations

Kimberly Nichele Brown, *Writing the Black Revolutionary Diva* (Bloomington: Indiana University Press, 2010)

Elisabeth Frost, *The Feminist Avant-Garde in American Poetry* (Iowa City: University of Iowa Press, 2003)

Barbara Henning, *Looking Up Harryette Mullen: Interviews on Sleeping with the Dictionary and Other Works* (Brooklyn, NY: Belladonna, 2011)

Harryette Mullen, *The Cracks Between What We Are and What We Are Supposed to Be: Essays and Interviews* (Tuscaloosa: University of Alabama Press, 2012)

STANLEY KUNITZ, "HALLEY'S COMET"

Poem from *Passing Through* (New York: Norton, 1995)

Sources of Quotations

Stanley Kunitz, *Next-to-Last Things* (New York: Norton, 1985)

Kunitz, *The Wild Braid: A Poet Reflects on a Century in the Garden* (New York: Norton, 2005)

MICHAEL PALMER, "LETTERS TO ZANZOTTO: LETTER 3"

Poem from *At Passages* (New York: New Directions, 1995)

Sources of Quotations

Vivienne Hand, *Zanzotto* (Edinburgh: Edinburgh University Press, 1994)

Michael Palmer, *Active Boundaries* (New York: New Directions, 2008)

Nerys Williams, *Reading Error: The Lyric and Contemporary Poetry* (Bern: Peter Lang, 2007)

Andrea Zanzotto, *Selected Poetry and Prose*, trans. and ed. Patrick Barron et al. (Chicago: University of Chicago, 2006)

ROBERT HASS, "OUR LADY OF THE SNOWS"

Poem from *Sun Under Wood* (Hopewell, NJ: Ecco, 1996)

Sources of Quotations

Robert Hass, *Twentieth Century Pleasures* (New York: Ecco, 1984)

Robert Hass, *What Light Can Do* (New York: HarperCollins, 2012)

Randall Jarrell, *Poetry and the Age* (1953; Gainesville: University Press of Florida, 2001)

Robert Lowell, *Collected Poems*, ed. Frank Bidart and David Gewanter (New York: Farrar, Straus and Giroux, 2003)

Liesl Olson, "Robert Hass's Guilt or The Weight of Wallace Stevens," *APR (American Poetry Review)* 36, no. 5 (2007): 37–45

C. D. WRIGHT, "KEY EPISODES FROM AN EARTHLY LIFE"

Poem from *Steal Away* (Port Townsend, WA: Copper Canyon, 2002); first book publication: *Tremble* (Hopewell, NJ: Ecco, 1996)

Sources of Quotations

David Abram, *The Spell of the Sensuous* (New York: Vintage, 1996)

Edward P. Casey, *The Fate of Place: A Philosophical History* (Berkeley: University of California Press, 1998)

Lyn Hejinian, *The Language of Inquiry* (Berkeley: University of California Press, 2001)

David Katz, *The World of Touch,* trans. Lester E. Krueger (1925; New York: Taylor and Francis, 1989)

Lynn Keller, *Thinking Poetry: Readings in Contemporary Women's Exploratory Poetics* (Iowa City: University of Iowa Press, 2010)

George Lakoff and Mark Johnson, *Philosophy in the Flesh: The Embodied Mind and Its Challenge to Western Thought* (New York: Basic Books, 1999)

C. D. Wright, *Cooling Time: An American Poetry Vigil* (Port Townsend, WA: Copper Canyon, 2005)

JUAN FELIPE HERRERA, "BLOOD ON THE WHEEL"

Poem from *Border-Crosser with a Lamborghini Dream* (Tucson: University of Arizona Press, 1999)

Sources of Quotations

Lauro Flores, "Auto-referentialidad y subversion: observaciones (con) textuales sobre la poesía de Juan Felipe Herrera," *Crítica* 2, no. 2 (1990): 172–181

"An Interview with Juan Felipe Herrera," *La Bloga*, February 21, 2008, http://labloga.blogspot.com/2008/02/interview-with-juan-felipe-herrera.html

Kevin Keckeisen, "Interview with Juan Felipe Herrera," *The Highlander*, May 8, 2012, www.highlandernews.org/3405/interview-with-juan-felipe

CARTER REVARD, "A SONG THAT WE STILL SING"

Poem from *Winning the Dust Bowl* (Tucson: University of Arizona Press, 2001)

Sources of Quotations
Ellen Arnold, ed., *The Salt Companion to Carter Revard* (Cambridge, UK: Salt, 2007)
Tony Horwitz, "The Horrific Sand Creek Massacre Will Be Forgotten No More," *Smithsonian*, December 2014
Dean Rader, "The Epic Lyric: Genre in Contemporary American Indian Poetry," in *Speak to Me Words: Essays on Contemporary American Indian Poetry,* ed. Dean Rader and Janice Gould (Tucson: University of Arizona Press, 2003), 123–142
Carter Revard, *Family Matters, Tribal Affairs* (Tucson: University of Arizona Press, 1998)
David Treuer, *Native American Fiction: A User's Manual* (St. Paul, MN: Graywolf, 2006)

ALLAN PETERSON, "EPIGRAPH"

Poem from *Anonymous Or* (Fort Montgomery, NY: Defined Providence, 2001)

Sources of Quotations
Richard Lewontin, *The Triple Helix: Genes, Organism, and Environment* (Cambridge, MA: Harvard University Press, 2000)
Zachariah Pickard, *Elizabeth Bishop's Poetics of Description* (Montreal: McGill-Queen's University Press, 2009)
Annie Wyman, "Against the Facts," *Los Angeles Review of Books*, October 9, 2012

RAE ARMANTROUT, "OUR NATURE"

Poem from *Veil* (Middletown, CT: Wesleyan University Press, 2001)

Sources of Quotations
Rae Armantrout, *Collected Prose* (San Diego: Singing Horse, 2007)
Rae Armantrout, Barrett Watten, et al., *The Grand Piano: An Experiment in Collective Autobiography*, 10 vols. (Detroit: Mode A, 2006–2010)
Tom Beckett, ed., *A Wild Salience: The Writing of Rae Armantrout* (Cleveland, OH: Burning Press, 1999)
Dan Chiasson, "Entangled: The Poetry of Rae Armantrout," *New Yorker*, May 17, 2010

ELIZABETH ALEXANDER, "RACE"

Poem from *Antebellum Dream Book* (St. Paul, MN: Graywolf, 2001)

Sources of Quotations
Elizabeth Alexander, *The Black Interior* (St. Paul, MN: Graywolf, 2004)
Langston Hughes, "Passing" (1934), repr. in Nella Larsen, *Passing*, ed. Carla
    Kaplan (New York: Norton, 2007), 281–283
Dan Sharfstein, *The Invisible Line* (New York: Penguin, 2011)

LIZ WALDNER, "A / PPEAL A / PPLE A / DAM A / DREAM"

Poem from *Dark Would (the missing person)* (Athens: University of Georgia
    Press, 2002)

Sources of Quotations
Sigmund Freud, *Civilization and Its Discontents,* trans. James Strachey (1930;
    New York: Norton, 2010)
Elisabeth Grosz, "The Labors of Love: Analyzing Perverse Desire," *differences* 6,
    nos. 2–3 (1994): 274–295
Liz Waldner, *Self and Simulacra* (Farmington, ME: Alice James, 2001)

KARI EDWARDS, ">> > >> > >> PLEASE FORWARD & > >>"

Poem from *Iduna* (Berkeley, CA: O Books, 2003)

Sources of Quotations
E. Tracy Grinnell et al., eds., *No Gender: Reflections on the Life & Work of kari
    edwards* (New York: Litmus / Belladonna, 2009)
Trace Peterson, "Becoming a Trans Poet," *Transgender Studies Quarterly* 1, no. 2
    (2014): 523–538

AGHA SHAHID ALI, "TONIGHT"

Poem from *Call Me Ishmael Tonight* (New York: Norton, 2003); first publica-
    tion, as "Ghazal": *Massachusetts Review*, vol. 37, no. 2, summer 1996.

Sources of Quotations
Kazim Ali, "Let Your Mirrored Convexities Multiply," Poetry Foundation
    audio podcast, March 9, 2010, www.poetryfoundation.org/features
    /audioitem/2064
Aamir Mufti, "The After-Lives of Agha Shahid Ali," *Dawn*, March 21, 2010

D. A. POWELL, "[WHEN HE COMES HE IS NEITHER SUN NOR SHADE: A CHINA DOLL]"

Poem from *Cocktails* (St. Paul, MN: Graywolf, 2004)

Sources of Quotations
Willis Barnstone, ed. and trans., *The Other Bible* (San Francisco: Harper and Row, 1984)
Samuel R. Delany, *Times Square Red, Times Square Blue* (New York: New York University Press, 1999)
Jasha Hoffman, "Cocktails for Two: An Interview with D. A. Powell," *Harvard Crimson*, November 9, 2001
Andrew Rahal, "Riding the Joy Bus: An Interview with D. A. Powell," *Nashville Review* 18 (2010)
Sam Witt and Sean Durkin, "Turning the Paper Sideways: An Interview with D. A Powell," *Poetry Flash* 284 (February-March 2000)

ANGIE ESTES, "SANS SERIF"

Poem from *Chez Nous* (Oberlin, OH: Oberlin College Press, 2005)

Sources of Quotations
Stephen Calloway, *Baroque Baroque* (New York: Phaidon, 1994)
Simon Garfield, *Just My Type: A Book about Fonts* (New York: Penguin, 2011)
Michael Krondl, *Sweet Invention: A History of Dessert* (Chicago: Chicago Review Press, 2011)
Karen Rigby, "Means of Transport, Medieval Mind: Dialogue with Angie Estes," *Cerise Press* 1, no. 3 (2010)
Charles A. Riley II, *Color Codes* (Hanover, NH: University Press of New England, 1995)
Heinrich Wölfflin, *Renaissance and Baroque,* trans. Kathrin Simon (Ithaca, NY: Cornell University Press, 1964)

W. S. MERWIN, "TO THE WIRES OVERHEAD"

Poem from *Present Company* (Port Townsend, WA: Copper Canyon, 2007); first publication: *The Nation*, vol. 281, no. 3, July 18, 2005

Sources of Quotations
Robert Lowell, *Collected Poems*, ed. Frank Bidart and David Gewanter (New York: Farrar, Straus and Giroux, 2003)
Jahan Ramazani, *Poetry and Its Others* (Chicago: University of Chicago Press, 2013)

BERNADETTE MAYER, "ON SLEEP"

Poem from *Scarlet Tanager* (New York: New Directions, 2005)

Sources of Quotations
Nada Gordon, "Form's Life: An Exploration of the Works of Bernadette Mayer"
        (1986), repr. *Read Me 4* (2001), http://home.jps.net/~nada/mayer7.htm,
        accessed January 10, 2016
Bernadette Mayer, *A Bernadette Mayer Reader* (New York: New Directions,
        1992)
Bernadette Mayer, *Ethics of Sleep* (New Orleans: Trembling Pillow, 2011)
Bernadette Mayer, *Scarlet Tanager* (New York: New Directions, 2005)
Maggie Nelson, *Women, the New York School, and Other True Abstractions*
        (Iowa City: University of Iowa Press, 2007)
Siobhan Phillips, "Sleep as Resistance," Poetry Foundation, www
        .poetryfoundation.org/article/247490, accessed January 10, 2016

DONALD REVELL, "MOAB"

Poem from *A Thief of Strings* (Farmington, ME: Alice James, 2007); first
        publication: *Conjunctions 45: Secret Lives of Children* (2005): 124

Sources of Quotations
SueEllen Campbell, "The Elements," in *Getting over the Color Green: Con-
        temporary Environmental Literature of the Southwest,* ed. Scott Slovic
        (Tucson: University of Arizona Press, 2001), 8–14
Donald Revell, *The Art of Attention* (St. Paul, MN: Graywolf, 2007)
Donald Revell, *Essay* (Richmond, CA: Omnidawn, 2015)

TERRANCE HAYES, "THE BLUE TERRANCE"

Poem from *Wind in a Box* (New York: Penguin, 2006)

Sources of Quotations
Terrance Hayes, *Lighthead* (New York: Penguin, 2010)
Jason Koo, "A Conversation with Terrance Hayes," *Missouri Review* 29, no. 4
        (2007): 58–78
Charles Rowell, "The Poet in the Enchanted Shoe Factory: An Interview with
        Terrance Hayes," *Callaloo* 27, no. 4 (2004): 1067–1081
Craig Werner, *A Change Is Gonna Come: Race, Music and the Soul of America*
        (Ann Arbor: University of Michigan Press, 1998)

JORIE GRAHAM, "FUTURES"

Poem from *Place* (New York: Ecco, 2012); first publication in *London Review of Books*, vol. 29, no. 13, July 5, 2007

Sources of Quotations
Calvin Bedient, "Toward a Jorie Graham Lexicon," in *Jorie Graham: Essays on the Poetry*, ed. Thomas Gardner (Madison: University of Wisconsin Press, 2005), 275–292
Jorie Graham, *The End of Beauty* (Hopewell, NJ: Ecco, 1987)
Timothy Morton, "Poisoned Ground: Art and Philosophy in the Time of Hyperobjects," *Symploke* 21, nos. 1–2 (2013): 37–50
Timothy Morton, "Victorian Hyperobjects," *Nineteenth-Century Contexts*, 36, no. 5 (2014)

LAURA KASISCHKE, "MISS WEARINESS"

Poem from *Lilies Without* (Keene, NY: Ausable, 2007)

Sources of Quotations
Laura Kasischke, *Boy Heaven* (New York: HarperCollins, 2006)
Liah Greenfeld, "When the Sky Is the Limit: Busyness in Contemporary American Society," *Social Research* 72, no. 2 (2005): 315–338
Kara Jesella and Marisa Meltzer, *How Sassy Changed My Life: A Love Letter to the Greatest Teen Magazine of All Time* (New York: Faber and Faber, 2007)
Brigid Schulte, *Overwhelmed: Work, Love, and Play When No One Has the Time* (New York: Farrar, Straus and Giroux, 2014)

FRANK BIDART, "SONG OF THE MORTAR AND PESTLE"

Poem from *Watching the Spring Festival* (New York: Farrar, Straus and Giroux, 2008)

Sources of Quotations
Jessica Benjamin, *The Bonds of Love: Psychoanalysis, Feminism, and the Problem of Domination* (New York: Random House, 1988)
Leo Bersani, "Is the Rectum a Grave?" *October* 43 (1987): 197–222
Frank Bidart, *Desire* (New York: Farrar, Straus and Giroux, 1997)
Frank Bidart, *Metaphysical Dog* (New York: Farrar, Straus and Giroux, 2013)
Frank Bidart, *Star Dust* (New York: Farrar, Straus and Giroux, 2005)
Frank Bidart, *In the Western Night* (New York: Farrar, Straus and Giroux, 1990)

ROBYN SCHIFF, "LUSTRON: THE HOUSE AMERICA HAS BEEN WAITING FOR"

Poem from *Revolver* (Iowa City: University of Iowa Press, 2008)

Sources of Quotations
Paul Barrett, *Glock: The Rise of America's Gun* (New York: Crown, 2012)
Amy Clampitt, *Collected Poems* (New York: Knopf, 2007)

MARY JO BANG, "Q IS FOR THE QUICK"

Poem from *The Bride of E* (St. Paul, MN: Graywolf, 2009)

Sources of Quotations
Patricia Crain, *The Story of A* (Stanford, CA: Stanford University Press, 2000)
Julia Kristeva, *New Maladies of the Soul,* trans. Ross Guberman (New York: Columbia University Press, 1995)
Brian Reed, *Nobody's Business: Twenty-First Century Avant-Garde Poetics* (Ithaca, NY: Cornell University Press, 2013)

LUCIA PERILLO, "VIAGRA"

Poem from *Inseminating the Elephant* (Port Townsend, WA: Copper Canyon, 2009)

Sources of Quotations
Mira Bellwether, *Fucking Trans Women* (n.p.: CreateSpace, 2010), repr. http://dymaxion.org/tmp/ftw.pdf, accessed March 24, 2016
Suzanne Koven, "How Are Drugs Named?" *Boston Globe*, July 14, 2012
Lucia Perillo, *I've Heard the Vultures Singing* (San Antonio, TX: Trinity University Press, 2007)
Lesley Valdes, "An Interview with Lucia Perillo," *APR (American Poetry Review)*, July-August 2014, 21–24

MELISSA RANGE, "THE WORKHORSE"

Poem from *Horse and Rider* (Lubbock: Texas Tech University Press, 2010)

Sources of Quotations
Walter Benjamin, *Illuminations* (New York: Knopf, 1969)
David Caplan, "Why Not the Heroic Couplet?" *New Literary History* 30, no. 1 (1999): 221–238

JOSEPH MASSEY, "PRESCRIPTION"

Poem from *At the Point* (Exeter, UK: Shearsman, 2011)

Sources of Quotations
Jennifer Groh, *Making Space: How the Brain Knows Where Things Are* (Cambridge, MA: Belknap Press of Harvard University Press, 2014)
Maurice Merleau-Ponty, *Phenomenology of Perception*, trans. Donald Landes (1945; New York: Routledge, 2013)
"New American Poets: Joseph Massey," Poetry Society of America, www.poetrysociety.org/psa/poetry/crossroads/new_american_poets/joseph_massey, accessed March 24, 2016
Peter Nicholls, "Modernising Modernism: From Pound to Oppen," *Critical Quarterly* 44:2 (2002): 41–58

DG NANOUK OKPIK, "DATE: POST GLACIAL"

Poem from *Corpse Whale* (Tucson: University of Arizona Press, 2012)

Sources of Quotations
Charles Wohlforth, *The Whale and the Supercomputer: On the Northern Front of Climate Change* (New York: Farrar, Straus and Giroux, 2004)

ROSA ALCALÁ, "CLASS"

Poem from *The Lust of Unsentimental Waters* (Exeter, UK: Shearsman, 2012)

Sources of Quotations
Poem from "Rosa Alcalá: An Interview, a Review," *Letras Latinas,* November 3, 2011, http://letraslatinasblog.blogspot.com/2011/11/rosa-alcala-interview-review.html, accessed March 24, 2016
Rosa Alcalá, *Undocumentaries* (Exeter, UK: Shearsman, 2010)
Jennifer Ashton, "Labor and the Lyric," *ALH* 25, no. 1 (2013): 217–230

GABBY BESS, "OVERSIZED T-SHIRTS"

Poem from *Alone with Other People* (Fairfax, VA: Civil Coping Mechanisms, 2013); first publication (under the name Gabby Gabby): *Illuminati Girl Gang* 1 (2012), http://vol1.illuminatigirlgang.com/gabbygabby

Sources of Quotations

Gabby Bess, "How to Be a Female Artist," *Dazed*, 2014, www.dazeddigital.com
/artsandculture/article/18712/1/how-to-be-a-female-artist, accessed
March 24, 2016

danah boyd, *It's Complicated: The Social Life of Networked Teens* (New Haven,
CT: Yale University Press, 2014)

Ana Carrete, *Baby Babe* (Arlington, VA: Civil Coping Mechanisms, 2012)

Marjorie Garber, *Vice Versa: Bisexuality and the Eroticism of Everyday Life* (New
York: Simon and Schuster, 1996)

Judith Goldman, "Hannah=hannaH: Politics, Ethics, and Clairvoyance in the
Work of Hannah Weiner," *differences* 12, no. 2 (2001): 121–168; repr. http://epc
.buffalo.edu/authors/weiner/goldman.html, accessed March 24, 2016

BRENDA SHAUGHNESSY, "HIDE-AND-SEEK WITH GOD"

Poem from *Our Andromeda* (Port Townsend, WA: Copper Canyon, 2012)

Sources of Quotations

Brenda Shaughnessy and Craig Morgan Teicher, "Our Enduring Discovery:
Marriage, Parenthood, and Poetry," *Poets & Writers*, September-October 2012

CLAUDIA RANKINE, "YOU AND YOUR PARTNER GO TO
SEE THE FILM"

Poem from *Citizen: An American Lyric* (Minneapolis, MN: Graywolf, 2014)

Sources of Quotations

Sara Ahmed, *Queer Phenomenology* (Durham, NC: Duke University Press,
2006)

W. H Auden, *The Dyer's Hand* (New York: Random House, 1962)

Claudia Rankine, *Don't Let Me Be Lonely* (St. Paul, MN: Graywolf, 2003)

Claudia Rankine, *Plot* (New York: Grove, 2001)

Claudia Rankine, Beth Loffreda, and Max King Cap, eds., *The Racial Imaginary: Writers on Race in the Life of the Mind* (Albany, NY: Fence, 2015)

BRANDON SOM, "OULIPO"

Poem from *The Tribute Horse* (Brooklyn, NY: Nightboat, 2014)

Sources of Quotations

Christian Bök, *Eunoia* (Toronto: Coach House, 2001)

Erika Lee and Judy Yung, *Angel Island: Immigrant Gateway to America* (New York: Oxford University Press, 2010)

André Lévy, *Chinese Literature, Ancient and Classical*, trans. William H. Nienhauser Jr. (Bloomington: Indiana University Press, 2000)

Marjorie Perloff, *Unoriginal Genius: Poetry by Other Means in the New Century* (Chicago: University of Chicago Press, 2010)

Louis Zukofsky, *Complete Short Poetry* (Baltimore: Johns Hopkins University Press, 1991)

ROSS GAY, "WEEPING"

Poem from *Catalog of Unabashed Gratitude* (Pittsburgh: University of Pittsburgh Press, 2015)

Sources of Quotations

Joanna Penn Cooper, "Interview with Ross Gay." *Cortland Review* 41 (2008)

Alison Gopnik, *The Philosophical Baby* (New York: Farrar, Straus and Giroux, 2009)

Dorothea Lasky, *Poetry Is Not a Project* (Brooklyn, NY: Ugly Duckling Presse, 2010), also online at http://www.uglyducklingpresse.org/archive/online -reading-old/poetry-is-not-a-project-by-dorothea-lasky/

Kyla Marshell, "Wild Love," Poetry Foundation, http://www.poetryfoundation .org/article/251308, accessed April 12, 2016

Mary Ruefle, *Madness, Rack and Honey* (Seattle: Wave, 2012)

Daniel Tiffany, *My Silver Planet: A Secret History of Poetry and Kitsch* (Baltimore: Johns Hopkins University Press, 2014)

Further Reading

LITERARY CRITICISM

Altieri, Charles. *The Art of Modern American Poetry.* Oxford: Blackwell, 2005.

Archambeau, Robert. *Laureates and Heretics: Six Careers in American Poetry.* South Bend, IN: University of Notre Dame Press, 2010.

Bendixen, Alfred, and Stephen Burt, eds. *The Cambridge History of American Poetry.* Cambridge: Cambridge University Press, 2014.

Bergman, David. *The Poetry of Disturbance.* Cambridge: Cambridge University Press, 2015.

Brown, Fahamisha Patricia. *Performing the Word: African American Poetry as Vernacular Culture.* New Brunswick, NJ: Rutgers University Press, 1999.

Caplan, David. *Questions of Possibility: Contemporary Poetry and Poetic Form.* New York: Oxford University Press, 2006.

Costello, Bonnie. *Shifting Ground: Reinventing Landscape in Modern American Poetry.* Cambridge, MA: Harvard University Press, 2003.

Culler, Jonathan. *Theory of the Lyric.* Cambridge, MA: Harvard University Press, 2015.

Friedlander, Benjamin. *Simulcast: Four Experiments in Criticism.* Tuscaloosa: University of Alabama Press, 2004.

Frost, Elisabeth. *The Feminist Avant-Garde in American Poetry.* Iowa City: University of Iowa Press, 2003.

Funkhouser, C. T. *New Directions in Digital Poetry.* New York: Continuum, 2012.

Grossman, Allen, with Mark Halliday. *The Sighted Singer.* Baltimore: Johns Hopkins University Press, 1992.

Halpern, Nick. *Everyday and Prophetic: The Poetry of Lowell, Ammons, Merrill and Rich.* Madison: University of Wisconsin Press, 2003.

Hejinian, Lyn, and Barrett Watten, eds. *A Guide to Poetics Journal: Writing in the Expanded Field.* Middletown, CT: Wesleyan University Press, 2013.

Keller, Lynn. *Thinking Poetry: Readings in Contemporary Women's Exploratory Poetics.* Iowa City: University of Iowa Press, 2010.

Kinzie, Mary. *The Cure of Poetry in an Age of Prose: Moral Essays on the Poet's Calling.* Chicago: University of Chicago Press, 1993.

Kirsch, Adam. *The Modern Element: Essays on Contemporary Poetry.* New York: Norton, 2008.

Logan, William. *Reputations of the Tongue.* Gainesville: University Press of Florida, 1999.

Longenbach, James. *Modern Poetry After Modernism.* New York: Oxford University Press, 1997.

———. *The Virtues of Poetry.* Minneapolis: Graywolf, 2014.

McClatchy, J. D. *Twenty Questions.* New York: Columbia University Press, 1998.

McLane, Maureen. *My Poets.* New York: Farrar, Straus and Giroux, 2012.

Nealon, Christopher. *The Matter of Capital: Poetry and Crisis in the American Century.* Cambridge: Harvard University Press, 2011.

Nelson, Cary, ed. *The Oxford Handbook to Modern and Contemporary American Poetry.* Oxford: Oxford University Press, 2014.

Nelson, Maggie. *Women, the New York School and Other True Abstractions.* Iowa City: University of Iowa Press, 2007.

Noel, Urayoán. *In Visible Movement: Nuyorican Poetry from the Sixties to Slam.* Iowa City: University of Iowa Press, 2014.

Perelman, Bob. *The Marginalization of Poetry: Language Writing and Literary History.* Princeton, NJ: Princeton University Press, 1996.

Perloff, Marjorie. *Poetry On and Off the Page: Essays for Emergent Occasions.* Evanston, IL: Northwestern University Press, 2004.

———. *Unoriginal Genius: Poetry by Other Means in the New Century.* Chicago: University of Chicago Press, 2010.

Rader, Dean, and Janice Gould, eds. *Speak to Me Words: Essays on Contemporary American Indian Poetry.* Tucson: University of Arizona Press, 2003.

Ramazani, Jahan. *Poetry and Its Others.* Chicago: University of Chicago Press, 2013.

Reed, Brian. *Nobody's Business: Twenty-First Century Avant-Garde Poetics.* Ithaca, NY: Cornell University Press, 2013.

———. *Phenomenal Reading: Essays on Modern and Contemporary Poetics.* Tuscaloosa: University of Alabama Press, 2010.

Shetley, Vernon. *After the Death of Poetry.* Durham, NC: Duke University Press, 1992.

Shockley, Evie. *Renegade Poetics: Black Aesthetics and Formal Innovation in African American Poetry.* Iowa City: University of Iowa Press, 2011.

Vendler, Helen. *The Music of What Happens.* Cambridge, MA: Harvard University Press, 1987.

———. *The Ocean, the Bird, and the Scholar: Essays on Poets and Poetry.* Cambridge, MA: Harvard University Press, 2015.

————. *Soul Says*. Cambridge, MA: Harvard University Press, 1995.

Wallace, Mark, and Steven Marks, eds. *Telling It Slant: Avant-Garde Poetics of the 1990s*. Tuscaloosa: University of Alabama Press, 2002.

Wang, Dorothy. *Thinking Its Presence: Form, Race and Subjectivity in Contemporary Asian American Poetry*. Stanford, CA: Stanford University Press, 2014.

Wiman, Christian. *Ambition and Survival: Becoming a Poet*. Port Townsend, WA: Copper Canyon, 2007.

Wojahn, David. *Strange Good Fortune: Essays on Contemporary Poetry*. Fayetteville: University of Arkansas Press, 2001.

Yu, Timothy. *Race and the Avant-Garde: Asian American and Experimental Poetry since 1965*. Stanford, CA: Stanford University Press, 2009.

ANTHOLOGIES

Ali, Agha Shahid, ed. *Ravishing DisUnities: Real Ghazals in English*. Middletown, CT: Wesleyan University Press, 2000.

Aragón, Francisco, ed. *The Wind Shifts: New Latino Poetry*. Tucson: University of Arizona Press, 2007.

Banerjee, Neelanjana, Summi Kaipa, and Pireeni Sundaralingam, eds. *Indivisible: An Anthology of Contemporary South Asian American Poetry*. Fayetteville: University of Arkansas Press, 2010.

Black, Sheila, Jennifer Bartlett, and Michael Nothen, eds. *Beauty Is a Verb: The New Poetry of Disability*. El Paso, TX: Cinco Puntos, 2011.

Bloom, Harold, ed. *The Best of the Best American Poetry, 1988–1997*. New York: Scribner, 1998.

Chang, Victoria, ed. *Asian American Poetry: The Next Generation*. Urbana: University of Illinois Press, 2004.

Charara, Hayan, ed. *Inclined to Speak: An Anthology of Contemporary Arab-American Poetry*. Fayetteville: University of Arkansas Press, 2008.

Dacey, Philip, and David Jauss, eds. *Strong Measures: Contemporary American Poetry in Traditional Forms*. Boston: Pearson, 1986.

Dumanis, Michael, and Cate Marvin, eds. *Legitimate Dangers: American Poets of the New Century*. Lexington, KY: Sarabande, 2006.

Dworkin, Craig, and Kenneth Goldsmith, eds. *Against Expression: An Anthology of Conceptual Writing*. Evanston, IL: Northwestern University Press, 2011.

Eshleman, Clayton, ed. *A Sulfur Anthology*. Middletown, CT: Wesleyan University Press, 2016.

Finch, Annie, ed. *A Formal Feeling Comes: Poems in Forms by Contemporary American Women*. 1994; Cincinnati: WordTech, 2007.

Giménez Smith, Carmen, with John Chávez, eds. *Angels of the Americlypse: An Anthology of New Latin@ Writing*. Denver: Counterpath, 2014.

Glenum, Lara, and Arielle Greenberg, eds. *Gurlesque: The New Grrrly, Grotesque, Burlesque Poetics*. Brooklyn, NY: Saturnalia, 2010.

[Jarvis, EE, Steve Roggenbuck, and Ray Younghans, eds.] *The Yolo Pages*. Tucson: Boost House, 2014.

McClatchy, J. D., ed. *The Vintage Book of Contemporary American Poetry*. New York: Vintage, 2003.

Niatum, Duane, ed. *Harper's Anthology of 20th Century Native American Poetry*. New York: HarperOne, 1988.

Nielsen, Aldon, and Lauri Ramey, eds. *Every Goodbye Ain't Gone: An Anthology of Innovative Poetry by African Americans*. Tuscaloosa: University of Alabama Press, 2006.

Peterson, Trace, and TC Tolbert, eds. *Troubling the Line: Trans and Genderqueer Poetry and Poetics*. Brooklyn, NY: Nightboat, 2013.

Pinsky, Robert, ed. *The Best of the Best American Poetry: 25th Anniversary Edition*. New York: Scribner, 2013.

Poulin, A., Jr., and Michael Waters, eds. *Contemporary American Poetry*. New York: Wadsworth, 2006.

Rowell, Charles, ed. *Angles of Ascent: A Norton Anthology of Contemporary African American Poetry*. New York: Norton, 2013.

St. John, David, and Cole Swensen, eds. *American Hybrid: A Norton Anthology of New Poetry*. New York: Norton, 2009.

Shepherd, Reginald, ed. *The Iowa Anthology of New American Poetries*. Iowa City: University of Iowa Press, 2004.

———, ed. *Lyric Postmodernisms: An Anthology of Contemporary Innovative Poetries*. Denver: Counterpath, 2006.

Silliman, Ron, ed. *In the American Tree*. Orono, ME: National Poetry Foundation, 2001.

Smith, Dave, and David Bottoms, eds. *The Morrow Anthology of Younger American Poets*. New York: Quill, 1985.

Stokesbury, Leon, ed. *The Made Thing: An Anthology of Contemporary Southern Poetry*. Fayetteville: University of Arkansas Press, 1987.

Young, Kevin, ed. *Giant Steps: The New Generation of African American Writers*. New York: Harper Perennial, 2000.

Acknowledgments

In some ways all books are collaborations, but all works of literary criticism are very clearly collaborations—you can't be a critic without relying on authors whose works you examine and might recommend, and I could not be a critic without what seems to me an uncommon, and an uncommonly generous, set of people who have helped.

First and last in that set comes Jessica Bennett, who had the initial idea for this book, provided the first and most important feedback for some of the claims and some of the poems chosen in it, and came up with the patience and the love that made it possible for me to finish the thing. I'm also grateful day and night for Cooper and Nathan, imaginative, generous creators themselves.

Harvard University, my employer, has been generous in its own appropriate ways, both in keeping me around and in defraying permission costs through the Rothenberg Fund and other funds. I'm grateful to my faculty colleagues and especially to James Engell and to James Simpson, who served as chairs of Harvard's English Department during the years in which I was writing this book. I'm also grateful, for a host of reasons, to my colleague Helen Vendler, whose work has set an example for mine since before I began to publish. She also read, and clearly improved, a few of the essays here. Graduate and undergraduate students at Harvard, singly and in groups, have read parts of this book, heard some of its arguments, and generally made it better: it would be foolish to try to list them all, but Ceci Mancuso, Christopher Spaide, and my current research assistant Aisha Bhoori deserve to be named, alongside all the other students who have taken English 50 and English 279. Individual essays also got better thanks to the expertise of other Harvard students, including but not limited to Julia Geiger, Tarina Quyrashi, Tili Sokolov, and Emmy Waldman. Nonfaculty staff in English (Lauren, Lauren, Lea, Sean, Anna, Henry, Gwen, Sol, and Case) made everything easier—and some things simply possible—as well. Bill Chapman at HFS, along with his coworkers, made a lot of copies. A lot of copies.

Parts of this book were read aloud to audiences, or discussed, in several sites on two continents over the past few years, among them the University of Chicago, the Library of Congress, and Charles University in Prague: my particular thanks to Justin Quinn, Rob Casper, Richard Strier, and Mark Payne for bringing me there. I'm grateful as well to my editors on other projects and at other presses, especially Jeff Shotts at Graywolf and Jim Sitar at the Poetry Foundation (where a few of these essays found their first home), and to Alison Granucci, Elaine Trevorrow, and the rest at Blue Flower Arts.

It's hard to imagine better treatment than I've received from Harvard University Press: John Kulka (again) liked both the idea of the book, before it existed, and the book itself, as it slowly coalesced out of separable parts; if he were anyone else the book would be less good. Joy Deng oversaw the minutiae, managed permissions, and deflected asteroids with pizzazz. Louise Robbins in Cambridge and Deborah Grahame-Smith in Westchester saw the book take final form. I'm grateful as well to the anonymous readers who evaluated the manuscript; most of their suggestions hit home.

Friends and allies outside Harvard also read parts of this book, or else let me talk about the parts, and the whole, with them at perhaps inordinate length; some also provided serious help with permission. A partial list of those friends and allies (besides those named above) has to include Clare Cavanagh, Langdon Hammer, Jennifer Lewin, J. D. McClatchy, Urayoan Noel, Trace Peterson, Carmen Gimenez Smith, Craig Morgan Teicher, and Monica Youn. I'm sure there are more I forgot. None of them—perhaps alas—have poems of their own in this book, in part because in a book of this kind (though not in other kinds of anthologies) it's poor form to include your closest friends, especially those of your own generation. Other friends and allies came in bunches, threads, circles, and gatherings via electronic media, some public, others hermetically sealed; I'm glad to be a passenger on several of those ships.

I am, finally, indebted to the contemporary poets who were able to read, or proofread, my essays about their own work, some of whom corrected serious errors; a few of their reactions (with their permission) are now quoted in the essays themselves. Any errors that remain are of course my own. To those poets and to the others who did not or could not read the essays about them—including those who passed away while this book was being assembled—I offer a final thanks.

Credits

Linda Gregerson, "Salt"
From *The Woman Who Died in Her Sleep: Poems,* by Linda Gregerson. Copyright © 1996 by Linda Gregerson. Reprinted by permission of Houghton Mifflin Harcourt Publishing Company. All rights reserved.

Kay Ryan, "Emptiness"
From *Atlantic Monthly,* vol. 272, no. 2 (August 1993), p. 81. Copyright © 1993 by Kay Ryan.

Albert Goldbarth, " 'A Wooden Eye. An 1884 Silver Dollar . . .' "
From *The Kitchen Sink: New and Selected Poems 1972–2007,* by Albert Goldbarth. Copyright © 2007 by Albert Goldbarth. Reprinted with the permission of The Permissions Company, Inc. on behalf of Graywolf Press, Minneapolis, Minnesota, www.graywolfpress.org.

Harryette Mullen, "honey jars of hair"
From *Recyclopedia: Trimmings, S*PeRM**K*T and Muse & Drudge,* by Harryette Mullen. Copyright © 1996 by Harryette Mullen. Reprinted with the permission of The Permissions Company, Inc., on behalf of Graywolf Press, www.graywolfpress.org.

Stanley Kunitz, "Halley's Comet"
From *Passing Through: The Later Poems, New and Selected,* by Stanley Kunitz. Copyright © 1995 by Stanley Kunitz. Used by permission of W. W. Norton & Company, Inc.

Michael Palmer, "Letters to Zanzotto: Letter 3"
From *At Passages,* by Michael Palmer. Copyright © 1995 by Michael Palmer. Reprinted by permission of New Directions Publishing Corp.

Robert Hass, "Our Lady of the Snows"
From *Sun Under Wood: New Poems,* by Robert Hass. Copyright © 1996 by Robert Hass. Reprinted by permission of HarperCollins Publishers.

C. D. Wright, "Key Episodes from an Earthly Life"
From *Steal Away: Selected and New Poems,* by C. D. Wright. Copyright © 1996 by C. D. Wright. Reprinted with the permission of The Permissions Company, Inc. on behalf of Copper Canyon Press, www.coppercanyonpress .org.

Juan Felipe Herrera, "Blood on the Wheel"
From *Border-Crosser with a Lamborghini Dream: Poems,* by Juan Felipe Herrera. Copyright © 1999 by Juan Felipe Herrera. Reprinted by permission of the University of Arizona Press.

Mary Jo Bang, "Q Is for the Quick"
From *The Bride of E,* by Mary Jo Bang. Copyright © 2009 by Mary Jo Bang.
Reprinted with the permission of The Permissions Company, Inc., on behalf of
Graywolf Press, www.graywolfpress.org.

Lucia Perillo, "Viagra"
From *Inseminating the Elephant,* by Lucia Perillo. Copyright © 2009 by Lucia
Perillo. Reprinted with the permission of The Permissions Company, Inc., on
behalf of Copper Canyon Press, www.coppercanyonpress.org.

Melissa Range, "The Workhorse"
From *Horse and Rider: Poems,* by Melissa Range (Lubbock, TX: Texas Tech
University Press, 2010). Copyright © 2010 by Melissa Range. Introduction © 2010
by Texas Tech University. Reprinted with the permission of The Permissions
Company, Inc., on behalf of Texas Tech University Press, http://ttupress.org.

Joseph Massey, "Prescription"
From *At the Point,* by Joseph Massey (Exeter, UK: Shearsman Books Ltd., 2011).
Copyright © 2011 by Joseph Massey. Reprinted by permission of the author.

dg nanouk okpik, "Date: Post Glacial"
From *Corpse Whale,* by dg nanouk okpik. Copyright © 2012 by dg nanouk
okpik. Reprinted by permission of the University of Arizona Press.

Rosa Alcalá, "Class"
From *The Lust of Unsentimental Waters,* by Rosa Alcalá (Exeter, UK: Shearsman
Books, 2012). Reprinted by permission of the author.

Gabby Bess, "Oversized T-Shirts"
From *Alone With Other People: A Collection of Prose and Poetry,* by Gabby Bess
(Fairfax, VA: Civil Coping Mechanisms, 2013). Copyright © 2013 by Gabby
Bess. Reprinted courtesy of the author and publisher.

Brenda Shaughnessy, "Hide-and-Seek with God"
From *Our Andromeda,* by Brenda Shaughnessy. Copyright © 2012 by Brenda
Shaughnessy. Reprinted with the permission of The Permissions Company, Inc.,
on behalf of Copper Canyon Press, www.coppercanyonpress.org.

Claudia Rankine, "You and your partner go to see the film"
From *Citizen: An American Lyric,* by Claudia Rankine. Copyright © 2014 by
Claudia Rankine. Reprinted with the permission of Penguin Books Limited in
the United Kingdom and The Permissions Company, Inc., on behalf of
Graywolf Press, www.graywolfpress.org, throughout the rest of the world.

Index